T0351836

From Old Regime to Industrial State

MARKETS AND GOVERNMENTS IN ECONOMIC HISTORY
A series edited by Price Fishback

Also in the series:

From Old Regime
to Industrial State

A History of German Industrialization from
the Eighteenth Century to World War I

RICHARD H. TILLY
AND MICHAEL KOPSIDIS

The University of Chicago Press
Chicago and London

The University of Chicago Press, Chicago 60637
The University of Chicago Press, Ltd., London
© 2020 by The University of Chicago
Published 2020
Printed in the United States of America

29 28 27 26 25 24 23 22 21 20   1 2 3 4 5

ISBN-13: 978-0-226-72543-7 (cloth)
ISBN-13: 978-0-226-72557-4 (e-book)
DOI: https://doi.org/10.7208/chicago/9780226725574.001.0001

Library of Congress Cataloging-in-Publication Data

Names: Tilly, Richard H., author. | Kopsidis, Michael, 1964– author.
Title: From old regime to industrial state : a history of German
    industrialization from the eighteenth century to World War II /
    Richard H. Tilly and Michael Kopsidis.
Other titles: Markets and governments in economic history.
Description: Chicago : University of Chicago Press, 2020. | Series: Markets
    and governments in economic history | Includes bibliographical references
    and index.
Identifiers: LCCN 2020004674 | ISBN 9780226725437 (cloth) |
    ISBN 9780226725574 (ebook)
Subjects: LCSH: Industrialization—Germany—History—19th century. |
    Germany—Economic conditions—19th century.
Classification: LCC HC285.T55 2020 | DDC 338.094309/034—dc23
LC record available at https://lccn.loc.gov/2020004674

♾ This paper meets the requirements of ANSI/NISO Z39.48-1992
(Permanence of Paper).

CONTENTS

This little book understands itself as a product of two elements. One is a book on German industrialization published long ago by one of the present authors: the German text *Vom Zollverein zum Industriestaat* (Tilly 1990). We think that the basic idea of that book—to offer a brief narrative account of German industrialization combining economic history with a bit of social history—is again overdue. The need for revision of a book published in 1990 is obvious. Thus, the second, more important element motivating the present work is the accumulation of evidence from new research since 1990 that traces the institutional roots of German industrialization back to the eighteenth century and also sheds new light on the nineteenth-century experience.

Though for the purposes of this book our narrative begins with the eighteenth century, we would not deny that some of the cultural roots of German industrial dynamism reach further back in time—to the seventeenth and sixteenth centuries and beyond. Their elucidation, however, would require a much different book. Here our focus is on the "transition to modern economic growth"—in our view, best described and interpreted on the basis of eighteenth- and nineteenth-century developments. This is a well-worked field, but it is often forgotten what an unusual period this was. In very long perspective it witnessed a true watershed of German economic history: the emergence of long-run economic growth in the sense of rising per capita product accompanied by rising living standards and change of the economic and social structure.

Here is the place to acknowledge help received along the road to publication. Special thanks are due to Tim Guinnane for comments on an earlier draft of this book and for help and encouragement throughout. We also owe a considerable debt to Ulrich Pfister for generous provision of empirical material and willingness to share with us his expertise on eighteenth- and early nineteenth-century economic history. We also wish to thank the three anonymous readers engaged by the University of Chicago Press for their constructive comments on the original book manuscript. Thanks, finally, to Price Fishback for including our book in this series.

Richard H. Tilly
Michael Kopsidis

Introduction, with Reflections on the Role of Institutional Change

The main theme of this history of German industrialization is the "transition to modern economic growth." Its analytical framework thus necessarily consists of the following propositions: (1) the transition to modern economic growth (MEG) was a very long-run, drawn-out process; (2) that transition depended on industrialization of the economy; (3) Germany's industrialization had a highly differentiated regional pattern; (4) industrialization and demographic change were closely linked, forcing some consideration of the transition from Malthusian to "post-Malthusian" conditions; (5) industrialization depended on institutions (understood as rules constraining both governmental and private individual behavior) and especially on institutional change; (6) industrialization depended on the development of human capital and technological change. These propositions deserve some elaboration here—a kind of guide to the book's structure.

On a Lengthened Transition

In his well-known typology of industrialization Alexander Gerschenkron defined Germany as the principal case of "moderate backwardness" that successfully caught up to the industrial leader, Great Britain, after a "big spurt." This "model" implied a rapid transition to modern economic growth—analogous to Rostow's "take-off." As in the British case (some years ago), it now seems time to offer a revised version of Germany's industrialization, one based in part on the argument that its transition to modern economic growth proceeded gradually and over a much longer period than previously believed. This also characterized demographic change (see below).

Recent work on individual regions of Germany has improved our knowledge of eighteenth- and early nineteenth-century developments to an extent that we think justifies reassessment of the country's industrialization. The Big Spurt and Take-Off models seemed to fit well the rapid growth of railroads and heavy industry that marked the important breakthrough period from the 1840s to the 1870s. The growth of these strategically important sectors, however, did not originate spontaneously and needs explanation. It depended on many conditions—political, social, and economic—that were long in the making. In this revision of an earlier text, we go back to the eighteenth century in a search for the roots of those conditions. By so doing we lengthen the period of "early industrialization" by four or five decades. This helps in understanding how certain German regions could respond smoothly to the British lead in industrial technology that became evident after 1815. It also helps in understanding why we can argue that, by 1840, many individual, local examples of rapid agricultural and industrial growth added up to a cumulative effect whose weight could have sufficed to induce the investment of the 1840s.

Industrialization as Prime Driver

As our history begins, the "German economy" was very much an agricultural economy, with perhaps 70 percent to 75 percent of its labor force and population in agriculture (Kaufhold 1983: 33; Pfister 2011: 5; Fertig et al. 2018: 27). More rapid technological change promoted the emergence and expansion of industry that necessarily diminished that preponderance, but the diminution of agriculture actually reflected its growing modernization and improvement, increasingly able to feed its own population and a rising share of those outside agriculture. That agricultural improvement was important for industrialization is an obvious point, but one worth noting.

The Regional Dimension

"German" industrialization was essentially a regional phenomenon. We thus begin discussion of its eighteenth-century antecedents with an explicitly regional approach (in part 1). This makes use, first of all, of Sidney Pollard's apt distinction between an "Inner" and an "Outer" Europe. The former, situated in Europe's northwestern corner, defined a territory whose outer boundary described an arc curving from the British Isles eastward and then southward down through the middle of Germany, curving southwesterly to the Upper Rhine and then across France to the Atlantic. By this phase of the early modern period it was here, in the Netherlands, that the prelude to European industrialization—an urban, commercial capitalism linked to handicraft techniques and rural industry—had begun, making Holland Europe's commercial center and turning large parts of the Europe around it into its agrarian and proto-industrial hinterland. It was here, as gateway to Europe's global trade and an expanding "Atlantic Economy," that the Dutch began to pull certain German regions into their orbit. In the eighteenth century, then, Great Britain became the center of this dynamism (Pollard 1981).

German lands straddled the border between an "Inner" and "Outer" Europe. Germany's "outer" European territories corresponded roughly to East Elbian Prussia, in this period dominated by large estates, powerful aristocratic landowners, and an "oppressive feudalism." In Germany's western half, in contrast, feudal rights were much less in evidence; tenant farmers, peasant agriculture, and small holdings were the rule. As we chart the course of Germany's industrialization in this book we shall repeatedly return to the theme of regional differences. The east-west development gap was by no means the only significant regional difference. A persistent north-south divergence also warrants attention; and there are others as well. This deserves mention here because we begin our historical narrative by describing eighteenth-century and early nineteenth-century developments in just three very different regions (part 1). These accounts lead the way into our understanding of Germany's nineteenth-century industrialization.

The distinction between "Inner" and "Outer" Europe also corresponds to recent descriptions of German demographic development from the early modern period to the middle of the nineteenth century. This is the opening chapter of part 1. Current demographic findings correct the older view, which placed escape from Malthusian conditions around the middle of the nineteenth century (Abel 1966: 244–57; Wehler 1987b: 641–702; Wehler 1995: 66–67, 92–94). They now place entrance into the "post-Malthusian era" in the second decade of the nineteenth century (Pfister & Fertig 2019, Fertig et al. 2018). Moreover, they show for the later part of the eighteenth century signs of a weakening of Malthusian influences, thus anticipating their complete disappearance at the beginning of the nineteenth century, a shift that ushered in a growing population. That description also shows how German demographic patterns in the eighteenth century tended to reflect the extent to which its regions were affected by the economic dynamism of northwest Europe, its "Atlantic economy," and the "Development Divergence" (Allen 2001) it produced within Europe as a whole, in

Germany's northwestern parts more than in the rest of the country. That tells us something about the forces, and especially the institutions, that affected the region.

Institutional Change and Industrialization

Institutions and institutional change represent an important part of our analytical framework. This is also the most difficult of our six propositions. Since our view of institutions differs somewhat from current fashions of economic history, we devote more attention to its elucidation here.

We begin with an "Ideal Type": ancien régime (Max Weber). The "ancien régime" embodied institutions that obstructed the transition to modern growth: the hereditary ruler of a state that supported and was supported by a number of "particularized" institutions, such as mercantile monopolies and artisan guilds, local town governments controlled by patrician elites supported by guilds, rural peasant populations subject to serfdom and local control by aristocratic landowners. Nevertheless, in our approach in this part of the book, we show that certain limits to the powers of regimes made possible the weakening, modification, even replacement of obstructive institutions, and thus the accommodation of growth-friendly interests.

One of those limits was political division. This meant that "public order" institutions faced important restraints, for eighteenth-century Germany, in contrast to its European neighbors (such as France, Great Britain, or czarist Russia), was not a nation-state, but a conglomerate of many hundreds of states, a few of them relatively large, such as Prussia. Saxony, Bavaria, Württemberg, or Hannover, the others much smaller, some of them no more than tiny lordships. A common language and shared culture bridged state borders to some extent, but the degree of political decentralization limited the impact of individual government actions on institutional change. That explains the regional approach used here.

Our starting point is the juncture of two dimensions of institutional change: its regional heterogeneity and its very long-run, gradual character. The leading regions of Germany's early nineteenth-century industrialization had already become its economically most advanced regions during the early modern period. Importantly, the structural transformation of these industrial core regions had successfully begun long before 1800—under the institutional conditions of the ancien régime.[1] Thus, "the centuries-long path to German industrialization must be understood as gradual institutional evolution in response to new circumstances, new opportunities, and new scarcities" (Kopsidis & Bromley 2017: 1). Note that a corollary of the juncture of regional leadership and gradual, long-run character of development is that regional disparities of the nineteenth century could hardly be the result of post-1800 policy changes.

This view contradicts those interpretations of the early nineteenth-century reforms as Germany's decisive institutional breakthrough to modern capitalism and modern economic growth—no matter whether that is attributed to an all-wise Prussian state, as in earlier German historiography (Sombart 1919: 30–46, 126–28, 334, 465; Weber 1906; Knapp 1887; critical: Kisch 1989: 214–18), or to the external shock related to the post-revolutionary French occupation of German territories, as one school of modern institutional economics believes (Acemoglu et al. 2011). Only those regions that had successfully launched gradual institutional reforms in the eighteenth century could quickly adopt and adjust to market relationships in the early nineteenth century.

We thus reject "Big Bang" interpretations, for such approaches focus unduly on state-ordered legal forms of institutions and ignore their capacity to leverage meaningful changes in behavior.[2] State-sponsored "public order" institutions were important agents of change, but their "supply" of radical reforms could only be effective if "private order" institutions—functioning markets coupled to secure property rights—could absorb and adapt to them easily; and this was only true for the "leading regions" referred to above, where commercialization of economic relationships had developed furthest.[3]

This was the case in those "leading regions." Here, the important "private order" institutions' secure property and contracting rights were embodied in the emergence of merchant-manufacturers in the eighteenth century. They helped promote rural industries (in textiles as in small iron wares) and, as merchants with contracting rights (internationally recognized and protected), linked those industries with international markets, thus gradually replacing the regime of guilds and merchants operating at arm's length. In chapter 2 we use the continuing development of export-oriented rural industry—"proto-industrialization"—in different parts of Germany as a kind of test of our approach. For "proto-industrialization," based on supra-regional markets, cottager labor, and capital in the hands of merchants, emerged within the context of the ancien régime—when and where merchants' marketing needs required closer control of production than craft guilds could accept. This generated conflict, but in some regions it also generated the labor supply and the cadres of skilled craftsmen and innovative industrial entrepreneurs who would promote nineteenth-century factory production.

We emphasize here that our approach differs methodologically from some recent contributions to the long-run growth impact of institutions (Cantoni & Yuchtman 2014, Becker & Woessmann 2009, Acemoglu et al. 2011).[4] These authors select a factor that is exogenous to the system of variables they wish to "explain": the fourteenth-century papal schism and the founding of universities as cause behind the growth of cities with functioning markets observed centuries later; the Reformation with its emphasis on education as cause of the distribution of the labor force, or degree of urbanization, observed some three hundred years later; and finally, the French Revolution and the extent of French occupation of German territories as cause of economic modernization—as measured by regional disparities in urbanization rates observed forty or fifty years later. This approach produces arresting facts, but it sweeps away the historical processes by which institutions are changed and become effective behavioral markers. It offers comparative statics, rather than dynamic processes, and it implicitly contradicts the idea that all change is part of a historical continuum—a touchstone of historical economics.

We single out the Acemoglu, Cantoni, Johnson, and Robinson study (Acemoglu et al. 2011) as an example of French impact on German development because of its prominence as a widely cited contribution to the topic of institutions and economic growth. We do not doubt the importance of French, and especially Napoleonic, influence on Germany's subsequent development, but we do not see its historical appearance as a starting point of German modernization.[5]

Thus, the revolutionary French unintentionally created the opportunity for launching fundamental liberal reforms, but their outcome—like most of the agrarian reforms—depended almost exclusively on the gradual institutional changes of the eighteenth century. By ignoring the historiography of German early industrialization, the paper by Acemoglu et al. (2011) can assert that French occupation determined not only the extent of reform in German regions after 1800 but also the subsequent regional growth paths—fifty years later. This curious lag is justified by war, occupation, and territorial changes, but remains unconvincing.

The account by Acemoglu et al. (2011) blots out the important role of the Prussian civil service bureaucracy—the principal architects of the reforms—for they fail to consider that it was in the eighteenth century that an efficient Prussian administration emerged and, influenced by Adam Smith's doctrines, proved perfectly capable of carrying out the "revolution from above" and establishing a modern capitalist economy against strong resistance from almost all layers of society. Prussia's ruling class and its bureaucracy saw economic reform as essential to the preservation of Prussia as a major power. This was the political goal of the reform program, not parliamentary democracy.

Germany's modernization, after all, proceeded differently from the Anglo-American experience, in which democracy and market economies emerged almost simultaneously. A close connection between liberal political reforms and liberal economic reforms seems to characterize most theories of the New Institutional Economics. Counter to the claims of Acemoglu et al. (2011), however, the higher the degree of political reform, the less the degree of economic reform (a claim documented with comparison of Prussia and the south German states in the following chapters of part 1). Prussia stands as the first instance of states successfully implementing market-oriented, "catch up" reforms under nondemocratic conditions. A capable, yet authoritarian, "modernization bureaucracy" was an essential element of this change. In this sense, the German states around 1800 were indeed a laboratory of modernity.

We remain unconvinced by Acemoglu et al.'s (2011) econometric results. The claim that their econometric model builds on a "treatment area" that qualifies as a "quasi-natural experiment" (Acemoglu et al. 2011: 3304) is vitiated by the heterogeneity of reform results achieved in the different French-controlled regions. The authors' reform index inadequately reflects these differences. In addition, the resort to urbanization and occupational statistics from the second half of the nineteenth century as evidence of early nineteenth-century French influence strains credulity. This eliminates a good deal of Germany's industrial history (for example, coal and its locational effects).[6]

Human Capital and Technological Change

"Human capital" refers to knowledge embodied in individual persons. It is acquired by investment in learning, through either schooling or on-the-job training, and can take the form of basic education (measured by literacy and numeracy), advanced special knowledge (measured by certification or years of schooling), and practical skills (craftsmanship, usually acquired by apprenticeship). Such investment is time-consuming and costly, but the consensus among economic historians suggests that its net returns in terms of lifetime earnings and other advantages have been considerable (Becker & Woessmann 2009). Its economic importance is based on two features: First, it is a valuable input into the production process, often regarded as a productive factor independent of capital and a source of technological change. Second, there is some agreement that human capital is closely linked to demographic processes, both reflecting family influence and also affecting family decisions about family size. Human capital, finally, can emerge as an external effect of contacts and interaction between concentrations of economic actors (Lucas 1988). Technological change, as here understood, follows from application of new knowledge to economic activity. It includes invention, diffusion, and innovation embodying the application in new production methods, new products, or both.

In this book the combined and separate effects of human capital and technological change are related to regional differences in industrial development, as a reflection of both the availability of highly skilled craftsmen and the distribution of educational facilities. This is seen to play an important role in the development of heavy industry during the "take-off" period. Somewhat more prominent were the contributions of human capital and institutions of higher education to the development of science-based industries in the 1870–1914 period. They are seen as an important element in the industrialization story of "Germany Overtaking Britain" at the end of the nineteenth century. Finally, human capital seems to have played an important role as co-determinant of the decline in German fertility that marked German demographic development from the 1870s to the 1920s, but we can offer little more in this text than acknowledgment of the fact and a few references to the relevant literature.

The rest of the book covers the years from 1815 to 1914 and focuses more generally on "German" industrialization as a whole, though regional differences remained considerable and also receive attention where that seems essential. Part 2 opens with chapter 5, centered upon the Zollverein, the German customs union. It covers the immediate post-1815 decades up to the 1840s, corresponding roughly to the classic stage of "early industrialization." This was a period of development that we see as a mixture of "recovery from war growth" (Pfister), technological borrowing from abroad, and increasing internal market integration, spurred by the development of the Zollverein and transportation improvements (paved roads, canals, and steam railways).

Industrialization progressed, bit by bit, though "interrupted" by the crisis of the 1840s and the revolution of 1848–49 (chapter 6). The 1840s nevertheless witnessed important signs of industrial progress: emergence of a railroad network, development of machinery-making and engineering firms, the growth of coke-smelted iron and deep-shaft coal mining, and of puddled steel, in short, the core of heavy industry. Immediate benefits from that progress no doubt reached no more than a limited circle of entrepreneurs, capitalists, and highly skilled craftsmen. The vast majority of contemporaries will have experienced few, if any, significant improvements in living standards. Economic growth in these years could just barely keep up with growth of the population. The signs of social tensions and political discord that marked the period were no doubt related to that condition. Nevertheless, seen in retrospect, the 1840s—even the revolution of 1848–49 itself—can be said to have helped lead the way to the phase of sustained industrial growth, the "take-off," that followed.

Part 3 covers the phase of development we feel is the book's centerpiece—for two reasons. First, it witnessed growth to maturity of Germany's heavy industry, the most striking feature of the country's nineteenth-century industrialization. Second, it moved the economy from a phase of growth just in step with population to one of increasing per capita income. Chapter 7 (on "Industrial Breakthrough") describes the syndrome of growth that linked railroads with heavy industry in the period from the 1840s to the 1870s, placing the relationships within a "leading sector" framework. Chapter 8 shifts back to description of the factors of production, capital and labor, emphasizing the surplus of labor and problem of income inequality that characterized the period. Chapter 9 suggests that agricultural development may to some extent be seen as a "forward linkage" effect of railroad growth, for the latter radically improved access of market-oriented farming to the urbanized industrial centers emerging in this period. Similarly, chapter 10 shows that the syndrome railroads/heavy industry made unprecedentedly great demands on the German financial system, arguing that their profitability and riskiness led to emergence of that historically unique institution, "universal banking," which may be seen, we suggest, as a kind of "backward linkage" generated by the railroad/heavy industry complex.

The book's last segment (part 4, "Germany's Emergence as an Industrial Power") takes up the more familiar topic of industrialization during the Kaiserreich (1871–1914). Sometimes called the "age of high industrialization" (in Rostow's terminology, "the drive to maturity"). It begins (chapter 11) by discussing growth trends and cycles, and asking whether the slowdown that followed the "boom and bust" of the early 1870s deserved the heading "great depression." The chapters that follow treat successively the development of industrial enterprises and their use of modern science and techniques (chapter 12), the role of finance and banks (chapter 13), the multidimensional topic of Germany's international relations (chapter 14), and, finally, a complex of questions covering the growth of cities, changes in social structure, and the development of strong municipal government, resulting in a remarkably comprehensive urban social policy (chapter 15).

The concluding section of the book summarizes its main components and arguments, asking whether individually, or taken as a whole, they constitute, a "German model" of development that distinguishes its industrialization from that of other countries.

PART ONE

Old Regime and Eighteenth-Century Origins of German Industrialization

Our introduction identified several arguments supporting the hypothesis that German industrialization was a much more drawn-out process than such concepts as "industrial revolution," "big spurt," or "take-off"—concepts that shaped a good deal of the earlier economic historiography—imply. One of the most cogent reasons for the "gradualist" position is the accumulation of evidence, quantitative and otherwise, on the extent to which important parts of the German economy had become integrated into the flourishing "Atlantic economy" in the course of the eighteenth century, a development that entailed the spread of rural industry—"proto-industrialization"—and commercialization of economic relationships in several key regions. For reasons that will become apparent, we focus here on the 1760–1840 period. In this part of the book, we begin with a short review of recent work on population and economy. We then turn to a regional perspective, introduced by an overview covering the geography of German industrialization. The next step is a survey of early industrialization in three of the oldest German industrial regions: Saxony, the northern Rhineland, and the south German state of Württemberg. It is followed by a chapter on agricultural development in Germany in this period. Description of institutional change during the eighteenth and the beginning of the nineteenth century, which culminated in the emergence of an identifiable market economy in the German lands, concludes this part of the book. We will show that regionally varying, gradual institutional evolution played a more important role in the long path to German industrialization than has previously been believed. As suggested earlier, we will contend that this set of experiences had influence on the German industrialization process that went far beyond the prosperity it created directly.

ONE

Population and the Economy

One component of the "gradualist view" of industrialization derives from recent work on the aggregates of population and real wages, and the relationships between them. This section thus begins with a brief review of that work. We adopt a macro-economic perspective, thus temporarily suspending consideration of the regional and sectoral sources of economic dynamism referred to above. The rest of the first section is devoted to discussion of the empirical evidence on population growth, the course of real wages, and the relationships between them. We conclude with a brief summary of the findings.

In a series of recent articles and monographs, Ulrich Pfister and his associates—summarizing and supplementing other recent work—have published new long-run estimates of population growth and real wages for Germany covering the period from 1500 to 1850 (Pfister & Fertig 2010, Pfister et al. 2012, Fertig & Pfister 2014, Pfister 2015, Pfister 2017a, Fertig et al. 2018, Pfister & Fertig 2019, Pfister 2019a, 2019b). This section attempts to explain their importance for the story we tell in this book, limiting ourselves to a few salient points. We emphasize the German-wide coverage these estimates offer, for—in the absence of other macro-economic data for this period—they represent a reference basis for comparison with other indicators of economic change and also facilitate backward extension of informed speculation about aggregate economic growth into the pre-1850 period.

The first point concerns new estimates of total German population covering the entire early modern period. We reproduce these in table 1.1, where the population numbers for the period 1500–1740 are highly tentative. It shows an upward trend beginning with the conclusion of the Thirty Years' War and continuing, with certain interruptions, until 1871 and beyond.

Table 1.1 **German Population, 1500-1871**

Population (in millions)		1500 = 100	Annual Growth
1500	7.2	100	
1618	13.5	188	1500-1618 = 0.55%
1650	7.9	110	1618-50 = -1.7%
1740	14.3	199	1650-1740 = 0.66%
1765	15.8	219	1740-65 = 0.32%
1790	18.0	250	1765-90 = 0.56%
1815	21.1	293	1790-1815 = 0.63%
1840	27.4	381	1815-40 = 0.97%
1871	34.3	476	1840-71 = 0.72%

Source: 1500-1740, Pfister & Fertig 2010: 5; 1740-1815, unpublished appendix to Pfister & Fertig 2010; 1815-71, Fertig et al. 2018: 31-33, our calculation.
Note: Germany is defined by the borders of the "Holy Roman Empire of German Nation" dissolved in 1806 by Napoleon, without the Habsburg Territories. This definition also excludes East Prussia, West Prussia, northern Schleswig, and Alsace-Lorraine, which later belonged to the Kaiserreich of 1871. The growth rates for the 1740-1871 period are calculated on the basis of annual values but only interpolated between two years for the period 1500-1740.

This long-term trend itself raises few doubts or questions. It reflected, however, a change in the relationship between population and the economy, our principal interest here. Population growth raises above all the question of its determinants. Ignoring noneconomic forces, we ask how economic conditions affected the positive trend in natural increase, that is, the balance of births and deaths, and net migration. In Germany, as in other European countries, births depended on marriage and female fertility, while these depended on economic conditions. Deaths reflected the population's health, also dependent, at least indirectly, on economic conditions.

One approach to our problem adopts what is called a "Malthusian framework," named after Thomas Robert Malthus (1766–1834), an English classical economist. In its modern guise, it distinguishes between the "preventive checks" of voluntary restraints on marriage and fertility and the involuntary "positive checks" of increases in mortality. In this scenario, the population of undeveloped, pre-industrial economies tends to grow to a ceiling set by the fall of labor productivity to sub-subsistence levels and then by rising mortality (the "positive check"). This happens because voluntary restraints on fertility and births were assumed to be inoperative, land fixed, and technology static, unable to offset the negative effect of population growth on the marginal productivity of labor. Economic conditions (or living standards) are represented by real wages or their proxies; these are positively related to fertility, but inversely related to mortality. Increases in population size negatively affect real wages (Clark 2007: 19–111).

According to the "Unified Growth" theory of Oded Galor (2005, 2011) and others, the transition from "Malthusian stagnation" to sustained "modern" growth was a long process, which led first through a "post-Malthusian" era. As Galor summarizes: "During the Post-Malthusian Regime the pace of technological progress markedly increased along the process of industrialization. The growth rate of output per capita increased significantly . . . but the positive Malthusian effect of income per capita on population growth was still maintained, generating a sizable increase in population growth . . . and offsetting some of the potential gains in income per capita" (Galor 2005: 185). New work by Pfister and Fertig (2019) describes this transition as a "Malthusian disequilibrium condition," which began to become effective in the eighteenth century and thus preceded the emergence of a "post-Malthusian regime." The long-term negative effect of population growth and falling real wages on death rates disappeared. While real wages continued to fall at an annual rate of –0.5 percent, the death rate showed not a correspondingly Malthusian rise, but a long-term decline (Pfister & Fertig 2019: 13; fig. 1.1). This suggests that death rates had become exogenous. In contrast to the positive check, restraints on marriage (and hence on fertility)—the "preventive check"—were present and responsive to real wages in Germany during the entire 1730–1870 period. Despite slowly declining mortality in the long run, it is appropriate to describe eighteenth-century Germany as a high-pressure Malthusian system because the positive checks repeatedly appeared in the form of sharp, short-run increases of the death rate in response to crop- and war-related income shocks.[1]

Thus, as far back as adequate data are available, a long-term Malthusian relationship between income and mortality did not exist.[2] In addition, birth rates adjusted only partially for income fluctuations and fluctuated in a narrow range between 30 and 40 per 1,000 inhabitants from the mid-1730s onward. Both developments, falling death rates and comparatively stable birth rates, resulted in a remarkable population growth of annually 0.4 percent despite falling real wages for the period 1740–90 (Pfister & Fertig 2019).

Because the long-run mortality was driven by forces exogenous to the Malthusian system, Germany's demographic regime differed substantially from other northwest European countries during the eighteenth and nineteenth centuries (Pfister & Fertig 2019: 8). Three developments help explain the decline in mortality during the eighteenth century: (1) the epidemic environment improved substantially compared to the seventeenth century (for example, the Black Death disappeared); (2) German grain markets became more integrated between 1650 and 1790 (Albers & Pfister 2018).

The relative stabilization ("the Great Moderation") of grain prices observed in these years reflected such improvements as well as slowly intensified, market-induced agricultural progress (Abel 1966: 182–204; Harnisch 1986). And (3) nonagricultural sectors—especially export industries or proto-industries—expanded more strongly from the late seventeenth century. Rising nonagricultural labor demand had the potential to stabilize household incomes despite falling real wages because of an increasing number of working days or longer working time per day (Pfister 2019a, Kaufhold 1986). All these developments corresponded well to the more rapid growth of population in this period (table 1.1) and to other signs of regional economic progress within Germany to which we later return.

The eighteenth century harbored changes that paved the way for the later demographic breakthrough: modernizing economic forces connected with the spread of trade and rural industry that facilitated—despite setbacks from war-related interruptions—a weakening of the "positive checks" and led to their virtual disappearance.

The recent research program mentioned above confronts the vital rates and population numbers with new, long-run estimates of real wages (Pfister 2017a) and extends the aggregate German demographic-economic history from the relatively familiar and time-tested picture of the nineteenth century into the less well-known early modern period. Despite its highly uncertain and tentative character, we find it useful to take a closer look here at some of its claims. Figure 1.1 illustrates these patterns, including the new, long-run estimates of real wages to indicate the connection between changes in demographic behavior and living standards.

A fateful development that accompanied German demographic expansion during the early modern period (and especially the eighteenth century) was the absolute and relative growth of the landless and land-poor population. Land-poor classes and not peasants dominated most of rural Germany around 1800 (Kopsidis 2006: 306–8). Recent work by Pfister and associates shows that this resulted not, as commonly believed, from over-reproduction of the poor, but from over-reproduction of the affluent landowning class in combination with a predominance of primogeniture inheritance rules. In a primarily agrarian economy such as that of pre-1800 Germany, this produced a substantial degree of economic inequality. In such a setting, the development of rural export industries represented a creative response, one that mitigated the decline of real wages during the eighteenth century. Rural proto-industrial growth was thus extraordinarily important for the development of German manufacturing and structural

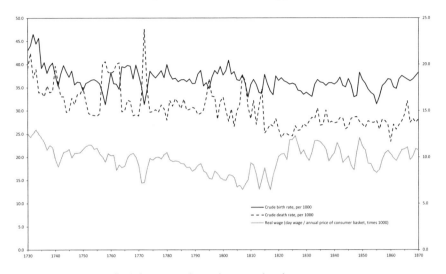

1.1 Crude Birth Rate, Crude Death Rate, and Real Wages, 1730–1870
Source: Vital rates in online appendix from Fertig et al. 2018: 31–33; Pfister & Fertig 2010.
Real wage from Pfister 2017a: supporting information S3; 2018: suppl. material A3.
Note: The dimension of the real wage (right axis) is the fraction of a consumer basket
consumed annually by an adult town dweller that can be purchased with
the summer day wage of an unskilled building laborer.

transformation until the early nineteenth century. This reflected the fact that Germany's urban system, compared to those of leading economic European regions like England and the Low Countries, was only poorly developed, and urbanization proceeded slowly until the middle of the nineteenth century, even in industrial core regions (table 1.2).

The intersectoral wage gap between agrarian and industrial occupations remained modest until the middle of the nineteenth century and widened only after 1850. During the second half of the nineteenth century the still existing gender wage gap also increased significantly, as will be described in later chapters (Pfister 2019b). Compared with some other Western European countries (such as England, Holland, or Sweden) for this period, Germany still experienced higher mortality rates that translated into much lower life expectancy (Pfister & Fertig 2010: 41, 54; Fertig & Pfister 2014: 6–7). Moreover, the new, long-run estimates of German real wages—with the important exception of Hamburg show levels well below those of the other northwestern European countries cited. However, those same demographic estimates suggest lower mortality rates (implying higher life expectancy) than southern European ones (Pfister & Fertig 2010: 41, 55;

Table 1.2 **Urbanization Rate and Share of Agricultural Population in Germany, 1500–1850**

	1500	1600	1650	1700	1750	1800	1850
Urbanization rate	9.2%	7.5%	7.6%	7.1%	8.7%	11.3%	14.3%
Employment share, agriculture	77.2%	80.0%	78.7%	77.0%	72.2%	63.8%	55.6%

Source: Pfister 2019a: 3.
Note: Urbanization rate is defined by the share of population living in communities with more than 5,000 inhabitants.

Pfister 2017a: 726). Germany's geography—its east-west and north-south differences—gave it a mixed demographic composition.

With the conclusion of the Napoleonic Wars in 1815, Germany's demographic regime changed dramatically. The new estimates show a rapid decline of mortality rates but more or less stable birth rates in the decades that followed. These, as suggested above, represented, in the Malthusian terminology, the virtual disappearance of "positive checks"—that is, "escape from the Malthusian Trap." The Pfister and Fertig (2019) study describes this post-Malthusian pattern of development as a situation "where the rate of increase of technology depended on population size"—scale-dependent productivity growth based on expanded markets that offset the negative impact of increasing population and labor intensity on marginal productivity. The disappearance "of a relationship between material welfare and mortality, that is of the positive check, points to the transition to a non-Malthusian regime" during the late 1810s (Fertig & Pfister 2014: 3; Fertig et al. 2018; Pfister & Fertig 2019). Neither demographic shocks nor food crises wholly disappeared after 1815, as we shall show, but the close relationship between demographic dynamics and real wages no longer reappeared at the national level. In no year after 1815 was the all-German natural population increase negative (Fertig et al. 2018, Pfister & Fertig 2019).

Peace also ushered in a period of rising real wages, ending a century-long trend. Some authors even see the upward jump from 1815 to the mid-1820s as a positive real-wage shock due to a series of bumper harvests. Within a few years real wages again reached the level at the beginning of the eighteenth century and then remained more or less stable until the 1880s despite a doubling population increase of annually 0.8 percent for the 1815–71 period. Much more research is necessary to improve our very limited knowledge about the acceleration of technical change after 1815. Uncertainties concerning agricultural productivity and grain markets remain as well, to which we must return below (Pfister et al. 2012, Pfister & Fertig 2010, Fertig & Pfister 2014).

We can thus summarize the aggregate picture that emerges from the new estimates as follows: Germany's demographic modernization, described here as "escape from the Malthusian trap," clearly began to take its mature form early in the nineteenth century—several decades earlier than the traditional view, which connects the industrial take-off starting in the 1840s with the overcoming of the Malthusian economy—all this happening within a comparatively short transition period (Abel 1966: 182–242; Wehler 1987b: 641–702; Wehler 1995: 66–67, 92–94). The "breakthrough" in 1815, however, represented the cumulative result of demographic-economic changes already begun and visible in the eighteenth century. These were shaped by modernizing economic forces that "influenced material welfare independent of population dynamics. They emerged later than in England and they were at first weaker than on the British Isles, but they were well established about 150 years before the onset of rapid industrialization" (Pfister 2017a: 718). This means, of course, that the revisionist view of population history presented here in capsule form depends, if indirectly, on revision of Germany's historical path to industrialization.

Before concluding this chapter, we must call attention to two qualifications of the view as summarized here. First, it ignores regional differences in demographic patterns. The better documented history of the nineteenth century shows important differences in demographic patterns between eastern, western, and southern parts of Germany. Much of the aggregate story, therefore, depends on the accuracy of the regional weights used in aggregation. Second, and rather less important, is the fact that the pattern of birth and death rates reported above introduces a second "demographic transition" into German development that preceded the nineteenth-century "demographic transition" that began in the 1870s. Both reflected the cumulative effects of social and economic changes on demographic behavior, and both had positive implications for human welfare, though different in character and effects. Our discussion of the "Empire period," below, will come back to this issue.

TWO

German Regions and the Beginnings of Early Industrialization

The Regions

During the period under consideration Germany contained most of Central Europe. From west to east it stretched over 1,200 kilometers from areas left of the Rhine to the Memel territory east of the river Neman, which is now divided between Lithuania and Russia. In a north-south direction it extended over almost 900 kilometers from the North Sea to the Alps. Early modern Germany's economic landscape was highly diversified—perhaps more so than that of any other part of Europe. The same may be said for Germany's political subdivisions: before 1815, it was not a state. The word "Germany" around 1750 described a population with a common language and culture, but politically subject to many hundreds of political entities, a few of them large, like Austria, Prussia, or Saxony, the rest small and spread across the vast territory described above. Prussia, for example, was the only European state that simultaneously encompassed regions belonging to the "growth nucleus" in the northwest of the continent and regions in the central and eastern "periphery." In fact, a strong west-east gradient marked the density of industrial activity during the early modern period—long before industrialization started. Contemporary statistics and experts, as well as all historical research, clearly support this contention. Moreover, as analyzed in greater detail below, industrial development during the eighteenth century and the first third of the nineteenth century was mainly rural in nature. The huge differences in industrial penetration of rural areas were what made the fundamental difference between the west and the east, while urbanization levels were roughly the same. Regional variations in industrial penetration of rural areas also do much to explain the large contrasts in population density (table 2.1).

Table 2.1 **Regional Variation in Prussian Population & Manufacturing, c. 1800**

	Population Density	Urbanization	Manufacturing Density			Manufacturing Rural Share
			Urban	Rural	Total	
Eastern provinces	22	25.3%	11.4%	1.0%	3.6%	20.1%
Central provinces	35	41.1%	15.2%	3.2%	8.1%	23.3%
Without Berlin	—	33.7%	13.3%	3.2%	6.6%	32.2%
Western provinces	47	25.7%	14.4%	8.0%	9.7%	61.7%
Total	27	31.1%	13.5%	2.6%	6.0%	29.7%

Source: Kaufhold 1978: 485, 504; our own calculation.
Note: Macro-regions around 1800 are defined as: (a) East (East Prussia and Lithuania, West Prussia and Netze District, Pomerania; data for Silesia are missing); (b) Center (Berlin, Kurmark, Neumark, Magdeburg, Halberstadt); and (c) West (Mark, Minden-Ravensberg, Tecklenburg-Lingen, Kleve, East Frisia). Population density = persons per square kilometer. Urbanization = share of urban population in percent (urban population refers to the population of settlements defined as towns by law independent of their size). Manufacturing density = share of all persons employed in manufacturing in urban, rural, and total population. Manufacturing rural share = share of rural persons employed in manufacturing in the total manufacturing labor force. The number of persons employed in manufacturing comprises all persons working in craft shops, employed in proto-industry, in manufactures, and in the few early factories. Mining is excluded.

A second, west-south gradient also existed. Its importance had been established by the second half of the eighteenth century at the latest, a fact indicated by real wage data for the early modern period (Pfister 2017a: 718–26). Indicators of regional disparities during German industrialization strongly support the continued existence of distinct economic discrepancies within Germany along the two gradients. Moreover, these indicators further verified that the west-south gradient was as strong as its oft-quoted west-east counterpart (Frank 1994: 54–55). Finally, if we look for arguments to back the importance of the pre-industrialization phase for German industrialization, none is weightier than the fact that the two by far fastest developing (proto-)industrial regions since the end of the Thirty Years' War, Saxony and the Rhine-Ruhr-area, also showed the strongest modernization dynamics in the period of rapid industrialization that began around the middle of the nineteenth century (Frank 1994: 55; Kopsidis & Bromley 2016: 178–85). It is of some interest to note here that the regional ranking of industrial development and modernity remained more or less stable between the beginning of industrialization and World War II. Only a few districts in the Middle Rhine and Neckar valley managed the transition from "rural backward" to "industrial-advanced" during this time (Frank 1994: 94–95). These features suggest that not only regional disparities but industrialization as well had deep roots in German history. Differing regional development paths emerged and strengthened long before industrialization, some of them possibly going back to the late Middle Ages. The subsequent chapters on Saxony, northern Rhineland, and Württemberg will further substantiate this historical approach.

In the following sections three leading premodern industrial regions will be analyzed more closely. Our approach will attempt to identify the driving forces of industrial growth during this period (c. 1760–1830). Having in mind that only a few industrial regions managed the transition to industrialization, while most rural industrial areas deindustrialized during the nineteenth century, causes of stagnation will be examined as well. We concentrate on the two successful early industrializers, Saxony and the northern Rhineland (including certain adjacent Westphalian regions), and contrast their development to Württemberg, which has been seen as the epitome of a region that began the early modern period as a major center of manufacturing based on rural industry, but then fell into a period of decline and stagnation that extended into the nineteenth century. It regained its industrial dynamism in the 1860s and may be classified as one

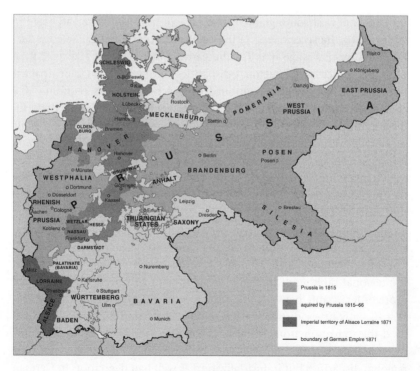

2.1 Germany, 1815–71
Source: Authors' own map based on a map from IEG-Maps (http://www.ieg-maps.de/).

Table 2.2 **Regional Differences within Germany, 1849**

Regions	Agriculture	Manu-facturing	Trade & Transport	GDP per capita (Germany = 100)	Franks's Moderni zation Index	Share in Total Population
Agrarian East	70.4	12.7	11.0	79.4	35.1	17.2
Silesia	59.1	28.6	6.2	100.4	46.2	9.5
Brandenburg	44.6	27.8	17.9	123.3	78.1	6.6
Prussian Province Saxony/Thuringia	50.7	32.6	9.0	113.3	60.6	8.5
Kingdom of Saxony	36.3	49.2	3.8	134.7	73.8	5.8
Agrarian Northwest	61.0	24.4	12.0	96.7	47.8	11.4
North Rhine–Ruhr area	41.0	39.8	12.8	134.7	74.7	7.4
Hesse/Rhenish-Hesse	55.5	26.6	10.4	106.5	49.0	8.3
Southwest Germany	61.1	24.7	6.9	98.0	37.4	11.3
Bavaria	71.6	20.9	2.7	77.6	28.0	14.0
Total (Germany)	58.6	26.0	9.0	—	48.2	—

Source: Our own calculation, using data from Frank 1994: x, xxx, appendix; www.hgis-Germany.de.
Note: Agriculture/manufacturing/trade & transport = sectoral share of employees in total labor force; mining and public service are excluded. GDP per capita = percent of German average (= 100). Modernization index = employment shares of modern sectors (manufacturing, trade & transport) as well as of urbanization share in cities with more than 5,000 inhabitants (Frank 1994: 50–56). Units are 62 administrative districts (*Regierungsbezirke*) for Prussia, provinces in all other states except Thuringia, aggregated petty territories in case of Thuringia.

of Germany's late-industrializing regions (Megerle 1982, Ogilvie 1996). The map of Germany in figure 2.1 (1815–71) can serve as a guide to the location of the states and regions discussed. Note that it traces both the expansion of Prussia and the unification of Germany in this period.

Guilds and Proto-industrialization

Before we turn to discussion of the individual regions during the period of early industrialization, a few general remarks on the controversial question of proto-industrialization and institutional change are necessary. They focus on the role of guilds. The historiography of European craft guilds, while in wide agreement that these institutions played a positive economic role in the late medieval and early modern periods—as protectors of product quality, human capital, and rights of urban labor—has tended to see their continuing existence in the eighteenth century as rent-conserving monopolies that held back technological change and economic growth potential. In contrast, that historiography has interpreted the spread of rural industry in the seventeenth and eighteenth centuries—proto-industrialization—as the fitting answer to guilds that hastened their disappearance and opened the door to progress and industrial growth. More recent work, however, has modified that picture. Since the three regional surveys of eighteenth-century development that follow focus on proto-industrialization, it may be useful here to describe that modified view of the role of guilds in this early phase of industrialization.

The recent work suggests (a) that eighteenth-century guild and proto-industrial structures were not necessarily antagonistic; and (b) that both fulfilled important entrepreneurial functions.[1] Cooperation between merchants and guilds took place more frequently than the older literature had indicated. Thus, in towns, where and when merchant- and master-manufacturers still operated on a small scale, they bought and sold at prices negotiated by the guilds. By so doing, merchants in effect made use of the guilds as provider of the entrepreneurial function, "delegated monitoring." In the long-distance markets that increasingly attracted merchant-manufacturers in the seventeenth century, the guilds' stamp of approval had guaranteed the product quality and reduced negotiating costs of merchants in those markets. Through control of members' work and remuneration, guilds also freed merchant-manufacturers from the need to engage in multiple (and time-consuming) negotiations with individual workers, important where their output represented an input for the finished product.

Nevertheless, the spread of proto-industrial production as "putting-out system" during the eighteenth century does suggest that budding merchant-manufacturers saw advantages in the assumption and execution of entrepreneurial functions: product specification, supply of the means of production (raw material or other inputs), direct contact with individual producers, and the higher profits related to the capital invested. Wage levels of rural workers were doubtless lower than those set by town-based guilds, but these were largely offset by the higher transaction costs of decentralized producing units (in the form of remuneration of intermediaries who delivered the input materials and collected the product for merchant-manufacturers). The consensus view now tends to emphasize instead the flexibility of adaptation to the changing demands of export markets and the corresponding upgrading of product quality as the factor behind the growing importance of merchants and commercial capital in the eighteenth century, a development documented by merchants' increasing use of their own individual trademarks on goods sent to distant markets.

Economic Policy during the Age of Mercantilism/Cameralism

Of concern here are the beginnings of economic policy as practiced by the territorial states that began to emerge in the post-1648 German Reich—

Austria, Prussia, Saxony, Württemberg. Policies focused on measures to improve agriculture, manufacturing, and trade, to encourage population growth, ultimately with the aim of increasing the revenues and power of the central government. This policy stance in the German states came to be called "cameralism" (from *camera*, or "treasury"), the German version of mercantilism as practiced by such Western European states as England or France. What differentiated German from French or British mercantilism was the strong emphasis on the state and its bureaucracy as an instrument for regulating economic life according to "natural law" and in the interest of the "general welfare" of all subjects as well as of the rising fiscal needs of the emerging modern state (Sokoll 2007; Münch 1996; Wehler 1987a: 218–40). Specific measures—such as the ban on exports of raw materials or on imports of finished cloth, subsidies and monopoly rights granted to manufacturers of armaments or of luxury goods, taxes imposed on river through-traffic, and so on—characterized the ambitions of German cameralism. Least successful of all were the colonial ambitions and projects of the German territorial states (for example, the Brandenburg-African Trading Company of 1682, or the *Seehandlung*, founded in 1772). All too often these represented contra-productive illusions, including belief in the government's ability to modernize the economies of these states, in part as substitutes for the nonexistent capitalist-liberal German bourgeoisie. Prussia's greatest eighteenth-century foreign policy success—Silesia—became a graveyard of repeatedly ineffective mercantilist policies. Even in Berlin, the capital, most of Frederick the Great's state-subsidized projects failed to create enterprises capable of sustained success without state help (Zimmermann 1885, Krüger 1958, Kisch 1989). The growing Prussian state apparatus proved most successful in its efforts to modernize the country's infrastructure, for example, the drainage and land improvement of the Warthe and Oder valleys, or canal-building, such as the canals linking the Oder and Havel rivers.

As we will show, however, German states that successfully centralized power in the post-1648 period at the expense of particularistic interests would have a clear advantage in creating swiftly the institutional framework of a modern market economy after 1800. In the absence of a modern, politically self-confident bourgeoisie, popular political participation in German states via premodern parliaments (*Landstände*) controlled by social estates nobility, clergy, or municipal notabilities—meant maintaining or extending privileges like monopoly rights to guilds that prevented the emergence of inclusive markets. Weak, highly indebted "non-absolutist" German states were forced to guarantee particularistic privileges in manufacturing and trade to ensure state financing. In the worst-case scenario, long-term economic stagnation was the consequence of an outdated and petrified institutional framework hostile to growth. As will be shown, Württemberg was a prime example for this kind of a German state (Ogilvie 1996: 290–96; Ogilvie & Carus 2014: 419–26; Carsten 1959).

The opposite was Prussia, where "enlightened absolutism" held sway. The early disempowerment of such institutions of particularism as parliamentary bodies embodying co-determination rights of the nobility, or the town councils dominated by urban patrician elites, facilitated the gradual emergence of a rational and self-confident bureaucracy that would find it possible to use its organizational skills to modernize the country's economy along competitive, market-dominated lines, making a start in reduction of the gap that separated Prussia from the leading Western European states (Roehl 1900: 16–88). Prussia was not the only state where administrative elites realized that radical reforms were necessary; but it was by far the most important and the only one with a bureaucracy able to implement them.

An essential feature of cameralist policy in many German states was population policy (*Peuplierungspolitik*). In Prussia this included an active "pro-immigration policy" to attract skilled workers and specialists to offset the high losses of the Thirty Years' War (1618–48). In a seminal paper Hornung (2014a) estimated that around 1700 the mass immigration of mostly high-skilled religious refugees—Calvinist Huguenots—from Catholic France to Prussia, which effectively guaranteed religious freedom to everyone, may have had a positive long-term impact on the productivity of the Prussian textile industry during the eighteenth century. Protestant religious refugees also played an important role for industrial development in Saxony and the Northern Rhineland (Zachmann 1997, Kriedte 2007, Kisch 1981).

Saxony

Saxony was the first German region to achieve the transition from an agrarian to an industrial economy—several decades earlier than the northern Rhineland and Ruhr area. Its fundamental modernization process had begun soon after the Thirty Years' War and continued to progress under the conditions of the ancien régime with both the manorial system and guilds still legally intact (Tipton 1976: 30–37; Pollard 1981: 103; Forberger 1982: 1–99; table 2.4). Our overview here is followed by a division of Saxon industrialization history into three periods: the first emphasizing developments in the eighteenth century up to the French, or Napoleonic, era; the second covering the French period (1792–1815); and the third taking Saxon industrialization up to about 1840 or 1850.

Table 2.3   Occupational Structure in Regional Comparison in 1849, 1861 & 1882

	Saxony	Germany	Saxony	Rhine/Ruhr	Germany
	1849	1849	1861	1861	1861
Agriculture (%)	37.4%	56.0%	28.8%	38.0%	51.7%
Industry (%)	45.6%	24.5%	51.2%	42.6%	28.8%
Services (%)	17.0%	19.4%	20.1%	19.4%	19.6%
Population (millions)	1,894	35,013	2,225	2,846	38,003
Employment (millions)	0,875	14,820	1,068	1,212	15,960

	Saxony	Rhine/Ruhr	Württemberg	Germany
	1882	1882	1882	1882
Agriculture (%)	23.5%	28.7%	56.3%	48.4%
Industry (%)	56.4%	51.5%	28.4%	29.6%
Services (%)	20.2%	19.8%	15.3%	22.0%
Population (millions)	3,105	3,953	2,137	45,719
Employment (millions)	1,325	1,647	1,083	19,958

Source: Tipton 1976: 37, 185, 191–193; Hoffmann 1965: 172–73, 204–5.
Note: The Rhine-Ruhr area comprises the administrative districts of Arnsberg, Düsseldorf, Cologne, and Aachen.

Radical liberal reforms often thought essential to implementation of the institutional framework and basic principles of a capitalist market economy came very late to Saxony—the agrarian reforms in 1831/32 and freedom of enterprise (*Gewerbefreiheit*) in 1861 when industrialization was very far along. In Saxony, fundamental liberal reforms thus followed, rather than led, century-long developments, as if the legal framework adjusted to economic reality, rather than shaped it. Nevertheless, German-wide comparison of modernization indices for the nineteenth century shows industrializing Saxony at the top, together with the Rhine-Ruhr area and greater Berlin (tables 2.2 and 2.3). No other German region showed such a combination of dynamic economic and population growth in the 1750–1914 period. In the following discussion we present Saxony as the epitome of gradual change—change that in the long run transformed the economy. For continuous change, and not swift radical change, explains Saxony's relatively early industrialization (Forberger 1982; Frank 1994: 55; Horster 1908; Kaufhold 1982; Kiesewetter 2007; Pfister & Kopsidis 2016; Pollard 1981: 103; Schäfer 2016).

Saxony's late medieval history bequeathed to Saxony's population the heritage of a weak manorial system—the *Mitteldeutsche Grundherrschaft*—and a flexible guild system (Haun 1892; Kötschke 1953: 89–185; Lütge 1957). The former gave the peasants personal freedom, based feudal obli-

gations on tenancy contracts, and thus empowered a large part of the peasantry with the freedom to sell, mortgage, and dispose of their land according to their will. Saxony's rulers practiced a policy of "peasant protection"
to secure those rights, probably as a means of securing their tax base. By so
doing, the central government in effect limited traditional property rights
of the local overlords. With the single exception of upper Lusatia, throughout Saxony a diversified and stable farm structure emerged with the mass of
the land belonging to holders of small and medium-sized, full-time family
farms.[2] The guild system—in the high Middle Ages a powerful institution
that restricted entry to handicrafts and regulated production standards—
had lost, by the eighteenth century, much of the support of Saxony's central state on which its monopoly rights had depended. Its continued viability required flexible adaptation to the competition of rural, non-guild
producers that was emerging in this period.

In much of rural Saxony, however, population growth since the second
half of the seventeenth century led to the emergence of a kind of proletariat with little or no land—cottagers and "gardeners"—forming households
that could not live from farming alone and would thus become ready recruits for employment in rural industry. Row 1 of table 2.4 gives an idea
of their growing importance. This explains the slow growth of urbanization, its overwhelmingly small-town character (73 percent of urban growth
1750–1834 was in towns with less than 5,000 inhabitants), and well illustrates Saxony's decentralized industrialization.

According to one historian (Blaschke 1967), by 1750, this land-poor
or landless proletariat had become the largest rural social group and represented about one-third of the country's total population. Their need for
employment did not always coincide with local opportunities and thus

Table 2.4 **Sectoral Structure of Saxon Population (percent)**

No.	Status Category	1720	1750	1780	1810	1840
(1)	Nonagricultural share of rural population (%)	29	34	37	41	56
(2)	Share of urban population[a](%)	39	41	40	36	37
(3)	Share of Leipzig + Dresden (%)	10	11	9	7	9
(4)	Agricultural population (%)[b]	61	55	54	52	35
(5)	Estimated total population	670,000	797,000	873,000	104,1000	1,408,000

Source: Pfister & Kopsidis 2015: 278; Kopsidis & Pfister 2013: 5.
Note: Territorial coverage relates to the kingdom of Saxony in the borders of 1815 excluding upper Lusatia.
[a] Communities having legal town status.
[b] = 100 – (nonagricultural share of rural population + Leipzig and Dresden).

led to migration to regions closer to mercantile centers, for example, the oft-cited migration from the agrarian north to southern Saxony (Schirmer 1996). That this took place on a considerable scale during the second half of the eighteenth century confirms the relative freedom of the Saxon population, cited above. These changes, however, depended on the development of rural industry, "proto-industrialization" as we will call it, and explanation calls for an answer to two questions: (1) How did an effective demand for labor emerge? (2) How were these proto-industrial employees supplied with food? The quick answers are (1) urban merchant-manufacturers able to overcome guild resistance; and (2) the availability of local subsistence supplies. Both require some elaboration.

Proto-industrial Development in the Eighteenth Century to 1790

In both cases a regional focus is essential, for protoindustrialization in Saxony concentrated in just two Saxon subregions, the districts of Erzgebirge (Ore Mountains) and Vogtland (Kaufhold 1986, Zachmann 1997). We look first at the Erzgebirge district and the role of merchant manufacturers (Sieber 1967; Schöne 1982; Keller 2001: 201–14). In late medieval times a center of silver and ore mining, it was gradually transformed in the early modern period into a major proto-industrial region, in the eighteenth century producing small iron wares (nails, needles, spoons) and increasingly textiles. Its textile industry had by this time replaced linen with cotton products (bobbin lace, embroidery, ribbon weaving). This transformation reflected the efforts of merchants from the district's larger towns, Zwickau or Chemnitz, who developed contacts with international markets, usually via Saxony's mercantile capital, Leipzig, and then began to recruit labor from among the cottagers and smallholders. The merchants specified what and how these villagers were to produce, and gradually became merchant-manufacturers. In so doing, they had to secure the cooperation of guild organizations; but, by the 1760s, this seems not to have raised severe difficulties. Merchants held the key to the changing demands of export markets, lending them considerable bargaining power with regard to guild resistance. In general, a cooperative pattern seems to have characterized Saxon guild relations to the spread of proto-industrialization.

A similar regime of decentralized manufacture connecting rural and urban manufacturing also characterized the production system in the district around Chemnitz (on the northern rim of the Erzgebirge). As in the other districts, merchants played the decisive role. In the 1760s, a boom in cottons in international markets began, spurred by British innovations, that reshaped export demand patterns and, by strengthening the role of merchant-manufacturers, in effect undermined the power of the guilds. From the 1780s on, the use of spinning jennies spread rapidly (by 1800 and 1810 to an estimated 2,000 and 9,000 [Forberger 1958: 288–90]). The Chemnitz district specialized in coarse cottons, thus adopting a strategy of avoiding direct competition with the fine cloth Britain exported.

In the textile district of Vogtland guilds played a somewhat more important role in the early eighteenth century. In cotton manufacturing, urban guilds succeeded in restricting cotton weaving and some finishing operations to the towns, such as Plauen. For a while this limited rural proto-industrial activity to spinning and providing the members of the weaver guild with cheap yarn. British competition was, of course, felt here too, enhancing the power of the merchant-manufacturers, who then reorganized the entire chain of production in response to British competition. In result, rural manufacturing as a "putting-out" system boomed in the district, despite renewed bans against it. The region's production of cottons grew rapidly from the 1760s to the 1790s. The fivefold increase of output in three decades would not have been possible in an effective system of guild controls (Bein 1884, Rätzer 1914, Kaufhold 1986). In one respect, however, the Vogtland, by concentrating on fine cotton cloth, followed the dangerous course of direct competition with Britain. We return to its consequences below.

Marketing of Saxon textiles depended on the Leipzig trade fair—one of the biggest in Europe—which traditionally served as an international gateway to eastern and southeastern European markets and in the later eighteenth century as a link between Saxony's rural industry and Hamburg and the Atlantic economy beyond. Every year in spring and autumn thousands of merchants from the czarist empire, Poland, and the Ottoman empire came to Leipzig to buy manufactured goods—mainly textiles—in great quantities. To make the fair attractive, Saxon governments followed a liberal, open-market policy, refraining from protectionism or trading monopolies. This included actions against local guilds when they threatened to strengthen monopoly privileges. Concessions for new manufactories free of guild regulations were granted liberally, official guild regulations standardized and carefully relaxed. In 1780, moreover, the government passed a law legalizing violations of guild restrictions (such as fixed wages or number of workers per shop) (Horster 1908; Tipton 1976: 32–33; Schäfer 2016: 46–64; Forberger 1958; Forberger 1982: 66–89).

The second and crucial basis of Saxony's "proto-industrial regime"—so to speak, its substructure—was the supply of food for its rural labor force.

The answer to this problem is important because it gives us the key to the most striking characteristic of Saxon industrialization: its rural and labor-intensive structure. Population pressure in rural areas led to labor-intensive and land-saving agricultural change. By the introduction of such crops as potatoes, clover, turnips, and pulses, it became possible for cottagers and smallholders to spin and weave for "putter-outers" and also to employ themselves as part-time gardeners on the small plots to which they had access. This pattern was especially pronounced in the southwestern parts of Saxony, throughout the Erzgebirge, in the district around Chemnitz just north of the Erzgebirge, and in the Vogtland district to the west. In these districts not only was population growth in the eighteenth century fastest, but also urban growth was most concentrated in small towns (of less than 2,000 persons) (Kopsidis & Pfister 2013).

In the upland districts where proto-industry spread, agriculture adopted highly labor-intensive, land-saving practices. Rough estimates of the crop structure in these areas suggest rising shares of potatoes, pulses, and oats, a pattern that reflected low-income diets. The limited extent of land-intensive animal production made meat and milk products relatively expensive. The rareness of such items in the consumption budgets of proto-industrial households thus mirrored the low-wage nature of Saxon textile production—in combination with its skilled craftsmen, the source of Saxony's principal competitive advantage (Pfister & Kopsidis 2015). Saxony's agriculture managed to feed a strongly growing industrial population during early industrialization, but food standards appear to have deteriorated in this period until around 1850. In the 1850s nutritional standards began to improve substantially (Kopsidis & Pfister 2013; Ewert 2006; Martin 1895: 150).

Grazing rights constituted one of the few spheres of conflict between noble estates and the land used by owners of small farms and cottagers during the late eighteenth and early nineteenth centuries. Intensification of agriculture occurred mostly by cultivating land hitherto left fallow with legumes, clover, and potatoes, which put pressure on pasture land. Since the 1760s, merino sheep husbandry had developed into a major activity on many noble estates, an activity that especially affected the densely populated proto-industrial uplands. Reactivation of manorial grazing rights—to secure the pasture land necessary for sustaining growing flocks of sheep—led to conflict with the peasant population in these areas. Peasants reacted by mass appeals to the courts—with some success—but conflicts continued, leading in 1790 to outbreak of a severe peasant revolt. After this, repeated and determined state intermediation led in some, but not all, regions to voluntary enclosures coupled with the redemption of grazing rights (Groß 1968: 17; Blaschke 1974: 72; Kopsidis & Pfister 2013: 11-12, 40-47).

The development of agriculture in Saxony during the eighteenth century thus followed a pattern that differed from its European neighbors on the North Sea rim. It adapted, with some help from government intervention, to the needs of its low-wage, proto-industrial-dominated economy. Nevertheless, over the long period from 1690 to 1780, Saxon aggregate agricultural productivity registered an annual rate of growth from 0.2 to 0.3 percent. Saxon agricultural development in this period was innovative, early in adoption of modern crop rotation systems, establishing permanent stable feeding of cattle as common practice by 1800. These innovations made Saxony's agriculture seem progressive (Groß 1968: 38-56; Ackermann 1911; Lincke 1842). Its history also demonstrated that institutions facilitating quasi-market transactions involving the sale of property rights in land and labor could become widespread practice, even without formal reforms and full privatization of land—which came much later (Schattkowsky 2007: 324-33, 358-66). One interesting question remains open, however. It concerns the institutional arrangements between peasant producers and landlords that made possible the simultaneous intensification of agriculture and expansion of the booming merino sheep husbandry. This deserves more research.

The Role of the State

Our story of Saxony's place in German early industrialization has emphasized the leading role played by capitalist entrepreneurs and the liberal, permissive policies followed by the political authorities. This assumes a view of Saxon political history that deserves some discussion here.

A starting point is the outcome of the Seven Years' War (1756-63). The elector-prince, titular head of a defeated and financially devastated power, sought help from the wealthy Leipzig bourgeoisie—a step that put a liberal, bourgeois reformer elite at the top of the government bureaucracy (Schlechte 1958; Matzerath 2006: 39-42).[3] At once strengthened by solving the state's financial plight, this elite took control over a newly created ministry—the Landesökonomie-, Manufaktur- und Kommerziendeputation (a kind of ministry of economics)—and by patronage and marriage created a self-perpetuating group of reformers that maintained control of economic policy for many decades. These reformers, however, did not follow a coherent "reform" program that aimed at the elimination of such institutional impediments to market forces as the rigid rules of urban guilds or feudal seigneurial rights. Instead, they gradually created through a liberal policy of concessions competitive alternatives, such as manufactories that de facto established formalized "putting out" systems, regions or activities to which guild rules did not apply; or they simply ignored older ones (for example, statutes calling for a ban on rural, cottage spinning and weaving operations) (Schäfer 2016: 27–154; Karlsch & Schäfer 2006: 15–22; Forberger 1982: 95–96; Hahn 2000; Schultze 2011; Zwahr 1981: 25–70). Saxon governments, however, did not directly suppress guilds, and in parts of Saxony outside the industrial belts, the restrictive, growth-inhibiting guild system continued to exist (Herzog 2000). By allowing rural industry to spread, the reformers even won the political support of the aristocratic owners of seigneurial rights, for such industry increased owners' revenues. Such a policy represented, in effect, official recognition of the power of capitalist entrepreneurs to succeed in growing competitive international markets and of the increasing number of rural households forced to earn a living outside agriculture and the guild system. Its effectiveness as a way of widening the scope of capitalist activity made direct attack on such institutions unnecessary.

The French Era from the 1790s to 1815

This entire period represented a sharp departure from the upward trend that had marked Saxony's eighteenth-century experience since the 1760s. Recent estimates imply an average decline in its aggregate agricultural crop output between 1791 and 1812 of –0.5 percent per year (Kopsidis & Pfister 2013). Scattered evidence suggests a similar decline in the incomes of proto-industrial households over the same years. In 1806 French ambitions in Germany led to an alliance with Saxony. From 1806 to 1813, Napoleon's influence dictated Saxony's participation as war ally, drawing manpower, animals, and food away from civilian uses for war purposes, and by making it a theater of war, exposed it to further wealth losses. Finally, the peace that concluded the war in 1815 also brought heavy losses—covering 60 percent of Saxon territory and 40 percent of its population.

The negative impact of French policies on Saxony included the effects of the continental system (*système continental*) and blockade (*blocus continental*) on trade with Great Britain that Napoleon imposed on the German states beginning in 1806/7.[4] Saxony's proto-industrial centers, like similar centers elsewhere in Germany (east of the Rhine), clearly experienced a slowdown. The important Voigtland district lost its markets for muslin cloth in Turkey, Russia, and Poland. Other districts, more specialized in coarse-yarn products, fared somewhat better in the central, eastern, and southern European markets. Nevertheless, access to its traditional overseas foreign markets and sources of raw cotton became difficult, if not impossible. True, the protection from British competition the blockade offered did induce a wave of investment in machine spinning in 1808–11; Saxony's spindle capacity jumped upward from 13,000 in 1808 to 276,000 by 1814 (Schäfer 2016: 114–18, 454). This expansion of capacity must have reflected—at least to some extent—demand impulses and the resilience of the Saxon proto-industrial centers. It may have also concealed, however, the limited ability of this capacity to match British competition in peacetime. In retrospect, indeed, the evidence suggests that the technical gap between British and Saxon textile producers widened between the 1790s and 1815. The boom of British yarn imports in the early postwar years offers strong support for that observation. It actually represented the industry's return to its successful pre-1790 path (Schäfer 2016: 83–154; Kiesewetter 1999).[5]

Saxony's Early Industrialization, 1815–40

As Saxony began to recover from the war, it soon became clear that its progress remained largely rooted in its rural textile industries and the skilled but low-wage labor on which they were based. One change worth noting concerns the shift to machine spinning in centralized workshops, factories driven by the water power available in these traditional upland centers. Breakdowns and repair needs of the early machine-driven cotton mills led to development of a growing supply of technicians, and machine shops located nearby, so that a kind of second pillar of Saxon industrialization gradually came into being.

Perhaps we may see this phase of industrialization as application of three strategies to save Saxony from deindustrialization and facilitate its recovery, a phase lasting into the 1830s. Those strategies were: (1) promotion of factory-based machine spinning (introduced in 1800) to replace hand spinning; (2) readiness of Saxon export industries to use imported intermediate goods—mainly British yarn—to reduce costs; and (3) avoidance of direct competition with British producers by focusing on market niches in which Saxony's competitive advantages of low wages combined with highly skilled labor came to full effect (Bodemer 1856: 49). Thus, the cotton industry in the Erzgebirge region and the area around Chemnitz survived because it specialized in production of coarse cloth (Schäfer 2016: 155–286, Zachmann 1997; Meerwein 1914).

In the decades following 1815, Saxon merchants and manufacturers looked to overseas markets, encouraging manufacturers to concentrate on the labor-intensive, high-price segment in which manual-skill and labor-cost advantages had their full impact and mechanization had made the least progress. They also exploited technical innovations that improved the productivity of manual labor in high-quality production, for example, the Jacquard loom, new stock knitting frames or Bobbinet machines, which rapidly spread across Saxony's industrial areas. Thus, Saxony's stocking-makers could even drive British competitors from the promising North American market.[6] In contrast, attempts by Saxon industrialists to introduce mechanical weaving and calico printing in the new British style in 1815 and 1820 proved unprofitable and had to be abandoned. Given the paucity of foreign trade statistics, we cannot go beyond scattered references here.

Up to about 1850 Saxony's development path remained largely decentralized, centered on its proto-industrial regions and its success based on low-wage, skilled labor. This was not because Saxon entrepreneurs were unaware of mechanized production methods based on steam power, used by their British competitors. It reflected the fact that Saxon steam-powered technology was not yet cost efficient as basis for export success (Wiek 1840: 18–19, 408–10; Forberger 1982: 312–28, 350–69; Kiesewetter 2007: 423–48). By this time, Saxon entrepreneurs as merchant-manufacturers had long replaced the simple purchase system (*Kaufsystem*) with sophisticated, vertically integrated putting-out systems (*Verlag*), the survival of which was based on concentration on high-quality fashion products sold in international markets. They controlled production as well as marketing—in contrast to the older purchase system, in which merchants bought final products from petty cottage producers. Steam-powered textile factories to centralize production only started to emerge on a larger scale after 1850, while companies based on decentralized homework and putting-out systems were still being founded until the 1860s (Zachmann 1997).

The first signs of change appeared in the 1830s, provoked in part by Saxony's worries about its possible exclusion from the Zollverein. Leipzig's merchants, encouraged by Friedrich List, proposed and formed two railroad companies: in 1836, the Leipzig-Dresden line, and in 1839, the important Leipzig-Magdeburg line, both joint-stock companies, but the latter requiring difficult negotiations between the Saxon and the Prussian governments. Exploitation of coal deposits in southwestern Saxony, the growth of machine-making workshops, including a Chemnitz enterprise that began to build steam locomotives, also began in these years, giving hints of future industrial growth possibilities. Nevertheless, it was not until the 1850s that railroads and heavy industry began to have any noticeable effects on Saxony's industrial growth.

Saxony's early industrialization, we have seen, reflected to some extent the role played by the state; historians have long argued about its liberal character. In the post-1815 years, the Saxon government began to consider abolition of the guild system (Horster 1908: 36). In the aftermath of Saxony's "July Revolution" in 1830, however, a constitution was introduced that significantly extended popular political participation. This made a radical anti-guild policy impossible, for the government recognized that the majority of Saxon voters clung to the illusion that guilds formed an effective protection against the feared "excesses of unleashed capitalism." This illusion may have weakened after the unsuccessful revolution of 1848—in which craftsmen feverishly fought for strengthening of the guild system. Nevertheless, it took another thirteen years until freedom of enterprise was introduced in Saxony (1861). Since Saxony's industrialization was well along by this point, we have reason to suspect that so late a declaration of freedom of enterprise reflected the fact that it had little to do with Saxon industrialization (Schäfer 2016: 445; Wieck 1840: 401–2).

Table 2.5 Number and Annual Rate of Growth of Cotton Spindles, 1800–1840

					Saxony	Prussia	Germany
	Saxony	Prussia	Germany		Annual Growth Rates (%)		
1800	3,000	15,000	22,000	1800–1815	35.4	9.0	20.5
1815	284,000	55,000	360,000	1815–25	0.5	0.9	0.8
1825	300,000	60,000	390,000	1825–34	2.5	5.2	3.2
1834	375,730	95,000	518,000	1834–40	4.6	7.9	7.9
1840	493,000	150,000	818,000				

Source: Our own calculation based on data from Kirchhain 1973: 39–42.
Note: Prussia almost entirely corresponded to the Rhineland.

Table 2.6 The German Textile Industry around 1840

	All Spinning[a]	Cotton Spinning[a]	Weaving[b]
Saxony	37.9%	56.3%	31.7%
Rhineland	17.6%	17.2%	7.6%

Source: Blumberg 1965: 55; Dieterici 1844: 340–41.
Note: Capacity of the German Customs Union = 100%.
[a] Percentages based on number of spindles.
[b] Percentages based on number of looms.

Northern Rhineland and the Ruhr
(Rhine-Ruhr Area), c. 1700–1840

The Rhineland's economic dynamism obviously owed much to the river from which its name derived. Trading opportunities along the Rhine meant wider markets and profitable employment for local capital and labor. During the sixteenth and seventeenth centuries, they linked the Rhineland to the economic potential of the Low Countries, Europe's most dynamic region, and the North Sea trade it served. Opportunities alone, however, would not have sufficed, had the Rhenish population not possessed the ability to exploit them. That it did reflected the region's medieval heritage of a weak manorial system and a degree of political fragmentation—in the seventeenth century no fewer than eight sovereign powers shared in its rule—that encouraged the development of a relatively free population; from this evolved a class of entrepreneurs with the needed ambitions and abilities, as well as a complementary class of free labor (Schulte 1959; Barkhausen 1954; Barkhausen 1958: 195–203; Ebeling 2000; Adelmann 2001).

To some extent the Rhineland's development duplicated that of Saxony (discussed above): its dynamism emerged largely in the rural countryside and focused mainly on the textile industries. One reason for this was that in the Rhineland, as elsewhere in Europe, cities, whose guilds regulated production techniques and product quality, proved inhospitable to ambitious, innovative entrepreneurs. Another was that in several parts of the Rhineland, certain rural areas marked by small holdings and growing populations bred a rising interest in industrial employment, which then gradually developed, often actively assisted by petty capitalists with contact to distant markets. In at least one respect, however, the Rhineland differed from Saxony: its iron, and iron- and steel-working, districts played a relatively more important role (Kisch 1981: 118–23, 225; Engelbrecht 1996: 99–122, 176–77; Gorißen 2002: 83; Kriedte 2007).

The development of what we might call the "Rhine-Ruhr" industrial belt seems to have accelerated during the two or three decades following the Seven Years' War. By around 1800 economic development in small and dispersed proto-industrial areas had crystallized into five main industrial districts (Schulte 1959; Kaufhold 1986: 149–63, 186):

1. On the left bank of the lower Rhine, in the duchy of Jülich, extending from the townships of Gladbach, Viersen, and Rheydt, where at first linen cloth

production for export and later cotton cloth dominated, northward to Krefeld, where a highly successful silk export industry developed.

2. In the border triangle between Germany, the Netherlands, and Belgium, with the region Aachen-Verviers-Limburg, a cross-border and highly differentiated industrial region emerged that was based on woolen cloth and metal processing.

3. On the right bank of the Rhine, in the duchy of Berg, the upland area centered in the Wupper valley (with the cities Barmen and Elberfeld) had first developed a linen cloth and finishing industry, but since the 1760s successfully switched to the production and export of cotton cloth. Nearby, in the same hilly area called "the Bergische Land," the towns of Remscheid and Solingen specialized in the production of fine steel wares (cutlery, household implements, tools).

4. The county of Mark covered the uplands (*Niedersauerland*) south of the Ruhr river around Hagen and Lüdenscheid, and essential parts of the at that time much more agrarian highly fertile Ruhr area. The uplands were characterized by metal-working activities, producing medium-quality ironware, wire, metal goods, and sewing needles. Textiles, woolen processing, linen weaving, and later, especially spinning and weaving for the Wupper valley's cloth industry, also played a noticeable role.

5. The Siegerland, southwest of the county of Mark in the Sauerland highlands, had iron ore mining and iron-working industries.

The Rhineland's two imperial cities, Cologne and Aachen, both influenced by Catholic political interests and powerful craftsmen guilds related thereto, remained largely outside the dynamism that characterized those five districts through much of the eighteenth century. They even experienced a severe "human and real capital drain"—mainly, but not only, Protestant entrepreneurs and craftsmen unwilling to accept their economic and religious discrimination. Their eventual integration into the "Rhenish economy" came with the French occupation of the region after 1790, and we return to it below (Kisch 1981: 162–316).

Rhenish agriculture, like its counterpart in Saxony, played a relevant role here. In no German region—not even in Saxony—was dissolution of the manorial system more advanced by the end of the eighteenth century than in the northern Rhineland (Aubin 1922: 135; Henn 1973; Kopsidis & Lorenzen-Schmidt 2013: 261–65; Kopsidis 2013: 286–93; Kopsidis et al. 2017). As in the bordering Low Countries, commercial tenancy and a highly intensive small-scale agriculture dominated. Proto-industrial households themselves engaged in small-plot subsistence farming, their contribution to local food security supplemented by a growing grain trade between the fertile Rhine valley and densely populated industrial regions of the nearby unfertile highlands. A long-distance interregional or international trade in foodstuffs played almost no role at all in this early period. The concentrated demand of population agglomeration such long-distance markets needed did not yet exist. By the beginning of the nineteenth century, however, a spatial pattern of "Thünen belts," with a small nucleus of highly intensive farming surrounded by an exterior belt of extensive farming, was already recognizable. Intensity as well as market sensitivity diminished with increasing distance from the rural-industrial demand centers and their immediate agrarian hinterland. Thus, the demand-driven character of agricultural development had become visible long before industrialization became an important shaping force (Kopsidis 2015: 351–57; Kopsidis 2009).

Three Textile Stories

The Rhineland's "dynamism," as suggested above, emerged first in what were very largely rural settings, "proto-industrial" regions, as they came to be known. The histories of the Rhenish textile industries offer prototypical examples. We look at three of these here, for they offer a key to the forces that determined the course of industrial development in the Rhineland. For the purposes of this book we confine our observations here largely to the progress since the middle of the eighteenth century.

The first, perhaps most typical, case concerns the Wupper valley with the "twin" towns of Elberfeld and Barmen, which began as villages that initially responded to demands for foodstuffs and raw materials emanating from the Rhineland's metropolis, Cologne. These villages were originally populated largely by freeholders or hereditary tenants, actors unimpeded by restrictive manorial claims or by powerful guilds hostile to change, and they quickly adapted, some of them becoming linen merchants. The district's growth was helped by a flow of migrants, largely Protestant dissenters fleeing the intolerance of the Catholic imperial city territories and the restrictive guild system there. It soon had become an important supplier of the Dutch markets, bypassing Cologne completely. By the 1750s its merchant-capitalists, who dominated both production and marketing, had begun to replace their success with linen fabrics by becoming major exporters of braids and ribbons and other articles made from half-cotton cloth—so-called *Siamoisen*—which went to other German states, to markets in Brabant, Holland, France, Britain, and overseas territories. The

Seven Years' War brought a hurtful time of occupation by Prussian and French troops, but the district rapidly recovered, innovating and widening its product assortment. Successful abroad in a growing world economy, the Wupper valley district had become, by the eve of the French and Napoleonic Wars, a major economic factor in the duchy of Berg. Hampered by the high living costs that came with its own prosperity, Elberfeld and Barmen merchant capitalists "farmed out" important input activities, such as yarn production, bleaching, and even dyeing, to villages and rural areas where underemployed and cheaper labor could serve as an attractive substitute. By the 1790s, with a population of close to thirty thousand inhabitants, the Wupper district was thought to employ, directly and indirectly, more than forty thousand persons! Such was its success (Kisch 1981: 162–257; Tilly 1981; Engelbert 1996: 163–87; Gorißen 2016a).

The Wupper valley textile district was probably the closest thing to a capitalist "open society and economy" that developed during the eighteenth century in the Rhineland. According to contemporaries, freedom of enterprise was de facto more or less existent in the duchy of Berg by the last third of the eighteenth century—even if it was never proclaimed. Freedom of enterprise, of course, meant that competitive pressure was ever present. If local costs of a production input became too high, the merchant capitalists had to look elsewhere for an alternative source, or lose the business to a rival. Their success had little to do with state policies, though the fact that the duchy's ruler placed no restrictions on immigrants and rarely intervened in local affairs proved to be advantageous for the region's growth. Success derived from careful control of the value-added chain from raw materials to final sale, and from careful attention to competitors. These self-made men par excellence, full of respect for market dictates, expected the same from those they employed. Over time, this generated repeated conflicts with weavers and again with bleachers, when costs threatened. Powerful corporate institutions like the *Garnnahrung* to organize the textile sector developed in the Wupper valley as elsewhere, in theory combining the interests of craftsmen with those of the internationally acting merchants. Almost from its beginning, however, the *Garnnahrung* was more market-oriented than any Cologne guild. The growing importance of the "Atlantic economy" for the Wupper valley de facto enhanced the power of its merchant capitalists within the guild. The latter's inability to defend the interests of craftsmen thus began to contribute to the descent of self-employed craftsmen to a de facto status of dependent wage laborers well before early industrialization had started—a transition that was not free of occasional violent protest (Kisch 1981: 169–73, 249–50; Reininghaus 2002: 79–81; Engelbrecht 1996: 271–76; Gorißen 2016b).

The second textile success story focuses on the lower Rhine city of Krefeld and its striking eighteenth-century ascent to prominence as one of Europe's most important producers of silken goods. It began in the seventeenth century with the arrival of Mennonites—members of a Protestant (Baptist) religious minority—in the lower Rhine area as refugees from the Spanish Netherlands where they were persecuted. As in the Berg territory, here too, the predominance of freeholding and tenant leaseholds suggests a relatively free population and hospitable territory for development of rural industry. Be that as it may, when the newcomers came to settle in the townships of Gladbach and Rheydt, the native population, both Catholic and Lutheran, viewed them with suspicion. Indeed, the speed with which Mennonite entrepreneurs began to prosper by specializing in the manufacture and trading of linen drew the negative attention of the local inhabitants. Mennonites, it was claimed, by virtue of their capital, were buying up flax still standing in the field, thus establishing a monopoly "that took the bread out of Catholic mouths" (Kisch 1989: 57). In truth, they were transforming into an industry an activity that local families had seen as an extension of their agricultural work, thus beginning to replace the Dutch merchants that had hitherto served local interests as buyers of their part-time labor services. Nevertheless, local agitation increased, eventually leading the duke of Jülich to expel the Mennonites, who thus emigrated to Krefeld, then a territory subject to the Dutch house of Orange. It was here that they established their reputation as effective business leaders. Their very names—van Aakens, ter Meers, von der Leyen—reflected their Flemish-Dutch origins.

The peculiarities of their religion made them "outsiders" in Krefeld, a place dominated by the Reformed Church. The Mennonites were a minority marked by clannishness, solidarity, and cohesiveness, characteristics strengthened by a high rate of intermarriage. Nevertheless they soon became noted for their hard work, their thrift, and their honesty in business dealings, and they began to prosper. By the early eighteenth century, as merchant-manufacturers, they had come to dominate Krefeld's linen export business. The more successful among them, however, were first and foremost merchants—their interest focused on market demands. It was this focus that propelled the ambitious von der Leyen family in the eighteenth century to its greatest success: the transformation of Krefeld into Germany's leading center of silk manufacture (and its emergence as one of the most important producers in Europe). They began as commission merchants, buying and selling silk and silken wares at the big markets in Frankfurt or Leipzig that were produced elsewhere; but as they recognized that the leading centers of silk goods production (such as Holland, or the city of Cologne) were becoming high-cost producers, they saw Krefeld's chance. The closeness to Holland facilitated the adoption of the "state of the art" Dutch production techniques. In the Rococo era, with its expensive fashions, the demand for silken fabrics soared, and Krefeld's silk industry along with it. By the 1760s it employed probably more than four thousand persons, some of them in nearby villages and many of them former linen weavers. The industry's leaders, the von der Leyens, realized enormous profits. The firm's net worth grew from around 30,000 thalers in 1730 to more than 1.3 million thalers in 1794! By this latter date, they were probably the richest merchants in the entire Rhineland. Perhaps it was no wonder that the king of Prussia, in 1787, had decided to award the von der Leyens a peerage. This recognition could have had something to do with the fact that Krefeld's success had been achieved with no royal or state support, while such support of Berlin's silk manufacture had proved to be an expensive failure (Kisch 1981: 66–161; Kriedte 2007).

A third textile story concerns the development of the woolen industry in the left bank region around the imperial city of Aachen. In the late medieval period, Aachen had been one of Europe's main centers of that industry, but in the early modern period England and the Low Countries developed rival centers, and Aachen, dominated by its inflexible guild institutions and the oligarchic political structure to which it was closely connected, could not adapt. In the late seventeenth century, alert and ambitious entrepreneurs among Aachen's clothiers began to move key operations—dyeing being the first—away from Aachen into the surrounding countryside (to Burtscheid, Eupen, Forst, and Leiden, later to Montjoie). Other finishing steps followed, and by the early eighteenth century, we see the entire operation of woolen cloth-making growing in these proto-industrial villages and towns, controlled by merchant- manufacturers eager to exploit the freedom from rigid guild restrictions on output and the cheapness of rural labor. Burtscheid, a nearby territory independent of Aachen and ruled by a Catholic women's abbey, offers an interesting example of the importance of economic motives, for the abbess used her policy of full religious and economic freedom to attract immigrants that would increase her revenues, and Burtscheid's subsequent development confirmed the wisdom of this stance. The most striking development of all, however, may have been the growth of fine cloth products introduced into Montjoie (Mondschau) by a local entrepreneur, Johann Heinrich Scheibler. The success of these products in European markets was so great that they brought him wealth, international recognition, and eventually a peerage. Such growth also led to shortages of labor, but the cost-efficient solutions Scheibler and his fellow merchant-manufacturers chose—recruitment of skilled workers (such as shearers) from southern Germany and of spinners and weavers in the nearby district of Limburg from among the peasant population (mostly dairy farmers) there—brought attacks from native shearers and weavers in the Aachen area. These men, employed by the Catholic clothiers in the coarse woolen cloth branch and used to the protection of traditional guild regulations, resorted to violence in 1762, while the Catholic clothiers filed formal charges against Scheibler and his compatriots with the ducal authorities of Jülich-Berg. The latter, however, proved reluctant to intervene. In the years that followed, repeated incidents of sabotage and violent protest over the same issues took place. In 1775, the Jülich-Berg government issued an edict—the so-called "Düsseldorf Mandate"—that supported the side of the fine cloth manufacturers, guaranteed their freedom of action, and in effect broke the power of the guilds as worker representatives. Violence would continue, but it could not and did not arrest the decline of guild-dominated industry, which continued into the nineteenth century (Kisch 1981: 258–316; Barkhausen 1954: 149–60; Barkhausen 1958: 187–94).

County of Mark

The county of Mark, since 1609 a Prussian territory, consisted of two contiguous districts, that comprising the Ruhr district, and the "south Mark" with the towns of Hagen, Altena, Lüdenscheid, and Iserlohn (Lange 1976, Reininghaus 1995, Gorißen 2002). We discuss the neighboring Siegerland (farther south in the high Sauerland) below. During the second half of the eighteenth century the county's economy depended heavily on metal production and metal-working, even more than on the textile industries. Table 2.7 shows an estimate of the situation in 1798.

Two characteristics stand out: first, industrial employment at the end of the eighteenth century had a strong rural base, even in the later Ruhr area; and second, at this date coal mining in the Ruhr area was largely a part-time job and the sector still too small to have much impact on the region's economy.

Metal production involved two main processes: the "osmond process," used to produce wrought iron for wire production; and the "strap-lift drop hammer," used to produce bar and plate iron suitable for production of

Table 2.7   Occupational Structure in the County of Mark, 1798 (number of male heads of households)

	Rural	Urban	Total	Share
Agriculture 1	11,224	1,293	12,517	50.5%
Farming as main occupation	7,973	232	8,205	33.1%
Industrial-agrarian workers	3,251	1,061	4,312	17.4%
Industry	6,185	5,804	11,989	48.4%
Metal	*1,884*	*1,535*	*3,419*	*28.5%*
Textiles	*1,649*	*1,478*	*3,127*	*26.1%*
Mining	*347*	*121*	*468*	*3.9%*
Other	*2,305*	*2,670*	*4,975*	*41.5%*
Public service	152	125	277	1.1%
Total	17,561	7,222	24,783	100.0%

Source: Our own calculation, using data from Reekers 1968: 106; Lange 1976: 16.
Note: Agriculture 1 = full farmers, farmers that owned a small farm (Kötter & Brinksitzer, Neubauern), and subpeasant strata that owned no land switching between agrarian and industrial occupation (*Heuerleute, Einlieger, Altsitzer,* and day laborers). Farming as main occupation = full farmers and farmers on a small farm (Kötter & Brinksitzer, Neubauern). This group comprises all male heads of households solely working in agriculture.

tools and small iron and steel wares. A third process, applying the "wrought iron and raw steel hammer" to produce steel for small items, was in rapid decline. Wire production took place largely in towns. Over the course of the eighteenth century, cartels were formed to control the production and price of wire. The Prussian government supported the interested producers, but the cartel had only limited success. As in textiles, here too, by the end of the century, merchants came to control the product and its marketing, evading cartel rules. The region's most important iron product category covered the production of finished iron and steel wares, such as buckles, buttons, needles, household utensils, agricultural tools, and so on. This branch employed roughly two-thirds of the industry's total labor force, about half of which lived in rural areas. These persons lived close to the location of the iron and steel hammers that produced the semi-finished goods they needed as inputs. Toward the century's end, this "proto-industrial" population also seems to have become increasingly dependent on food imports, mainly from elsewhere in Westphalia. The merchant-manufacturers who dominated this segment of the industry intermediated most of these needs (Kaufhold 1976a). Of some interest, finally, is the Prussian state's attempt to impose the tax system applied in its East Elbian territories to the Mark, a system designed to restrict industrial activities to towns that included a ban on rural manufacturing. Despite that official ban on all rural manufacturing producing for supralocal markets, the estimated share of rural production in all export production in manufacturing was 47.4 percent of the value of production in 1788 (Lange 1976: 157; Gorißen 2002: 98–107).

The Siegerland

The "Siegerland" in the southern Sauerland highlands provided the pig iron and crude steel inputs the Mark's metal-working industry required. The region's rich reserves of high-quality ores delivered correspondingly high-quality pig iron—the basis for high-quality steel or wrought iron—and it would remain western Prussia's most important source until the second half of the nineteenth century. Its importance was based on its most striking characteristic: its cooperative institutional form, the "*Haubergwirtschaft.*" Every landowning farm family had a claim on a share of the highlands' wooded slopes (with oak and birch trees). Partible inheritance rules had created by the eighteenth century a plurality of small holdings, dictating that most families supplemented farming with employment in ore mining or smelting. The Siegerland's hundreds of mines and hammer-and-hearth smelting units were small-scale cooperatives owned jointly by local landholders. These cooperatives, sanctioned by the Prussian government, operated according to a timetable that ensured orderly exploitation of a scarce resource—wood suitable for charcoal production—but they could only achieve this by limiting the annual consumption of charcoal (edicts of 1516 and 1731). This would change in the nineteenth century and will be discussed below (Gleitsmann 1980, 1982, Lorsbach 1956).

Several generalizations about this early period of Rhenish-Ruhr industrialization under the conditions of the ancien régime may be offered here as a kind of summary of the developments up to the advent of the French influence that came in the 1790s.

One concerns the effect of the ancien régime, understood as a system of government by hereditary rule, on industrial change. From our survey, we infer that political fragmentation within the Rhineland weakened such governments by subjecting them to competition. This encouraged the mobility of labor and capital. Thus, both ambitious merchants and alert craftsmen could circumvent discriminating guild regulations by migrating to a neighboring, more liberal territory. Of some importance, finally, was the fact that the two most important rulers—the king of Prussia (sovereign of the county of Mark and the duchy of Kleve) and the duke of Jülich-Berg—lived far away, the former in Berlin and the latter in southern Germany (Mannheim or Munich), for absentee rule seems to have encouraged a policy of neglect and nonintervention (Barkhausen 1954; Barkhausen 1958; Schulte 1959; Volckart 1999: 28; Volckart 2002: 180–234; Reininghaus 2002: 72–75).

That raises the question of the effect of Prussia's eighteenth-century economic policies on the Rhineland's development. Its neglect of the Rhineland may have been a blessing in disguise. Its mercantilist policies included a ban on exports from Rhineland and Westphalian producers into its East Elbian core territories. This region apparently was to be reserved for its subsidized Berlin and Silesian producers. The western region found profitable export alternatives in the Low Countries and the growing Atlantic economy, while the limited success of Prussia's policy in the east does not suggest that intervention in the Rhineland-Ruhr region would have improved the results (Kisch 1959; Kisch 1968; Kisch 1981: 93, 361–66; Fremdling 1986; Boldorf 2004).

The eighteenth century witnessed the growing influence of merchants in the guilds they worked with, reflecting their interest in control of the value-added chain attached to their marketing work, an interest that derived from the need to react quickly to the rapid shifts in the fashions that increasingly characterized the international markets they served. In the century's second half, that interest manifested itself in the form of merchant-manufacturers' attempts to concentrate that value chain in centralized workshops, some of which succeeded brilliantly (for example, von der Leyen in Krefeld, or Johann Scheibler in Montjoie). These Rhenish merchant-manufacturers were gradually transforming themselves into industrial capitalists, though their ideas about how the economy and society should be organized retained a curious corporatist, even mercantilist character (Kisch 1981: 283–98; Reininghaus 2002; Gorißen 2000; Gorißen 2016a; Ebeling 2000). Not until around the 1830s did their thinking on the organization of the economy begin to abandon corporatist views (Boch 1991).

The Period of French Influence

From the 1790s to around 1815 French influence strongly affected development of the Rhine- Ruhr economy. Some of these effects were positive, others less so. This section offers a brief resume of the issues—a kind of (verbal) balance sheet.

By the mid-1790s, France became the political master of the entire Rhineland for the next twenty years. French troops occupied the left bank in 1794, incorporating that area into the French economy, and France ruled the right bank territory by means of commissariats it established there. The French revolutionary reforms abolished feudal master-servant relationships without compensation, declared religious discrimination illegal, confiscated and secularized monastic lands, all but abolished the guilds, and radically reformed the judicial system by abolition of patrimonial courts and introduction of trial by jury. Somewhat later came introduction of the Napoleonic version of revolutionary law: the famous *cinque codes* (Five Codes), which included the *Code civil* (1804), *Code de procédure* (1806), *Code de commerce* (1806), *Code d'instruction criminelle* (1808), and the *Code pénale* (1810). French reforms also directly affected business interests, for example, by the introduction of chambers of commerce to represent the interests of capitalist entrepreneurs, or the establishment of *conseils de prud'hommes*, commercial courts to regulate industrial disputes. These courts notoriously favored independent capitalist employers, significantly weakening the rights of wage laborers. A repressive system of labor control—the legal introduction of workbooks (*livrets d'ouvriers*) introduced in 1803—strengthened this tendency by noticeably limiting the mobility of workers (Kisch 1981: 317–60; Wischermann 1992: 40–44, 424–44; Bernert 1982). Simplifying somewhat, one may claim that members of the Rhenish bourgeoisie—merchants, industrialists, and bankers—were the principal beneficiaries of the French reforms, and the social gap between them and the working class widened during the Napoleonic era (Diefendorf 1980). French influence in the Rhineland also included contributions of French capital, entrepreneurs, and technology to the early development of the region's coal mining and metallurgical potential, for example, in the establishment of a mining school in Geislautern in 1802, or in reorganization of coalfields in the Saarland and Aachen district (Cameron 1961: 223–42; Banken 2003: 1:66–89).

For many years, historians have debated the significance of these reforms. On one side are those who see the "French era" as a milestone in the Rhineland's development, enabling it to play its well-documented leading role in German industrialization (Cameron 1961; Kisch 1981). A second position argues that the Rhineland's progress during the eighteenth century had first made it capable of benefiting from the French reforms (Barkhausen 1954, 1958, Schulte 1959). We tend toward this second position. We neither deny the potential impact on local institutions of an external shock nor doubt that the reforms went further and with more effect in areas under direct French rule than elsewhere. But a recent study by Acemoglu et al. (2011), using econometric estimates based on rates of urbanization for 1850, is unpersuasive, as some historians have already argued (Kopsidis & Bromley 2016, 2017). We note, for example, that the speedy establishment of chambers of commerce in the duchy of Berg reflected the fact that entrepreneurs had already begun to group themselves voluntarily in formal organizations before the French era. We call attention to the facts that (a) liberal reforms did not induce industrial development outside the traditional industrial areas; and (b) the shortness of the period of reform on the right bank practically precluded their having significant, lasting effects on institutions. This period was too short to change the "institutional landscape" radically, especially during turbulent times of war when most of the scarce administrative capacities were needed to meet pressing military needs. In the strongly industrialized county of Mark, finally, we see the short period of French reforms as part of a Prussian reform continuum begun in 1786, after the death of Frederick the Great. In 1791, the tax system protecting guilds and penalizing rural industry had already been abolished there, and the establishment of centralized workshops made no longer dependent on royal concessions (Kaufhold 1982: 73–85; Wischermann 1992: 4–39; Gorißen 1992; Gorißen 2002: 85–105, 197–210).[7] In areas such as this, French influence must have played a minor role at best.

The French period also included wrenching short-term economic changes related to the Napoleonic War aims and the continental system devised to implement them. Almost all Rhenish enterprises supported the prohibition of British imports, and this measure stimulated a boom in the production of linen and cotton cloth in the Rhineland. This was not the reaction, however, of those producers located in the (right bank) duchy of Berg to the prohibition of their exports to the French empire market, enacted in 1806, for it had a disastrous effect on the textile industries there, transforming the export boom that had characterized the 1798–1806 years into a period of stagnation that lasted until 1814. The Rhineland's left bank districts, annexed by France, fared better. Enjoying full access to France and its empire, the woolen industry in the Aachen district experienced a boom, and even the city itself, freed from guild regulations, participated (Kisch 1981: 258–360; Kriedte 2007: 223–424). Under the hothouse conditions of the continental system, the linen and cotton industries of Gladbach and Rheydt could also expand, cotton spinning mills could be founded, even factories, these changes reflecting the exclusion of British competition (Crouzet 1964: 563–86; Dufraisse 1981).

The overall effect of the continental blockade and continental system on Rhenish industry is hard to judge. Its enforced withdrawal from overseas markets turned the latter into British spheres of influence. Recultivation of a clientele there after 1815 required adjustment; and this proved difficult since the years of separation had led to a widening of the technical gap between British and continental cotton producers (Crouzet 1958; Crouzet 1964; Heckscher 1922: 295–323; Tárle 1914; Fehrenbach 2008: 228–34).

Of course, in summarizing the French influence on Rhenish economic development, we must go beyond the direct effects of wartime measures and consider the long-run effects of that influence on economic institutions, above all, on those that affected the status of capitalist entrepreneurs, their property rights, and their relationship to other social classes. Apart from the collapse of the guild system, secularization of the monastic lands, and the preservation of French civil law reform in the left bank territories after 1815, what we see is a strengthening of the Rhenish bourgeoisie; but that tendency began long before the revolution and reflected long-run forces. Unknown, however, remains the path that Prussian Rhineland policy might have taken in the absence of French influence. A later chapter takes up this and other reform-related questions.

The Rhine-Ruhr under Prussia, 1815–40

In 1815, many Rhenish business leaders appear to have worried about their fate under Prussian rule—a feeling reflected in the comment (attributed to a Cologne private banker) that "we have married into a poor family" (Krueger 1925: 11). There was obviously some truth in this comment. That did not apply so much to the prospect of hostile or unsympathetic policies from Berlin as to the industrial backwardness of the East Elbian territories. Table 2.8 offers an illustration, around 1800. In 1816, the share of East Elbian Prussia's population (excluding Berlin) that made its living from agriculture was more than double that of the Rhineland (Hohorst 1975: 260, 283, 343).

Our focus on textiles here is to emphasize their importance in these early post-1815 years. In Wuppertal—contemporaries called it the "German Manchester"—a short boom of spinning mills took place, but it quickly petered out. Throughout the next few decades Wuppertal manufacturers relied on imported British yarn and concentrated on less mechanized operations (dying, bleaching, and weaving) and their traditional fine specialties (lace, ribbons, bed quilts of cotton, silk, and half-silk). As in Saxony and the lower Rhineland, concentration on high-quality textiles based on manual labor for market niches was the chosen strategy. Lower labor costs made this the only feasible response to Prussia's free trade policy and the British imports it facilitated. In the 1820s Rhenish textile centers began to attract machinery-making firms and to install steam engines, but the transi-

Table 2.8   **Manufacturing in Prussia around 1800**

Annual growth rates, 1782–97 (number of looms)					
	Silk	Wool	Linen	Cotton	Total
Kingdom of Prussia	3.7%	0.1%	−1.1%	4.6%	0.1%
Eastern provinces	1.6%	0.4%	−3.7%	1.3%	−1.6%
Central provinces	4.0%	0.4%	−1.6%	4.3%	0.4%
Western provinces	4.5%	−1.9%	0.0%	7.9%	0.2%

	Looms		Labor Force in Manufacturing		Share of Textile
1802	Urban	Rural	Urban	Rural	Workers
Kingdom of Prussia	63.8%	36.2%	67.0%	32.8%	81.9%
Eastern provinces	87.9%	12.1%	76.2%	23.8%	75.3%
Central provinces	77.3%	22.7%	75.4%	24.4%	85.3%
Western provinces	15.1%	84.9%	33.3%	66.3%	78.0%

Total Number & Shares of Total (Prussia)			
1802	Population	Looms	Labor Force in Manufacturing
Kingdom of Prussia	4,335,462	45,551	266,194
Eastern provinces	51.7%	13.2%	27.0%
Central provinces	36.5%	62.8%	52.5%
Western provinces	11.9%	23.9%	20.5%

Source: Our own calculation, using data from Kaufhold 1978: 487–90, 515–19.
Note: For definition of macro-regions, see table 2.1. Manufacturing = total labor force employed in manufacturing (persons); share of textiles = share of textile workers in total manufacturing labor force.

tion to mechanized factory production in textiles first began in the 1850s. Despite its considerable weight, the Rhenish textile industry does not seem to have been the catalyst that sparked the Ruhr district's "take-off" in the 1840s. True, in 1815 textiles formed the leading industry in the Ruhr district. As early as the mid-1820s Wuppertal capitalists promoted the construction of a railway between the Ruhr and Wuppertal, powered by horses, to bring coal for the latter's industries. This was a sign of what was to come, but only a sign (Boch 2016, Adelmann 1986).

By around 1830, coal mining and iron production in the Rhine-Ruhr region had become nonnegligible factors. The hundreds of small-scale producing units accounted in the aggregate for more than half of all Prussian coal and more than one-third of iron production (Holtfrerich 1973, Fremdling 1986, Däbritz 1925), and in the 1830s, entrepreneurs began to see more clearly the possibilities based on techniques demonstrated by British, Belgian, and French producers. Many of these entrepreneurs came from old merchant dynasties familiar with the industry's trade, represented, for example, by names like Stinnes, Krupp, Harkort, or the firm of Jacobi, Haniel & Huyssen (Köllmann 1990). These capitalists provided the financial basis for early experimental investments in larger operations. Iron smelting with coke and bar iron by the puddling process began. These first steps, however, remained quite modest in the 1830s, for two main reasons: (a) thanks to Prussia's low tariffs, English and Belgian iron was much cheaper; and (b) thanks to limited mastery of the technique of coke-smelting, Siegerland charcoal offered a more reliable and cheaper fuel than coal. The true breakthrough came in the next decade with two changes. First, the exhaustion of shallow pit mining in the Ruhr district led to use of steam power to bore deeper shafts. In 1839–40, Matthew Stinnes and his technical staff succeeded in boring through a layer of marl and sinking a deep shaft that reached rich seams of high-quality coal. By 1841 this mine, the "Graf Beust," could begin to produce. The demonstration effect of this success was considerable. This was the point at which the Ruhr's production began to leave the other Rhenish coal regions behind it.[8] Second, as the railroad network began to expand more rapidly, industrial entrepreneurs pressed for higher protective tariffs on iron products, pressure that led in 1844 to the desired Zollverein duties. At this point a period of rapid replacement of charcoal smelting by coke began, followed by import substitution. We return to this theme in chapter 7.

Württemberg

Today one of Germany's most wealthy and highly industrialized regions, in 1800 Württemberg was an industrial backwater. Like Saxony and the Rhineland, Württemberg had a long tradition of export-oriented manufacturing that went back to the late medieval period. In the sixteenth and seventeenth centuries, it was a major center of linen and woolen (worsted) production. In contrast to the experience of those two early industrializers, however, substantial parts of Württemberg's formerly vibrant textile sector slipped into stagnation during the last third of the eighteenth century (Ogilvie 1997a; Ogilvie 1997b: 109; Medick 1997: 85; Troeltsch 1897: 172–99; Flik 1990: 234). True, the shift of international trade from Central Europe and the Mediterranean to the North Sea rim and "Atlantic economy" in the eighteenth century adversely affected producers in Württemberg to a greater degree than it did their counterparts in Saxony or the

Rhineland. Nevertheless, the successful adaptation of Switzerland's proto-industries to that geo-economic shift throws some doubt on the decisive importance of location (Pfister 1992). We thus need to look further—to the role of economic, social, and political institutions.

We quickly rule out the importance of quasi-feudal restrictions affecting rural populations, for in Württemberg by 1700 little remained of manorial rights, and peasant landholders had strong property rights (Hippel 1977: 278–304; Ogilvie 1997b: 110–13). With the proto-industrial histories of Saxony or the northern Rhineland in mind, we look then at the role of guild organizations. In the early modern period these institutions had played a strong role in Württemberg's most important industries—linens and woolens—even where much of the production took place in rural settings. This has been attributed to their ability to serve as guarantors of product quality. By the second half of the eighteenth century they had attained their mature form, in which large merchant companies with monopoly power controlled production and marketing, and craft guilds controlled entry to their crafts. One company, the Calwer Zeughandlungs-kompagnie, which controlled the worsted industry in the eastern part of the Black Forest, had become by 1700 the largest in the entire industry. A second large enterprise, the Leinwandhandlungs-Compagnie, founded in 1662 in Urach, regulated linen production in the Swabian Alb region. A sister company with similar rights began to operate in the district around Heidenheim, a town on the eastern border (Ogilvie 1997a; Troeltsch 1897; Medick 1997; Flik 1990: 88–108).

Both companies and guilds successfully maintained their dominance of the linen and woolen industries until the end of the eighteenth century. This reflected the duchy's peculiar political economy: the dukes, weakened by military and other central government expenditures, sought to raise funds by the sale of monopoly privileges, but this could not suffice, and thus they repeatedly turned to its estates assembly, the Landstände, for funds. Unique in Germany, this body was not controlled by the nobility, nor did it reflect a capitalist-friendly bourgeoisie, but rather consisted of persons who belonged to what one might call Württemberg's "honorable citizenry" (*ehrbare Bürgerschaft*). This group enjoyed full communal citizenship, the right to operate a business, and the right to use the communal commons. Its leadership fell to an elite group, the so-called *Amtsbürger*, a relatively small number of educated and wealthy citizens who alone possessed the right to hold a municipal or state office. Throughout Württemberg local governments led by these elites set and collected taxes and enforced guild regulations, penalizing violations with fines. In exchange for transfer of revenues to the central government, they demanded guarantees for protection of local autonomy and guild regulations, and these were forthcoming. Guilds thus depended on local governments to defend their interests, while local ruling elites expected guilds to contribute to local prosperity as well as to their support in local political affairs. Frequent overlap (when guild officials also held public office) eased cooperation between the two. This "system" proved self-sustaining, for it was popular as a guarantor of stability—at least among those groups that possessed political power in Württemberg—even though those achievements arguably came at a considerable cost of foregone innovation, technological progress, and economic growth. Women, for example, were systematically excluded from guilds and forced into low-paid, low-skilled occupations (Ogilvie 1997a, 1999, 2003, Medick 1990, Carsten 1959, Vann 1984, Ogilvie & Carus 2014: 419–22).

Some concrete facts on the behavior of privileged companies and guilds may help convey a sense of how the result just described could come about. We begin with the Calwer Company, a formalized cartel of "putter-outers" of worsted cloth. Its "natural" strength built on the crucial importance of dyers and merchants for export market success in the worsted industry, but with its charter of 1650 came the additional force of the monopoly right to export. Its Black Forest partners, the weavers, had agricultural reserves plus their guilds to rely on, but by the second half of the eighteenth century most weavers had become dependent on the "putter-outers." Over the years, the company had used bribes and cheap loans to government officials to ensure passage of laws enhancing its privileges, for example, those making it the weavers' exclusive buyer at maximum prices set by the company. The weaver's guild responded by restricting entry to their trade, limiting workshop size, setting maximum prices for spinners (mostly women), and using what the company regarded as lax quality controls. Price incentives to improve the latter were not forthcoming. This combination appears to have resulted in a product that initially enjoyed some export success, but became, by the last third of the eighteenth century, internationally noncompetitive. Nevertheless, the one weaver-friendly provision of the partnership—the company's obligation to buy all of the weavers' output—turned out to be its ultimate downfall: in 1797, under pressure from war complications and international competition, the company dissolved (Ogilvie 1996, 1997a, Troeltsch 1897).

A somewhat different picture emerges from a look at the linen industry and a second privileged merchant company, the Urach Linen Trading Company (Leinwandhandlungs-Compagnie), founded in 1662. This was a kind of cartel formed by Urach merchants to serve as a "putter-outer" in the Swabian Alb region of eastern Württemberg, the original intention being to reduce the influence of merchants from nearby imperial cities, such as Reutlingen, Ulm, or Augsburg. A sister company in Heidenheim, on the eastern border, also came into being. For roughly similar reasons, linen weavers of the region had developed a guild, and it became the Urach company's principal labor source. Over the course of the eighteenth century, however, company-guild conflicts broke out over questions of quality of product and prices; the system of disincentives cited earlier prevailed here as well. Throughout the region, but especially in villages and districts closer to the eastern border, weavers demanded from the government a "free trade" regime, by which they seem to have meant the right to sell their cloth at prices that corresponded to quality (and would also vary with the price of food). The companies proved unable to maintain control of the region's development. The example of Laichingen, a district south-east of Urach, is instructive. Here we see weavers, usually small landhold-ers, "kulak-like," acting as rural cloth merchants (and "putter-outers") for poorer (possibly landless) neighbors, ignoring guild and company regu-lations and marketing the product at competitive prices. Laichingen, in fact, proved very successful in this regard, creating a degree of prosperity in the district lasting until the early 1800s, when French influence over-whelmed the entire region. The district's linen cloth exports grew steadily, since the 1750s faster than those of the Urach company, and by the 1780s it exported more than twice as much (measured by the export duties paid) as that monopolist. Weaver demands for repeal of the hated export duties remained unheeded. A different development seems to have characterized the Heidenheim district, where a successful transition from linen to cotton cloth production began in the 1780s, though linen weavers protested vio-lently against it at the time (Flik 1990, Medick 1997).

The Early Nineteenth Century

At the turn of the century Württemberg's entire linen and worsted indus-try began to face difficulties that pulled it into a severe structural crisis, one that would last until the mid-1820s. The Napoleonic Wars generally, and the continental system in particular, disturbed its foreign trade, while the wartime alliance raised the tax burden to oppressive levels. Linens as well as worsted woolens lost market shares to cotton; even so, in German-wide comparison its own cotton industry remained minuscule. Eventually, the most promising "survival strategies" would be found by specializa-tion in production of labor-intensive, high-quality goods. In the meantime, however, Württemberg's laboring population exploited its traditional shield against poverty—the agricultural ties that it had never completely severed—thus protecting itself from utter destitution and (perhaps) also helping to stabilize the economy (Medick 1997: 229–63; Loreth 1974: 68; Megerle 1982: 106; Boelcke 1973: 454).

In the years 1806–14 Napoleon made his influence felt in other ways. His alliance with Württemberg's ruling house in 1806 turned the state into a kingdom, enabling its ruler, King Frederick I, to dissolve the diet, end all constitutional and democratic experiments stimulated by the French Revolution, and begin a period of autocratic government. With Napoleon's backing, Frederick I ruthlessly carried out a policy of absolutist reform (earning him the title "Swabian Czar"). His efforts created a centralized, powerful, and reform-oriented administration for the new kingdom of Württemberg (enlarged by its absorption of petty states). The period of absolutist rule ended in 1814 and thus proved too short for realization of substantial concrete reforms. The constitution of 1819 established a constitutional monarchy, restoring strong local self-government, but also providing for a strong central government subjected to limited parliamentary checks. The position of reform-minded civil servants remained strong in Württemberg, both in the administration and in parliament, where they dominated debate. The bureaucracy's leverage as political force, however, fell far short of the "Prussian model."[9]

The constitution of 1819, in effect, reinforced a political constituency—probably a strong majority of voters—that believed in and clung to the guild system. Most voters were artisans or tradesmen who favored guilds, and probably most intellectuals shared the same fear of their abolition (Medick 1990: 62–72; Langewiesche 1974: 48, 71–82; Dipper 1996a). The power of local governments supported their view, for they had long benefited from guild support. Residential rights and thus migration in Württemberg remained under strict municipal control until 1870 (Matz 1980, Knodel 1967, 1972). In effect, therefore, municipalities also controlled industrial location. Under these conditions, liberal attachment to free employment laws (Gewerbefreiheit) had little chance of success. This ruled out open abolition of guilds as policy option, but as one historian put it, not legislative éclat, but administrative finesse was what rendered guilds ineffective (Tipton 1976: 37).

Württemberg, in fact, like some other German states, took another "road to Rome": it followed its reform bureaucracy along what one might call a "soft liberal" policy course. In 1828, it took a first constructive step by concluding a customs union with its neighbor, the kingdom of Bavaria.

Table 2.9   **Structure of Nonagricultural Employment in Württemberg in 1832**

	Status			Share of Labor Force (in %)	
Occupation	Master/ Owner	Employee/ Helper	Total Number	Of Total Population	Of Total Male Adults
Handicrafts	113,943	30,981	144,924	9.18	27.47
Factories	269	6,852	7,121	0.45	1.35
Retail trade	7,892	16	7,908	0.50	1.50
Wholesale trade	2,666	1,110	3,776	0.24	0.72
Mills etc.	5,342	272	5,614	0.36	1.06
Inns/taverns	12,012	764	12,776	0.81	2.42
Brewing/distilleries	9,263	154	9,417	0.60	1.78
Sum[a]	151,387	40,149	191,536	12.14	36.30

Source: Megerle 1982: 94.
[a] Megerle describes this sum as that of the "gewerblich Tätigen" (employees in all manufacturing).

This would soon lead it (in 1834) into the German-wide Zollverein, thus reflecting abandonment of its traditional protective policy and a turn toward freer trade and a more open economy. Its second step came in that same year, with its industrial code of 1828. Partly a response to rekindled entrepreneurial interest, the code introduced full economic freedom for larger industrial firms and certain crafts deemed essential for their operations, thus legitimizing a system by which the central government granted concessions for centralized workshops or factories planned to produce goods on a large scale and for which guild regulations were suspended. A liberal licensing policy ensured that restrictive guild regulations could not and did not prevent a growing number of factories (Flik 1990: 82; Megerle 1982: 82–93; Langewiesche 1974: 32–40; Köhler 1891: 108–75). Nevertheless, guild protection of those occupations that provided so-called "necessities" and accounted for around 80 percent of all handicrafts remained officially untouched by this approach, perhaps to ensure social peace. Therein lay the "softness" of this measure (Dipper 1996a: 144, 155–56).

The result of this hesitant policy was that in the early 1830s, barely 6 percent of employees in mining and manufacturing worked in factories or centralized establishments. Moreover, 60 percent of those so employed worked in the textile industries. It is of some interest, finally, that in the few large enterprises that employed more than 100 persons, 57 percent of those worked outside the factory as outworkers, a condition suggesting ties to agriculture (Megerle 1982: 95–99).

Two features of Württemberg's industrialization policy course stand out: (1) its cautious avoidance of an openly liberal, pro-market stance, limiting its liberal voice to issues of foreign trade that interested only a small minority of merchants and industrialists, though trade would eventually affect guild restrictions more than a policy of open confrontation; and (2) its adaptation to the spatially dispersed and agriculturally oriented labor force of the region, an approach that left intact for decades the traditional dominance of enterprises that combined factory production and outwork within the same enterprise.[10] In both respects, we may interpret this stance as catering to the preferences of Württemberg's labor force and rejection of a policy of forcing it into market-driven paths.

In the decades that followed, the policy stance just described had mixed results. Estimates suggest that Württemberg's economy grew steadily from the 1820s through the 1840s, though its industrial growth lagged well behind that of Saxony and the Rhineland in these years (Loreth 1974: 93–111). Membership in the Zollverein encouraged agricultural exports, but also imports of manufactured goods that put pressure on domestic producers, especially in textiles. Its policy of encouraging the survival of rural industries combined with agriculture suffered a serious setback in the late 1840s and early 1850s, when a series of harvest failures turned thousands of smallholders and cottagers into paupers. A mass emigration resulted, mainly to North America, reaching dimensions that clearly outstripped all other German regions (Boelcke 1973: 485–97; Megerle 1982: 161–62, 200–204; Hippel 1976; Loreth 1974: 16–19). Württemberg's population shrank over the next ten years, and its growth in the decades that followed remained well below the German-wide average (own calculation; Kraus 2007 [1980]; Sensch 2004).[11] The same crisis also revealed the bankruptcy of its backward-looking policy of supporting the dying rural linen industry. This revelation had the merit of leading to a shift toward promotion of vocational education—a policy that would eventually be widely adopted in many German states—but its long-run beneficial effects did not become visible in the period of concern here (Medick 1997: 157–71; Megerle 1982: 177–78, 220–26; Boelcke 1973: 445–46, 485–504). That same stricture applies to the advent of railroads in Württemberg in the 1850s: their importance for this "landlocked" region was enormous, but immediate effects were overwhelmed by the negative agricultural and demographic developments of these years (Boelcke 1973: 450–59).

We sum up: from the perspective of industrialization Württemberg was not a "leading region," such as the Rhineland-Ruhr or Saxony. Instead, its history identifies it as a region whose proto-industrial past did not lead directly to industrialization, for its emergence as an industrial powerhouse first became visible in the early twentieth century (Megerle 1982, Loreth

1974). In that respect, it was a latecomer. Nevertheless, Württemberg's century-long familiarity with rural industries and handicrafts does not permit its classification as "backward" in the same sense as regions such as Prussia's agrarian East Elbian territories. Historians have long stressed the dispersed character of the region's industrialization and the pulling force of part-time agriculture on which it rested. It remained strong: around 1860, two-thirds of the nonagricultural labor force was active in farming (Langewiesche 1974: 43, 46).

THREE

Agricultural Change from the 1760s to the Early Nineteenth Century

German agricultural history of the pre-1850 period suffers from the lack of accessible and reliable data on output, especially for Prussia, the largest state. Nevertheless, the vast secondary literature does permit the broad generalizations offered here, and we are able to draw on a small number of micro-studies that reinforce the points we wish to make. Those points are as follows: (1) the sustained rise in food prices in the second half of the eighteenth century reflected both more rapid population growth and the rising demand of export markets; (2) the supply response took the form of an increase in the cultivated land area and an intensification of land use; (3) the growth of output that constituted the supply response reflected two different groups of actors, the owners of large estates (mainly in East Elbia) and peasant landholders in several different parts of Germany; (4) modernization of German agriculture and its principal actors did not depend on the celebrated Prussian agrarian reforms; (5) modernization of agriculture meant, above all, commercialization and specialization, and these changes depended on the extent of the market and trading costs. All in all, German agricultural development c. 1750–1914 was mainly a demand-driven process.

Food Prices

We look first at the pattern of price development. Rye was the main German staple food during the period under consideration. Thus, here we use rye prices, but the long-run pattern would apply to wheat as well. A sustained rise in agricultural crop prices over the second half of the eighteenth century, which accelerated during the Napoleonic Wars, is well established (Abel 1966: 182–204; Slicher van Bath 1963: 221–39). Figure 3.1 is based

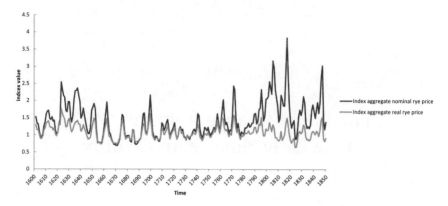

3.1 Index of Nominal and Real German Rye Prices, 1601–1850
Source: Albers et al. 2018: 93.
Note: 1731 = 1.0. Unbalanced sample, 30 cities, 1601–1850. A consumer price
index was constructed to deflate nominal rye prices in order to adjust for inflation.

on data from a geographically well-distributed sample of thirty German
cities that confirm the rising trend. Nominal prices can be justified by reference to "monetary illusion": as contemporary sources indicate, agricultural
producers reacted to changes in nominal food prices. They did so because
German farm wages were sticky, adjusting slowly to secular changes in
food price trends (Pfister 2019a, 2019b, Abel 1966: 182–89). For the sake
of completeness, figure 3.1 includes part of the seventeenth and nineteenth
centuries as well; but we postpone discussion of the later, post-1800 period
here. Improvements of international and regional grain markets during the
eighteenth century—described as the "Great Moderation"—led to reduced
volatility and dispersion of prices and made them better guides for producers (Albers & Pfister 2018).

Supply Response

As food prices rose faster than wages, supply responded by intensification
of land use, including colonization of new land on a larger scale (*Lan-
desausbau*), conversion of pasture into arable, and planting of hitherto fallow land with legumes (notably clover), in general increasing the labor-
to-land ratio with the aim of raising total crop output, regardless of the
depressing effect on yields (output per acre of land) and on labor productivity.[1] The share of cultivated land increased substantially, in part a result
of state-sponsored land-clearing and drainage projects. A limited role was

played by German intellectuals who took an interest in agriculture as a field of applied science, especially in the second half of the eighteenth century, as societies for agricultural science were founded; some large estates experimented with new planting techniques, new livestock breeding methods, and new crops (for example, the "Americas" of potatoes, corn, and sunflowers); and numerous publications on the subject appeared (Abel 1962: 253–65).

The supply response reflected the activities of a broad spectrum of producers, from large estate owners to small peasant landholders down to land-poor households working tiny plots, and it included very different kinds of farms in very different parts of Germany, from the northeast to Saxony, and from the northwest to the southwest. We emphasize this point because the importance of Germany's peasant producers in this period has not been generally recognized.[2]

The dominance of peasant family farming in Germany represented a sharp contrast to England, where a landlord's "agricultural revolution" eliminated peasant holdings and radically reduced labor inputs. Only in a few coastal agrarian export regions did the nobility remain sufficiently powerful to enforce mass eviction of peasants and implement a profitable extensive (and labor-saving) farming system of convertible husbandry (the *Koppelwirtschaft*, which combined arable with pastoral farming) (Kopsidis 2015: 355–56; Engelbrecht 1907: 100–101, 262–69; Kopitzsch 2003: 289–92; Hötzsch 1902: 258–65; Dipper 1980: 69–74). That kind of agriculture, with labor shedding in British style (described paradigmatically by Allen [1992]) was observable during the eighteenth century in the Baltic region—namely east Holstein, Mecklenburg, and Swedish Pomerania. In most parts of Germany, however, even in some areas east of the river Elbe before the Emancipation Act of 1807, peasant farmers were the main actors of agricultural development. They remained in this role in their post-emancipated guise as free family farmers.[3]

Historiographical neglect of the importance of small-scale agriculture is a bit of a puzzle. One factor that contributed to this result was the preoccupation of generations of historians with the East Elbian landed aristocracy—the Junker—and their large "grain factories" (Schumpeter 1939) when the historians considered agrarian matters. In the nineteenth century, finally, writers such as those of the German Historical School in its stage theories of development saw peasant agriculture as a tradition-bound condition of social and economic backwardness to be overcome (Sombart 1919, Weber 1906, Knapp 1887).

Demand Sources

The demand for food that underlay the above-mentioned price movements had two very different dimensions. One of these originated in international markets and stimulated German exports. In regions close to Germany's external borders, such as parts of the Rhine valley and the southwest, farms responded to Swiss, French, and Dutch demand. Large estates in East Elbia with access to the Baltic ports (Stettin, Danzig, or Stralsund) exported large amounts of wheat to the Netherlands and especially Great Britain from the 1770s to the early 1800s. The export boom led to a speculative boom in land. Prices of large estates rose to dizzying heights, by one estimate between the 1760s and the 1790s in Silesia by 73 percent and in the province of Brandenburg by more than 100 percent. Prussia's defeat at Jena in 1806 and the continental system, however, put an end to both booms.[4] These markets have probably received more attention, perhaps because of the political importance of the East Elbian landowners (the Junker), than their economic importance warrants.

Far more important—indeed, dominant—were domestic rural demands even in food-exporting regions. In this period, most agricultural markets were local ones, used largely by poor households dependent on subsistence crops, such as rye and potatoes, or frugal grains, such as oats. There were some exceptions, of course. Thus, growth of interregional trade developed to feed the growing populations in less-fertile highland regions. For example, the densely populated eastern Westphalian proto-industrial textile regions around Bielefeld were supplied with foodstuffs from the adjacent plains around Paderborn and Warburg. In the neighboring proto-industrialized southern Westphalian highlands, a dense string of market towns developed during the second half of the eighteenth century, which supplied those highlands with grain from the adjacent and highly fertile plain in the north between the Lippe and Ruhr rivers (Kopsidis 1996: 244–59; Gehrmann 2000: 198; Müller-Wille 1981: 225; Bass 1991: 180). To some extent this applied to Saxony, but here too, proto-industrial households were very largely self-sufficient on a subsistence-crop basis (potatoes and oats).

The Prussian Agrarian Reforms

The well-known Prussian agrarian reforms of the early nineteenth century played a smaller role in the development of German agriculture than traditional historiography has claimed. They appear to have had their greatest

Table 3.1 Annual Growth of Crop Production and Population Growth in Selected German Regions & the Netherlands, 1720–1860 (in percent)

		Crop Production	Population
Saxony	1743–99	0.3	0.3
	1818–49	1.0	1.1
Anholt (northwest Germany)	1740–99	0.4–0.7	−0.2
	1821–58	0.7	0.4
Netherlands	1720–1800	0.3	−0.3
	1821–58	0.9	0.9
Bavaria	c. 1800–1860	0.6	0.6

Source: Kopsidis et al. 2017: 38.
Note: Definition of crop production for Saxony: wheat, rye, barley, oats, potatoes, pulses, buckwheat, and maslin (Pfister & Kopsidis 2015); for Anholt: wheat, rye, barley, oats, and buckwheat (Kopsidis et al. 2017); for Bavaria: all grains, pulses, and potatoes (Böhm 1995: 380). For the Netherlands (1720–1858): estimates of national product from entire arable farming (wheat, rye, barley, oats, buckwheat, potatoes, cole seed, beans, and peas) (van Zanden & van Leeuwen 2012).

effects in East Elbian agriculture, where peasant dependence on landowners was strongest. We note here that reliable statements about the impact of the reforms in the Prussian east require new research. Before discussing that region, we first summarize the development of three areas in central and west Germany where those reforms had little effect and for which micro-studies exist: Saxony, the Prussian province of Westphalia, and Anholt, a tiny state close to the northeast corner of the Rhineland. Table 3.1 also shows results for Bavaria and the Netherlands, to offer a comparative perspective.

Our data for Anholt, a small sovereign lordship, have the merit of offering detailed information on the relations between peasant farmers and their landlord, and their effects on production and the markets it served. Peasants held land on leasehold and sharecropping contracts, paying a fixed rent. In the eighteenth century, output concentrated on buckwheat and oats, subsistence crops sold in adjacent proto-industrial districts of the western Münsterland. At the end of that century we see signs of a shift from those crops to wheat, a price-driven shift reflecting access to improved transportation facilities and more distant markets (via the Rhine) (Kopsidis et al.: 2017). The Prussian reforms (offering division of commons and separation of individual plots of land) appear to have had little impact here at this time.

Saxony's agriculture had introduced root crops (clover, potatoes, turnips) in the eighteenth century, and by 1800 stall feeding of livestock was well established. Its output supplied largely staple crops (rye, oats, and potatoes), though its rapidly growing proto-industrial population also produced subsistence crops—most important, potatoes—for own consumption.[5] The fact that, with a constant ratio of per capita food consumption and production, the share of agricultural employment declined (tables 2.3 and 2.4) suggests that average productivity of Saxon agriculture grew respectably in both periods. As noted earlier, Saxony's agricultural structure and growth were hardly affected by the formal reform of tenures and peasant obligations to landlords that came very late in 1831–32 (Pfister & Kopsidis 2015).

The individualization of farming, which included improved peasant property rights, a better legal status of peasants, and a more intensive use of commons based on strengthened individual user rights, was a long process that proceeded over the entire early modern period in large parts of Germany west of the river Elbe. This process intensified in most of Germany during the eighteenth century, even in important Prussian territories east of the river Elbe. Farther west, in Westphalia, we have a prime example of a successful gradual individualization of farming since the end of the medieval period (Kopsidis 2006: 277–374). Not until the 1850s did commutation of feudal dues and fees become important for the bulk of peasants. In Westphalia, therefore, the Prussian agrarian reforms had no more than faint effects (for the land market, see Fertig 2007).

Such qualification of the Prussian agrarian reform program does not apply to East Elbia—the Prussian heartland—with the same force. Nevertheless, by 1800 most large and middling peasant landholders had reasonably secure tenures. For this reason, the incentive effects often attributed to the reforms remained weak, for their implementation involved time-consuming negotiations plus loss of land or high credit costs. Except for parts of the Rhineland, the North Sea area, and the Prussian heartland—the main "target area" of the reforms—full ownership first became a realistic option for peasants in the 1850s, when state-sponsored land banks were founded and offered attractive conditions. Up to that time, in Prussia, only the large estate owners enjoyed the benefits of land banks—the *Landschaften* founded in the 1770s.[6] Nevertheless, peasant farmers at great sacrifice—some 500,000 hectares went to the estate owners for commutation of feudal services—had managed to maintain the lion's share of their holdings, and by the end of the 1840s, the bulk of farmland in East Elbia had been privatized (Harnisch 1984: 136–47). The large and middle peasant landholders remained important actors in East Elbian Prussia—despite the losses of land imposed by the reforms.

One part of the reform argument—that agricultural modernization related positively to industrialization—was surely correct. Modernization

Table 3.2   Estimates of Agricultural Productivity in the East Elbian Region of Prussia and in the Western Prussian Province of Westphalia, 1800–1880 (annual rates of growth in percent)

	Labor Productivity	Land Productivity	Land–Man Ratio
	East Elbia[a] (total gross crop production in tons)		
1800–1840	0.43	1.22	−0.58
1840–60	0.76	1.95	−0.93
	Westphalia (total gross agricultural output in 1880-prices)		
1830–80	0.96	1.50	−0.54

Source: Our own calculation based on data from Dickler 1975b: 286; and Kopsidis & Hockmann 2010, unpublished data.
[a] East Elbia: East Prussia, West Prussia, Posen, Pomerania, Brandenburg, Silesia, and the Prussian province of Saxony.

of agriculture, we argue, depended on markets. For large estates in those districts in the eastern provinces with easy access to Baltic ports, export markets for their wheat, wood, and wool had long been important. Dickler shows for East Elbian Prussia that technological change in the first period (c. 1800–1840) was land-saving, a change brought about mainly by the increased land area used to produce potatoes—the staple food of the smallholding and land-poor rural population (Dickler 1975b, table 3.2). This trend strengthened during the second period (c. 1840–60), as a switch away from sheep to tillage took place, which reflected competition from overseas wool producers and Britain's liberalized grain market. Table 3.2 shows farming productivity in Westphalia in the 1830–80 period as following the same trends as in East Elbia between 1800 and 1860 (Kopsidis & Hockmann 2010, table 3.2).[7] Growing labor productivity despite rising labor and capital intensity very likely seemed to be a common German trend in the post-Malthusian period. After 1815 the pace of technical change in farming seemed to have substantially accelerated, compared to the eighteenth century. Estimates for animal production, agricultural population, and farm capital for Prussia, 1816–49, point in the same direction (table 3.3).

The Importance of Markets

We hypothesize that these changes were market-induced. A growing number of cities began to draw their food supplies from a widening ring of farm producers. Berlin, the Prussian capital, had long served as a market

Table 3.3   Indices of Animal Output, Agricultural Capital & Farming Population in Prussia, 1816–49

Year	Index Animal Production	Index Agricultural Population	Index Capital[a]
1816	100	100	100
1831	131	121	116
1849	198	137	150

Source: Tilly 1978: 388–441, text and appendix.
[a] Livestock, farm buildings & seed.

magnet for farms in the region around it, but in the 1830s, the growth of trade and industry greatly magnified its dependence on those suppliers. Other industrial centers, such as the twin textile cities of Barmen and Elberfeld in the "Wuppertal," or the metal-working town of Iserlohn and the region around it in southern Westphalia, depended on intraregional trade to cover their needs. Even the mining district of the Ruhr region, whose miners were known for their self-sufficiency, had by this time begun to employ growing numbers of workers unable to produce their own means of subsistence (Tenfelde 1977). Intraregional markets were the answer. The transportation improvements facilitated efforts of growing industrial centers to ensure their food supplies, and may have contributed somewhat to a spatial widening of market integration (Kopsidis 2009). Evidence for Westphalia for the 1820s on road building supports this notion (Uebele & Gallardo-Albarrán 2015). In this period, however, Prussia showed few signs of a developing interregional trade between eastern agrarian and western industrializing regions based on specialization according to comparative cost advantage (Kopsidis & Wolf 2012).

In long-run perspective, it seems that in this early phase of industrialization, agriculture in most parts of Germany was just able to keep up with accelerated population growth. That farming could not yet achieve more reflected certain conditions, especially the limited extent of market integration as brakes on growth. For market integration depended on the development of stable and continuous relations between suppliers and consumers. Transportation costs affected these, of course, but so, too, did those principal intermediaries of continuous trading relations, merchants. Their strength was in their special knowledge of market rules and market conditions—their human capital. Their aim was to profit from the other transaction costs of trade: uncertainty concerning the quality of the product, the appropriate price, the rules and laws governing particular markets, and the behavior of competitors. By the early decades of the nineteenth century, they had become important actors in international grain markets, where trade volumes were high and competition strong, but their human capital and the fixed costs of trading could be better amortized (Kopsidis 2013). Local and intraregional agricultural markets, in contrast, where smaller volumes of lower priced products, such as rye, oats, or potatoes, were traded, seem to have had less attraction for such merchants. They may have represented a kind of bottleneck in early industrialization, for the skills they possessed were scarce. The question deserves more attention, but the time would come when industrial growth had produced sufficiently high concentrations of households with no direct means of subsistence, and these would open the door to development of long-distance markets. We return to that theme in a later chapter.

FOUR

Institutional Change and the Role of Early Nineteenth-Century Prussian-German Reforms

Liberal reform programs were undertaken in most German states in the early nineteenth century, directly or indirectly responding to French influence (Fehrenbach 2008; Wehler 1987a: 347–485; Nipperdey 1983: 11–82; Koselleck 1967). The Prussian variant, however, was the one that, rightly or wrongly, has come to dominate German historiography. These reforms had many advocates, fiscal needs, political ambitions, and, not least of all, developmental goals. Economic historians have focused largely on the latter, but whatever the emphasis, both design and implementation of the reforms were carried out by the state bureaucracy. In this chapter, we concentrate on the Prussian variant, emphasizing that the reforms were not only a sudden response to emergency conditions, but long in the making.

The Historical Roots: Changes in the Manorial System

In order to understand the reforms, it is important to know what needed to be reformed. This was first and foremost a matter that concerned agrarian institutions, and it is there that our discussion must begin. The rearrangement of property rights between lord and peasant that constituted the heart of the agrarian reforms had, in fact, begun gradually in the late medieval period and, by the late eighteenth century, had already brought about considerable changes in the lord-peasant relationships of the German manorial system. We look first at some of the most distinct regional differences.

In the western, northwestern, southwestern, and central parts of Germany, the shared property rights of the manorial system had moved in favor of peasants. "Full" peasants enjoyed personal freedom; held their land as virtually heritable property, paying the lord legally fixed rents and fees, either in kind or in money; and farmed as they saw fit (though constrained by tradition and custom). Personal status depended on the legal rights and obligations attached to the land peasants occupied; by the late eighteenth century, though serfdom had vanished, in most rural areas many peasant households of lower status coexisted with "full" peasants. They were also free, but conversion of their obligations to the lord into fixed rents and fees required higher payments than those due from "full" peasants—a rough measure of status difference (and of the value of obligations owed the lord) (Robisheaux 1998; Wunder 1996; Prass 2016, Kopsidis & Lorenzen-Schmidt 2013; Hippel 1977: 278–304; Henn 1973; Reinicke 1989; Lütge 1957, 1963).

East of the Elbe river and in certain parts of the northwest, agrarian institutions developed differently during the early modern period. The power of the lords increased, enlarging the share of demesne land (the lord's estate) at the expense of peasant land. Pressure on the peasant population in the form of greater demands on its labor and livestock rose to such an extent that historians have called this change the "Second Serfdom" (Kaak 1991). Indeed, in regions such as the duchy of Mecklenburg, east Holstein, or Swedish Pomerania, the vast majority of peasant households were un-free—in effect, serfs who worked on the lord's estate—and they remained so until the end of the eighteenth century. By this time, however, those three regions had become exceptional. Throughout most of the East El-bian territories, serfdom had disappeared and the number of peasant land-holders with secure property rights had grown considerably. According to one recent study of Prussia's East Elbian peasant conditions at the end of the eighteenth century, "a majority, possibly the vast majority, of peasant farms were held under a pretty secure form of tenure" (Eddie 2013: 85). This striking claim—which differs from traditional views—demands explanation and is a subject of the next section.[1] Nevertheless, the need for reform of peasant tenures doubtless remained greater in East Elbia than in the more developed regions to the west and south.

Historical Roots: Market Forces and the State as Agents of Agrarian Reform

The regional differences in agrarian structure sketched above were associated with different demand and supply patterns. Simplifying somewhat, we may say that in East Elbia, large estates played a much more important role, dominating the supply response to international demand for grain, while peasant landholders and land-poor population were principal actors in the hundreds of local food markets that emerged over the eighteenth century throughout Germany. In the more developed regions of the west and south, peasant family farms responding to intraregional markets based on the food demand of proto-industrial districts had become, by 1800, a feature less evident in the eastern regions. Peasant farmers in the west, moreover, were doubtless much more familiar with commercial, market relationships than their counterparts in the east. Nevertheless, here too, local markets predominated.

The state's interest in agrarian reforms, of course, concentrated on its heartland east of the Elbe, and was initially related to noneconomic concerns. Early in the eighteenth century, the Prussian king and some of his top advisors, worried about the state's slender finances and their effect on the army, began to see improvement in the condition of the peasantry as a potential, if long-term, solution. Nothing came of an early plan affecting the royal domains, but its aims, elimination of serfdom and empowerment of the peasantry, were followed doggedly.[2] Two laws opened the door to a permanent and cumulative improvement in the status of the peasantry: (1) in 1717 a law abolishing serfdom protected many low-status peasants from the arbitrary power serfdom gave to owners of large estates on which they worked, transforming them into hereditary tenants (subject to *Erbuntertänigkeit*); and (2) a law in 1748 that announced (or restated) the state's intention to protect the status of peasant landholdings (*Bauernschutz*) (Harnisch 1994a, Hötzsch 1902, Hintze 1898, Schmoller 1886). This law forbade the conversion of temporarily unoccupied peasant landholdings into demesne land. Both of these measures, to be sure, took decades to implement, mainly because their application had to be adapted to the specific characteristics of each of the different provinces. By the 1770s, however, peasant landholders proved able to legally defend themselves in royal courts against landlord attempts to increase their claims on peasant resources. By such support, the Prussian monarchy strengthened peasant property rights, thus providing positive incentives and a necessary if not sufficient condition for development of a strong peasant farming sector (Neugebauer 2009: 304–14).[3] The number of peasant farmers in Prussia, in any case, did not decline during the eighteenth century, but even increased.[4]

Indeed, we may see the eighteenth century as a period of ongoing agrarian reform, marked by gradual institutional changes that by around 1800 had brought a majority of Prussian peasants increasingly secure ownership status, thus making mass eviction of Prussian peasants after 1806 impossible. The redemption legislation that authorized the reforms that followed the Edict of 1807 was in fact based on legal principles developed under the ancien régime, thus provoking the historian Neugebauer to speak of the "self-liberation" of the Prussian peasants as an essential part of the long history of Prussian *Bauernbefreiung* (liberation of peasants) (Neugebauer 2009: 310; also Kopsidis & Bromley 2017: 1121–23).

During the last third of the eighteenth century, both the conversion of weak peasant tenures into secure holdings and commutation of labor and livestock obligations to the lord into fixed money rents accelerated noticeably in the eastern provinces. This change of pace reflected the unprecedented agricultural boom of the period, for the widening of market opportunities motivated peasants to invest in secure ownership—to buy themselves, so to speak, "out of *Laß* [land held at the landlord's will] and into *Erbzins* [hereditary] tenure" (Eddie 2013: 110).[5] The rise of agricultural prices and increased peasant prosperity that came with it, of course, was not confined to East Elbia, but was German-wide and related, at least indirectly, to the expansion of the northwest European and "Atlantic" economy referred to in previous chapters. Nevertheless, despite the limited impact of the rural industries that drove growth elsewhere, agricultural producers in Prussia's eastern provinces—both peasant farmers and large estate owners—experienced rising market demand based on (1) East Elbia's growing numbers of land-poor and landless households that were not self-sufficient in the supply of food; and (2) export markets in northwest Europe—mainly for producers with good access to the Baltic seaports. Both deserve more attention.

Rapid growth of the rural population in Prussia's eastern provinces in the second half of the eighteenth century reflected largely the increased numbers of landless or land-poor households (Peters 1970; Kocka 1990a: 83–86; Dipper 1996b: 64–66). They played a significant role in two respects: (1) their dependence on others for food motivated them to seek employment as (wage) laborers; and (2) their demand constituted the basis of the hundreds of local food markets that developed in Prussia over the last third of the century. We add here that in many parts of Germany, peasant farmers and landlords seem to have organized local food distribution in the form of so called "interlocked markets," designed to organize the exchange of labor, food, leaseholds, and loans with the largely landless rural classes they employed (Mooser 1984; Schlumbohm 1994; Küpker 2008; Kopsidis 2006: 136–97, 308–24; Kopsidis 2013: 297–98; Kopsidis 1996: 396–483).[6]

Consider first the latter, especially the markets' dimensions. By the end of the century these land-poor and landless households represented a majority of the rural population. For Prussia east of the river Elbe, estimates suggest that by 1800 no more than one-third of the rural population was self-sufficient in staple grains; they also suggest that about three-quarters of the entire Prussian population depended on markets (or on payments in kind) to secure its grain supply (Eddie 2013: 138–56). Since peasant producers were important suppliers in these rising markets, they will have accumulated, by the 1800s, considerable positive experience with market-oriented agriculture—long before the legendary era of "peasant emancipation" of the decades that followed (Harnisch 1986).

The role played by the "sub-peasant" population of land-poor as labor recruits was only slightly less important. For the owners of large estates, eager to exploit the continuing strong foreign demand for grain, they represented a welcome source of cheap, "day wage" labor—all the more so, since commutation and "peasant protection" laws increasingly limited their claims on the labor, tools, and animal power of the peasant landholders. In their place, estate owners acquired and provided the labor they employed with their own farming capital (animals, tools, and implements). Mobilization of this labor force helped turn large estates into economically viable production units, thus providing the region's ruling elite, the Junker landowners, with an economic pillar (Harnisch 1984: 27–58; Hagen 2002: 524–92; Hagen 2005). This transformation, however, did not take place without state financial help. That came indirectly, in the form of the *Landschaften*, state-sponsored institutions that provided mortgage credit based on the estimated value of such estates (Weyermann 1910, Mauer 1907, Wandschneider 2015). The historical importance of this development was such that it deserves some additional explanation here.

Through most of the early modern period not even owners of the large private noble estates—the *Rittergutsbesitzer*—had easy access to credit.[7] The feudal lord-vassal relationship that marked such entities only began to loosen after 1717, when the king renounced his overlord claims, but by the 1770s, most estates had become heritable private property, transferable and hence credit-ripe. This had two significant consequences: first, it enabled the estate owners to profit from the rise in land prices related to the grain export boom, since higher prices will have most likely improved their credit status; and second, it tempted many noble landowners—and even non-nobles—to engage in speculative buying and selling of such estates. Wandschneider's study (2015) shows that the institutional design of the *Landschaften*—based on unlimited liability of all members and "double recourse"—was well suited to protect them from their most speculative members. In any case, the end product of these changes that had emerged in East Elbia by 1800 was a ruling class that exhibited a curious mixture of feudal social forms and capitalist profit-oriented behavior.

One further element of "pre-reform era" agricultural development in the eastern provinces also deserves mention here, because it illustrates roughly the same mixture of state policy and market forces that characterized the changes already discussed. It concerns the royal domain lands (mentioned briefly above). The agrarian edicts of 1717 also initiated the policy of leasing entire domain districts exclusively to nonnoble agrarian entrepreneurs, who undertook to improve the profitability of the districts they oversaw.[8] The state officials set high standards and high leasing fees. Some of the districts were very large and could contain as many as 10,000 inhabitants; by the end of the century they averaged about 2,100 acres each, the leaseholders paying between 3,000 and 30,000 thalers per year and lease. Though their direct sphere of influence covered no more than 5 percent of the region's agricultural land, they are thought to have contributed significantly to the spread of new techniques and practices among the peasant farmers there. Moreover, these *bürgerliche Pächter* (bourgeois leaseholders) were not confined to royal domains, but also began to play an increasingly important role as managers of the *Rittergüter*, some of them even becoming themselves owners (Müller 1965, 1966, Heegewaldt 2012). Thus, they added a further dose of capitalist market orientation to two of the principal actors in the era of reform that would begin in 1806. The third actor—the state bureaucracy—demands a somewhat more detailed description, which forms the subject of the next section.

"Enlightened Absolutism" and State-Building as Reform Prerequisites

The concept of "enlightened absolutism" is a shorthand way of describing the nature of certain monarchical governments in the eighteenth century, designed to suggest the legitimacy of rulers whose policies appeared to reflect the rational principles of the Enlightenment. The term has been applied to Prussia under Frederick the Great (1740–86), in part since Frederick liked to think of himself as a leader of the Enlightenment: he patronized the arts, philosophers, and scientists, and he himself had occasionally written on such subjects. To what extent did his policies actually conform to this ideal?

The short answer must be: to some extent; but a more satisfactory response requires first going back to the reign of Frederick's father, Frederick

Wilhelm I (1713–40). The overriding policy goal of his reign was survival of the Prussian state, vulnerable as it was with its scattered territories, and in a Europe full of potential enemies. To this end his highest priority was always the maintenance of an oversized army. He increased its size, ensured the supply of troops by dividing the rural districts into separate units (cantons) in which peasants would serve as soldiers, their Junker landlords as officers. Covering its high costs—between 1713 and 1740 military expenditures grew from 62 percent to 81 percent of total state revenues—demanded careful attention to financial matters, and in this respect the Prussian monarch had no peer.[9] He built up a strong central bureaucracy, but managed it with an iron hand and harsh discipline. Thanks to his continued watchfulness, by the end of his reign he had paid off all debts to the estates and towns, added to the state's domains, balanced the budget, and accumulated a state treasure of nearly 9 million thaler. Moreover, his reforms of the central government—for example, the shift from regional to functional division of ministries, or the systematic opening of the bureaucracy to nonnoble talent—made it a formidable weapon of domestic policy that he used, together with the standing army, to tame the ever ambitious landed aristocracy. The splendid condition of the state finances made it impossible for the nobility to use the traditional bargaining tool, the "power of the purse," to extract concessions.[10] This was the heritage the "soldier king" left to his son, Frederick II (Neugebauer 2009, Hintze 1900, 1920).

This development of an efficient bureaucracy contradicted the claims asserted by those organs of the traditional early modern corporate state—the assemblies of the landed nobility and representatives of the towns (*Landstände* or *Ständeversammlungen*)—and solidified those gains already made by Prussian rulers earlier. As this bureaucratic machinery strengthened, the central state's ability to modernize the country's institutions increased with respect to traditional corporatist interests.

Unlike his father, Frederick II had a truly strong interest in cultural matters, music, literature, and the sciences, and he took steps to promote the spread of Western ideas and practices in Prussia. His government policies, however, like those of his father, had a strong Prussian state and a powerful army as their main goals. He did not continue his father's systematic undermining of the landed aristocracy, but restored their privileged positions, believing them indispensable for the effective functioning of the army. There is reason to believe that the deepening of the rural "canton system" of military organization under Frederick II—described as "the militarization of rural society"—may have worsened the social conditions of peasant

Table 4.1 **Enrollment Rates in Primary Schools in Prussia, 1816**

Provinces	Population (6–14)	Pupils (6–14)	Enrollment Rates
East Prussia	166,568	97,696	58.7%
West Prussia	110,109	41,084	37.3%
Brandenburg	234,840	155,246	66.1%
Pomerania	135,497	77,260	57.0%
Posen	163,953	31,523	19.2%
Silesia	401,386	263,328	65.6%
Saxony	239,046	184,757	77.3%
Westphalia	221,814	151,231	68.2%
Rhineland	328,372	167,559	51.0%
Prussia	2,001,585	1,169,684	58.4%

Source: Unpublished data from Cinnirella & Hornung 2016. We thank both authors for their willingness to provide us with these data.

life, for it certainly increased peasants' dependence on the lords (Winkler, 2000: 28; Büsch, 1962).

A lasting achievement of Prussian enlightened absolutism was its education policy. Compulsory schooling was first introduced in 1717 by Frederick Wilhelm I, but with little effect. Reintroduced in 1763 by Frederick II, it now began to have an impact on schooling despite setbacks (Neugebauer 1985). This, after all, offered a broader base for popular influence, one in harmony with Enlightenment ideals and likely to attract support of the educated class (*Bildungsbürgertum*)—the recruitment basis of the bureaucracy. By 1816 Prussia had established itself as the world leader in primary schooling (Lindert 2004) with an enrollment rate in primary schools of close to 60 percent in the age class 6–14 (table 4.1). Only the newly acquired Polish territories (West Prussia and Posen) and the catholic Rhineland showed significantly lower rates.

We may add here that the importance of Prussia's school policy for its positive contribution to Germany's subsequent industrialization and (decades later) its "catching-up growth," built in large part on the effects of human capital, has been the theme of several recent econometric studies (Becker & Woessmann 2009, Becker, Hornung & Woessmann 2011). Such findings rightly suggest the constructive and progressive character of Prussia's eighteenth-century enlightened absolutism, the force that gave birth to the primary schools. Whether that policy could have had such long lasting economic effects, however, remains an unsettled question and deserves further discussion—for several reasons (Edwards 2018).[11]

Although he tolerated a high degree of intellectual openness, Frederick II avoided radical changes that might question the rule of the nobility and the hierarchical structure of estates on which its rule rested. He feared uncontrollable upheavals that could endanger the state's military power, its economic strength, or its very existence. Thus, though he personally deeply disdained serfdom as a "crime against humanity," he took no action to abolish it. True, he did fight to eliminate the worst practices of the manorial system—such as peasant mass eviction, as in neighboring Mecklenburg—especially when these practices weakened Prussia's military power. This conservative attitude did not mean standing still. It reflected what German historians call a social conservative development dictatorship (*sozialkon-servative Entwicklungsdiktatur* [Niedhart 1979: 208]). This strategy aimed at partial modernization (in the fields of economics, administration, and judiciary) with the goal of ensuring national stability—the indispensable foundation of both state and army. Despite certain inconsistencies, this represented a development strategy that could serve as prerequisite for institutional and economic modernization (Harnisch 1994a).

Frederick II was more than a soldier-king, of course (Blanning 2016). Like his father, he took an interest in social, political, and economic affairs that went beyond military aims. His economic policies consisted largely of mercantilist measures, few of which had positive results. They also included some positive achievements, such as state-sponsored immigration, state-run land-clearing, and transportation improvements. More important, however, were the steps he took to unify the legal system, and to reform the dispensation of justice. Thus, he limited the right of administrative officials to adjudicate in legal conflicts. This improved the judicial system (Behrens 1985: 99–109). In 1748 the procedures for court cases were made more uniform and transparent. His long-run goal in this was the codification of a general set of laws that "would prevent all unnecessary legal complications and delays and which would in consequence remove an 'incubus' from his people so that 'we may have more clever merchants, industrialists, and artists who will be of use to the state'" (Behrens 1985: 106). His strong interest in this matter reflected his intellectual curiosity about law and lawmaking, but the event that led to the ALR (Allgemeine Landrecht für den Preussischen Staaten, or General Law for the Prussian State) was his famous intervention in a court case in the 1770s, the so-called Miller-Arnold controversy, for his reversal of a patrimonial court decision shocked Prussian jurists, who saw it as a blatant violation of judiciary independence. With codification, he thought, such wide differences of opinion on legality would disappear. A cabinet order of 14 April 1780 authorized this compendium, which first became law with its publication in 1794.[12] The ALR, in any case, embodied a contradictory mixture of future legal rules and existing laws, reflecting, as it were, Prussia's transitional position between feudal past and capitalist-industrial future (Koselleck 1967).

In spite of his preferential treatment of the nobility, Frederick II, like his father, concentrated recruitment of personnel for the civil bureaucracy on nonnoble applicants (Wehler 1987a: 210–14, 254–67; Straubel 2010). Their inferior social status made them more willing "servants of the state," and their education was more suitable for administrative work, while its pietistic quality internalized a strong work ethos and achievement orientation. The bureaucracy's hierarchical chain of command fostered a culture of strict obedience, enhanced by the high costs of punishment for negligence or dishonesty. Early on, the monarchy had developed a system of spies to monitor the several ministries and their departments, especially where corruption endangered the state. Positive incentives, however, were by no means negligible. Thus, relatively high salaries, pensions, or social prestige represented rewards especially valued by the many nonnoble members of the bureaucracy and surely strengthened their loyalty. The end result of this system of incentives and sanctions was the emergence of a cohesive body of highly motivated civil servants, an invaluable instrument of state policy (Behrens 1985: 57–66, 173).

We will see that states such as Prussia, which had fostered the rise of a powerful, "enlightened" bureaucracy during the eighteenth century and begun with modern state-building, would be in the best position to respond to the challenge of Napoleon. The long period of state formation in the spirit of the Enlightenment would enable their leaders to undertake radical reforms quickly and help create the institutional framework of a modern capitalist market economy (Berding 1996; Berding 1973; Blanning 1989; Sperber 1985; Behrens 1985: 176–98; Wehler 1987a: 218–67; Demel 2010).

By creation and development of an efficient civil bureaucracy, the two Hohenzollern monarchs, father and son, had recognized its importance for a state with Great Power aspirations. It was perhaps their most important institutional achievement. In the course of time, however, as the levels of education of those in the upper segments of the bureaucracy rose, there was a corresponding increase in ideas that collided with the traditional privileges of birth observable in the ruling circles and society of Prussia: individual freedom, merit, competition, equality. Since the 1770s a small number of these individuals had been exposed to liberal doctrines at the Prussian universities of Königsberg and Halle, where the ideas of Immanuel Kant, of John Locke, Adam Smith, or David Hume, played an important role. In retrospect, we can see that such changes as the abolition of manorial and guild controls, or the replacement of cameralist and mercantilist policies by market competition, could become desirable goals in the minds of such civil servants, though not realizable under Frederick II (Treue 1951; Garber 1979; Forstmann 1995; Behrens 1985: 44, 128, 186–89; Vopelius 1968; Vogel 1988; Hintze 1896).

A more decisive move toward liberal possibilities may have come with Frederick's death and the accession of Frederick Wilhelm II in 1786. Certainly, the civil bureaucracy became more "bourgeois": by 1806 the share of new "councilors" (*Räte*) of nonnoble origins had risen to over 80 percent (Wehler 1987a: 1:261–63). In these very same decades, however, the shock of the French Revolution and subsequent French influence in Prussia—as elsewhere in Germany—had effects on reform willingness we judge to have had greater importance. We thus turn to that topic in the section that follows.

French Influence, Institutional Reforms, and Modernization in Prussia and Southwest Germany, 1790–1820

The impact of the French Revolution in Germany was strong, if diffuse (Fehrenbach 2008). By the mid-1790s it had certainly strengthened what one might call counterrevolutionary sentiments in ruling circles (Rumler 1921ff.). These varied, but in the increasingly powerful Prussian bureaucracy they encouraged the belief in change guided by the state—a "revolution from above," as the Prussian minister von Struensee called it (Rosenberg 1958: 161; Winkler 2000: 43). We have already mentioned some of the characteristics of this social group, including the exposure of its members to liberal ideas. One of the most striking developments was the great significance and hope that some of these civil servants attached to the views on political economy laid out in Adam Smith's works. They seemed to see his *Wealth of Nations* as a handbook of economic development that perfectly fit the needs of the relatively backward, agrarian-dominated Prussia east of the Elbe (Kopsidis & Bromley 2017, Vogel 1983). For these reformers, the task of the state was to ensure that individual freedom, self-interest, and achievement, rather than birth or special privilege, served as bases of economic decisions to produce and consume. Applied to Prussia, this meant the emancipation of peasant producers and their land-poor neighbors from feudal and manorial controls, freedom of occupational choice, an end to the restriction of manufacturing to towns and to the ban on its spread to the rural countryside, an end to state monopolies, and, in general, a preference for free trade and mobility of population over mercantilist restrictions. In the writings of some contemporaries, references to economic conditions in the Rhineland and parts of Westphalia—and also to the effects of French reforms there—appear in policy discussions as an implicit measure of what could be done.

Most of this "reform blueprint" (Wehler 1987a: 405) was ready in the minds of reformers, but in the 1790s the "counterrevolutionary" reaction of the nobility had persuaded the king to revise the Prussian legal code (the ALR), reinserting aristocratic privileges and transforming the veto right of the bureaucracy into an advisory function. De facto, the final revision (1794) restored the king's control. The "old regime" was back in charge. Reform plans thus had to be shelved for the time being (Wehler 1987a: 241).

The reformers' moment came in the fall of 1806, after Prussia had joined the Coalition against Napoleon. The shattering defeat of the Prussian army in the double battle of Jena and Auerstedt revealed its embarrassing comparative deficiencies. As defeat loomed, the rapidity with which commanders surrendered and the extent to which the army's retreat became headlong flight, marked by desertion of thousands of troops and even many officers, threw harsh light on the Frederician image and wholly discredited the Junker elite believed responsible for the army. The peace of Tilsit that ended the war exacted harsh conditions: territorial and population losses of half the kingdom, and high reparation claims. These catastrophic results naturally led to military reforms, but they also opened the door to the so-called Stein-Hardenberg Reforms—reforms based on roughly the same ideas motivating the reformer faction of the bureaucracy in the 1790s.

In the autumn of 1807, in spite of the existential threat and some confusion in Prussia's government center, its rulers were determined to reestablish Prussia as a major power. This explains their readiness to entrust a small group of high-level civil servants with a radical program of reform. As Smithian liberals, they believed in the quick effectiveness of market-friendly reforms. Elsewhere in Germany—for example, in parts of the German west—we see no such determination (Vogel 1980: 4–5; Landes 1980; Fehrenbach 2008: 109–10). As the historian Elisabeth Fehrenbach wrote, only the Prussian reformers favored a defensive modernization "not *with* but *against* Napoleon" (2008: 109; italics in original). This commitment to confront Napoleon, and to fight him again in the future if necessary, imposed great demands on Prussia's modernization agenda. And it explains the more elaborate and comprehensive Smithian economic reforms compared to what is found in the French "model states" of Berg and Westphalia—as well as in the other *Rheinbund* states (Vogel 1983: 224).[13]

The sweeping character of Prussian reform aims became clear with publication of the famous "October Edict" of 9 October 1807. It announced the end of aristocratic legal privileges based on "estates" (*Stände*), declared the right of free choice of a profession, created a fully free land market, and abolished all forms of peasant bondage (serfdom and inherited subjection [*Erbuntertänigkeit*]). Indeed, the edict marked the end of premodern estate-based society. It read as a statement of general constitutional principles, and contemporaries understood its historical meaning to be just that, labeling it the "Prussian Magna Carta" (Koselleck 1967: 160). The details of reform implementation were left to other laws that followed. The law establishing freedom of occupational choice and of enterprise (*Gewerbefreiheit*) came in the form of two laws enacted in October 1810 and September 1811 (Vogel 1983): the first opened most trades and businesses to all who paid the appropriate tax, sweeping away guild monopolies (Ziekow 1992: 329–59). Countless royal monopolies for certain manufactures, enterprises, and merchants, which characterized the mercantilist Prussian *Fabriksystem* (industry system), were revoked. A second law abolished the requirement that residents use only seigneurial mills and inns, and that they buy and sell only in seigneurial-specified markets; but thanks to the protest of their seigneurial owners, the abolition of the profitable seigneurial monopoly of distilling rights proved short-lived (Vogel 1983: 176–79).

As implementation of the reforms begun, the overriding importance of financial motives and improvement of the state's threatened financial status—it was close to bankruptcy—became clear. In 1810, on the heels of the October Edict, came a land tax that fell on peasant holdings, and with occupational freedom, a tax that fell largely on urban trades. Further taxes were planned, but their realization first came, like the rest of the reform program, after the war ended: in 1820–21, with a tax on urban consumers of meat and flour, a customs duty, and a class tax (which fell on rural households). In the meantime, borrowing dominated state finance policy, and huge debts accumulated. These led to the well-known State Debt Law of 1820, which included a promise of popular political representation, but the crucial further step—making the power to tax dependent on the will of a representative body—was not taken. Avoiding this issue produced a timid, almost backward-looking system of taxes that fell far short of liberal reform principles and dictated a parsimonious, debt-conscious financial policy in Prussia during the following decades (Schremmer 1994: 118–36; Tilly 2003, 48–54).

Recognition of this fiscal problem may have served as motivation for the agrarian and manufacturing reform programs. It was possible to imagine an increase in the number of peasants with full property rights in their land and creation of an agrarian middle class based on family farms that would yield more tax revenues.[14] Appropriate reform design could make reforms affordable. The reform "vision" had "Old Prussia" (east of the Elbe) in its sights: a territory plagued by a century of mercantilist policy that forbade rural manufacturing—thought to protect town craftsmen—but left the rural hinterland surrounding towns only poorer, thus limiting town markets. Deregulation of manufacturing (*Gewerbefreiheit*) and spread of rural industry would offer the emancipated peasants not only employment but also markets for agricultural products. The two together would represent growing markets for the towns (Vogel 1983: 135–54).

Thus, the reform architects may have been the first in history to embrace a multisectoral strategy of rural development. A poor countryside caused poor towns, and vice versa. Reformers grasped the idea that an expanding domestic market required improved rural incomes to stimulate consumption, and that this would then break the cycle and create positive feedbacks in which both rural and urban growth would become linked and mutually reinforcing. The solution to stagnation for each was mutual growth for both. In the spirit of Adam Smith, Prussian reformers rejected the idea that the growth of one sector could only be achieved at the expense of the other (Vogel 1983: 141–54; Harnisch 1976; Harnisch 1978b: 254–63; Kopsidis & Bromley 2017).

With the Regulation Edict of 14 September 1811 (Regulierungsedikt) had come the announcement that peasants with weak property rights would be offered the opportunity to become full owners. Once again, however, protests of the nobles gained the support of the minister of justice, who saw the planned law as violation of noble property rights. Five years later, an amendment to the regulation of 1811 in the Declaration of 29 May 1816 (Deklaration zum Regulierungsedikt) formally revoked the measure and strictly limited the number of peasants allowed to acquire full property rights in their farms. It was followed by the redemption rules published in a decree of 7 July 1821 (the Ablösungsordnung), regulating the acquisition of full ownership rights for all peasant tenants with strong rights. Another law in that same year (Division of Common Land by Edict, or Gemeinheitsteilunsgordnung, of 7 June) paved the way to enclosure of all commons.[15] Further extension of redemption chances down the peasant hierarchy had to wait until the revolution of 1848 (Harnisch 1978b; Harnisch 1984: 58–101; Dipper 1980: 55–69).

Looking back at the Prussian reform program from the perspective of, say, 1848, two important characteristics stand out. First, in spite of the massive redistribution of land from peasant farmers to noble estates that commutation of manorial dues and enclosure of commons demanded, peasant farms still owned more than half of all agricultural land in the eastern provinces, and the number of "full peasants" did not decline.[16] This amounted to rejection of a policy "model" based on the English enclosures of the eighteenth century—which had effectively eliminated small peasant holdings (Harnisch 1984: 96, 136–47; Wehler 1987a: 422; Berthold 1978: 102). East of the Elbe, Prussian agriculture retained its dual structure of large estates and peasant family farms.

As a result of their relatively swift implementation, the agrarian reforms were largely completed in Prussia's old provinces by 1840. Over this period, subservient peasants had gradually been transformed into a solid class of capitalist family farmers of varying sizes. Politically conservative, they gradually developed into a pillar of the Prussian monarchy under the leadership of their former landlords (Harnisch 1984: 136–47, 168–85, 352–54; Harnisch 1996: 164; Wehler 1987b: 704–15). Indeed, this process could only emerge as quickly as it did because enlightened reformers enforced a historical compromise between peasants and nobility against the will of the latter (Kopsidis & Bromley 2017). Unlike developments in the "French-treated" south and west of Germany, the Prussian reformers engaged in serious confrontation with the nobility.[17]

Second, the reforms reflected the initiative of an authoritarian state, driven by its reformist-oriented bureaucracy, clearly a "revolution from above" that repressed democratic forces. Thus, the abolition of compulsory guild membership for many trades, or freedom of residence choice, came without consultation by the disempowered guilds or municipal authorities and the interests they represented. Such measures, in effect, amounted to the extension of executive power to judicial functions and represented weakening of an important democratic balancing of power ("due process"). By excluding consideration of interests negatively affected by reforms—with the important exception of the noble estate owners—the way to radical economic reforms became easier (Vogel 1983: 161–67, 188–223; Fehrenbach 2008: 116; Harnisch 1996: 166–70). This course stood in marked contrast to the reform program implemented in the states farther south that had belonged to Napoleon's Confederation of the Rhine States. A comparative look at that experience is instructive.

From 1806 on, the three states of Baden, Württemberg, and Bavaria undertook reforms, first aiming at administrative unification of their enlarged territories, then considering the questions of popular representation, civil liberties, and finally, financial and economic reforms. All three states gave administrative and political reforms highest priority. By the mid-1820s they all had constitutions that tied government-executive measures to parliamentary assent, though the opaque electoral rules ensured disproportional representation of elites—the well-born (aristocracy) and the wealthy and well-educated bourgeoisie. This executive-legislative nexus reflected state financial problems inherited from the Napoleonic era, and financial reforms were its most tangible achievement (Ullmann 1986, 2009). In contrast, reforms of the manorial system of claims and controls affecting peasant agriculture in these states made little progress before 1848 (Hippel 1977: 310–54, Dipper 1980: 85–88). One reason was the opposition of the politically influential aristocratic landowners to change. Their opposition gained support from the fact that secularization of church properties had made the state a major claimant of manorial dues, and these had become an important component of state revenues.[18] Reform of urban-based guild restrictions on entry into handicraft occupations also had to be postponed, for guilds represented an important force in local town government—too strong for reformers in the central government to attack. The same judgement applies to local government restrictions on in-migration, which were tantamount to hindrance of free population mobility (Matz 1980; Schomerus 1981: 103–5; Ehmer 1991).[19]

The contrast between the policy course followed by these three states and Prussia in this period of reform could hardly be greater. It reflected the great influence of the reform faction of the bureaucracy. It alone had ready a rescue plan, and it assigned highest priority to liberal economic reforms.[20] In Prussia, therefore, an authoritarian state, driven by its bureaucracy, pushed through a program of reform of agrarian, commercial, and financial policies that did not yet need to take account of democratically mobilized vested interests. In the south German states, where the opposite sequence prevailed, a strong decision-making power at the municipal level enabled the "premodern" pressure groups to impede radical change of economic institutions (Fehrenbach 1983: 51–55; Fehrenbach 2008: 93, 115–16; Vogel 1983: 227; Dipper 1996a: 154–55; Nolte 1990: 19; Wehler 1987b: 704–11; Tilly 1996; Kopsidis & Bromley 2017; Kopsidis & Bromley

2016; Koselleck 1967: 168–214, 287–328).[21] The economies of these states fell well behind those of Prussia and Saxony industrially, commercially, and in output per capita (Frank 1994). Though the benefits of popular representation in government—present in the three south German states and missing in Prussia before 1848—surely had much weight for the affected populations, we may doubt whether the limited extent of the electorate really offered equivalent compensation for the deficit in economic welfare borne by the entire population of those states.

PART TWO

Early Industrialization, 1815–1848/49

FIVE

Early Industrialization, Government Policies, and the German Zollverein

Our story of early industrialization up to 1815 has emphasized regional centers—"islands" might be a better description—of largely export-based development and the related role of agricultural changes. "German" industrialization, however, depended on development of closer interrelations between the different regions and sectors of the economy—in a word, on domestic markets. The postwar peace that arrived in 1815 brought Germany the benefit of a large reduction in the number of independent and sovereign territories (Pfister 2017b). Nevertheless, the development of internal markets still faced formidable barriers—high communication and transportation costs and political borders embodying customs duties—that needed to be overcome. The task of this chapter is to describe how and how well German business and political leaders reacted to that need in this early phase of industrialization.

Our description centers on the Zollverein—the German customs union begun in 1834—not only because of its prominent place in German historiography, but also because of its singular importance as a market-friendly instance of state-sponsored economic reform. It created a widening free trade area within Germany; and it was to serve well Prussia's hegemonic ambitions. Its historical importance depended on both of these features.

Financial Concerns

Most of the enlarged German states that emerged from the Napoleonic War and the Congress of Vienna in 1815 faced serious financial problems in the early postwar years—heavy debts and depleted treasuries—and though most had survived as monarchies, banker loans to the sovereign secured by domain properties and other sovereign rights no longer sufficed. Some form of popular consent to the sovereign power to tax was deemed essential. In the south German states (Baden, Württemberg, Bavaria, and Hesse-Darmstadt) constitutions creating limited electorates and periodic budgets brought stability. In heavily indebted Prussia, a power to tax based on the king's promise of a constitution achieved the same. In retrospect, it is with Prussia's fiscal reforms that the Zollverein story must begin.

These fiscal reforms represented, in effect, continuation of the program of institutional change begun with the October Edict of 1807. The promise of a constitution seemed portentous. To meet its immediate refinancing needs, in 1818 the government contracted a long-term loan of £5 million with the Rothschilds, secured by a lien on the royal domain lands. Clause 2 of the loan made any additional Prussian loan dependent on consent of a representative assembly, and was thus indirectly responsible for the Edict of 17 January 1820. This measure, intended to be made public, presented for the first time a published record of Prussia's national debt—including the constitutional promise.[1]

The fiscal reforms that came in the form of royal edicts, however, were shaped by Prussia's Janus-faced bureaucracy. Tax reform began with the tariff of 1818, a forward-looking measure that transformed the old excise tax on goods entering towns into an import duty levied on Prussia's external borders (to which we return below). A backward-looking law of 1820 imposed on the larger towns and cities a milling and slaughter tax (on flour and meat). Its rural counterpart was the class tax levied on the putative incomes of individual rural households, sorted into five classes. Two additional direct taxes—the land and occupational taxes—also had archaic features: the land tax was based on local estimates of the amounts "historically" raised in each province and distributed across all landholders (though most owners of noble estates in the eastern provinces were exempted); the occupational tax was distributed among each district's tradesmen according to a complex key based on estimated earnings. Indirect

Table 5.1   **Government Expenditures, Direct Taxes & Debt per capita in Prussia, 1821–50 (in thalers)**

Year	Expenditures per capita	Direct Taxes per capita	Debt per capita
1821	4.65	1.53	19.5
1841	4.13	1.25	12.3
1850	4.16	1.19	10.2

Source: Schremmer 1994.

"consumption" taxes (especially on beverages) rounded out the system. A step toward fiscal stability had been taken, its effect reflected in the decline of direct taxes and state debt per capita.[2]

The tariff of 1818 was a measure designed to integrate the kingdom's traditional territories in the east, largely agrarian, with its new, more commercialized and industrialized acquisitions in the west: the provinces of Saxony, Rhineland, and Westphalia. The domestic political orientation of this measure seems unmistakable, though it also represented Prussia's answer to the post-1815 restrictive trade policies of neighboring countries, such as Great Britain, the Netherlands, Russia, or France (Freymark 1898: 46–75).

Though long ignored by German historiography, fiscal motives lay behind the Tariff Law of 1818. Nearly as soon as the law had been published, the customs system's civil servant authors recognized its unexpectedly large financial benefits (Ohnishi 1973, Dumke 1994, 1984). Most recently, Wolf and Huning (2019) have stressed its decisive role. Moving the customs tax collection to the borders not only eliminated internal trade barriers and boosted commerce (and tax revenues), it also vastly reduced the ratio of collection costs to those revenues. These indirect tax revenues, moreover, brought the additional advantage that they—in contrast to direct taxes—were free from the "Constitutional Promise" made by the king and his ministers in 1815, when the state's finances had seemed so precarious, and embodied in the 1820 Edict (Witzleben 1985: 192–93; Klein 1965; Spoerer 2004; Richter 1869).

The importance of Prussia's own "customs union" of 1818 not only rested on financial benefits, it also had foreign policy implications. By moving its customs offices to its new external borders, Prussia forced the smaller enclave statelets (like Schwarzburg-Sonderhausen) to negotiate new agreements, and it motivated other states whose "normal" trading routes crossed Prussian territory to consider doing the same. Prussia, as recent work reminds us, was Germany's gateway to the northern seacoast (Keller & Shiue 2014), this strategic position a result of British diplomacy at the Congress of Vienna in 1815 (Wolf & Huning 2019). Moreover, other German states realized that Prussia's policy aimed at a union of its geopolitically separated eastern and western provinces, and this gave some of those states a bargaining chip. Prussia, with its lower collection costs, could respond by offering all members a share of net revenues based on their populations, a subsidy that would ease their accession.

Rolf Dumke's important study built its interpretation of the Zollverein around this point. The Prussian tariff was moderate and became the basis

Table 5.2 **Estimated Rates of Prussian Tariff (c. 1831)**

Type of Commodity	Specific[a]	Ad Valorem
Raw materials	1.95	16.3 %
Luxury consumption goods	6.83	73.7 %
Industrial inputs	1.33	18.9 %
Semi-manufactured goods	2.13	12.4 %
Final manufactured goods	18.75	19.1 %

[a] Prussian thalers per zentner (100 pounds).
Source: Dumke 1994: Appendix, p. 72.

of the Zollverein duties. Though it was a specific duty (based on weight), Dumke's estimates suggest the above-cited ad valorem rates (1831):

In 1818 the intent of the tariff was to levy extremely low duties on raw materials and a rate of no higher than 10 percent on manufactures (Ohnishi 1973: 44–46). Declining prices made the tariff more protective, but it nevertheless provided a growing source of revenue. Dumke thus saw the moderate Prussian tariffs as revenue producers and noted that smaller states, with high border lengths relative to area, had higher collection costs (= difference between gross and net revenues).[3] The study also argued that many small states had relatively high per capita governing costs and rulers faced with popular hostility and challenges to their power to tax. The princes who ruled such states were vulnerable to the offer of tariff revenues free of parliamentary controls, and thus were willing to surrender sovereign control over tariff policy to the Zollverein as a quid pro quo. Accession of the Hessian states—Hesse-Darmstadt (1828) and especially Hesse-Cassel (1831)—fits this interpretation perfectly.

Dumke's view emphasizes that Prussia's leaders directed their attention to the interests of the rulers of the states with which they negotiated, not necessarily to their economies. This reflected how Prussia's high bureaucracy saw their own domestic needs: a focus on expected benefits that served the welcome aim of strengthening rulers against democratic claims on power. Dumke made use of statistics on intra-Zollverein trade between Prussia and Bavaria, Württemberg, and Baden in 1837 to estimate (static) welfare effects of union and found them to be slight (little more than 1 percent of putative income)—a finding that supported his argument. In the years that followed the Zollverein's founding, it was thus arguably not economic success, but good financial results—the per capita revenues of the member states between 1834 and 1842 rose by c. 5 percent per annum—that made the further development of the customs union so attractive.

The Sequence of Zollverein Formation

The Dumke study depicted Prussia's tariff-revenue solution to its own financial problems as the basis of Zollverein expansion, implying not only Prussia's primacy but also the cumulative, almost automatic, effect of its policy on Zollverein expansion—a kind of "snowball effect." His emphasis on Prussia's decisive role was surely correct. Its size alone made it impossible to ignore. In 1833, it was four times as large as its largest potential partner (Bavaria), accounting for about 60 percent of the future Zollverein's population and two-thirds of its territory. Moreover, its geographical position in Germany gave it a strategic advantage over all but a few German states. Dumke's interpretation, however, failed to consider one factor of great importance: the sequence of accession and nature of negotiations that underlay that expansion. More recent work by Florian Ploeckl (2010) has recognized the importance of that factor. Ploeckl analyzes negotiations leading to the Zollverein as a bargaining game, with Prussia as "agenda-setter" that negotiated sequentially, in order to form coalitions with those states which otherwise—outside its customs union—were most able to impose negative externalities on Prussia. Ploeckl's insight was that customs unions formed to expand trade between two states were likely to divert trade away from neighboring nonmember states, and in some cases, to isolate them completely from important trade routes. Income losses in such states associated with that diversion represent negative externalities of the customs union.

A map illustrates the geopolitical structure of the Zollverein's expansion and can supplement our discussion (fig. 5.1).

In addition, with the help of table 5.3, we try to convey an idea of the dynamics of Zollverein development. Our description necessarily includes how other German states reacted to Prussian initiatives.

We begin by noting that in January 1828 a customs union between the south German states of Bavaria and Württemberg, after years of negotiation, was concluded. This gave rise to Prussia's (justified) fear that their further expansion could block the desired connection between Prussia's eastern and western provinces. That motivated Prussia to offer the duchy of Hesse-Darmstadt an agreement that was one-sidedly generous to the latter (financially) but enabled Prussia to block further expansion of the Bavaria-Württemberg customs union (thus imposing on that union a "negative external economy").[4] Similarly, the "Middle German Union," formed in 1828, brought together a diverse collection of seventeen medium and small states and some tiny dominions united only in their hope to block

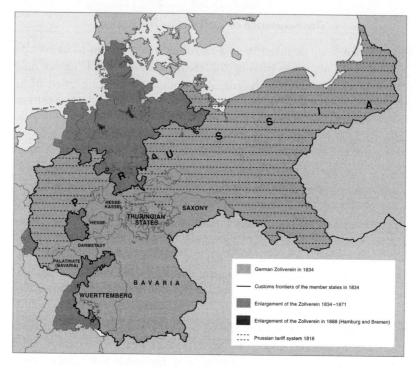

5.1 Prussian Tariff System and German Zollverein, 1818–88
Source: Authors' own map based on a map from IEG-Maps (http://www.ieg-maps.de/).

Table 5.3   Zollverein Timetable, 1818–36

Order	Date	Name of State	Status	Border/Area
1	May 1818	Prussia	Customs Union	0.22
2	1819–31	Row 1 + 11 enclave territories	Customs Union[b]	0.22
2	January 1828	Bavaria & Württemberg	Customs Union	0.25/0.48
3	February 1828	Prussia & Hesse-Darmstadt	Customs Union	0.22/1.06
4	September 1828	17 middle German states	Trade Agreement	n/a
5	August 1831	Row 3 + Hesse-Cassel[a]	Customs Union	0.22/1.13
6	22 March 1833	Row 5 + Bavaria & Württemberg	Customs Union	0.22/1.13
7	30 March 1833	Row 6 + Saxony[a]	Zollverein	0.22/0.59
8	May 1833	Row 7 + Thuringian Union[a]	Zollverein	n/a
9	May 1835	Row 8 + Baden	Zollverein	0.75
10	December 1835	Row 9 + Nassau[a]	Zollverein	0.67
11	January 1836	Row 10 + Frankfurt[a]	Zollverein	8.0

Source: Dumke 1994: 94–97.
[a] Formerly member of the "Middle German Trade Union." [b] No vote.

or modify Prussia's plans. Prussia, however, had no interest in negotiating with this "trade bloc" as a whole and concentrated on the smaller states (such as Hesse-Cassel), its need making those offers more generous than they would have been otherwise. That the offers could be generous reflected Prussia's unique position, for it could promise the leaders of those relevant smaller states the higher net revenues that derived from its relatively large size (economies of scale in revenue collection) (Dumke 1984, 1994). This lay behind its next step: the treaty with Hesse-Cassel in 1831 that gave Prussia the long-sought, duty-free territorial link between its eastern and western provinces.[5] As Ploeckl noted, this dealt the "Middle German Union" a fatal blow. By dividing it into two geographically unconnected parts, Hesse-Cassel's accession imposed on the association a decisive negative externality; it also ended the expansion plans of the Bavaria-Württemberg union (another negative externality) and led to its union with the Prussia-Hessian Union. The same fate befell Saxony and the small Thuringian states—which were now also isolated. Thus, a week later Saxony, and two months later the Thuringian states, joined.[6] In 1834, the Zollverein began operations.[7]

The founding of the Zollverein shocked further members of the Middle German Union into accession negotiations. Nassau, hitherto satisfied with the trade potential of its location and access to the Rhine, was first, joining in 1835. This left Frankfurt cut off from the Rhine—a main source of its importance as commercial center—and it followed Nassau into the Zollverein in 1836. The accession of Baden in 1836 completed the first round of Zollverein growth. Baden's geographic position (on the Rhine bordering France and Switzerland) gave it a good bargaining position, but fear of isolation from the bigger German market proved decisive (Ploeckl 2010). A change in the character of Zollverein accession matters came in the early 1850s, when Prussia alone negotiated a treaty with Hannover, confronting the other member states with a *fait accompli*—which they felt forced to accept in 1854. In 1862 Prussia again tested its hegemony with conclusion of a free trade treaty with France, and once again, the important countries to its south judged the costs of resistance too high.[8]

The Zollverein and Trade: Catalyst of Industrialization?

The *raison d'être* of the Zollverein was surely the expansion of trade among its members. That was one of the declared aims of its Prussian architects (such as the finance minister, von Motz). The shift of customs barriers to the external borders that accompanied its birth, however, put an end to generation of the information (trade flows) needed to measure that expansion directly. Dumke's estimates of trade between Prussia and Bavaria, Württemberg, and Baden as of 1837 shed light on (static) welfare effects; but he could not estimate its change over time. More recent work by Keller and Shiue (2014) has shown that it is possible to infer the economic impact of the Zollverein on members' trade expansion from the narrowing of wheat price differences between German cities within and outside the Zollverein in the long period from 1820 to the 1880s. This conforms to the logic of a "single market," but there is a problem: did the Zollverein create trade, or did trade bring about the Zollverein? Keller and Shiue see this problem of "reverse causation," and they also recognize that factors other than the Zollverein (such as changes in institutions or transportation costs) could theoretically explain the observed changes. These problems are neatly resolved (econometrically). Thus, the authors make use of an instrumental variable "distance to coast" (modified to work exclusively via the Zollverein), and they add other explanatory variables. The results are as follows: (1) price convergence of cities in states joining the Zollverein in 1834 was higher than for "non-joiners," so the "customs border" effect was significant; (2) distance to Prussia's Baltic and North Sea coast and international markets motivated accession, since the early joiners were exclusively states to the south of Prussia; (3) as the Zollverein became larger, the net benefit of joining (an expanding market) increased. By stressing market access as major motive, Keller and Shiue explicitly reject Friedrich List's emphasis on tariff protection as justification for customs union. Instead, the Zollverein can be seen as an instrument of market integration and market widening—elements of the growth paradigm associated with Adam Smith.

State Policies and Signs of Industrial and Economic Growth

Did integration and widening of German food markets also imply a link between Zollverein expansion and the country's industrial and economic growth? The Dumke study cited above showed that the exports of the "North Zollverein" (Prussia-Hessia, Saxony, and Thuringian states) to the "South Zollverein" (Baden, Bavaria, and Württemberg) in 1837 were large, and their structure was dominated by manufactured goods (87 percent), their imports by foodstuffs and raw materials (70 percent). That suggests the importance of intra-Zollverein trade for industry, though it is just one point in time.[9] In the following discussion, we look at several available indicators of industry that show change over time, asking what they can tell us. Table 5.4 opens that theme.

Table 5.4   **Selected Indicators of Industrial Growth in Prussia & Germany, 1820–40** (values in current prices)

Indicators	1820	1830/31	1839/41	1820s[c]	1830s[c]
Employment, cotton spinning[a]	12,300	13,600	19,500	0.92	3.33
Employment, cotton weaving[a]	65,000	110,000	194,000	4.90	5.29
Cotton yarn output (millions of marks)[a]	11.78	12.56	20.7	0.58	4.65
Cotton finished goods output (millions of marks)[a]	52.5	55.2	130.5	0.46	8.14
Employment, coal mining, Prussia	3,556	4,457	8,945	2.07	6.54
Hard coal output, Prussia (millions of marks)	5.14	7.7	15.4	3.74	6.50
Metals output,[b] Prussia (millions of marks)	——	11.5	21.8		5.99

Source: Kirchhain 1973, Holtfrerich 1973, Tilly 1978.
[a] Germany. [b] Zinc, copper & iron. [c] Annual growth rates.

The numbers tend to show a more rapid increase in the 1830s, especially for the most important sector, textiles, but what information we have on the size of firms suggests very small-scale operations: for Prussia in 1843 Dieterici (1846) lists the following: 48 cotton spinning mills with just 4,127 workers, 228 wool spinning mills with 6,142 workers, and 15 silk spinning mills with 1,730 workers. Most textile industry employment was still spread across the countryside—in proto-industrial regions, such as Saxony, the Rhineland, or Lower Silesia—where thousands of individual family units spun yarn and wove cloth to be finished in small-scale proto-industrial workshops. Even as late as 1846 less than one-third of all industrial workers had "factory" employment, and these were mostly small-scale units, with an average of 5.5 workers. Coal production and employment grew, but slowly, restricted as it was by tight state regulation. The iron industry, still mainly small scale, used traditional charcoal technology. The recruitment of Belgian and British skilled workers, and absorption of the superior British technology, had begun, but—as in textiles—the switch to new techniques took time and satisfactory market conditions did not seem to dictate haste (Fremdling 1986: 117–34; Dumke 1994).

Thus, Prussian industry grew somewhat in the 1830s, but there is little evidence of scale economies or heavy regional concentrations that could cause economies of agglomeration related to the Zollverein. Railroad-building had begun; its economic effects would first be felt in the 1840s. Here, as elsewhere, the customs union doubtless helped, contributing to long-run German growth, but most of the changes mentioned here were just as likely to represent continuation of progress realized in the 1820s.

One kind of industrial change related to the Zollverein—intraregional shifts in response to accession—is discussed in a highly original article by Florian Ploeckl on Baden, which joined in 1836 (Ploeckl 2013). The grand duchy of Baden was a small state in Germany's extreme southwest, bordering on France and Switzerland. Accession gave its borders with the latter a substantially higher tariff and duty-free access to the bigger Zollverein market. Drawing on regional, unusually detailed data on manufacturing enterprises and employment, Ploeckl uses the "New Economic Geography" to test for market access effects. A marked increase of firms and employment in manufacturing accompanied accession, but though aggregate effects were small, disaggregation by gender shows male employment in northern districts closer to the German markets (Stuttgart and Frankfurt are used as magnets) with expected positive pull effects, while female employment shows a strongly positive effect from nearness to the Swiss border. This resulted from Swiss foreign direct investment in cotton textile firms, undertaken with aim at the Zollverein market. The conclusion supports the idea of a positive Zollverein effect on industrialization. Ploeckl's approach might deserve extension to other German states.[10]

Another piece of new research on Baden's history has reminded us that the Zollverein, by stimulating trade, also promoted the spread of new technological knowledge (Donges & Selgert 2019). This spread has been documented in that state's patent history, in the 1840s and 1850s reflected in innovations in steam power applications, textiles, machine-making, and other industries. Most of these innovations and patents originated outside Baden, thus reflecting both that state's imitating actors and the interest of the "foreign" patent applicants in sharing in the economic fruits they produced.

The Role of Transportation

In 1815 Prussian policymakers had immediately recognized the importance of state-supported investment in the transportation network, for it represented a potentially strategic condition of integration and development of its new western territories, and it soon had the same importance for the regional markets that the Zollverein promised to offer. To some extent, this development benefited from the improvement in financial conditions that marked this early period (see chapter 10).

Table 5.5   Growth of Transportation Network in Prussia, 1816–1851/53
(length in kilometers)

Sector	1816	1830	1840	1850
Waterways[a]	1,593	1,623	1,870	1,966
Paved roads	3,836	7,301	11,009	16,689
Railroads	——	——	185	3,602
Total capital invested[b]	——	146.6	373.2	1404.4

Source: Tilly 1978: 412–17; Fischer et al. 1982: 80–81.
[a] Canals. [b] Cumulative total in millions of marks.

High transportation costs naturally limited interregional division of labor and the advantages of specialization, especially where resources dictated concentration on bulky products with high weight-to-value ratios. We
concentrate here largely on Prussian policy, but we emphasize that other
German states also undertook transportation improvements at this time.

The growth of the transportation network suggested in table 5.5 reflected the combined effect of local economic interests and central government policy aims. Improvement of Germany's most important natural
waterways—the Rhine and Elbe rivers—required cooperation at the government level between the affected sovereign states. Exploitation of the
Rhine raised difficulties, for its access to the North Sea lay in Dutch territory; and the Congress of Vienna in 1815 had given Holland the right
to impose transit tolls on German shipping. The traditional transit control rights of the cities of Cologne and Mainz, coupled to the guilds that
claimed exclusive rights of shipping employment, represented further
impediments to development—until vigorous Prussian intervention led
to the Rhine Shipping Act of 1831, which resolved the first two of these
hindrances. Farther to the east, the Elbe Shipping Act of 1821 had already
resolved similar difficulties (involving Prussia, Austria, Saxony, Denmark,
Hamburg, and so on). From the 1820s on, steam-powered shipping became more important, contributing greatly to the weakening of the third
impediment (guild power), though guilds retained control over the Rhine's
downstream timber-raft shipments well into the second half of the century (Gothein 1903). Canals also played an important role in widening of
the network, accounting, by mid-century, for nearly one-third of the length
of German waterways.[11] The joining of the Oder and Elbe rivers via Berlin
(and the Havel), enhancing that city's commercial importance, exemplifies
that role. As was true of road and railway development, intercity competition probably spurred development of the network, even if it created some

overcapacity and raised coordination problems for government policy (Gothein 1903). Germany's waterways probably carried most of the country's long-distance freight shipments in this period and were first replaced by railroads in the 1850s. In 1850 German waterways were estimated to carry 900 million ton-kilometers of freight, its railroads about 300 million (Fischer et al. 1982: 83–84).

Nevertheless, in this period roads and highways doubtless carried by far the largest share of movements of persons and goods, in Prussia and elsewhere in Germany, though our statistical knowledge is scanty. From contemporary accounts we can infer that overland freight movements were overwhelmingly short distance, their high costs limiting the extent of the market they served. Prussia's readiness to expand its network of paved roads offered an early response to this limitation. By 1850 public and private agents had spent more than 400 million marks on this network. This appears to have regularized and speeded up freight traffic, but with costs of 15–30-some pfennigs per ton-kilometer (depending on product), they must have remained a trade hindrance (Kumpmann 1910: 16; Schwann 1915; Steitz 1974: 37–38; Reininghaus 1995: 335). For the Prussian grain trade in this period, we have two studies of market performance in the province of Westphalia based on price movements (1780–1850s).[12] They both reveal an increasingly well-integrated market, and while Uebele's study emphasizes road-building, the Kopsidis study sees railroads as the decisive integrating force.[13] We return to this question in a later chapter.

The Zollverein and Foreign Trade

The modest import duties imposed by the Prussian Law of 1818, proven to be fiscally "productive," served as basis for the German Zollverein. What effect did this have on the importance of foreign influence on the German economy? The older historiography tended to stress the positive role of the Zollverein as a bulwark against foreign influence (Tilly 1967).

This argument has some validity. To the extent that one may see the customs union as a "quiet" approach to the strengthening of German political integration, the Zollverein had foreign policy implications. Moreover, the Zollverein did directly influence access to markets. Its international bargaining power doubtless brought its members better foreign trade agreements than they could have negotiated individually. Its widening came just in time to profit from the spread of trade liberalization across Europe initiated by Great Britain and France with the Cobden-Chevalier trade treaty of 1860 (Lazer 1999; Lampe 2009). In addition, it gave land-locked states, such as Württemberg or Bavaria, duty-free access to the north German coast, thus contributing to the growth of German foreign trade. Finally, its protective tariffs in the 1840s and 1850s probably accelerated the process of import substitution in some German industries, for example, iron or cotton (Borries 1970, Fremdling 1986, Kirchhain 1973).

Nevertheless, in two respects, emphasis on negative foreign effects points in the wrong direction. First, foreign influences had positive effects. The duties, moderately protective and higher for finished goods than for raw materials and intermediate products, encouraged the supply of inputs for domestic industry (as the "infant industry" argument intends). From no region could German enterprises have acquired cheaper and better cotton and woolen yarn or iron goods than they received from Great Britain during the first half of the nineteenth century. These served as basis for German industry's growth and its own export success. These imports also delivered news about existing domestic demand and "models" that potential German competitors could imitate and supply. They facilitated the adoption of new technologies, such as the "puddling process" in the iron industry. Here the first step that followed imports involved the employment of immigrant British and Belgian "puddlers" in Germany, which began in the 1820s. The next steps led via imports of raw material and half-finished goods as inputs to complete import substitution. In addition, most of Anglo-German trade was financed in Britain and thus represented a cheap and welcome form of capital import (Clapham 1964: 1:254–56; Tilly 1967: 194). Such facts were blocked out of the collective memory by the short and dramatic British "export offensive," which immediately followed the end of the Napoleonic era and was long remembered, especially by historians.

Second, such historical myopia obscured the facts (a) that the import and gradual imitation of foreign products and technologies had begun before the Zollverein was launched; and (b) that the successful adoption of these modern technologies could have other causes, such as technological change, human and physical capital, and natural resources.

Dumke's work included another argument for positive assessment of Anglo-German trade in the Zollverein period. He emphasized British demand for primary products from East Elbia (mainly wheat, but also wool and wood), which pulled the region's incomes upward, generated demand for consumer goods from the more industrialized western regions, and indirectly stimulated the latter's demand for imports of intermediate goods (mainly cotton and woolen yarns and iron) from Britain. According to

Table 5.6 Indicators of Prussian and Zollverein Foreign Trade and Its Relation to Great Britain, 1820–65

(1) Period	(2) Hamburg Imports from Great Britain		(3) Hamburg Imports of Finished Goods		(4) Zollverein: $(X - M)/X + M$	
	Ratio of Yarn to Finished Goods		Ratio of German to British Imports		European Foodstuffs	Finished Goods
	Cotton	Woolens	Cottons	Woolens		
1820	0.48					
1825	0.84				1.4[a]	1.5[a]
1833	1.11					
1838–43	2.3	0.34			1.8	0.6
1854–56	1.8	1.48	1.0	2.2	1.2	0.65
1860–65	1.6	2.93	0.99	1.9	?	0.5

Source: Dumke 1994, von Borries 1970, Dieterici 1846.
[a] Prussia.

this argument, Anglo-German trade indirectly promoted the east-west economic integration that transportation costs still hindered. Table 5.6 summarizes these arguments.

The table makes three points: first, column (2) showing the relative growth of yarn imports reflects the substitution of domestic finished cottons for British imports of that product. Second, the positive ratios of column (3) show that German textile firms (especially those in woolens) could compete successfully in international (third) markets. Third, column (4) shows net export surpluses for both European foodstuffs and finished goods in this period, suggesting that Zollverein Germany enjoyed a comparative cost advantage in both product categories in this period.

From the 1830s to the 1850s the Zollverein's foreign trade grew more rapidly than estimates of its domestic production—a result that applies to both exports and imports. That the "German economy" became more "open," while raw material imports and exports of intermediate and finished goods grew, supports a benign view of the interdependence between Zollverein, foreign trade, and industrialization, hinting a degree of causality.

Some Long-run Consequences of the Zollverein

The "Zollverein project" enhanced, at least implicitly, the utility of supra-regional monetary integration. The Prussian Tariff Union of 1818, quickly followed by the Coinage Law of 1821 that unified the Prussian currency, provided a kind of model. Distribution of the Zollverein customs revenues among the member states having different currencies required agreement on the exchange rates between those currencies. Though all had silver-based currencies, differing weight measures and *seignieurage* charges made calculations difficult and time-consuming. The treaties of 1837 and 1838 solved this problem through recognition of two currency zones, the south German Gulden area and north German thaler area, and by reaching agreement on the rate of exchange between them. Austrian interest in joining the Zollverein led to yet another treaty in 1857, which clearly recognized the dominance of the Prussian thaler as the basic monetary standard. This was reflected in the exchange rates: 1 thaler = 1.5 Austrian Gulden = 1.75 south German Gulden; and it found expression in the fact that the one-thaler coin became the basic Zollverein coin in both thaler and Gulden areas. This same treaty also pioneered an agreement that explicitly forbade the issue of nonconvertible paper money. That underlined the commitment of the German states to establishment of a stable currency—an important element of monetary integration—though it also reflected Prussian power politics against Austria (Rittmann 1975, Holtfrerich 1989). Another important, but often overlooked, contribution to monetary integration was the unification of German laws regulating bills of exchange—the General German Bill of Exchange Statute of 1849—a measure initiated in the Zollverein and passed by the National Assembly in Frankfurt in 1848 (Pannwitz 1998, Bergfeld 1987). Since bills of exchange were the main means of payment in German wholesale trade, the law's contribution to monetary integration was by no means negligible.

A second long-run consequence of the Zollverein's dynamics may be seen in the development of the spatial pattern of intra-German trade and the railroad network that helped shape it. The Zollverein influenced trade flows and led to the fear on the part of commercial centers in the several German states that their own trade was at risk. Avoiding that fate constituted one of the most cogent arguments for joining the customs union; and improvements of the transportation network offered a suitable answer to the risk of being left out. In the 1830s that included railroad-building, and thanks to interregional competition for trade, more rapid development. Thus, the Zollverein gave impetus to German railroad growth, and the chronology of its expansion doubtless shaped the spatial pattern of the network that emerged. It is interesting to remember that in the 1830s, Friedrich List named these two factors as the "Siamese twins" of the German modernization he envisioned (List 1841, Fremdling 1985, Beyer 1978).

The story of German early industrialization and its Zollverein development, finally, had an important European dimension: it became possible to conceive of a united German political economy that might change the balance of power within Europe. In the long run that happened. In the Zollverein's early years, however, financial and modest economic benefits were what stood out. The latter included the beginnings of "catching-up growth" that would eventually challenge the undisputed leader in the period, Great Britain.[14] Progress in Germany, fueled in part by emulation of its neighbors, did produce some "catching up." Knowledge of Britain's key industrial technologies, for example, spread quickly. Thus, cotton mills with centralized and mechanized spinning operations, use of the Watt-type steam engine, coke-smelting of iron, and even steam-driven railroads appeared on the Continent (and in Germany) within a decade of their British birth (Clark 2007: 304). Sheer knowledge, however, was not widespread application, which depended on profitability and, hence, on countries' exposure to foreign competition and their endowments of factors of production. In 1850 German raw cotton consumption and pig iron production were both less than one-tenth of Britain's—a result of imports from that country (discussed above)—and its railway network about half as long. The overall quantitative picture, summed up by estimates of "levels of industrializa-

Table 5.7a **Per capita Levels of Industrialization in 5 Countries, 1750–1860 (UK 1860 = 100)**

Country	1750	1800	1830	1860	ROG[a]
United Kingdom	28	30	39	100	3.2%
Belgium	14	16	22	44	2.3%
Netherlands	—	14	14	17	0.6%
France	14	14	19	31	1.6%
Germany	13	13	14	23	1.7%

Source: Broadberry & O'Rourke 2010: 172.
[a] Annual rate of growth, 1830–60.

Table 5.7b **GDP per capita in 5 Countries, 1820–70 (in 1990 $)**

Country	1820	% of UK	1870	% of UK
United Kingdom	1,707	100	3,191	100
Netherlands	1,821	107	2,753	86
Belgium	1,319	77	2,697	85
France	1,230	72	1,876	59
Germany	1,058	62	1,821	57

Source: Maddison 2000: app. table A1-c.

tion" and GDP growth in the period (tables 5.7a and 5.7b), illustrates how elusive the goal of "catching up" might have seemed.

This measure shows Germany's place in the "catching up" story: it fell further behind Britain and Belgium, 1830–60, but at least began catching up with its continental neighbor France. Maddison's GDP estimates tell a similar story: Germany gained on France, but by 1870 had fallen even further behind Britain and Belgium.[15]

SIX

The Crises of the 1840s

The 1840s represent a turning point in German history. Political institutions in several German states came under pressure. Historians have written of the incomplete "bourgeois revolution" of 1848–49, which ended in a historic compromise between the traditional aristocratic elites and the *third estate*. A brief period of bourgeois ascendancy ended with the old aristocratic elite in control of the state, and the political power of the bourgeoisie remained limited. Nevertheless, the state clearly upgraded the economic demands of capitalists as criteria of policy. Its rulers assigned higher priority to economic modernization, so long as it did not endanger conservative control of the polity. This combination became a main and problematic feature of German history until the end of the Kaiserreich (Wehler 1987b: 641–784; Winkler 2000).

The 1840s doubtless deserved the "crisis" label even without the revolution that followed. Industrialization and the rise of industrial capitalism, as well as the decline of pre-industrial manufacturing, had clearly begun well before the revolution of 1848–49. What made the 1840s a decade of crisis was the coincidence of three fundamental crises:

1. The hunger crisis of 1845–47 after severe crop failures, which culminated in the last all-German economic crisis of a "type *ancien*." Its spread reflected the long-term structural crisis of premodern manufacturing, namely, in proto-industry and skilled crafts and trades, as well as unresolved rural conflicts concerning land use and land tenures.
2. The commercial and financial crisis that struck the newly emerged modern sector in 1847 and terminated the first boom of modern industry.
3. The revolution of 1848–49 as expression of a legitimacy crisis of the old political and social order.

These three crises interacted. The list can begin with the series of bad harvests and the hunger crisis that began in the mid-1840s and forcibly drew public attention to the spread of what was called "pauperism." Its negative social and economic effects were enhanced by the commercial and financial crisis that broke out in 1847, and it was most likely the combined effects of these changes that motivated the social protest actions that spread across much of Germany at this time. These laid bare the structural changes under way that in more stable times were invisible to contemporaries: the widening commercialization of agricultural production, the connection between population growth and incidence of poverty, the importance of regional differences in welfare, the seemingly unbalanced, discontinuous character of industrial capitalism, and the complex relationship between economic conditions, social protest, and government actions.

Although our focus here is on German conditions, it is useful to see those crises as part of a European-wide experience that earned the name of the "Hungry Forties" and that included the devastating famine in Ireland (which killed as many as 1 million persons). The coincidence of potato blight and poor grain harvests affected Belgium and the Netherlands as much as, if not more than, Germany, while the important economic, social, and political changes that followed—reform, revolution, or mass emigration—took place in other European countries as well (Vanhaute, Paping & O' Grada 2006, Berger & Spoerer 2001). Germany's experience was thus not wholly unique, and we might say that it reflected here, as later, the connectedness of Western European industrialization.

A Structural Crisis?

In line with European trends, contemporary and recent anthropometric and food studies point to falling living and food standards for Germany during the early stages of industrialization. Whatever was happening to real wages in the urban sector (this is contested), living standards in general probably deteriorated during the first half of the nineteenth century. Decreasing body heights have been said to reflect this decline, and some evidence on food consumption also suggests falling standards (Ewert 2006: 51–88; Baten 1999; Kopsidis & Pfister 2013). German experience in this period showed striking parallels to Great Britain's earlier development. Historical demographers have argued that by the 1820s, Germany's economic growth did not suffice to keep living standards stable. Many contemporaries saw population growth as cause of this decline in living standards that they observed and called "pauperism" (Jantke 1965). Some evidence

(Köllmann 1974a) suggests that the potential labor supply grew more than twice as fast as employment in the 1840s! Under the circumstances of the time, this "gap" meant a rise of underemployment and a decline in living standards for those affected. The growing number of tax-exempt craft workers and the shrinking size of their tiny shops reflected that result, as did the wage decline of those employed in "declining branches" (estimated at –5 percent per year for such workers as the hand spinners or linen weavers). Such estimates, of course, are subject to the reservation that they rest on uncertain assumptions concerning the extent of employment in the "proto-industries" during these years.[1] For this reason we need to focus more clearly on the true crisis years of the mid-1840s.

Agrarian and Hunger Crisis

The crisis of the 1840s reveals itself above all as an agrarian crisis caused by the weather-determined harvest failures of 1845 and 1846, failures that affected not only grain production but also the increasingly important harvest of potatoes. Contemporary observers had begun to worry about the disappointing harvest of 1842 that marked some regions, but in 1845 such worries began to spread in Prussia's important Rhine province. The Lennep chamber of commerce, a quasi-public body, reported that throughout the province hopes for a satisfactory potato harvest had been dashed by the spread of blight, and that this immediately raised the specter of a catastrophic decline in the living conditions of the region's working class—"who will be helpless when its main and often only means of subsistence is missing" (Obermann 1972: 142).

In Prussia's bureaucratic center, Berlin, such reports multiplied in 1845. The fear surfaced that a general hunger crisis threatened. For the western provinces, officials estimated that the endangered population was now much larger than that affected by the crises of 1816–17 and 1830–31: as much as half of the population was seen at risk. In the 1840s grain prices rose sharply. In 1846 the crisis was repeated, officials predicting a shortfall for rye and potatoes of about 40 percent (or an estimated 7–8 million bushels of each). Figure 6.1 (using hitherto unpublished price data) shows the change of rye prices.

The standard scenario assumed the shortfall would fall on consumption and depended on prices alone: an average household of 5 persons consumed 17 bushels of rye and 25 bushels of potatoes annually. At the "normal" prices of 1.5 thalers for rye and 10 silver groschen for potatoes, this added up to annual outlays of 33–34 thalers, within the budgets of

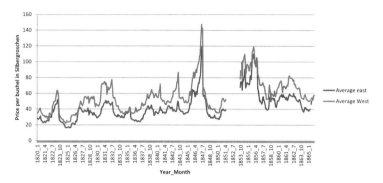

6.1 Average Monthly Rye Prices in the Western and Eastern Parts of Prussia, 1820–65
Source: Our own calculation; data from Secret State Archives, Prussian Cultural Heritage Foundation (GSTA, I. HA Rep. 120 Ministerium für Handel und Gewerbe, Abt. A V 1ff, Nr. 1ff, Bd. 1ff).
Note: The rye price series for the east represents an unweighted average of monthly notations from 35 market towns in the provinces of East Prussia, West Prussia, Silesia, Posen, Pomerania, and Brandenburg. The rye price series for the west represents an unweighted average of monthly notations from 18 market towns in the provinces of Rhineland and Westphalia.

even the poorer households with incomes of 50–60 thalers per year. In the crisis years 1845/6 and 1846/7, however, price increases meant a doubling of outlays and, in the absence of outside help, an unhealthy decline in food consumption. Such immiseration was not confined to Prussia. For southern Germany similar developments were reported. In Baden, for example, households that normally hovered on the subsistence minimum—estimated at 150–65 Gulden per year—fell in 1846/7 to about half of that figure. According to F. W. von Reden, projections of the calculations (made on the basis of price and typical household consumption quantities) to the entire German population would involve an expenditure increase of more than 200 million thalers, a sum equivalent, by one estimate, to the country's total investment (Tilly 1990: 13–14).

Focusing on price changes unfortunately gives us no more than an incomplete indication of the welfare loss households suffered through the reduction in food consumption. There are alternatives, however. Demographic data, available for Prussia in regionally differentiated form, offer an instructive example. We may assume that a large share of the growing population lived on the brink of subsistence in the 1830s and 1840s and had few reserves. We may also assume that the shortfall of the 1840s could have had disastrous effects on the health of this population, effects reflected in demographic change: increasing morbidity, increasing mortality, declining birth rates, and increased emigration. Figure 6.2, which shows

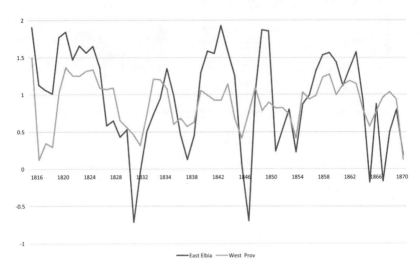

6.2 Annual Rates of Population Growth in East Elbian and Western Provinces of Prussia, 1816–71
Source: Our own calculation based on data from Bass 1991: 39–46.

the sharp declines in the rate of population growth associated with the rise in death rates and decline of births that accompanied hunger crises, illustrates the effects we have in mind.[2]

The relative sensitivity of the East Elbian population to crop failures and food price peaks is unmistakable. Hardest hit by subsistence crises was the agrarian Prussian east (East Prussia, West Prussia, Posen, Silesia)—Prussia's poorhouse—where living standards were lowest, growth of the population in normal years fastest. More than 80 percent of the worst crises (labeled "very serious") took place here (Bass 1991: 39–46).

Some of the worst news came from Silesia. In 1847 a report from Breslau stressed local problems, but added: "In several parts of our province, especially in Upper Silesia, conditions look even worse. It is not especially unusual to hear that people have been found lying dead on the roads or in their houses, victims of starvation. Only a few days ago two such cases were reported for the district of Oppeln. Bread has totally disappeared in many places; and many are known to eat grass, the potato plants, bran, or the pea straw, stolen from the fields and spiced with herring gruel" (*Augsburger Allgemeine Zeitung* 1847: 975).

The food crisis of 1845–47 hit Upper Silesia with great force.[3] Nevertheless, as figure 6.2 suggests, other East Elbian regions were not much better off. The province of East Prussia suffered on roughly the same scale as Silesia even if food prices were the lowest in the Prussian kingdom. What stands out most in broader perspective is the remarkable contrast between the western and eastern provinces of Prussia in these years. A close look at the regional distribution of agricultural prices in this period (see figure 6.1) reveals the striking fact that food prices rose much more in the western than in the eastern provinces, though the demographic effects of food shortage were much more pronounced in the latter. Harvest failure in the agrarian east of Prussia, it seems, directly lowered real incomes and with them the effective demand for food. Food "entitlements" shrank (Sen 1982). Dramatically tragic in this connection was failure of the potato crop in 1845 and 1846, for it was not only worse in East Elbia but also more important for the poor there. Rural laborers in that region partly depended on potato production on household plots to survive. High transaction costs, in addition, prevented interregional trade in potatoes from playing a price/shortage equalizing role, as contemporary observers such as Wilhelm Roscher (1852) noted.

One of the bitter ironies of the East Elbian crisis was the fact that the region's own big grain producers and merchants reinforced local shortages through the export of grain to the wealthier countries of Western Europe. Even in the crisis year 1845–46 Prussian grain exports, mainly from the eastern provinces, held steady at about 5 million bushels. The devastating effects of this development shocked even a market-friendly observer such as Roscher, who conceded that "we have often had the deplorable experience that harvest failures have not been accompanied by a corresponding reduction of exports, so that increased reductions in local grain consumption and the substitution of potatoes, etc. is the result. Thus, in April and May of 1847, the Province of Prussia, in spite of its acute shortage, could not prevail against richer foreign buyers in the competition for use of its own product" (Roscher 1852). The very uneven distribution of land in East Elbian Prussia magnified the effects of the food crisis in the poorest regions, whose economy was based on an export-oriented, large-estate agriculture. In contrast, intensified trade in the industrializing and economically diversified western provinces, whose working population earned higher wages, limited the development of famine conditions in regions suffering food deficits. What happened during the disastrous Irish famine, as British landlords continued to export grain to England, thus had its counterpart in Prussia.

The food crisis of the 1840s had high social and economic costs, as we have tried to show, and they did not end with the direct effects of hunger and health damage. Important indirect effects soon made themselves felt in the demand for nonagricultural products and for the labor that they embodied. The decline in agricultural production and incomes reduced the demand for nonagricultural goods and services, and a decline in employment soon followed.[4]

Contemporaries were painfully aware of this connection. In 1843, a dyestuffs manufacturer attributed the decline in sales to the subnormal harvest of potatoes experienced in 1842:

> Well known are the effects of a good or poor potato harvest on the prosperity of the poor and the laboring classes; and last year's potato harvest affected our business especially, for high potato prices forced the poorer classes to spend their incomes on food, leaving them almost nothing for other needs such as clothing. In consequence, the commodities usually sold to the poorer classes such as crude cotton fabrics remained unsold, and the demand for dyestuffs and the chemicals needed for its production—for example, our sulphuric acid, iron alkali, vitriols, etc.—also stagnated or even declined. (Harnisch 1977: 83)

This view soon dominated interpretations of the economy in the later 1840s, as repeated, for example, in numerous chamber of commerce reports, and invariably focused mainly on the textile industries—by far the main source of nonagricultural employment in Germany. According to one estimate, between 1840 and 1844 textile production had grown by around 17 percent, but between 1845 and 1847 it shrank by about 5 percent. Reliable unemployment statistics are missing for these years, but reports of idle looms in textile towns suggest a serious decline of employment. This had negative effects on the livelihood of numerous craft workers, reflected, for instance, in the exemptions from taxes in Prussia (which rose by 63,000 persons between 1845 and 1847). The situation deteriorated still further in 1848, but by this time the immediate cause was the collapse of confidence that stemmed from the revolution itself.

German producers, disappointed by their own domestic market, may have aimed their hopes at foreign markets, but because other European countries were also suffering from poor harvests, not only did their demand for German products decline, but their competition in third markets also became sharper. For the Zollverein economies, the "zero" export-import balance of finished goods up to 1848 could still have been seen as a success, at least in the sense that it precluded negative "income multiplier effects" (Spree 1977, Blumberg 1965).

The "crisis of the 1840s," unsurprisingly, generated repeated popular demands for government intervention. These aimed at two types of activity: (1) alleviation of widespread hunger by direct intervention in the distribution of foodstuffs; and (2) government spending to finance employment-creating projects. The governments in the various German states responded to the first demand in varying ways. In Prussia, the state proved reluctant to act. Even in May 1847, as the food crisis neared its peak, the measures remained modest. A grain tariff was reduced, regional reductions of the milling and slaughter tax were authorized; but the government would allow neither an export ceiling nor the frequently demanded ban on spirits (*Branntwein*) and their production by grain and potato producers. This form of consumption—which absorbed 2.6 million bushels of grain and 19 million bushels of potatoes annually—reduced the supply of food for thousands of households, but it also served the financial interests of the powerful East Elbian estate owners, who ran most of the distilleries, and who successfully blocked any short-term intervention in food markets to support the hungry rural poor in the east. This probably strengthened the noninterventionist attitude of the bureaucracy.

It is of some interest to observe the contrast between the important role of Prussian government intervention in the hunger crisis of 1816–17 and that of 1846–47, especially in the western provinces. The need to integrate these new territories in 1816 no longer troubled the Berlin bureaucracy in 1846–47. Eventually, however, the state did release stocks of grain from the military stores and authorize grain dealers to buy and distribute additional stocks to local communities. For the province of Westphalia, the amount distributed through these channels was not negligible: 4 million pounds of bread grain corresponded to the needs of one-fourth of the population for thirty days! The state, to be sure, saw itself as financial intermediary, and expected reimbursement of its outlays from the city and county authorities (Wischermann 1983: 198; Tilly 1990).

This qualification identifies an important point: effective crisis measures depended largely on local government and voluntary actions by local elites. They bought bread grain and organized public kitchens, and often criticized central government intervention as too late and poorly executed (even complaining that its actions raised the cost of local food purchases). This may have applied mostly to Prussia, especially its western provinces. In the industrializing parts of the Rhineland, Westphalia, or Saxony, the presence of a politically more active bourgeoisie with an interest in social stability and a peaceable working class had created an active civic society that was less dependent on the central state. In rural East Elbia, controlled by the large estate owners (the Junker), different conditions prevailed. In other German states, central governments seemed somewhat readier and quicker to intervene. In 1847, for example, both Württemberg and Hesse-Darmstadt made public registration of private grain stocks obligatory and introduced price controls (Medick 1985, Herzog & Mattheier 1979, Roscher 1852).

The motivation behind public actions may have differed in some respects from region to region, but a strong interest in political stability was doubtless common to them all. According to Hans Medick, government intervention in the food market embodied a kind of "moral economy from above" (E. Thompson). which anticipated—and could hopefully obviate— the threat of a "moral economy from below." This claim usefully introduces the important relationship between social protest from below and public action from above, a relationship visible in the hundreds of food riots that marked the crisis year 1847 (Gailus 1990). The aim of such protest actions was to establish social control over the distribution of food, and particularly the primacy of local needs over the "rules of the market" and the profits of foodstuffs dealers. Numerous studies have shown that these actions were often successful, resulting (at least temporarily) in state-ordered distribution and rules in place of market forces. In a typical case (in Hermeskeil, a small village close to Trier), on 19 April 1847, a crowd of "lower class" inhabitants gathered to hinder a local dealer from the "export" of a wagon full of potatoes, which they saw as a violation of existing rules; the threat of violence was avoided by the intervention of the local tax collector, who paid the dealer "his price" and agreed to distribute the potatoes to the local inhabitants (no price was cited). Similar reports multiplied throughout Germany in April and May 1847. The protests did not always end as harmoniously as the one just cited, however. Violent mishandling of farmers at weekly markets, forced sales of food at prices dictated by angry crowds, plundering, and, finally, an end brought about by military counter-violence also belonged to the protest scenarios of 1847 (Gailus 1984).

One of the striking features of the food protests of 1847 was the difference between Prussia's eastern and western provinces. In the latter, where food prices were highest, protests were rare, whereas east of the Elbe prices rose much less, but protests were much more frequent and often violent. In the largely rural and agricultural east, incomes were lowest and local government was seen to be in the service of big grain producers, who, as mentioned above, remained significant exporters of food. In the more developed western provinces, we may speculate, household incomes were higher and effective demand for food stronger, a "market solution" less troubling.

Local government was also more responsive to the needs of working-class households, in hard times better able and more willing to provide poor relief than its counterparts in the east (Bass 1991: 240). Local governments desired and called for state-financed, employment-creating programs; but little came of such demands in 1846 and 1847. This did not change much until the revolution of 1848.

Emergence of a Modern Sector: Investment Goods

Despite the grim developments just summarized, the 1840s did witness a remarkable breakthrough driven mainly by private enterprise, and which generated additional employment opportunities on a large scale: private capitalists and bankers formed joint-stock railroad companies that needed construction workers. Thus, railroad-building in Germany between 1841 and 1846 led to an increase in employment from 30,000 to 178,000, accompanied by a significant rise in income from around 3 million to 22 million thalers per year (Fremdling 1985). State governments helped here somewhat, for example, by offering interest rate guarantees on about 20 percent of the railroad companies' capital. This was welcome, but hardly decisive for the growth that took place. This "breakthrough," moreover, involved more than railroads. It represented the development of what we may call the "modern leading sector" of the German industrial economy, which therefore deserves a comment here.

We offer a fuller discussion of this development later. Here it must suffice to stress the anomalous character of modernity emerging within the crisis context of the period. Its story focuses on a syndrome of development initiated by railroads and continued through a sequence based on industries producing machines, iron, and coal—that is, heavy industry. The newness of this syndrome lay in the time-shape of its effects on the economy as a whole: what came to be called the "trade cycle" or "business cycle." In contrast to consumer goods production, the development pattern of which was dominated by movements of real wages or incomes, the new syndrome appeared to be autonomous. Railroad investment, initiated by the profit expectations of private capitalists, set the "cycle" in motion (Spree 1977, Fremdling 1985). Influential capitalists in cities like Cologne or Leipzig, typically wealthy merchants or private bankers, quickly mobilized relatively large amounts of capital for railroad companies—sums hitherto limited largely to investment in government debt. From 1841 to 1846 the value of this investment rose from around 50 million to well over 400 million marks. The stock market boom from 1842 to 1844 was stopped short in 1844, however, when the Prussian government banned futures trading (Bergmann 1976, Leiskow 1930, Kubitschek 1962). Contraction in the capital markets shifted the financial burden back to the private bankers, and credit became scarce. Expansion slowed in the later 1840s as uncertainty about financial stability increased, with the standstill continuing through the revolutionary months of 1848. Signs of recovery and upswing first appeared in 1849.

The Revolutionary Years, 1848–49

The revolution of 1848–49 can be seen as a dramatic heightening of the crisis of the 1840s. Commercialization, industrialization, and population growth were altering the economic and social structure, and making the need for a reordering of the political system appear imperative. We concentrate our attention here on just two basic problems: (1) the connection between economic crises, government intervention, and government finances; and (2) the link between social protest and government regulation of the so-called "agrarian question."

Liquidity and credit problems in many German commercial centers had been growing since late 1847, but when they broke into the open with the failure of a prominent Karlsruhe private bank, Haber & Co., in January 1848, bad news spread to other commercial centers, such as Berlin, Leipzig, and Frankfurt am Main, and the number of failures multiplied. The news of revolution in France and Austria in February 1848 further enhanced the spread of uncertainty and mistrust. In March 1848 the largest banking firm in the Rhineland, A. Schaaffhausen & Co. (Cologne), failed, in part due to its large holdings of bad debt. At the time it was said that 40,000 jobs were thereby threatened. Dozens of firms failed, while many others, some of them large ones such as Krupp, Borsig, or Stinnes, dismissed their workers or limited working time. Contemporary observers, therefore, became familiar with the nexus between credit shortages, unsold inventories of goods, and unemployment; this delivered the argument behind the appeals for government intervention that multiplied at this time.

In pre-1848 Prussia, Germany's largest state, such appeals had rarely evoked a strong response. The revolution, however, powerfully affected the "political economy" of Prussian public finance. Up until 1847–48, Prussian public finances reflected a policy of extreme parsimony, which was based on a quasi-constitutional link between government borrowing and parliamentary controls. Back in 1820, in order to consolidate its financial position, the monarchy had been forced to include the clause in a new law authorizing borrowing: "should the state in the future find it necessary for its survival or the promotion of the common welfare, to contract new loans, it may only execute this through consultation with and approval by a yet-to-be created national assembly of the 'General Estates' ('*Reichsstände*')" (Tilly 1966).

Royal antipathy to the possibility of constitutional restraints on royal actions, and strict opposition of the ruling Prussian elites to any increase in popular political participation (including the bourgeoisie), explains the state's parsimonious policy, which extended in the 1840s not only to necessary public investments in infrastructure (namely, the railway), but to military spending as well (although nothing was more important for its survival). The importance of a ready army must have been clear to the king and his advisors in the first revolutionary week in March 1848, for in response to a much feared popular challenge, they quickly decided to move the (secret) "state treasure" of about 15 million thalers from Spandau to Berlin, to finance mobilization of the army, seen at the time as an option against the threat of violent disturbances.

Scarcely ten days after the violence of 18 and 19 March, however, the king appeared to change course and appointed, for the first time, representatives of the liberal bourgeoisie to run the government. The new government, headed by two business leaders from the Rhineland, Ludolf Camphausen and David Hansemann, acted quickly and did not recoil from unorthodox measures. To stop the collapse of the bank system and financial markets, it converted the insolvent but important Cologne private bankers, Schaaffhausen & Co., into Prussia's first joint-stock commercial bank, turning some of the debt into equity shares. In April, the same ministry founded so-called loan offices in the country's major cities, endowed with 10 million thalers (30 million marks) consisting of government treasury notes (a form of paper money). In addition, the newly activated Estates Assembly empowered the ministry to contract loans to the amount of 25 million thalers. Most of these funds seem to have gone to big enterprises, such as the Rhenish Railway Company; this resulted from the fact that distribution depended on local interest groups, which often reflected the largest (and most influential) employers. Local initiatives also played a role: for example, the Ruhr Coal Miners' Society (Knappschaft) was authorized to pay miners' wages despite the stagnation of coal sales; and in the Rhenish city of Barmen, the combined efforts of state, city council, and private persons founded an association for the "promotion of emergency employment" that financed jobs for 1,200 unemployed workers (Tenfelde 1977: 135–36; Köllmann 1960).

Government intervention during the revolutionary years was not confined to Prussia. We cannot offer a comprehensive account here, but an example from the Saxon industrial city of Chemnitz is instructive. In March 1848 the city administration and the Saxon state agreed to grant substantial credits and advances to finance employment-intensive projects, for example, in railroad construction. This was said to reflect the protest potential of the city factory workers, who were reputed to be well organized, if only informally; there were complaints from towns and villages nearby that nothing comparable had been offered their local workers (Strauss 1960).

All told, between 1847 and 1850 the circulation of government paper money in Germany rose from around 25–30 million thalers to about 53 million thalers—a growth rate of 100 percent! In addition, the Prussian government alone financed new investment by means of new loans to the amount of 33 million thalers. Though not trivial, these sums could not wholly offset the decline of effective demand caused by the crisis and its effects on employment and incomes. Nevertheless, they helped to stabilize the economy and to alleviate the social crisis in the short run, and it was the "short run" that counted.

In Prussia, however, political changes fundamentally altered the political economy of public finance. Negotiations in 1849–50 produced a constitution favorable to the interests of the well-to-do bourgeoisie: a parliament (Landtag), based on a three-class electoral system, that controlled the government's annual budget and its right to tax.[5] This greatly reduced the tensions that had previously accompanied public investment and spending plans. It also gave rise to high expectations. In a speech in a session of the parliament in 1849, the banker (and MP) Friedrich Carl aptly expressed the new consensus: "The previous administration may have been guilty of too frequently withholding approval of the funds that would have sufficed to further cultivate our country. Now, however, we stand behind the government, and we will always approve the means that are designed to improve our transportation, commerce and industry, and agriculture; and though the governmental budget may grow in result, nevertheless, we may see such expenditure as an investment which will yield a good return" (Tilly 1966). In the next chapter, we shall return to discuss the validity of this contemporary view.

The second government response to the revolution focused on the so-called "agrarian question." In Prussia, where east of the Elbe institutional reforms had gone furthest, well over 100,000 smallholders, cottagers and landless households had derived virtually no material advantages from the liberal reforms; instead, they had the continued weight of quasi-feudal conditions, such as the work load, loss of access to common resources, and revived hunting rights. This discrepancy between claims made for the liberal reforms and reality led to a considerable degree of solidarity among these socially rather heterogeneous groups, and it made them capable of a massive demonstration of social protest. This applied especially to Silesia, where so-called *Rustikalvereine* mobilized to engage in actions that persuaded the Prussian government, at the end of 1848 and early in 1849, to enact further reform measures that extended commutation of feudal claims to these groups as well. With this measure, it is argued, the peasantry east of the Elbe disintegrated as a revolutionary force (Wehler 1987b: 660–787).

In 1848, however, the agrarian question had considerably more protest potential in the south German states, especially Baden and Württemberg. Large numbers of relatively small farms dominated here, most of them operating on the brink of subsistence; the bad harvests of 1845 and 1846 left many of them in destitution in 1847. Protest was directed mainly against the slowness and harshness with which the elimination of feudal rights had been proceeding, especially for those rights claimed by the petty states within the state (*Standesherrschaften*) that dotted both Baden and Württemberg. These represented a heavy economic burden for most rural households. In 1848 protests multiplied, and almost everywhere they soon brought the state to act: it curtailed aristocratic hunting rights, the right of petty princes to administer justice, and, above all, it effected a significant reduction of the various quasi-feudal dues that burdened the farms. Nowhere did these actions bring about a change comparable to the French Revolution. The financial burdens of redeeming feudal duties that remained were considerable for the peasants, but they were no longer prohibitively high and ceased to motivate social protests. In addition, the foundation of peasant-friendly agrarian banks facilitated and accelerated the process of "peasant liberalization." It is likely that the compromises favoring peasants and consideration of their demands prevented further spread of revolutionary fervor across rural areas. The changes that had come about seemed to "pacify" the rural population in these territories in the decades that followed, and that was a positive achievement. Nevertheless, in none of these states did social peace reflect a satisfied population, for they experienced a great wave of emigration in the 1850s and early 1860s. The economic effects of the agrarian reforms, therefore, remain an open question. If they were positive, they doubtless took a long time to work themselves out. Empirical investigation of an earlier case (Saxony) certainly raises doubts that institutional reforms yielded quick results (Dipper 1989, Wirtz 1981, Kopsidis & Hockmann 2010, Pfister & Kopsidis 2015, Kopsidis et al. 2017).

Consequences?

The revolution of 1848–49 brought an important change in German political institutions: a contender outside the ruling polity—the non-aristocratic upper-middle class, the bourgeoisie—had been peaceably accepted into the ruling center of power, even if only as junior member, and at the cost of excluding broader popular participation. It also brought changes in economic policy (discussed below). Nevertheless, from the perspective of economic history, the direct consequences of the revolution were by no means as far-reaching as they were for German political history, which, according to most of its historians, experienced in those years what amounted to a seismic shock (Wehler 1987b; Winkler 2000; Siemann 1985).

PART THREE

The Growth of Industrial Capitalism up to the 1870s

The discontinuous character of economic development raises the problem of the relationship between short-run and long-run changes. Investment embodying important innovations or major institutional changes, for example, can have cumulative effects that only become identifiable in a longer term context. This applies to some of the changes that marked the 1840s, for it was their continued development or influence that dominated industrial change in Germany during the 1850s and 1860s.[1] In this period we observe a growing share of the economy moving into the capitalistic, market-dominated orbit and also the relative growth of those segments of the economy already capitalistic, such as commerce and finance, flanked by the strengthening of institutional rules and practices that supported capitalist entrepreneurial activities. We describe these changes as growth of industrial capitalism not only because the share of industry was rising but also because agricultural growth, as we will show, increasingly depended on urban-industrial markets.

SEVEN

"Industrial Breakthrough" and Its Leading Sectors

This chapter focuses largely on the emergence of heavy industry and its sectoral interdependence. That development reflected both technological change—especially the spread of steam power—and institutional changes that encouraged private capitalist investment. The growth of heavy industry that characterized this depended on institutional changes that emerged, so to speak, as fruits of the revolutionary years. The advent of constitutional government in Prussia in 1849, described in the previous chapter, brought with it a major shift in financial and economic policy. Two consequences stand out in retrospect: first, the government's increased readiness to spend money on development of the economy, especially for railroads; and second, its willingness to reduce its control over key parts of the economy. Between 1848 and 1865 the Prussian government's debt grew by almost 90 percent (per capita by 75 percent). Most of this growth reflected expenditures on railroad expansion, in the form of shareholdings, interest guarantees, or loans. The change in the government's regulatory stance was reflected in a more generous grant of concessions to form industrial joint-stock companies. Neither Prussia nor any other important German state allowed free incorporation for business purposes, and they reserved related rights (such as limited liability) to specific government concessions authorizing activities believed to promote the public good. The early railroad boom of the 1840s had already led to a Prussian law of 1843 that standardized conditions for company formation as corporations with limited liability, and this had helped; but not until the ADHGB of 1861 did a uniform, German-wide business law exist.[1] Between 1800 and 1850 just 32 such companies (with a total capital of 15 million thalers) had been founded; by the end of the 1850s their

Table 7.1 Joint-Stock Companies Founded in Prussia, 1800–1859 (number & capital in 1,000 thalers)

Category		1800–1840	1840–49	1850–59	Totals
Industrial companies	Number	15	17	107	139
	Capital	6,281	9,828	107,761	123,870
Railroad companies	Number	5	26	7	38
	Capital	13,552	147,428	192,200	353,180

Source: Blumberg 1960: 165–208; Bösselmann 1939: 19–202.

number had increased by more than 100 companies with a total capital of more than 100 million thalers (300 million marks). Table 7.1 illustrates the contrast.

The liberalization of coal-mining operations also indicated a shift in regulatory policy. In Prussia up to 1850, coal mines were managed and directed by state-trained civil servants—in the belief that the private owners of the mines did not possess the necessary know-how. In the eighteenth century, there had still existed some justification for this belief, but by the 1820s private owners were demonstrating its limits (Holtfrerich 1973, Fischer 1961). The liberal Co-Ownership Law of 1851 (and its extension in 1853) began at last the long overdue transfer of decision-making power to the private owners of the mines.[2] A substantial increase of investment in coal mining, for example, in the all-important Ruhr district, followed almost immediately (Holtfrerich 1973: 26–30, 80–84; Fischer 1961: 141–43). State influence in mining, however, did not disappear completely, remaining important for the education and supply of mining technicians and managers (Pierenkemper 1979: 56–60).

These changes greatly enhanced the growth of a market-oriented heavy industry and, in retrospect, the emergence of the railroad-dominated leading sectors that became so characteristic of German industrial capitalism between 1850 and the 1870s. Before turning to their description, we present an overview under the heading "Trends and Cycles."

Trends and Cycles in the Breakthrough Period

Description of the overall trends is straightforward, as we can compare Burhop and Wolff's (2005) revision of Hoffmann's estimates of net national product growth with those of Reinhard Spree (1977), who also estimated the NNP 1840–80 trend:

Spree (1840–80) = 1.05% p.a.

Spree (1851–80) = 0.95% p.a.

Burhop/Wolff (1851–80) = 0.95% p.a.

Our description of cyclical coincidence between the leading sector complex and movements of the overall economy draws on the pioneering work of Spree (1977). It sees German economic growth in the period from the 1850s to the 1870s—a period known in some texts as "the take-off"—as a cyclical phenomenon. As we have shown, the roots of this relationship go back to the nascent signs of an emerging leading sector complex that appeared in the 1840s. The characteristics of this complex became more and more visible in the following decades. Not only did the railroads, coal-mining, and iron-working sectors continue to grow faster than the economy as a whole, but the increase in their overall weight in the economy transmitted the instability of the complex—a result of the competitive conditions that prevailed in these years—to the cyclical movements of the overall economy. It is noteworthy that this cyclical pattern was carried over into the financial sector (banks and financial markets), a point important enough to deserve discussion under a separate heading. Spree's selection of indicators exaggerates somewhat the "macro-economic" importance of the economic actors in the dynamic modern sectors.[3] We accept this "cost," for we are more interested in the behavior of these sectors. The reason is that they reveal more clearly what was changing than a perspective that assigns more weight to the aggregate behavior of agricultural producers and household consumers—who constituted the majority of the German economic actors of the 1850s and 1860s. For the later phase of an industrially developed economy, a different perspective might well be preferable.

Our summary description of the "take-off" period's growth cycles (we exclude the 1840s, discussed earlier) begins by drawing on a reproduction of Spree's graphical depiction of turning points (the curve shown in figure 7.1).[4]

The remarkable strength and length of the upswing of the 1850s undoubtedly had something to do with recovery of economic actors from the loss of confidence and instability of the revolutionary years 1848–49. Structural changes, however, were at least equal in importance. Import substitution in iron consumption, for example, reflected the rapidly growing demands of German railroad construction on domestic suppliers. Similar change marked development of the German engineering and machine-building sector, though its impressive growth rate of 17 percent per year

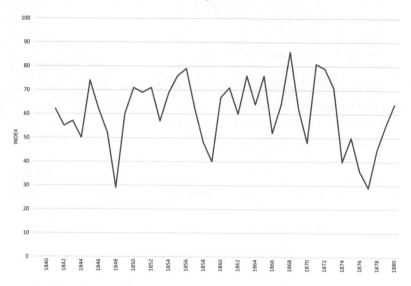

7.1 Index of Economic Fluctuations in Germany, 1841–80 (based on 42 indicators)
Source: 42 indicators from Spree 1977: app., 372–500.

between 1850 and 1857 did not depend on railroad-building alone (Spree 1977: 494, 552; Schröter & Becker 1962). Import substitution, finally, also marked growth of the cotton industry, as it proved increasingly able to re-place British cotton yarn with its own product (Kirchhain 1973: 33). The upswing of the 1850s, in addition, benefited from the global expansion of the economy in these years, which pulled German industrial and agricul-tural exports upward. Correspondingly strong were the negative effects on the German economy when the downswing began and a world-wide crisis broke out in 1857 (Rosenberg 1974 [1934]). International credit links fur-ther strengthened the negative crisis effects in Germany.

A depression followed the crisis of 1857 and lasted into the early 1860s—in part a reflection of the increased capacity of heavy industry cre-ated in the previous upswing but now too large for a shrunken demand and hence profitless. During these years, exogenous political events, such as the "constitutional crisis" in Prussia, which began in 1862, or the two Prussian wars of 1864 and 1866, may have weakened business firms' readi-ness to invest; but the principal cause surely lay in stagnation of the RHIC (Railway and Heavy Industry Complex). The situation changed quickly in the second half of 1866, as banks and capital markets again began ex-panding their credit operations and the RHIC responded positively. Invest-ment activity began to take on boom character in the late 1860s, but its growth impulses were blocked off by outbreak of the Franco-Prussian War of 1870–71—"and with the result that the new decade began as a phase of cycle weakness" (Spree 1977: 351).

The Role of Leading Sectors: Railroads, Iron and Steel, and Coal

We use the concept "leading sector" here to make clear the interdependence of railroads, the iron and steel industry, and coal mining, and also to emphasize that railroads were the initiator, the "senior partner." The concept itself goes back to the pioneering work of Albert Hirschman in the 1950s, though later popularized by the economic historian W. W. Rostow in his well-known book, *Stages of Economic Growth* (Hirschman 1958, Rostow 1960, 1962). The latter emphasized four criteria: (1) technical progress and productivity increase; (2) a high rate of growth; (3) significant and increasing weight in the overall economy; and (4) linkages that stimulated growth in other sectors. The importance of intersectoral linkages implies an unbalanced growth process driven by profit expectations, with these, in turn, based on market demand. The idea emerged as an alternative to planning. A glance at available data suggests some reasons why railroads qualify as leading sector.

Railroads show a rapidly growing capacity, a more rapidly growing output, and a falling price (over a period in which the overall price level moved, but at the period's end was at the same level as in the 1840s). Other data round out the picture: according to Fremdling (1985) and Hoffmann (1965), German railroads in the 1840s accounted for about 20–30 percent of aggregate investment, and for about 15–20 percent in the 1870s. The annual growth rate of railroad "output" between 1852 and 1874 was about 14 percent, much higher than the estimated growth of the economy as a whole (about 2.6 percent). Total factor productivity of the railroads grew at an annual rate of 3.4 percent. Table 7.2 lists some of the indicators. Railroads thus clearly satisfied three of the leading sector criteria.

What were the linkages? Linkages identify the dynamic contribution of a leading sector and consist of (a) "backward linkages," which represented the effect of the increased demand of railroads for inputs (such as capital, iron, or coal) on the investment and production developments in other sectors that produced such inputs; and (b) "forward linkages," which represent the effect of falling transportation costs or improved transportation quality on investment and production developments in other sectors. In discussions of these linkages, economic historians—namely Rainer Fremdling and Carl Ludwig Holtfrerich—have constructed "input-output"

Table 7.2 Indicators of German Railroad Development, 1844–81

Years	Pfg. per Ton-Kilometer	Price Level (1913 = 100)	Output (in millions of ton-kilometers)	Network in Kilometers
1844–46	13.5	78	27.1	1,600
1854–56	7.5	99	643.7	5,300
1864–66	5.6	87	2,162.7	8,700
1874–76	4.8	97	7,600	16,600
1879–81	4.2	80	9,000	20,700

Source: Fremdling 1985: 18–20, 48, 57; Jacobs & Richter 1935.

tables (see table 7.4). To illustrate both of these linkages, we draw on the relationship between iron production, coal mining, and railroad growth.

Backward Linkages and the Role of Tariff Policy

We turn, then, to the "backward linkages"—the effects of railroads on the demand for certain important products used as inputs. This followed not only from chronological precedence, but also from the growing weight of railroads in the overall economy. Starting from zero weight in 1835, railroad investment in the mid-1840s accounted for nearly one-third of total net investment, a magnitude that influenced other parts of the economy and began to shape the business cycle. The railroad investment explains the relatively rapid growth of the German heavy industry in the 1840s. The growing demand of the railroad companies for steam locomotives, iron rails, and other materials was large in relation to the country's existing quantitative and qualitative capacity in these areas, and this represented business that went to foreign suppliers. The profits of such suppliers stimulated German producers to emulate them, and import substitution began. Whereas in 1841 none of the 20 locomotives used in Prussia was of domestic origin, in 1849 that share exceeded 95 percent (Fremdling 1985). Import substitution of iron rails proved a more formidable hurdle, but by the end of the 1840s German enterprises were supplying around 25 percent of the domestic market; by the 1860s that had risen to more than 85 percent. That increase, of course, reflected changes in supply and costs as well as in demand.

Interpretation of these changes, however, requires some consideration of tariff policy. The Zollverein Iron Tariff of 1844 (mentioned earlier), raised duty on both pig iron and bar iron by 50 percent, but a treaty with

Belgium (that same year) lowered the duties on pig iron and on bar iron imports from that country by half, adhering to the basic principle of the 1818 Prussian tariff (lower rates on raw and intermediate goods). The large increase in Zollverein pig iron imports that followed gave rise to sharp criticism of the treaty (especially by Rhenish-Westphalian pig iron producers using charcoal as fuel); but as Fremdling showed, the rapidly modernizing Rhine and Ruhr puddling furnaces and rolling mills— producing rails—could only compete with British and Belgian rivals by access to their cheaper pig iron.[5] The sample data of table 7.3 show that by the 1850s some German firms could undercut British suppliers of pig iron in the German market, but satisfying the country's overall demand still required imports (last row of table). German progress in the 1840s and 1850s had reduced its cost disadvantage, but dependence on imports continued, weakening in the late 1850s. In 1852 the treaty lapsed, but Belgium's share of Zollverein pig iron imports had already peaked, and along with it the share of all imports in Zollverein consumption of pig iron. By 1862, when Prussia concluded its trade treaty agreement with France (subsequently confirmed by the Zollverein states), its competitive position in both primary products (pig iron and bar iron) had strengthened, and the iron duties began to fall, eventually approaching a free trade level in 1870. Tariff protection had helped, but it was no longer needed.

The buoyant demand for iron rails that induced modernization of German pig iron production naturally stimulated demand for coking coal. The response was slow to emerge, for in addition to foreign competition, the lengthy gestation period of investment in these branches also meant that it first could become noticeable in the 1850s. By this time, nearly one-third of coal output went to the iron industry.

Table 7.3 Tariff Rate, Selected British & German Iron Prices in Germany, and Import Share of German Iron Consumption, 1830s–1850s (marks per ton)

Indicator	1832–35		1844–47		1850–54	
	Pig Iron	Wrought Iron	Pig Iron	Wrought Iron	Pig Iron	Wrought Iron
Tariff	0	60	20	90	20	90
British price	106	216	106	172	96	251
German price	104[h]	326	130[b]	272	87.5	276
(M–X)/ P[a]	0.08	0.014	0.33	0.31	0.39	0.04

Source: Fremdling 1986.
[a] Import share of German consumption. [b] Charcoal-smelted.

Table 7.4   Input-Output Table of Railroad Leading Sector Linkages, 1850s (coefficients in percent of consumption)

Deliveries to:	Railroads	Coal Mining	Iron Working	Total Consumption = Production + (Imports − Exports)
Deliveries from:				
Railroads		1		
Coal mining	2	7	12	100 = 102 − 2
Iron-working	36			100 = 96 + 4
Pig iron		.	88	100 = 72 + 28

Source: Fremdling 1985: 235.

The closeness of the input-output connections is illustrated in table 7.4

Note the asymmetry: railways influenced coal and iron much more than coal and iron influenced the railways. Railroads absorbed more than one-third of German finished iron production in the 1850s, and thus, indirectly, more than 4 percent of coal-mining production, while those sectors took no more than 1 percent of railroad output. Dynamic effects, however, were important. In the 1840s, for example, the railroad network expanded by about 20 percent per year, in the 1850s by around 10 percent per year. In the 1840s, however, coal output in the Rhenish-Westphalian district grew by about 4.5 percent annually, in the 1850s doubling to 9 percent. The difference reflected the changing capacity of the Rhenish-Westphalian iron industry: in the 1840s, a fairly large share of the railroads' demand for iron was supplied, as mentioned above, by imports from Belgium and Great Britain, but by the 1850s, thanks to modernization and enlargement of German iron-producing firms, they began replacing imports with their own output.

The input-output relationships of table 7.4 give us a long-run view of the linkages and resultant growth process. It is important to emphasize the short-run expectations and uncertainty that influenced the investment decisions that generated growth. Capacity shortages tended to suddenly produce increases in price and profit expectations, with these—under competitive conditions—leading to uncoordinated surges of investment, creation of capacity that outran existing demand, and eventually to a situation characterized by overproduction and even sales at below-cost prices. Below-cost prices spelled danger for the sellers, but cost economies for the buyers that could spur further investment. Ruhr coal mining between 1850 and the 1890s offers a classic example. The current supply in this coal market, owing to the length of time needed to bore and drain new mine shafts, tended to reflect the prices and profitability that had prevailed seven or eight years earlier. In the short run, some extension of capacity was possible, but the sharply rising prices and profits of the early 1850s and 1870s attracted new firms and led existing ones to open new mines. The resultant combination of competition, uncoordinated expansion, and time lag tended to produce excess capacity, oversupply, and falling prices. The high fixed costs of drainage and other overheads, however, limited restriction of production, with the result that the enlarged supply kept pressure on prices until demand again began to rise.[6]

Coal production thus appears to have depended on prices and profits determined by the demand for coal. New investment came about in response to growth of the iron industry and the railroads, but the competitive, uncoordinated expansion of coal production had positive effects on the iron industry (and other coal-using branches), since it brought with it cheapened inputs—at least until an effective cartel could be formed (it first came in 1893). We find it not at all far-fetched to argue that the limited coordination and foresight of coal-mining entrepreneurs in the third quarter of the nineteenth century enabled their industry to play a growth-inducing role in the sense that they would not have invested so heavily had they known—seven or eight years earlier—how prices and profits would develop. The "overinvestment" so deplored by individual producers may well have had social benefits—in the form of additional output and income in the iron industry—that outweighed the private losses suffered.[7]

The interpretation of coal mine behavior just offered can be seen as a "fruit" of Prussia's economic liberalism, for the Mining Law of 1851 radically reduced the state's former control of coal prices and sales. It repudiated therewith its traditional policy of avoiding excess capacity and overproduction—thus promoting the very result that could generate growth impulses in coal-using branches of industry (Fischer 1961: 5–28)! Figure 7.2 attempts to illustrate the price and output movements that accompanied the relationship described.

The discontinuous character of growth of this leading sector syndrome also stemmed from the nature of the railroad companies' investment behavior. As we noted earlier, railroad investment and expansion depended largely on the profit expectations of the companies' owners and directors, with these based largely on the development of revenues. Figure 7.3 clearly shows the cyclical pattern of investment. The demand for railroads' transportation services proved sensitive to rate reduction, and this response ensured that revenues kept in step with investment. The companies were able to pay average dividends of 5 percent per year—at least as high as, if not higher than, comparable alternative investment opportunities. These

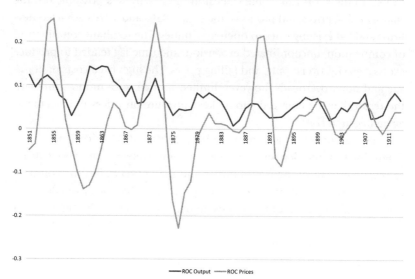

7.2 Rate of Change of Prices and Output of Ruhr Coal, 1851–1913
Source: Holtfrerich 1973: Tables 1 and 2.

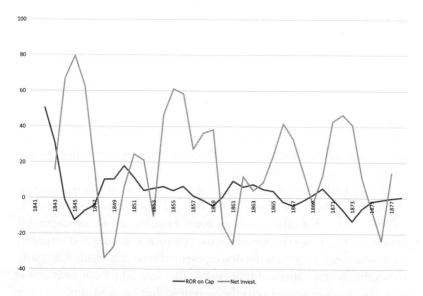

7.3 Rate of Change of Return on Railroad Capital and Net Investment of
Prussian Railroad Companies, 1841–79 (in percent)
Source: Fremdling 1985: 150–54.

connections suggest that railroads were not a "premature" innovation that came into existence before a demand for it existed. Nevertheless, profit expectations rested on a somewhat uncertain basis: not only on projections of revenues and costs, but also on the opinions of capitalist investors about railroad share prices as expressed in Germany's growing capital markets. These varied considerably. To some extent, therefore, the higher returns of railroad shares reflected a risk premium (Fremdling 1985: 132–58).

This result deserves emphasis: the first important railway lines were connections between commercial centers and were promoted by private business interests motivated by expectations of profit, and not by the state—which in the 1830s often hindered railroad development, though it subsequently provided subsidies that helped some lines to completion.

A Further Linkage: Steam Power and Growth of the Machine Industry

The growth of the heavy industrial sector and the spread of steam power that accompanied it had significant effects on the machine industry. Over the first third of the nineteenth century that industry had begun to emerge in Germany, largely driven by the widening possibilities of steam engines. These led beyond their traditional application in coal-mining and metal-working manufacturing employment into textiles, flour-milling, sugar-refining, and several other branches. The breadth of this development has led some historians to see steam power as the "general purpose technology" of this period, the main force shaping the spatial and sectoral structure of industry (Broadberry & O'Rourke 2010: 172–75; Jovanovic & Rousseau 2005: 1188). As access to coal improved, entrepreneurial enthusiasm for steam power did grow; it was reflected in an increase in the number and horsepower of installed steam engines, estimated for Prussian manufacturing industries between 1849 and 1861 as in table 7.5.

The number and size of German machine factories grew in step with those of steam engines—their star product. From 412 factories and 12,463 employees in 1846, the Zollverein's machine industry expanded to an estimated 665 factories with about 20,000 employees in 1861 (Schröter & Becker 1962). Table 7.6 uses a wider definition of the industry to show its growth to 1875.

Given the closeness of linkages to mining, railroads, and iron producers, the growth of the capital stock in these branches will have corresponded to a substantial part of the output of the German machine-making industry. Steam engines supplying power, heat, and blowing pressure were an impor-

Table 7.5   **Number & Horsepower of Steam Engines in Germany**

Sector	1849[a]		1861[b]	
	Number	Horsepower	Number	Horsepower
Mining & metallurgy	332	13,695	1,528	60,387
Flour milling	95	1,111	1,111	8,101
Textiles	274	3,691	738	16,152
Metal-working	192	5,298	3,398	24,874
Machine-making	91	1,354	373	4,139
Other	92	3,396	338	2,913
Total	1,076	28,545	6,689	137,377

Source: IPEHDB, Factory, Tech (1849); Zollverein, Tabellen der Handwerker, etc. (1861).
[a] Prussia. [b] Zollverein states (total excludes railroads, shipping, and service branches).

Table 7.6   **Machine Industry Employment in German States, 1861 & 1875**

Year	Prussia	Saxony	Bavaria	Württemberg	Germany
1861	98,319	18,225	20,375	11,291	171,494
1875	174,599	32,198	32,621	17,305	322,029

Source: Engel 1881.

tant part of that capital, for coal mining (pumps and hoists), iron and steel production (for blast furnaces, melting furnaces, steam hammers, and so on), and of course for railroads (locomotives). Machine-industry output also included machine tools, such as turning lathes, planing and drilling machines, or screw- and bolt-cutting machines. One study of this connection (Wagenblass 1973) focused on railroad demand for iron rails as the force that stimulated formation and growth of the progressive iron-making firms of the period—the ones that transformed the iron industry (by promoting coke smelting, rolling mills, cast steel, and so on). These newer (and bigger) firms, most of them in the Rhenish-Westphalian industrial district, accounted for more than 60 percent of the shift to coke-smelted pig iron and coke-fueled production in the bar and wrought iron sector between the mid-1840s and the 1860s. They were the agents that accelerated the import substitution mentioned earlier (Fremdling 1986: 343–51). The need of such firms for modern equipment had demand effects stimulating the growth of the larger machine-making firms.

Only good-sized firms could produce the locomotives and other heavy equipment demanded. Between 1841 and 1861, the 39 firms of the Wagenblass sample delivered 2,647 locomotives to railroad enterprises (mostly in Zollverein states). By 1861 these same firms represented just 4.5 percent of the Zollverein's total number of 861, but they employed 17,000 persons, well over one-third of the industry's 47,000 workers.[8] Big and capital-rich firms (such as Borsig in Berlin, Hartmann in Chemnitz, or Maffei in Munich), however, were exceptions in an industry typically organized as small-scale enterprises. A slight widening of the industry's definition—for example, by adding such craft occupations as locksmiths or instrument-makers—greatly increases its numbers and reduces the average size of producers. The success of these producers depended on the technical skills of their managers and workers, that is, on *human* capital, rather than physical and financial capital. We return to this topic again below (chapter 8).

Forward Linkages: Railroads and Coal

Forward linkages may be seen in the massive shift of coal shipments from water to rail transport that took place in Germany between the 1850s and 1870s—especially, but not exclusively in heavy industrial regions—coupled to the surges of investment in coal productive capacity in such regions. The Ruhr area offered a classic example: by the 1860s and 1870s coal accounted for more than 50 percent of the freight of railroads operating there—in part a result of substantial tariff reductions. Table 7.7 shows the connection.

In addition, Fremdling (1985: 55–74) showed that the impact of the railroads was not limited to heavy industrial districts. For Berlin and Magdeburg, the share of coal shipments via waterways fell from about 60 percent around 1850 to less than 30 percent in 1881 in favor of railroad transport, this resulting directly from improved and cheaper rail service. A more recent study by Hornung, finally, goes even further. It concludes (for Prussia) that cities linked to main network lines grew more rapidly than other cities, 1838–71, and had, moreover, larger firms. In his view, therefore, "railroads had a significant causal effect on urban population growth."[9]

Table 7.7 **Transport Tariff for Ruhr Coal and Share of Railroads in Total Transported**

Years	Pfg. per Ton-Mile	Years	Share of Railroads in Transport
1836	15.0		
1840–48	4.2		
1853	3.1	1851–52	30%
1858	1.9		
1863	0.8	1861–62	67%
1876	0.8	1871–72	77%
1877	0.5		

Source: Holtfrerich 1973: 136–38.

Readers may note that such statements about the causal effects of innovations like the railroads are, in effect, a kind of "counterfactual history" implying an economy without the innovation. In 1879 Ernst Engel, an important German economist, gave us an example. He compared for the entire period from 1844 to 1870 the price for transport of goods and persons by rail with the rates paid for overland transport before railroads (1840s). He multiplied this difference by the volume of traffic, then interpreted the resultant figure as an estimate of economic benefits attributable to railroads. This is not the place to discuss the vulnerability of such estimates, above all that of the ceteris paribus assumption that only the railroad tariffs would have changed, for a vast literature is devoted to the subject.[10] Nevertheless, such an experiment does underscore the potential importance of forward linkages related to railroads.

Regional and Spatial Dimensions of Industrial Growth in the Take-Off Period

The sectoral interdependence described above had an obvious spatial counterpart: The high costs of moving coal made coal mines a powerful attracting force for producers of iron and most other metals and for most metal-working industries. With the spread of the steam engine that characterized this period, moreover, coal's heat and energy-spending qualities made it an important locational force for other industries as well. An excellent study of this question is available for the later period, 1875–1907 (Gutberlet 2014), but, unfortunately, not for 1849–75. For our purposes here, a few impressions must suffice. Gutberlet's estimates for 1875 offer a benchmark starting point. They show, for example, a relatively high degree of geographic concentration of metals, of silk and cotton textiles, and also of producers of instruments (all of these at least partly attributable to coal). It appears that 1875 was the high point of regional concentration of industries and of coal's locational effects, though several industries evidenced continued influence of coal.

By 1849 steam power had already appeared in most parts of the German economy, if only with minor effect. It may have begun to affect the more industrialized districts of Prussia: textiles in the northern Rhineland, Lower Silesia, in Berlin and other parts of the Brandenburg province, and it had naturally arrived in the coal-mining and iron-producing districts of Upper Silesia, the Ruhr, the Saar, and the lower Rhine areas. Entrepreneurial interest in steam power grew in the 1850s, but we observe few dramatic shifts in the location of manufacturing. One study of that entrepreneurial interest showed that applications to local government for installation of steam engines—necessary due to negative external economies, such as noise and air pollution—first began to boom in the late 1860s, then becoming a cascade in the early 1870s.[11] Thus, there may be little reason to expect substantial locational shifts of entire industries before the 1870s.

In addition, we must keep in mind the role of steamships and steam railways. As the rail and waterway network thickened, the reduction of transportation costs in effect brought coal closer to industry. Upstream and water-to-rail overland shipments eased adoption of steam power away from coal. This strengthened the links between coal, metal production, and metal-working, a good example being the small-scale iron-ware and steel-ware industries in the Berg and Mark districts, where in 1861, 22 percent of Prussia's metal-working employment was located.[12] A more striking example is the development of Berlin as a major center of machine-making and metal-working, a role that prepared the way to its later importance as a center of the electro-technical and chemical industries (Baar 1966: 104–38; Kocka 1969). Berlin's example also reminds us that industrial agglomerations had causes other than fuel costs. Its highly skilled machinists, engineers, and instrument-makers represented a pool of human capital that other industries might draw on, a kind of external economy. This pool owed its growth in large part to Berlin's vocational schools and polytechnical institute, where technical industrial problem-solving was given a scientific basis. It was in the polytechnicals, in Berlin and other cities, that the industry's technical leaders—its engineers—originated (Becker 1962).

Reference to technical education thus returns us to the question of spatial distribution of industries. For the machine industry we have a study of "factories" founded between 1850 and 1870, which shows their overwhelmingly urban locations (Becker 1962: 216–24). Table 7.8 summarizes the results.

Table 7.8   Estimated Number & Location of Machine Factories Founded in Zollverein States, 1850–70

Location	Number of Cities	Factories in Cities	Other Factories
Prussia	18	50	23
Saxony	4	36	7
Bavaria	5	8	5
Württemberg	1	4	9
Hessen	2	7	2
Baden	2	5	7

Source: Becker 1962: 216–24.

Becker (1962) suggests that these results conform to pre-1850 tendencies, strengthening the importance of cities in the more industrialized regions. His conclusions offer a modest, if somewhat diffuse interpretation that stresses both supply and demand factors: markets in districts with dynamic industries (Chemnitz with its textile industry, Magdeburg with its sugar-refining industry and nearby lignite mining, the Rhenish-Westphalian cities of Aachen, Düsseldorf, or Dortmund with nearby mining and metallurgical districts); access to pools of skilled labor and to raw materials in cities such as Berlin or Dresden. In the absence of a more detailed study for this period, such as the Gutberlet work cited above, we suggest that Becker's emphasis on access to markets and skilled labor usefully supplements interpretations that stress energy sources as locational determinant.[13]

EIGHT

Labor and Capital in the Industrial Breakthrough Period

Our account up to now has followed the conventional historiography in describing the industrial upswing from the 1840s to the 1870s as the "take-off," and has emphasized the profit expectations, entrepreneurial decision-making, and investment readiness of "leading sectors." Willingness to invest in "leading sectors," however, implied an economic and social structure congenial to investment and the availability of factors of production, such as labor and capital and technical knowledge. In this chapter, therefore, we must turn to the supply side of the growth process. What follows is a description of the development of these "factors" of production and related changes in the distribution of income and social structure.

We begin with a concept taken from development economics known as the "labor surplus model" (of W. A. Lewis). This model assumes the existence of a surplus of labor employed in a subsistence sector having very low productivity and wage levels, but large enough to have macro-economic effects analogous to Marx's "reserve army of the unemployed"; that surplus labor promotes economic growth in the modern sectors by holding wages at low (subsistence) levels, while the share of profits and capital in the revenues produced grows.[1] If this economic surplus is continuously reinvested, the capital stock of the economy, that is, industrial plant and equipment, will grow, modernize, and encourage a higher rate of technical progress. How well does this "model" fit the period's economic history?

The classical Lewis model is used here because it seems to fit cases showing a significant gap between labor potential and labor demand, such as Germany in the pre-1870s period. It corresponds to evidence of migration from stagnating regions to more dynamic ones in these years (Köllmann 1974a). The observed stagnation of real wages in the period supports the notion of labor surplus. There are problems with this interpretation, however. First, some neglected empirical evidence supports the hypothesis that individual labor time per day and year was rising during these years (Kocka 1990b: 481–86; Kirchhain 1973: 76–89; Meinert 1958). This is consistent with the accumulation of evidence from twentieth-century experience in underdeveloped countries that more rapid rural population growth, often labeled as "overpopulation," was needed to feed the growing population and tended to be accompanied by rising workloads, unchanging labor incomes, but not by rising structural underemployment. Equally important, in addition, is the evidence available for Germany of increased farming intensity and labor workloads in the nineteenth century (Boserup 1965, 1981; Kopsidis 2006: 86–101). Second, there is virtually no direct evidence of unemployment or underemployment for the period under discussion. The few reports of municipal or state government spending on work-finding or work-creating programs that exist reflected unusual situations and do not offer a satisfactory substitute (Strauss 1960; Köllmann 1960: 170–72). Until further evidence is uncovered, the notion of underemployment thus remains questionable. A surplus of labor, we conclude, affected workers by downward pressure on wages or upward pressure on workloads, in agriculture as in industry and mining.

Where did this labor surplus come from? One traditional answer has looked to the role of population growth. In the decades following 1815 the rate of growth doubled, rising to nearly 1 percent per year. Figure 8.1 shows the results of new estimates for the 1815–71 period.

Heralded as sign of a "post-Malthusian era," the evidence shows at the national level a natural increase of the population—the surplus of births over deaths—that remained positive in every year of the period. This is an important finding, especially in international comparative perspective, and it merits the attention of historians interested in demographic change. In the 1840s, as we have seen, contemporaries worried about population growth as cause of an oversupply of labor (Jantke 1965, Conze 1954); but did this apply to the "take-off" period? We look first at the aggregate data.

Aggregate data for the period 1849–75 show an annual growth rate of employment of about 0.8 percent, roughly equal to the estimated population growth rate (see table 8.1).

Estimates of the participation rate of the agricultural population are largely guesswork, as Hoffmann pointed out (Hoffmann 1965: 186–87). In a largely agrarian economy such as Germany's was at this time, we might expect the main source of a labor surplus to lie in the growing rural agricultural population. In fact, between 1849 and 1871 the agricultural labor force grew much more slowly—from 8.3 million to 8.5 million—than any

8.1 Birth and Death Rates in Germany, 1816–71 (per 1,000 inhabitants)
Source: Fertig et al. 2018 and own calculations.

Table 8.1   **Growth of Labor Force in Germany in 3 Sectors, 1849–75 (in 1,000s)**

Year	Agriculture[a]	Manufacturing[b]	Mining[c]
1849	8,298	3,491	95
1871	8,541	5,017	255
1875	9,230	5,153	286

Source: Hoffmann 1965: 204–5.
[a] Includes forestry & fishing. [b] "Industry & craft." [c] Includes lignite & ore mining.

plausible estimate of the birth surplus among agricultural families could imply. We may thus conclude that around 1 million persons left agriculture in the period.[2] This happened in spite of the fact that agricultural prices were rising throughout this period relative to other prices, the demand of urban centers for agricultural products growing in importance. Indeed, agriculture may have shed more labor than left proto-industrial employment in these years: about 400,000 persons between 1850 and 1875, according to Henning (1973: 20–23), while the estimated birth surplus from that base should have produced an increase of about 400,000.

Net migration in the 1850s and 1860s—marked by overseas emigration of nearly 3 million persons—no doubt absorbed part of the surplus (Köllmann 1974a; Hoffmann 1965: 172–73, 194–205; Fischer et al. 1982: 25).

Table 8.2   **Annual Growth Rates of Population in Cities & Regions and Net Migration, 1846/49–1871 & 1849–65**

Region	Growth Rate, 1846/49–1871		Net Migration, 1849–65	Employed in Industry & Handicrafts, 1861	
	Cities (%)[a]	Regions (%)	Region (Numbers)	Region Numbers	% of Population
Northeast Prussia	2.97	0.94	−87,000	222,894	5.1%
Kingdom of Saxony	4.11	1.32	+48,000	485,321	21.9%
Province of Saxony	2.71	0.73	−83,000	247,153	12.5%
Rhine Province	3.88	1.07	+3,053	436,550	13.6%
Westphalia	9.02	0.87	−52,000	198,975	12.3%
Baden	1.81	0.43	−135,000	182,515	13.4%
Württemberg	3.00	0.28	−203,000	257,331	15.0%

Source: Köllmann 1974b, Tilly 1990.
[a] Cities with at least 20,000 inhabitants.

The questions of labor surplus and changes in its supply, however, remain unmanageable at the aggregate level. It is necessary to look at the regional distribution of labor and labor's interregional movements. From various accounts in the historical literature, we can point to regional "winners" in the redistribution of labor—above all, the Rhenish-Westphalian industrial district, for instance, the lower Rhine, the former duchy of Berg, the Ruhr, parts of the Mark area (in Westphalia); and then there are the industrial parts of Saxony, the Vogtland, Berlin, and Upper Silesia. Among the "losers" were especially the proto-industrial regions, such as east Westphalia, parts of Hessen, the Eifel, and possibly parts of Lower Silesia. Certain agrarian regions were also among the losers: this applies to the areas of partible inheritance rules in the southwest; but the regional losers also (and increasingly) included the East Elbian region. On the whole, one can say that regions with the higher rates of urbanization and higher levels of income experienced the highest net migration (see table 8.2).

There are some puzzles in the picture, to be sure. "Westphalia" masks the district difference between Minden (with out-migration) and industrializing Arnsberg. Saxony may have received more net migration than its economy could absorb. Both of the south German states, Baden and Württemberg, may have lost more labor via emigration than was good for their industrial growth potential; their labor force grew but little in this period.[3] If so, that could represent negative confirmation of the "Lewis model." Proto-industrial regions apparently contributed disproportionately to the emigration from Germany in this same period (Kamphoefner 1983).

The most important component of the period's labor migration, however, may have been short-distance migration from rural to urban-industrial localities. This took place very largely within the several Prussian provinces and German states, and would not be captured by the standard indicators of internal migration cited above (Langewiesche 1977; Grant 2005: 62–65). Typical was the migration from rural villages to the nearest city, and an uncertain part of this represented seasonal migration, reflecting a switch between agricultural and urban employment. This especially characterized work in the textile industries and in construction, and involved largely unskilled labor (Baar 1966, Jackson 1980, Lee 1978, Köllmann 1974b). In the cotton industry, urban factories recruited a substantial share of their early labor force from nearby declining proto-industrial regions (Kirchhain 1973; Laer 1977; Ditt 1982, 61–77; Hoth 1983, 96–103). Here, where most workers were unskilled and trained on the job, wages seem to have lagged behind rising labor productivity (Kirchhain 1973). Employers in this industry did experience labor recruitment and training problems, but, generally speaking, enjoyed access to an abundant labor supply, in part the result of their own expansion, which came in part at the expense of rural, proto-industrial employment. Proto-industrial productivity remained low, along with it wages, and there was a significant urban-rural wage differential. This mechanism benefited the manufacturers of the growing industrial towns of Barmen, Elberfeld, Duisburg, or Essen, who thus covered their seasonal and cyclical swings in demand for labor.

Note that this description applies largely to textiles. Next to its offshoot, the garments industry, the textile industry was Germany's largest manufacturing employer. We list the "top five" in table 8.3.

Textiles, like construction, were branches organized largely as small-scale operations. In 1861 mechanized spinning in all 4 branches (cotton, wool, silk, and linen) employed slightly less than 100,000 persons in 3,695 factories (about 26 persons per factory). Weaving and finishing operations employed another 300,000 persons, but most of these were organized on a

Table 8.3 **Employment in 5 German Industries, 1849–75 (in 1,000s)**

Rank	Branch	1849	1861	1875
1.	Clothing	816	966	1078[b]
2.	Textiles	789	813	966[b]
3.	Food & drink	493	586	676[b]
4.	Mining & metals	138	255	436[b]
5.	Metal-working[a]	290	378	601[b]

Source: Hoffmann 1965: 195–206.
[a] Includes machines. [b] Includes Elsass-Lothringen.

putting-out, domestic-producer basis (Hermes 1930: 139–44). Even as late as 1875 the small scale dominated textiles, where 98 percent of the establishments (374,059) employed 55 percent of the industry's workers (Engel 1880), many of these still as domestic producers. An abundant labor supply, self-exploitation, and low wages continued to characterize much of this highly competitive industry.

For the period's leading sectors, however, the labor supply was less abundant. Here, we may see evidence of long-distance labor recruitment and migration. The dependence of the iron and machine-building industries on foreign workers from Belgium or England offers an example. It had to do with recruitment of workers with comparatively scarce skills (such as puddlers in the iron industry), and thus still frequently involved fairly long-distance movements—in sharp contrast to recruitment of the unskilled (Becker 1960, Lee 1978). This opens a different perspective on the question of labor supply, for unsurprisingly, skilled workers could demand and achieve higher wages than their unskilled counterparts. Figure 8.2 offers a comparative illustration.

Readily apparent is the rising gap between incomes of cotton textile workers and those of the other branches, especially the machinists. It reflected the different quality of work involved. The supply of labor was not

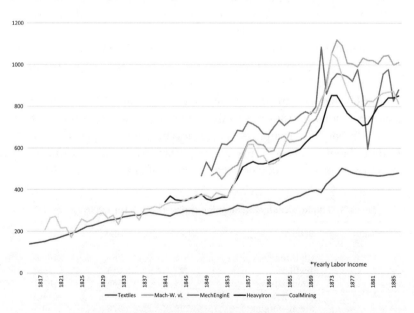

8.2 Workers' Wages* in 5 German Industries, 1817–86 (in marks)
*Annual labor income.
Source: Pfister 2018: Online Appendix.

Table 8.4   Growth of Real Wages and Skilled/Unskilled Wage Gap in 5 Branches

Branches	Annual Growth Rate, 1840–80 (%)	Years	Wage Gap, Machinists/ Cotton Factory Workers[a]
Cotton industry	0.1–0.2	1850–54	130
Coal mining	0.9	1860–64	140
Railroads	0.3	1870–74	160
Iron industry	0.7	1875–79	160
Machine industry	0.7	1880–84	170

Source: Kirchain 1973: 158; Spree 1977: 448, 463, 532, 540; Laer 1977: 239; Fremdling 1975: 24.
[a] Wage level of cotton workers = 100 (nominal wages compared).

homogeneous, and was marked by significant differences between skilled and unskilled workers. In most of the growing industrial centers in Germany in this period, the chronic shortage of skilled workers noted in the 1820s continued to raise problems. Many of these workers, especially in the iron, steel, and metal-working branches of industry, had experienced apprenticeships in the artisan tradition, and thus embodied, so to speak, "human capital" that was in short supply and required an adequate return. Machinists, indeed, represented almost the classic case of labor shortage, a fact confirmed by the data in table 8.4, where their wages are compared with those of workers in the cotton industry.

The Role of Human Capital

Our capital-labor dichotomy thus seems less persuasive when we consider skilled labor; and we turn to the concept of human capital, in recent years an integral part of many models of economic growth, to offer a different perspective (Becker 1964, Schultz 1961, Galor 2011, Jones & Romer 2010). Human capital is the investment in knowledge embodied in persons, acquired by "learning by doing" (craftsmanship skills) and by formal education (ranging from basic literacy and numeracy to scientific theory). Acquisition of knowledge represented a time-consuming process, but one that is generally believed to have yielded positive returns in the form of higher lifetime earnings and other advantages. Sweeping claims have been made for its contribution to technological progress and industrial growth; and we shall return to those below, where we consider the developments from the 1870s to 1914. Like many economic historians, we long believed that human capital first became an important productive input for economic growth during the "second industrial revolution" in the last quarter of the nineteenth century (Landes 1969, Tilly 1990, Galor 2011, Ogilvie & Carus

2014). That now seems to be no more than a half-truth. Several German economic historians have investigated both the extent and effects of human capital investment, drawing on data covering literacy, school enrollments, and outcomes (such as income or patent activity) that reflected its effects. For the period of "take-off" treated here, less readily useful patent data are available.[4] Attention is thus focused on basic education, "learning by doing," and accumulation of craftsmanship skills. A recent study by Cinnirella and Streb on the causal effects of human capital on innovation has drawn on data from this period and suggested that basic education and practical skills were important inputs for certain types of innovation (Cinnirella & Streb 2017: 192–227). High literacy rates in a region could have facilitated the spread of new technical knowledge, and relatively high numbers of skilled craftsmen (in relevant occupations) could ease the application of such knowledge. It is surely no accident that the regions characterized as "innovative" were locations of important machine-building centers.

The geographical distribution of "innovative" districts with skilled craftsmen coincided pretty well with the country's growing industrial centers (Saxony, the Ruhr, Berlin, parts of Silesia, and the Rhineland). The development of the machine-building industry offers a good illustration. By the 1830s the demand of textile firms for spinning and weaving equipment and of mines and railroad companies for steam engines had created an expanding market for machines, and a first generation of machine-making firms began to respond. A study of seventy-two of the firms in existence before 1850 reckoned nearly half of the founders to handicraft trades (mechanics, cabinetmakers, carpenters, blacksmiths), another quarter to a group named as "machine-builders" (mostly entrepreneurs from machine-using branches), and the rest to merchants or machine-interested individuals with varied (middle-class) backgrounds (Schröter & Becker 1962).

Prussia's high literacy rates doubtless reflected its early development of a comprehensive system of primary education; with enrollment rates (of children aged six to fourteen) in 1849 of more than 80 percent, it was well ahead of most European countries. In the following decades, not only did enrollment rates rise (to above 90 percent), but the system of secondary schooling also expanded, its distribution largely dovetailed with industrial regions. Unsurprisingly, perhaps, the largely agrarian northeastern and eastern parts of Prussia, characterized by large noble estates and a high degree of concentration of ownership, lagged behind the central and western parts of the country in school enrollments and literacy rates. In the Prussian census of 1871, literacy rates per hundred persons age ten or older were, for the northeast, 0.73; for the central region, 0.95; and for the west,

0.93. Elementary school enrollment rates (per hundred six-to-fourteen-year-olds), taken from other sources, show for 1864 a weaker contrast: northeast, 0.73; central, 0.81; and west, 0.81.[5]

A useful recent study of the relationship between land concentration and school enrollments reveals a persistent negative association between those two phenomena for the nineteenth century, attributing it to a landowner power structure hostile to peasant education. This nexus weakened after 1849, thanks to peasant emancipation, but the long-term damage to the region's population could not be easily or quickly undone. The study offers an interesting example of how socioeconomic inequality can negatively affect the accumulation of human capital (Cinnirella & Hornung 2016).[6]

Such studies also underline the argument being made here: the growth mechanism based on labor surplus and downward wage pressure did not apply to an important core of the leading sector complex based on railroads. Here, we find a somewhat different mechanism at work: the relationship between technical progress, skilled labor, and human capital. In branches such as metal-working, engineering, or iron- and steel-making, employers and employees were both technicians. Entrepreneurial success in these branches depended more on mastery of the relevant techniques than on accumulated wealth, that is, on human more than on financial capital. Workshops gradually turned into factories to the extent that masters, by successfully imparting their technical skills to their workers, were turning themselves into entrepreneurs. These industrial leaders saw their authority as lying in their own technical competence, more so than in their wealth, as the biographies of such entrepreneurs as August Borsig, Alfred Krupp, or Werner Siemens clearly imply. This, they felt, was the basis of the prestige they increasingly enjoyed in Germany during the 1850s, 1860s, and 1870s. This should not blind us to the important role played by family wealth, commercial ability, or the sheer persuasive power of a strong personality in such careers; but the emphasis on training rules and absorbing new techniques in these branches contrasted sharply with those other sectors in which capital, abundant labor, and lower wages dominated. Until the 1870s most machinists and mechanics obtained their skills as apprentices (normally involving a period of three years). Since the 1860s, however, the machine industry had begun to attract growing numbers of graduates of technical schools, employing them as technicians charged with training new employees or for research and development purposes. In the following decades, they would become an important part of the industry's middle management (Becker 1962).

Thus, the "take-off" period of German industrialization depended on development of a dualism based on relatively scarce technical skills and

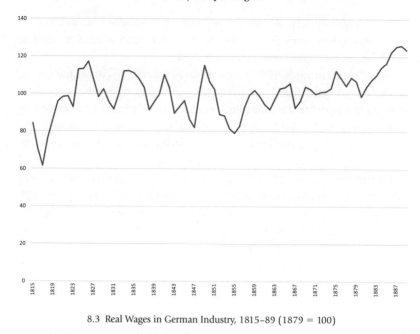

8.3 Real Wages in German Industry, 1815–89 (1879 = 100)

relatively abundant labor. It may be helpful to summarize our results by a look at estimates of real wages. What do they show us about this period? Our response here draws on the most recent study of the question, by Ulrich Pfister (2018). A special merit of his study is its simultaneous use of both regional and time-series data for seven different branches of industry (combined in a panel analysis). It offers a regionally more balanced view of real wage development than hitherto available and also a new and broader consumer price index. Its results are summarized in figure 8.3.

Like the older estimates, those of figure 8.3 show cyclical up-and-down movements and a modest upward trend. Estimating the period trend from cyclical trough to cyclical trough, we arrive at a long-run growth of real wages of about 0.5 percent per annum (Pfister 2018).[7] Comparison of this rate with the estimated growth rate of real social product per head for the period (Burhop & Wolff 2005), however, shows quite a difference: the latter is about 1 percent per year, or about twice as high as real wages.[8] The constellation of a nearly stationary real wage level with a clearly rising per capita product corresponds to the above-mentioned model of a "labor surplus economy." Rising per capita product reflects increasing productivity, but when coupled to strong competition among labor for employment, the result is a declining share for wages, in the extreme falling to the subsistence levels of the cheapest available laborers.

Capital's Share and Income Distribution

We tentatively conclude that a relatively abundant labor supply helped promote German industrialization in the period between the 1840s and the 1870s. Downward pressure on wages could permit a higher rate of capital accumulation, and this in turn promoted innovation and technical progress, since one may assume that the introduction of technical innovations is to some extent dependent on the rate of capital investment (Gould 1972, Crafts 1985). Investment embodying technical progress, in turn, should have positively influenced the rate of productivity growth.

The labor conditions described are consistent with the notion of redistribution of aggregate income from "labor" to "capital," that is, recipients of income from capital gained relative to wage earners. Since capital incomes under capitalist conditions were more unequally distributed than labor incomes, increasing inequality of income distribution in Germany must have resulted. Some historical evidence does confirm this suspicion. For the largest German state, Prussia, several studies based on that state's income tax statistics have clearly shown the expected rise in inequality of the personal income distribution, in this case for the period from 1851 to 1913 (Grumbach 1957, Hoffmann 1965, Dumke 1991). According to the data reported by Hoffmann (1965), increasing measured inequality in the income distribution went hand in hand with the rising share of capital income in total income over the period from 1851 to the 1870s. To the extent that the cited income tax data are representative of the period's actual income distribution, the relationship mentioned above identifies an important point that deserves some discussion here.[9]

First, however, to give readers an idea of the kind and extent of income inequality involved, we offer a sample of evidence based on the Prussian tax returns for the period from 1852 to 1873. These returns were based on tax officials' assessments of the lowest income groups and on self-classification by the higher income receivers. The highest annual tax was set at 7,200 thalers, levied on incomes of 240,000 thalers (720,000 marks). This left an uncertain and surely increasing amount of income of the wealthiest households tax-free, and it suggests that the returns represent a lower bound estimate of income inequality. Table 8.5 shows several standard measures of income inequality based on the Prussian tax data. The Gini coefficient is a rough measure of the divergence from perfect equality of income shares of all income classes (= 0). Rising coefficients indicate increasing inequality.[10]

All measures show an increase in inequality. This trend would continue in the following decades, but already had two characteristics worth men-

Table 8.5   Changes in Personal Income Inequality in Prussia between 1852 and 1873

Inequality Measure	1852	1866	1873
Gini Coefficient	.38505	.42061	.45686
Top 5[a]	.268	.295	.34
Top 1[a]	.13	.153	.177
Bottom 50[a]	.31	.288	.264

Source: Tilly 2010: 183; Engel 1868, 1875; our calculations.
[a] Share of bottom 50 and top 5 and 1 percent of taxpayers in total income.

Table 8.6   Political Effects of the Prussian Three-Class Electoral System Illustrated (1861)

Class	Number of Taxpayers	Share of Total	Amount of Taxes (in Thaler)	Share of Total Tax	Participation Rate in Election
I	158,019	0.05	8,865,058	0.35	0.56
II	451,592	0.013	8,140,461	0.33	0.42
III	2,741,004	0.82	7,977,690	.032	0.23
Total	3,350,615	1.00	24,983,209	1.00	0.27

Source: Engel 1868; our own calculations.

tioning here. First, income inequality was higher in urbanized and commercial regions than elsewhere, reflecting the wealth of their merchants. Second, it provided the basis of Prussia's plutocratic three-class electoral system, which assigned one-third of the total electoral votes to each group paying one-third of the tax total. Thus, Group I represented the top third, Group II the middle, and Group III the rest. This strengthened the country's political inequality. Table 8.6 shows the effects on political participation in the Prussian Landtag election of 1861: the disincentive effects for the majority of Group III, recognizable here, would continue to characterize Prussia's politics until 1914.

In spite of the pernicious effects of increasing income inequality on political development, it is possible to see a positive side. The trend of rising capital income coupled to increasing economic inequality most likely had a positive effect on investment and contributed to acceleration of the pace of industrialization during this period. Capitalists possessed incomes far in excess of their consumption needs and were thus major contributors to the economy's flow of savings, which financed new investment activity. These wealth-holders—merchants, private bankers, industrialists, and rentiers—dominated the top of the income tax lists, but represented no more than 1–2 percent of all households. They also dominated the lists of shareholders and bondholders of many of the companies founded during these years; it was this same group whose deposits backed the lending activities of private bankers and the public saving banks that helped finance growth of the leading sector RHIC (Tilly 1966, 1974). Despite the growth of the banking sector at this time, however, industrialists themselves embodied a crucial component of capital income—the reinvestment of profits that represented an important source of industrial finance in the nineteenth century (Coym 1971; Klein 1971: 123). Here we see most clearly the direct and positive link between high capital incomes and high levels of investment activity, and it was surely here that the closest and most positive effect of chronic labor surplus would have been felt.

This emphasis, however, does not devalue the interpretation emphasizing the juncture of rising productivity and per capita real income and virtually stagnant or only slowly rising real wages. Such a combination, we repeat, meant a shift in income distribution favoring capital incomes in relation to labor incomes, as the population dependent on the latter grew relatively in the period to the 1870s. Nevertheless, though "labor's share" declined, it does seem clear that real wages were also growing in the period, if only slowly. This constellation is noteworthy in one further respect. The substantial absolute and relative growth of nonagricultural employment, which between 1849 and 1871 increased by around 2.3 million persons, coupled to rising average incomes in the same period, would have been impossible had agricultural productivity not also grown significantly, for agriculture produced the "wage goods" (above all, food) the nonagricultural population depended upon, and without agricultural productivity increase those "wage goods" would have been much more expensive and reduced real wages, nonagricultural employment, or both. In fact, both magnitudes increased, and these reflected the increased productivity of agriculture. The latter did not keep pace with the productivity growth of industry, and the terms of trade turned in favor of agriculture: the trend of agricultural prices relative to industrial ones was upward between around 1850 and the early 1870s. Nevertheless, sufficient room for a modest increase of real wages had been created—a notable achievement of the agricultural sector and an important component of the period's growth. In the next chapter, therefore, we offer a closer look at agriculture.

NINE

Agriculture in the Period
of Take-Off and Beyond

German agricultural growth (and its benefits described above) owed much to the emergence of the railway and the RHIC during the decades between the 1830s and the 1880s. Such was the closeness of this relationship that we might see the nexus between industrial-urban growth and agricultural change as a kind of forward linkage generated by railroads. Since early in the nineteenth century Germany's industrial development had begun to indirectly influence the modernization of agriculture, opening the door to the breakthrough sometimes called the "agricultural revolution." Railways and the connected expansion of urban-industrial agglomeration based on coal and iron powerfully affected German agricultural development, simultaneously inducing fundamental changes on the supply and demand sides of agricultural markets in two ways. First, the swift expansion of industrial belts generated a long-lasting "demand push," especially for high-value-added food like meat, dairy products, and vegetables. Second, for the first time in German history, variants of cost-intensive but very productive "high farming" became profitable in more and larger parts of the country. It is interesting to note that these findings were anticipated to some extent by nineteenth-century research on demand determinants; we shall return to this connection below.[1]

In the following account, the growth of the Rhine-Ruhr area plays a prominent role. This fits its unique importance as Europe's largest industrial belt, but it also reflects the well-researched status of the agricultural response to its expansion (Kopsidis 1996, 2015, Kopsidis & Hockmann 2010). Over the second third of the nineteenth century, local increases in the value of agricultural land in Westphalia were observed to reflect improved transportation facilities—mainly the railroad network—but the

9.1 Agrarian Regions around the Ruhr in Westphalia, 1865
Source: Authors' own map.

cause was the growing Ruhr population itself, for by the 1860s and 1870s it already represented to Westphalian farmers an unprecedented opportunity. A hierarchy of reaction was observable. Best positioned were the smaller farms that ringed the "Ruhr" district itself (comprising the counties of Bochum and Dortmund; see figure 9.1) and the fertile counties east of the "Ruhr" (counties of Hamm, Soest, and Lippstadt), both of which strongly increased land-intensive dairying and meat production (especially pork). Both regions were agriculturally especially well favored.[2] On the Ruhr's north border, and third in the hierarchy, the "Core-Münsterland" was on its way to becoming Westphalia's leading milk and meat producer, and also number one in wheat production. The other, less fertile and more isolated regions—the "Sand-Münsterland" on the northwest and eastern borders of Westphalia and the highland region on the southern tip of Westphalia—were less favored and started to be deeply integrated into the Ruhr food belt only after 1880 with the coming of the railway. Thus, the hilly and densely populated "lower Sauerland" directly south of the Ruhr district became a milk-producing greenland belt for the Ruhr (Kopsidis 1996: 211–33). Table 9.1 summarizes the region's status in the 1861–65 period, though extending to 1883.

Table 9.1   Westphalian Agricultural Regions and Their Characteristics, 1830s to1880

Region	Ranking	Land Tax Value in Thaler[a] (1861–65)	Population Growth, 1828–80 (1828 = 100)	Share of Agricultural Population 1882 (in percent)	Land Quality: Percent of Average & Above-Average
"Ruhr" district	1	3.08	575	7.6	53–70
"Hellweg"	2	2.72	155	38	46–84
"Core" Münsterland	3	1.39	135	44.8	16–54
Lower Sauerland	4	1.38	236	12.3	42–58
"Sand" Münsterland	5	0.90	106	58.7	4–34
High Sauerland	6	0.62	157	34	2–26

Source: Kopsidis 1996: 132.

[a] Net income per unit land (*Morgen*) in thaler (*Morgen* = 0.62 acres). Land refers to total surface area (as the best indicator of intensity of land use). The land tax value was based on a census (land tax assessment) designed to estimate the profitability of individual holdings and tax them accordingly (Meitzen 1868).

The influence of the food demands of the Ruhr district did not stop at Westphalia's borders, and its need for grains began to spread northward. Nevertheless, before the 1870s, evidence of farm supply response from more distant locations is virtually nonexistent. Prussia's eastern provinces, despite their pronounced agricultural economic structure, never became a supplier of the industrializing Rhenish-Westphalian district. True enough, as the Prussian transportation infrastructure thickened, throughout the country agricultural producers, large and small, began in the 1860s to supply urban-industrial districts, even in the east, forming what we might call "Thünen rings" around such centers as Berlin, as well as industrial cities in Saxony or Silesia. This development followed pretty much the Westphalian pattern. High population densities, land rents, and labor-intensive, high-value products with high transportation costs (perishable products such as fresh vegetables and fruits) characterized the innermost rings, surrounded by a series of rings moving outward along a declining plane to ever lower rents, labor intensity, and transport cost sensitivity—a movement from meat and dairy products to grains of ever lower value.[3] It was the case of the Westphalian Ruhr district, however, that seems to have impressed contemporaries most. The head of the Prussian Statistical Office, Ernst Engel, observed the rapid increase in grain prices since the 1850s and attributed it to the syndrome of growth based on railway links between farming areas and heavy industry with its concentration of high-wage workers able to pay for more and better foods. He also noted the profitability and high rents of the farms that produced them (Engel 1867: 108).

The farms that responded to the urban-industrial food demand just described were predominantly medium-sized family farms. Sustained demands encouraged them to combine livestock and animal production with crop production, to practice "mixed farming." Mixed farming imposed high demands on the timing and flexibility of farmers' decision-making. These medium-sized and smaller units were better adapted to the changing needs of urban consumers. Economies of scale did not characterize this kind of farming, nor did its absence appear to materially slow the adoption of technical change in these years. Only grain farming showed limited signs of profiting from scale effects (Kopsidis 1996, 2006, Kopsidis & Hockmann 2010). We turn to those in the next section.

Agricultural Growth from the 1870s to 1914

In the 1870s, the effect of Ruhr workers' demands for meat and milk products began to spread more rapidly and farther across northwest Germany (Schleswig-Holstein, Oldenbourg, Hannover). As the long-distance transport infrastructure improved, farmers increasingly replaced the "traditional" indirect supply response of feed grain sales to livestock farms closer to the Ruhr by turning themselves into livestock, or "mixed," farms. The northwest German plain had long faced the problem of its less-fertile, sandy soils, but livestock investment led to better fertilization and increased yields. In the following decades, the spread of mineral- and chemical-based fertilizers further supported this trend. This same development also explains a marked improvement of arable yields in East Elbian agriculture, both for large estates and many of the region's smaller farms. East Elbian growth was even greater (Grant 2005: 215–52; Grant 2009; Kopsidis 2015: 366–67).[4]

A second important change of the 1870s came with the "grain invasion" of Germany's market by North American producers, supplemented by Russian producers of cheap feed grain. This development encouraged farmers in the northwest to shift more into livestock farming, a shift especially concentrated on pig-raising. This change had an interesting "side effect": "pig farming" (as it came to be called) did not require large tracts of land and thus attracted small landholders, who joined the ranks of small farms producing for the market, broadening somewhat the social structure of the agricultural sector and—by stopping a trend of depopulation—slowing the relative decline that industrialization was thought to imply (Engelbrecht 1907: 244–49; Mütter & Meyer 1995: 23–28, 47–55; Lichter 1994: 106–7; Lorenzen-Schmidt 2003: 386).

The "grain invasion" of the 1870s by North American wheat powerfully affected the Prussian northeast and its large grain-producing estates. The loss of traditional export markets forced the Junker landowners to look more closely at domestic markets and to demand protective tariffs. Tariffs on grain imports came in 1879, becoming clearly protective in the 1880s. The tariffs doubtless encouraged modernizing investment, and were also supplemented by the thickening and improvement of the Prussian railway network that came with its nationalization in the 1880s (Ziegler 1996). We return to the question of agrarian protectionism and its political implications again below (chapter 14). In the 1880s, then, northeastern German agriculture became the principal supplier of the region's industrializing centers around Berlin and in Silesia; in the central region covering the Saxon territories and Thuringia, local sources more than sufficed.

We can perhaps best summarize the long-run development of German agriculture with the help of some quantitative data. First, for Germany as a whole, table 9.2 offers several measures of growth rates covering the entire 1850–1913 period.

Two results deserve mention. First, the difference between crop and total output reflects agriculture's response to an increasing demand for meat and other nongrain foods (for example, dairy products). Second, the difference between net output (column 3) and net value-added (column 4) suggests increasingly efficient use of inputs from other sectors, which seems plausible and also fits in with the rising labor productivity shown in column 5.

With a second table, we attempt to summarize a somewhat longer run perspective on agriculture and Germany's regional differences (table 9.3).

The table confirms the view of an acceleration of growth around mid-century, also that of a more slowly growing Bavaria. The righthand column,

Table 9.2 **German Agricultural Growth, 1850–1913 (annual growth rates, 1913 prices)**

(1)	(2)	(3)	(4)	(5)
Period	Net Crop Output	Total Net Output	Value- Added	Labor Productivity of (4)
1850–80	1.5%	1.7%	1.6%	—
1880–1913	1.1%	1.7%	1.6%	1.5%
1850–1913	1.3%	1.6%	1.5%	1.2%

Source: Hoffmann 1965: 52, 204–5, 310, 320–23; our own calculations.

Table 9.3   Agricultural Growth in Germany and Its Regions, 1800–1910 (annual rates of growth in percent)

Land/Region	1800–1850/80	1880–1910
	Crop Production	
Bavaria	0.7	0.7
Saxony	1.0	1.3
Westphalia	1.6	2.3
	Agricultural Net Product	
Germany[a]		1.9
Northeast		2.4
Central		1.8
Northwest/west		2.1
South/southwest		1.1

Source: own calculation. Data for 1880–1910 from Grant 2002: 35–42, 1880–1910 = 1880/84–1905/7; data for Westphalia 1830–80 (1822/35–1878/82) from Kopsidis 1996: 196–97; data for Bavaria 1800–1870 from Böhm 1995: 386; for Saxony 1790–1830, Kopsidis et al. 2014: 67, and for 1818–49, Pfister & Kopsidis 2015: 284.
[a] Without Alsace-Lorraine.
Note: northeast = East Prussia, West Prussia, Pomerania, Posen, Silesia, and Mecklenburg; central = Berlin/Brandenburg, Prussian Saxony, Saxony, Thuringia; northwest/west = Schleswig-Holstein, Hannover, Westphalia, Rhineland; south/southwest = Hesse-Nassau, Bavaria, Palatine, Württemberg, Baden, and Hesse. All pre-1880 output data except for Westphalia are measured in grain equivalents. All Westphalian output data and all post-1880 data are measured in real prices.

in addition, shows a rapidly growing northeast during the Kaiserreich—a result that reflected the progressiveness of both large- and small-scale farming. The lagging development of the south and southwestern regions is also apparent, though a ready explanation for this is not at hand.

Over the course of the nineteenth century, an agricultural sector emerged in Germany that proved able to generate sustained increases in productivity based on technical change. It was surely no chance coincidence that examples of this development first appeared in areas affected by the food supply of emerging industrial belts. These achievements of the agricultural sector had their heyday in the age of high industrialization, 1871–1914, but their roots (as we have attempted to show in the preceding chapters) went far back, directly to the decades that began with the acceleration of industrial growth in the 1850s, indirectly back to the late eighteenth century. Nevertheless, toward the end of the Kaiserreich, the progress of German agriculture allowed it to be seen as an asset in the drama of "catching-up growth" that marked the Anglo-German rivalry, even if the productivity gap favoring British agriculture did not disappear until the eve of World War I, as seems to have happened in manufacturing (Grant 2009; Broadberry 1997; Burhop 2011: 49–65).[5]

TEN

Money and Banking in the Railway Age

Railroads and the industry they stimulated in Germany developed in tandem with the country's financial system. On the one hand, thanks to Prussian and Zollverein coinage reforms, their financing benefited from an increasingly stable and uniform currency. On the other hand, they provided banks and other financial actors with promising investment opportunities—at a time when other sources of demand seemed to be drying up. In this period from the late 1830s to the 1870s, banks, mainly private banking firms, served as an integral part of the leading sector complex driven by railroads. Indeed, the activity of the larger of these banking firms during this period may be said to have planted the roots of what became the "universal banking system" so characteristic of German economic development. To some extent, therefore, we can even consider the creation of the universal banking system as a kind of backward linkage effect of railroad building! In order to describe the nature of the structural connection, however, we need to look at the historical origins and earlier development of the financial system and the "universal banking" practices it brought forth.

The early nineteenth-century German "financial system" comprised a few hundred private bankers, mostly in cities like Berlin, Hamburg, or Frankfurt; money changers; a few collective institutions, such as the Prussian *Landschaften*, which provided East Elbian landed estates with mortgage credit financed by the sale of bonds to capitalists; state-controlled banks, such as the Prussian *Seehandlung* or the Royal (Prussian) Bank in Berlin; a small number of local savings banks; and, of course, the thirty some sovereign German states, which were the principal borrowers and also the main providers of the country's currency (coin and paper money). The stabilization of the currency in the 1820s and 1830s (noted above) facilitated interregional market integration, both within and between the several states,

Table 10.1   Total Stock of Currency, "Money Substitutes," and Bank Credit in Germany, 1815–65 (in millions of marks)

Year	Metallic Coin	Total Currency[a]	Money Substitutes[b]	Bank Credit
1815	590	610	—	—
1835	845	929	98	84
1850	1,195	1,447	273	205
1865	1,626	2,309	1,067	2,138

Source: Tilly 2015; our own calculations.
[a] Coin + paper money. [b] Bank short-term liabilities.

and this stability served as the basis for the expansion of credit that characterized the "financial system" in this period. Table 10.1 offers some rough estimates of this development.

Private banking firms were the main actors in this story. The money substitutes corresponded roughly to the bill of exchange drawing rights they extended to their current account customers. These "substitutes" served as means of payment in place of coins and paper money, thus supplementing a supply that, thanks to the growing monetization of economic activity, was seen to be inadequate. It is of some importance to realize that note-issuing banks and a central bank of issue first appeared in the 1840s; and that their effects remained at first modest, if not negative. Here we see private bankers as commercial bankers.

Many private bankers, however, went beyond that role. The fact is that one can recognize a forerunner of "universal banking" in the prerailroad age, even as early as the eighteenth century. The comprehensive management by "court bankers" of the financial affairs of the princes and other aristocrats who ruled the several German states then offered both long-term loans and the short-term payment services and credits related thereto. These transactions often arose from the states' need to finance military spending in wartime, a need that became especially acute at the beginning of the nineteenth century, even extending to provision of military supplies. The legendary rise of the Frankfurt Rothschilds took place within this context (Ferguson 1998: 1: chap. 4; Krüger 1925; Schnee 1953–55). By this time, the more successful of these bankers had already succeeded in developing a network of wealthy capitalist clients, the start for what was to become a hallmark of German universal banking: close ties to big borrowers and wealthy depositors/investors.

The end of the Napoleonic Wars in 1815 ushered in a phase marked by substantial growth of capital markets dealing in state loans, located in cities such as Berlin, Karlsruhe, Leipzig, Frankfurt, or Cologne, and these markets became increasingly interconnected. A knowledgeable contemporary, Gustav von Gülich, noted (in 1830) that "in the past decade the mass of this paper traded has grown enormously and become, more than any other commercial instrument, the market's principal object of speculation" (Neidlinger 1930: 375). He might have added that the buoyancy of these markets and declining rates of interest also reflected an accumulation of financial capital that exceeded existing demands in Germany. This fact helps explain the export of capital intermediated from the financial center of Berlin in these years and may have characterized Germany as a whole (Brockhage 1910, Borchardt (1961).

The financial market conditions described by Brockhage (and others) formed an important part of the environment in which Germany's railroad age began. Both financial capital and organized financial markets were potentially available for railroad companies, but they had to be mobilized. This was the job of the private bankers. We thus find these bankers in the center of the organizing and financial efforts of the early railroad companies, which began in the late 1830s and early 1840s. They helped secure the needed concession, managed the issues of shares and bonds, served as the companies' bankers, and usually held influential positions on the boards of directors.

A well-documented example of the bankers in their role as "universal banks" in this period can be seen in the early history of the Rhenish Railway Company (Rheinische Eisenbahn-gesellschaft, or REG). This company was originally conceived by a group of Cologne merchants and bankers as an answer to Dutch control of the Rhine's outlet to the North Sea. Merchants and bankers in Aachen joined the project, and when the company was founded in 1837, its route was to run from Cologne via Aachen to Antwerp. Its capital of 3 million thalers made it the largest private enterprise in all of Prussia at this time. This enhanced the role of bankers, for a sum of this size could only be mobilized inter-regionally—that is, by the bankers. The first official shareholders' meeting revealed that an insider group of bankers—thanks to the proxy shareholdings of their customers—in effect controlled the company. How the bankers used this control is an interesting story, but it has been told elsewhere and the details need not be repeated here (Tilly 1966).

This pattern was repeated in the development of other railroads. The important Cologne-Minden Company that would link the Rhenish-Westphalian industrial district with Berlin (founded in 1843) depended on the same private bankers. Other regions were also affected. Leipzig bankers played a leading role in organizing and financing the first Saxon railroads, the Leipzig-Dresden and the Magdeburg-Leipzig lines (Benaerts 1933: 270; Beyer 1978). Bankers also promoted and helped organize manufacturing companies, especially in the Rhenish-Westphalian region. Important enterprises such as the Hoerder Bergwerks- und Hüttenverein (1852), the Phönix AG (1852), and Bochumer Verein (1855) are examples. Promotion and financing of manufacturing firms, however, involved greater risks for bankers, and in the 1850s and 1860s their shares and bonds usually had to be placed privately. Berlin bankers (such as Bleichröder or Mendelssohn) proved helpful here, though only with the bigger and more established enterprises (Krüger 1925, Däbritz 1931). The "financial community" needed time (and a "track record") to form opinions on the securities of such firms. This was "universal banking" in the making.

The developments just described form the background for the appearance of the joint-stock banks that would eventually play, as "universal banks," such a prominent role in German economic historiography. The first of these, the Schaaffhausen'sche Bankverein, mentioned earlier, emerged from the failure in 1848 of the Cologne private banker, Abraham Schaaffhausen. In 1853 came the Bank of Darmstadt, in 1851 and then in expanded form in 1856 the Disconto-Gesellschaft in Berlin, and in 1856 several more, such as the Allgemeine Deutsche Credit-Anstalt Leipzig and the Berliner Handelsgesellschaft (Burhop 2002, Poschinger 1878–79: vol. 2; Tilly 1967). These new banks were founded largely by private bankers, who saw them as a means to enlarge their financial operations. For this reason they were described as "private banks of a higher order." Gustav Mevissen, a well-known Rhenish entrepreneur who played a key role in the development of these banks from the 1850s to the 1870s, described the role of these "mixed banks" as follows: "The banker is in high degree the irreplaceable confidant of industry and capital, the regulator of economic activity in general. In the degree to which banks and bankers extend or restrict industrial credit, is industrial production either encouraged to accelerate or wisely retarded. The banker is in equal measure the confidant of the capitalists, who as a rule follow his advice" (Hansen 1906).

As Mevissen himself privately acknowledged, however, the business model he had in mind concentrated on governments, big businesses, and wealthy capitalists—assistance for the strong (Tilly 1986). This became, in fact, the center of the business of these big banks.

The development of these "mixed banks," however, depended not only on the preference of bankers, on the needs of the leading sector related to railroads, or on large-scale enterprise in general, but also on the way monetary and banking policy developed in Germany. During the second third of the nineteenth century, public debate concerning banks focused mainly on note-issuing institutions as they had been developing in Britain and the United States. For various reasons—the most important of which was state policy—in Prussia note issue remained practically a monopoly of government. In the 1850s and 1860s, some private note-issuing banks operated in several German states—for example, in Saxony or Bavaria—but their impact tended to remain quite local. The Prussian Bank, moreover, had to learn how to operate as a "central bank": in the financial crisis of 1847–48 it had protected its cash reserves and restricted discounts, and in the crisis of 1857 it again contracted procyclically. By the 1860s, however, it began to become a dependable market stabilizer (Thorwart 1883). The circulation of its notes began to spread through other German states. By 1860, their circulation equaled approximately 70 percent of the German total. This left little room for the private note-issuing banks. For private investors, therefore, interest in such banks cooled and died.

From this development emerged as historical result a kind of division of labor in which most paper money and a growing share of short-term commercial credit was provided by government-controlled institutions, and in which industrial credit and capital market transactions fell to private banking firms and their creations, the joint-stock "mixed banks." Increasingly, these bankers and banks could rely on the "government" institutions to execute their interregional payments and—in times of monetary tightness—to provide emergency liquidity help.[1] Thus, in this respect as in others, the state played an important role in shaping the development of German industrial capitalism in this period. Not only could it ease mobilization of capital to the leading sector RHIC, but also it set the institutional rules along which the German banks—as the most important financial intermediary—could develop.

The evolution of private banks into "universal banks" may not be the only financial story of this period worth telling. From the 1840s on, local savings banks began to play a role, mobilizing local savings and contributing to the finance of local small firms and infrastructural projects. Between 1850 and 1870 the deposits in German savings banks grew from about 160 million marks to over 900 million marks. For 1870, the total number of savings banks has been estimated at about 1,500. That is, savings banks represented a widely accessible institution with enough financial weight to have made a difference, though too little is known about the lending side of their business for researchers to do more than speculate on the question (Ashauer 1998, Trende 1993 [1957], Voigt 1950).[2] In the 1860s, in addition, credit cooperatives appeared. These were institutions designed to foster a self-help form of finance for both small craftsmen and tradesmen in towns and small farmers in rural areas. These petty enterprises represented high credit risks for potential local lenders and accordingly faced very high borrowing costs. These reflected the high costs of obtaining information on borrowers' quality. Credit cooperatives pooled members' information about one another's credit-worthiness. Their rapid growth in their first decade suggests their success: their total assets were estimated in 1870 at close to 200 million marks. Moreover, their operations seem to have improved the credit-worthiness of both of these groups quickly, but, once again, we have too little information to generalize on their impact before the 1870s (Faust 1967; Hoffmann 1965: 736; Guinnane 2002; Crüger 1912).[3] What is certain is that both savings banks and credit cooperatives were definitely here to stay. We will return to them below, in our discussion of the 1870–1914 period.

PART FOUR

Germany's Emergence as an Industrial Power, 1871–1914

German historiography has classified German economic development in the period from 1871 to 1914 under a variety of headings. Thus, we have "The Rise of Monopoly Capitalism," "The Age of High Industrialization," the "Drive to Maturity," or the transition "From Agrarian to Industrial State." These reflect differing interpretations of the period, but they all have one thing in common: they all imply that German industrial development was already well under way as the period opened. The basic driving forces of that development remained, as in the preceding five decades, the mobilization of labor and capital, coupled to technical change. As was the case before 1871, economic growth remained unbalanced and discontinuous, the up-and-down rhythm of the business cycle still reflecting investment goods production. As in the preceding decades, economic development went hand in hand with deep changes in the social and political structure of the country.

The years between the empire's founding and World War I, however, did witness some important social, economic, and political changes that justify their treatment in a separate set of chapters. These include the shift in government policy away from economic liberalism and to a more interventionist course marked by protectionist tariffs and a state-sponsored program of social insurance; a related growth of organized economic interest groups (business associations, labor unions, cartels); the rise of large-scale industrial enterprises and banks; the growing integration of science and industry (the so-called "Second Industrial Revolution"); and rapid urbanization of the population.

ELEVEN

Growth Trends and Cycles

From the perspective of long-term economic growth, the empire period presents itself as one of rising prosperity. All available estimates show an economy that grew faster than it had between 1850 and 1870. The higher rate of growth of total net national product after 1870 reflected more rapid population growth in the later period, but the per capita NNP figures also show more rapid growth: 0.8 percent per annum as opposed to 0.4 percent, 1851–71 (Burhop 2011: 32–47; Metz 2015: 189).[1] Estimates of aggregate real labor incomes, finally, also showed a higher rate of growth after 1871: 0.6 percent per annum, over 0–0.3 in the earlier period.[2] Taken together, these imply a more widely shared prosperity than earlier, a shift that began to reshape the social and political structure of Germany, as we will attempt to show in later chapters.

The secular trend of rising real income rested on increasing productivity in both agriculture and industry. In spite of measurement problems, the trend seems indisputable. Table 11.1 shows the pattern.

The period difference in productivity change reflects the special role of the 1870s, a point to which we return below.

We see here the remarkable growth of the industrial sector, whose net output was about double the size of the primary sector by 1913. Nevertheless, the productivity figures imply that the German transition from agricultural to industrial economy also included modernization of the agricultural sector (see chapter 9). Without that sector's productivity growth, the huge numbers moving to industry over the period—estimated at several million persons—would have remained needed in agriculture as food producers.

The secular trend of production offers a useful long-run perspective on German economic history of the empire period. Its most obvious limit, however, is its failure to recognize the discontinuous character of the coun-

Table 11.1   **Share of Employment and Annual Rate of Growth of Labor Productivity in 3 Sectors in Germany (in percent)**

Sector	Employment Shares		Labor Productivity	
	1871	1913	1871–1913	1881–1913
Primary sector[a]	49	34	1.01	1.36
Industrial sector	29	38	2.02	2.22
Tertiary sector	22	28	0.4	0.4
Aggregate economy	100	100	1.34	1.53

Source: Our own calculations from Hoffmann (1965: 204–5); Burhop & Wolff (2005).
[a] Includes forestry & fishing production.

try's economic development in that period. Like most other industrializing countries, Germany industrialized at an uneven pace, with longer periods of rapid change alternating with periods marked by slower growth, a fluctuation that seemed quite independent of the more commonly recognized business cycle of six to ten years. Whether these deviations from trends ought to be understood as recurring, longer run cycles or historical "artifacts" is an unsettled question, for a generally accepted theory of such fluctuations does not exist.[3] Nevertheless, the phenomenon's presence in the history of the industrial countries seems indisputable.

Boom and Bust of the 1870s and the "Great Depression"

The empire's founding in 1871 took place against the background of a cyclical upswing that had begun to manifest itself in 1866–67 (Spree 1977). The Franco-Prussian War of 1870–71 interrupted this upward movement, which then continued, buoyed up by the war's successful outcome. The free incorporation law enacted by Prussia in 1870 facilitated investor exploitation of the euphoric expectations and bull stock market that followed the peace. Between 1870 and 1873, more than 900 corporations were founded, adding more (nominal) capital than that of all previously existing corporations combined. Belief in the positive effects of the war indemnity imposed on France—the infamous "5 billion"—coupled to monetary expansion further strengthened the boom (Mottek 1966; Baltzer 2007; Spree 1977: 362–67; Soetbeer 1874). The upswing, however, did not rest only on financial impulses: it had a "real economic core." For one thing, powerful demand effects came from resumption of investment in the leading sector RHIC: the railroads doubled their network and their capital (with investment estimated at more than 3 billion marks, 1868–74). Most of the decisions behind this investment had already been made in the 1860s, but they will nevertheless have affected expectations in the 1870s and spurred readiness to invest in the industries that supplied and used the railroads. A second upward impulse came from investment in urban building (mostly hous-ing). This, in turn, represented a supply response to the unparalleled popu-lation migration to cities that had begun in the late 1860s, but one that was carried upward by stock market speculation in land and construction companies, many of them newly formed corporations.[4]

Not only was this great wave of investment very large—producing be-tween 1868 and 1874 an increase in the country's capital estimated at roughly 60 percent—but also much of it was based on expectations about future profits, an inherently uncertain outcome. The same nexus applied to the growth of banks and credit creation, which further strengthened the investment boom. As in earlier cycles, what had gone up like a kite came down like a rock. In May 1873 the stock market wobbled and then crashed. Many hundreds of joint-stock companies had to be liquidated, and thousands of enterprises failed in the months and years that followed. The borrowing of the boom years now emerged as an unwelcome burden, especially in heavy industry, where falling prices magnified the real costs of debt finance. Crisis was followed by a long depression, which first bot-tomed out in 1879.[5] Depression conditions in Germany were reinforced by the simultaneous decline of economic activity in other industrializing countries (Great Britain, France, Austria, and the United States) (Burhop 2011: 75–76; Thorp 1926: 74–100). One indication of the negative effects of the "Gründer" crisis of the 1870s can be seen in the returns of investors in German equities. In table 11.2 we list estimates of the rate of return on a sample of shares for the period 1871–81. This experience will not have helped the reputation of equities as financial investments. Even if an inves-tor had had the foresight to pick survivors, he still would have been better off investing solely in government bonds.[6]

We dwell on the crisis and depression of the 1870s because it has played an important role in German historiography of the nineteenth century, and because that importance deserves further discussion. A. Spiethoff, a Ger-man pioneer of business cycle research, noted that the signs of recovery in 1879–81 that seemed to mark the end of the depression of the 1870s were brief, and—in spite of the strong upswing from 1887 to 1890—he classi-fied the entire period from 1874 to 1894 as *Stockungsspanne*, or "stagna-tion phase" (Spiethoff 1955: 69–78, 123–30).[7] Spiethoff focused mainly on economic indicators that reflected and affected business perceptions, such as profits, wholesale prices, credit availability, security prices, and

Table 11.2 **Rate of Return on Equities in Company Sample, 1871–83 (in percent)**

Branches	Survivor Firms[a]		All Firms		Failed/ Liquidated
Category	Number	Rate of Return	Number	Rate of Return[b]	Number
Mining/metallurgy	49	6.1	89	0.5	11
Machine-makers	29	1	61	−.1	25
Construction	17	−2.56	48	−22.5	20
Chemicals	6	6.1	14	0.2	4
Textiles	11	4.16	26	1.9	11
Breweries	16	4.4	30	1.96	7
Banks	72	4.65	183	2.5	88
Total	204	3.28	449	−2.35	166

Source: R. van der Borght 1883.
[a] Firms existing in 1871 & 1881. [b] Includes losses of failed firms (−7% p.a.)

interest rates. The historian Hans Rosenberg took up this notion with verve and—drawing on analogous treatment of economic stagnation in Great Britain—he described German history from 1874 to 1894 as "Great Depression and Bismarck Era" (Rosenberg 1967).[8] The study assumed that general economic conditions could affect how individuals and especially socioeconomic groups perceived society and how they behaved. A deterioration of economic conditions thus produced pessimistic views, bred mistrust in capitalist, market-oriented changes, and led to appeals for government intervention, seen as needed to reduce uncertainty and stop or reverse their distributional effects. During this "Great Depression"—the *Stockungsspanne* 1874–94—Rosenberg saw an ideological shift that he called "the discrediting of liberalism," and which was accompanied by a series of major changes in German economic, social, and political institutions, for example, the dramatic shift of commercial policy toward protectionism in 1879, the beginnings of a comprehensive, government-sponsored system of social insurance, or the more restrictive Corporation Law of 1884.

Rosenberg's study captured an important element of the period, but was based on an outdated economic historiography. Few economic historians today would share his description of the 1870s and 1880s as a "Great Depression era." In both decades, years of expansion alternated with years of recession; and over the entire period the economy grew by about 60 percent—a rate of 2.3 percent per year (Burhop & Wolff 2005; Burhop 2011: 70–71; Sarferaz & Uebele 2009). Revision especially applies to agriculture. What Rosenberg described as "agricultural depression" actually corresponded to the end of an unprecedentedly long period of prosperity benefiting agricultural producers. In the 1870s, however, that situation changed fundamentally. Railroads and steamships created a global market for agricultural staple products, a change that deprived German producers of their strong position in West European markets. While in the 1850s German grain had supplied more than one-quarter of the British market, in the 1870s that share shrank to less than 10 percent! American and Russian producers made even the German market a contested market. Increase in the worldwide supply of grain caused a dramatic fall of grain prices, in Germany as well as elsewhere. In the 1880s, grain prices were 20–25 percent below the level of the 1870s. Falling prices for grain-producing agrarian landowners continued into the 1890s and meant increased debt burdens, thus strengthening the pessimism and protectionist bent of those producers. This especially applied to the large estate owners in East Elbia. Smaller family farms proved better able to adjust, by specializing in the supply of animal products (meat, eggs, dairy) to urban markets. The politically important East Elbian "grain magnates" responded with political agitation, the label "Great Depression" supplying a convenient justification.

Thanks to their political influence in Berlin, these aristocratic landowners were the natural leaders of the shift to agrarian protectionism. As grain producers, they were hard hit by the falling prices, especially since they proved unable to achieve comparable cost reductions. In 1876 they founded the "Vereinigung der Steuer- und Wirtschaftsreformer" (Association of Tax and Economic Reformers), with the declared aim of "defending the material and professional interests of the large and medium-scale farms against the overweening power of commercial, financial, bank, and industrial capital" (Rosenberg 1967).[9] Their immediate goal, however, was tariff protection against the "foreign grain flooding into Germany." Reich Chancellor Bismarck made adept use of this plea, combining it with demands of the organized leaders of heavy industry, the association CVDI (Centralverband deutscher Industrieller), into the well-known "marriage of iron and rye" embodied in the Tariff Law of 1879. We return to this agrarian dimension of the period in chapter 14.

The "Great Depression" period 1874–94 had one pervasive economic characteristic, which it shared with other industrializing countries: falling prices. Figure 11.1 illustrates this important point.

This common denominator may well have reflected a sluggish growth of the precious metals coupled to growing real output of goods and services. The movement of several important countries to the gold standard in the 1870s pressed on a limited supply and called forth, among other things, demands for a return to the silver standard and an enhanced interest in

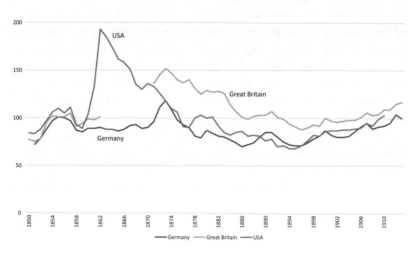

11.1 Wholesale Price Indices for Germany, Great Britain, and the United States, 1850–1913
Source: Jacobs & Richter 1935; *Historical Statistics of the United States,
Colonial Times to 1970*, Chapter E; Mitchell 1973: 815–19.

bimetallism (Kindleberger 1984). In the 1890s, however, this tendency weakened, the global picture changed, and price levels began to rise (as figure 11.1 suggests). Before leaving the topic, we note that figure 11.1 points to a more dramatic fall in prices in Great Britain than in the United States or Germany. This could reflect the absence of an effective protectionist movement in the former country, where commercial policy still responded to its role as "workshop of the world," while in both Germany and the United States, agricultural interests agitated powerfully for what they saw as agrarian-friendly commercial and monetary policies (Nocken 1993, Ritter 1997, Tilly 2003).

In the mid-1890s, the tendency reversed, and a period of generally rising prices (stimulated by the discovery and exploitation of new mines in the 1890s and a significant increase in global gold production) continued virtually unbroken until 1914. According to Schumpeter, these years corresponded to the beginning (upswing) phase of "The Third Kondratieff" long wave, marked by credit-financed innovations, while Spiethoff emphasized the positive interactions between rising prices, profits, and investment demand.[10] Cyclical downturns were not wholly absent, as the banking crisis of 1901 and worldwide crisis of 1907 demonstrated, but, on the whole, growth seems to have been higher and smoother in this period.

Heavy industry continued to play a major role as "cycle-maker," but the new science-based industries (chemicals, electro-technique) were factors of growing weight. Urbanization, in addition, brought with it heavy investment in housing and related infrastructure investment (water, gas and electrical works, local transportation networks), replacing the tapering-off of longer distance railroad building. In any case, up to 1914, German industrial growth showed no more than weak signs of slowdown in the 1870s, and these were soon reversed in the 1880s. (Figure 11–2).

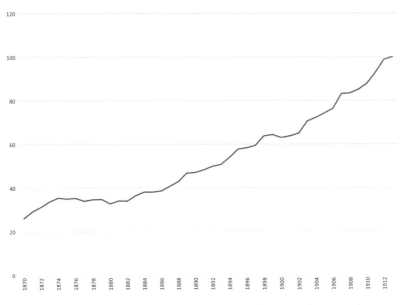

11.2 Industrial Production in Germany, 1870–1913 (3-year moving averages)
Source: Burhop & Wolff 2005: Appendix, Table 3.

TWELVE

The Growth of Industrial Enterprise, Large and Small

Industrial growth in Wilhelmine Germany reflected the operations of thousands of individual enterprises, large and small, public and private. The country's growing economic power and prestige depended strongly upon the achievements of its industrial enterprises. Success of the latter, in turn, depended largely on their ability to productively cultivate and mobilize human capital and new technological knowledge. That gives this chapter its framework of analysis. Thanks to important work on German patent history (especially by Streb, Baten & Yin 2006, Streb, Wallusch & Yin 2007, Richter & Streb 2011, and Cinnirella & Streb 2017), we have a periodization shaped by successive waves of innovation in successively different branches of industry. This development was marked in addition by distinct regional patterns that reflected, in part, innovations that affected the relative importance of energy sources (on these, Streb et al. 2006; Gutberlet 2014).

Innovation and Patents: Temporal and Regional Patterns

First, however, it is important to note that we are discussing operation of a "public order" institution that mattered: the Patent Law of 1877 establishing the German Imperial Patent Office. This had reflected recognition by increasing numbers of industrial leaders of the need for some nationwide protection of inventiveness (perhaps also of the growing connections between science and industrial technology). With establishment of the Imperial Patent Office, public control at the national level seems to have stabilized the handling of patents, turning them into a secure form of property, which facilitated the development of a market for patents in Germany. This "market" may have enhanced collective enjoyment of the benefits of the public good "innovation" (Burhop 2010: 921–39; Wischer-mann & Nieberding 2004).

Burhop's study (2010) presents several indicators that support his argument. First, most applications to the Patent Office were rejected. Second, there were very few (reported and contested) infringements of patent rights, and very few accepted patents were ever repealed. Third, the law stipulating a patent's use within three years ensured application, and it also stimulated a relatively high frequency of transfers—including a substantial increase in the importance of interfirm transfers in the high-growth period of the 1900s (Burhop 2010).

The use of patents in economic history—first possible on a national scale from 1877 onward—has to face up to the problem that their sheer number mixes important with unimportant innovations and can involve large measurement errors (Streb et al. 2006: 349, citing Grilliches). German patent law, however, contained a provision for renewal enabling patentholders to extend protection by paying a fee, which could rise to a maximum of 700 marks for the fifteenth year. We can assume that a patentholder would renew if he judged the present value of expected returns to the patent to exceed the present value of costs of maintaining it. This reasoning leads to identification of a subclass of "valuable patents"— Streb and colleagues (2006) settle for a sample of patents held up to ten years—that can be allocated to different branches of industry.[1] This supplies the basis of the following description.

The first wave—the "railway boom"—characterized the 1877–86 years and was marked by innovations focused on processes and products related to steam engines and steam boilers, railway equipment, machine parts, and metal processing. This reflected the continued importance of mechanical engineering and the linkages between railroads, heavy industry, and machine-making that had marked the take-off period from the 1850s, up to and including the boom of the early 1870s. It is a point of some interest that this development corresponded to Schumpeter's view of the period as part of the "Second Kondratieff" long wave based on "railroadization" of the economy and innovations related thereto. Railways would continue to be a focal point of linkages between heavy industry and mechanical engineering until the end of the century. These linkages probably included exchange of information concerning new technologies, indirectly reflecting "spillover effects" of knowledge from one branch of industry to another (Streb et al. 2006). This entire sectoral "cluster" had its geographical-regional counterparts. The northern Rhine and Ruhr industrial districts of

Düsseldorf and Arnsberg, greater Berlin, and the industrial heartland of Saxony (Chemnitz, Dresden) showed the greatest concentrations. This mirrored the pattern that had characterized emergence of the mechanical engineering industry in the "take-off" period and also reflected the importance of market access as location factor.

The success of German firms in the area of mechanical engineering owed much to the supply of literate skilled craftsmen. In the 1870s a "catching up" to England probably began, presumably helped by the relative cheapness of Germany's skilled labor. This by no means characterized comparison with the United States, whose relatively scarce and high-priced labor encouraged mechanization, and with it, world leadership in the production of machine tools. By the 1870s, therefore, German machine-tool firms had begun to imitate American products. A study by Richter and Streb (2011) using German patent data describes how imitation helped German producers to become innovators in some important machine-tool branches (such as agricultural machinery) between 1877 and the end of the century, a wave of imitation to 1900 followed by a wave of innovation up to World War I. By the early twentieth century, indeed, German exports of machine tools to the United States exceeded imports.[2]

The second wave of valuable patents reflected the activity of dyestuff firms, 1887–96. Their subsequent rise to world leaders marked the advent of "the Second Industrial Revolution," based on the closeness of ties between science and industry. One study of this industry (Murmann 2003) argues that Germany's Patent Law of 1877 had come at exactly the right time: before one or two large firms had come to dominate the market and use patents to stifle competition (as in Great Britain in the 1860s). Fierce competition among German firms in the early 1870s had weeded out weaker firms, and with patent protection the survivors began to expand research and development departments, switching from imitation of foreign dyes to invention of new, synthetic ones.

The success of German chemical firms stimulated foreign and domestic competitors to imitate their products—not covered by the process protection clauses of the patent law. Lobbying by the imitated firms, however, led to extension of patent protection to products in 1891. In the 1890s, then, the diversification of chemical firms, helped by their research laboratories, into the production of pharmaceuticals and synthetic fertilizers generated a third wave of valuable patents in the 1897–1902 period. The commercial importance of "heavy chemical" companies, however, continued to rest on their success as dyestuffs producers. Noteworthy is a link between dyestuffs and dyeing processes, and the marketing success of cotton textiles that also had a distinct spatial-locational pattern (Streb et al. 2006, Gutberlet 2014). The fourth and final wave of innovations marked the period from 1903 to 1918 and reflected the inventive and commercial success of electrical engineering. The effectiveness of electric motors for mechanization had been demonstrated in the 1880s, though the direct current (DC) used could not yet be transmitted over longer distances.[3] Nevertheless, the fourth wave of valuable "electricity" patents followed, rather than led, an expanding electro-technical industry. Between 1875 and 1895 it grew from 81 plants with 4,600 employees to 1,326 plants employing more than 26,000 persons; by 1907 the census showed 5,391 plants with 142,171 employees. The center of this innovative activity was Berlin (which built on its previous leadership in mechanical engineering). The Streb et al. study (2010) notes that the industry's two giants—Siemens and the AEG—produced less than 20 percent of the fourth wave's patents. This observation, however, may underestimate the technological and organizational vision of Werner von Siemens and especially of the Berlin engineer Emil Rathenau, whose competitive cooperation widened the scale and scope of the industry (Kocka 1969, Pinner 1918).[4]

As suggested above, patent activity had a distinct set of regional patterns. Berlin remained leader in all four waves (including dyes and chemicals), and was distinguished, toward the end of the period, by its electrical engineering cluster (spillover among subbranches of electrical applications and with linkages to scientific instruments). Nearby Potsdam hosted a mechanical engineering cluster (combining vehicles, railway equipment, and so forth). The Düsseldorf district, which remained number two throughout, also hosted dyestuff firms, but its mechanical engineering cluster was based on spillover (for example, between metal-working and machine tools). The nearby Arnsberg district (with the Ruhr) developed a mining cluster based on the variety of technical equipment that deep-shaft mining involved (pumps, fuel, machine tools, and so on). These were metropolitan areas in which market access played an important role. Farther south, Wiesbaden and the Palatinate formed clusters based on chemicals, access to raw materials, and water provided by the Rhine.

The regional distribution of industrial employment unsurprisingly coincided roughly with that of patent activity. It was shaped by access to markets, raw materials, and other productive inputs (including human capital). The Gutberlet (2014) study cited earlier emphasized the importance of energy sources. From the 1870s to the 1890s steam power and coal contributed to the growing concentration of metals, metal-working, chemicals, cotton-spinning, and other branches of industry. From the 1890s to World War I, the spread of electrical power led to a noticeable regional deconcentration of industrial employment, accompanied by some weakening of the locational power of coal.[5] For some industries, however, the importance of steam power and access to coal continued to grow. This was true of cotton-spinning, silkens, chemicals, and metals. The coincidence of cotton-spinning and chemicals could be related to the link between dyes and textiles reflected in patent history (mentioned earlier).

Iron and Steel and Technological Change

The "Railway Wave" (1877–96) cited in the previous section included innovations affecting iron-making, but the momentous changes in the importance of iron and steel that had just begun deserve some elaboration here. The "heroic age" of German iron-makers had been the successful switch to coke-smelting and growth of finished iron of the 1850s and 1860s. As Fremdling (1986) showed, by 1870 German iron-makers had considerably reduced the British lead in productivity, using the import of British pig iron as a "forward linkage" that encouraged growth of the output of finished iron. Britain remained number one. In the early 1870s it produced four times as much pig iron as Germany and about as much as the rest of Europe together (Mitchell 1975). Change in the technology of steel-making, however, would open a new chapter in metallurgical history.

Steel was already known to be a superior form of iron, just as hard, but with greater strength per unit of weight or volume, and more elastic. British advances in the development of crucible and puddled steel had clearly identified the critical importance of carbon content,[6] but the labor time and fuel still required for a ton of puddled steel left it three or four times as expensive as a ton of wrought iron. In 1856 a British "tinkerer," Henry Bessemer, found the key solution: he devised a converter that forced blasts of air through the molten metal, thus raising the heat in the furnace and holding the iron liquid until decarburization was completed. It could produce 3–5 tons of steel within 20 minutes (as against 24 hours for puddled steel). The German firms Krupp, Bochumer Verein, and the Hörder Union were early licensees, but the new process had certain deficiencies that delayed its replacement of puddled steel. All costs considered, it was not cheaper than puddled steel, and its quality (especially its greater durability), except for rails and railways, won no new markets.

In 1864 a second innovation appeared, the Siemens-Martin process, by which the waste gases of oxidization in the converter were utilized in a "re-generative" process that made use of a separate heating unit using cheaper coal. This not only generated much higher temperatures, but also made possible the use of scrap iron mixed with pig iron—an advantage that grew over time. Despite these innovations, a "take-off" of steel production did not occur. A major drawback of the Bessemer converter was its inability to utilize iron ore containing phosphorus, for non-phosphoric ores were rare and more costly than ordinary ironstone. It so happened that Britain was blessed with a major deposit of such ores (hematite)—in contrast to France and Germany, both of which depended largely on imports from Spain. Thus, Britain soon added dominance of steel production to that of iron.

At the peak of British dominance, in 1879, a year in which Britain produced more steel than Germany, France, and Belgium together, two Englishmen, Sidney Gilchrist Thomas and his cousin Sidney Gilchrist, devised a converter that neutralized the acid effects of phosphoric ore, utilizing the basic Bessemer process. It was an immediate success. German firms were quick to adopt it, the first licensees being the Hörder-Verein and Rheinische Stahlwerke. Commercial production of the new (Thomas) steel began in 1879. Other firms soon followed. Within a decade, German steel producers had closed the gap to British ones, and in the 1890s the curves of output crossed. Table 12.1 shows the changes between 1865 and 1913.

Landes and others have interpreted this example of "catching-up growth" as the result of superior entrepreneurial quality—top executives with engineering training and the ability to manage large-scale operations. Its obverse is the thesis of British entrepreneurial failure. There is some support for the focus on entrepreneurship in the literature; for example, Pierenkemper's study of Westphalian heavy industrialists observes for the last quarter of the nineteenth century a rising share of owners and top managers with university and engineering school degrees—in sharp contrast to British steel executives, among whom comparable qualifications first

Table 12.1 **Steel Output in Germany & United Kingdom, 1880/84–1910/13 (in millions of metric tons)**

Years	Germany	United Kingdom.
1880–84	0.99	1.82
1890–94	2.89	3.19
1900–1904	7.71	5.04
1910–13	16.24	6.93

Source: Mitchell 1975.

appeared between fifty and sixty years later (Erickson 1959, Pierenkemper 1979, Berghoff & Möller 1994, Nicholas 2014).

Landes, however, was particularly impressed by the size of German steelworks, for instance, the fact that in the early 1900s an average German blast furnace turned out 60 percent more pig iron per day than its British counterparts. This suggests the importance of scale economies. Steven Webb's (1980) study of the German steel industry confirms this. In his analysis two institutional changes of the 1870s facilitated the achievement of scale economies: the protective tariff of 1879 and the formation of strong cartels that flourished under its influence. Falling iron and steel prices and zero tariffs in the 1870s had led to cartel formation—the rail cartel founded in 1876 was the first—and steelmaker demands for tariffs. More cartels followed enactment of the 1879 tariff. Jointly, the two protected German steel producers from foreign and domestic competition, but the main beneficiaries were the small number of large and vertically integrated producers of heavy steel products. Cartels protecting inputs of the finished steel producers—coal, coke, pig iron, and half-rolled steel—stimulated these large steel firms to integrate still further backward, while the tariff-cartel combination kept domestic prices high enough to cover their high fixed costs.[7] Vertical integration and relatively stable domestic prices promoted investment in the newest technologies: larger furnaces, power generation from waste gas, continuous rolling mills, and mechanized movement of materials. The payoff came in the form of productivity gains that by the early 1900s put German steelmakers 10–15 percent ahead of their British competitors—a result reflected in the large share of German steel exports to Great Britain in these years (Webb 1980: 322–27; Buchheim 1983; and chapter 14).

Human Capital, Science, and Industrial Innovation

We can probably make the clearest case for the story of "Germany overtaking England" with the development of the German chemical industry, for no other industry illustrates so well the importance of education, science, and human capital as productive factors. Between 1875 and 1907 overall employment in the German chemical industry tripled to 155,370 persons, a growth rate of 3.5 percent per annum. Between 1880 and 1913 output grew at an annual rate of 6.5 percent (Hoffmann 1965) This suggests a respectable increase in productivity (and higher than the 4 percent reported for the British industry by Kennedy [1987]).

In the 1870s, however, Britain was still the undisputed leader in production of alkalis (for soap and bleaching purposes), and although strongly committed to the field of inorganic chemistry, it also led in the first practical discoveries made in the organic chemical industry (with the help of Germans working there). The first aniline dyes appeared there in the 1850s and 1860s, and in 1869 alizarin, the first to replace a natural colorant (madder). Experimentation with coal tars probably went further in Britain than in any other European country, but, as Landes remarked, "in Britain, the coal-tar amateurs were out of their depth" (Landes 1969: 273). Development stagnated.

This was Germany's opportunity. The 1860s and 1870s were a period of growth and consolidation of chemical firms, marked by mergers and takeovers. The BASF itself was a merger of two firms. By the end of the 1870s, a smaller number of larger firms began to stand out—Bayer, BASF, Hoechst, and Agfa—and they had begun to enlarge their collective share of the world dyestuffs market. These firms developed in tandem with the country's educational system and scientific activity. A growing system of secondary education supplied students, and German universities, in a tradition going back to Justus Liebig (a "founder" of German chemistry), produced graduates trained in a combination of chemistry theory and laboratory experimentation, with practical applications in view. These chemists became industrial technicians, some of them managers, transferring academic practice in laboratory research and discourse into the organization of the German chemical industry. The laboratory run by Carl Duisberg (Bayer Works) produced a growing number of Bayer patents that enlarged the range of its products (rising from around 200 in 1886 to nearly 2,000 in 1911). These laboratories played a crucial role, but they could also generate intrafirm conflict between the respective directors of research, production, marketing, and finance. The history of BASF offers an example of leadership impatience with the slow development of a synthetic dyestuff, indigo blue. The conflict even led to a change in the firm's leadership. Nevertheless, the research lab—human capital—was the industry's main resource. In this case it produced a concrete illustration of the importance of human capital for firms in this industry. In 1880 BASF concluded a contract with the Munich professor Adolf Baeyer (who held the patent for the synthetic dye indigo blue). The contract transferred the patent rights to BASF in exchange for a payment of 100,000 marks plus 20 percent of net profits from the dyestuff up to a maximum of 500,000 marks if reached by 1887, otherwise up to a maximum of 1 million marks! This was risky investment, and it so happened that development of a cost-covering production of the dyestuff could first be realized in 1897. At the century's end, the top management wondered whether indigo had been worth the trouble and expense it had involved.[8]

Reassuring for many firms, however, was the thought that applied science not only could solve immediate production problems, but also could reveal chemical processes at work that led to further applications and further profitable products. Landes called this "Imperial Germany's greatest industrial achievement." He added: "the scientific principles that lay behind artificial colorants were capable of the widest application. There was the whole range of products derived from cellulose, that remarkable family of carbohydrates that constitutes the chief solid element of plants" (Landes 1969: 276). He went on to cite examples such as explosives, photographic plates, film, or celluloid.[9] Another study has noted the emergence of a "network of knowledge" linking universities, professors, chemists, and their firms in a kind of "scientific community" (Murmann 2003: 28, 78–82). The surge of "high value" patents in the 1890s, one study suggests, was due to these research and development departments of the larger firms (Streb et al. 2006: 354). Britain had nothing comparable, its secondary school system not yet able to provide British universities with the needed students. The documentation of German leadership is overwhelming. Between 1885 and 1900 the number of German registered patents for chemical products was eleven times as high as that of British ones, and the number of articles by Germans on the subject appearing in British scientific journals was six times the number of those written by Britons. In 1900 there were around 4,000 chemists in Germany, more than twice as many as the 1,500 reported for Britain (Murmann 2003: 37–45).

The history of German engineering offers another example of an increasingly science-based industry that outstripped its British counterpart in this period. The engineering labor force grew by about 4 percent per year between 1875 and 1907, and its estimated output grew by 5.5 percent during those same years (Hoffmann 1965: 537–38). In some respects, the performance of this industry was more important for "catching-up growth" than chemicals, for productivity increases here could boost productivity in many other branches of the economy. Even more so, if we include the contribution of electrical engineering (for which an output in 1913 valued at 1.3 billion marks has been cited [Landes 1969: 290]). In comparison, British engineering output grew about half as fast, 1870–1913 (Kennedy 1987: 60). The economic history of electrical engineering has focused largely on the two most successful giants, the Siemens and AEG groups. The historian A. Chandler attributed their success to the entrepreneurial ability to exploit key innovations, invest strategically, and realize economies of scale and scope (Chandler 1990: 463–74). He might also have added that they benefited from a growing supply of human capital (Kocka 1975: 106).

Several studies have noted the growing demand of the mechanical engineering industry for highly skilled technicians (Cinnirella & Streb 2017, Streb et al. 2006). In the 1850s and 1860s the expanding network of vocational secondary schools had played an important role in satisfying the demand. By the 1880s, however, engineering firms, particularly those of the electro-technical branch, began to turn their sights on the technical colleges. As early as 1872 Siemens & Halske in Berlin "expanded its technical physics research program by institutionalizing it in a laboratory directed by a professor of physics" (Kocka 1975: 106). This tendency strengthened in the 1890s as the number of technical colleges in Germany began to expand more rapidly, and the supply of engineers grew. Thus, by the beginning of the twentieth century, German technical universities were turning out around 3,000 engineers per year—more than eight times the number reported for Great Britain. For Germany, indeed, there is even some evidence suggesting an oversupply of scientifically trained technicians by the 1900s (Pierenkemper 1987: 74, 76, 88, 191; Kocka 1969: 275–79, 364, 470–71; Laer 1982).

From Otto Motor to Automobiles: An Illustrative Case

It is possible to see mechanical engineering as the principal basis of Germany's nineteenth-century prowess. This section offers a case in point: the Otto Gas Engine. The wave of innovations based on steam power and railroads, discussed earlier, gave birth to a variety of innovations. One of these—the gas engine, a device using a piston and cylinder to compress gas and generate pressure—embodied properties that would eventually lead to the internal combustion engine and the automobile. The initial goal was a small engine that would better serve the interests of small businesses than the steam engine. Its first practical version was developed by a French inventor, Lenoir, in 1861, and its potential fired the inventive imagination of a German autodidact, Nikolaus Otto. With the help of a mechanic, he built an engine in a rented workshop in Cologne. Though imperfect, the engine sufficed to give him a patent for England, and it served as basis for the founding of a firm, "Gas Motor Factory in Deutz" (in Cologne), in 1864. Otto's patent was his capital; the firm's liquid capital (of 10,000 thalers) was supplied by a partner, Eugene Langen, a trained engineer, inventor, and member of a well-known, business-owning family in Cologne. The first two or three years, however, brought just two sales, returned engines, and customer complaints.

The engine's first major commercial successes began with the Paris Industrial Exhibition of 1867. The turning point came with a public test of competing gas engines that revealed the Otto version to consume significantly less gas per horsepower than its rivals. Soon thereafter, orders poured in. The firm, which now held patents in Prussia and some other German states, was too small in scale (with just fourteen employees) to meet the demand. It thus licensed other machine factories for production and delivery to northern and eastern Germany, while it concentrated on Rhineland and Westphalia and the southern states. The initial success proved short-lived. The licensed patents brought few returns, and complaints about the malfunctioning of the engines multiplied. Langen, Otto's partner, became worried, for he had lost, up to 1868, some 40,000 thalers (120,000 marks). The firm was reorganized on the basis of a new contract, which reduced Otto's share in the firm and its profits. Then came the boom of the early 1870s. It induced Langen and Otto to bring in additional capital by forming a corporation, Gas Motoren Fabrik Deutz AG, in 1872, with a capital of 300,000 thalers (1,500 shares of 200 thalers). Langen and his associates held the capital, Otto was technical director. They were able to absorb potential competitors by offering Gottfried Daimler (a trained engineer) and Wilhelm Maybach, two Swabian inventor-entrepreneurs, co-directorships in the firm. This marked an important improvement. The newly organized firm focused attention on precision of machine parts, finding that for some needed inputs, ordering them from Belgian or English firms led to more efficient engines. By 1874–75 the firm had a turnover of more than 1 million marks, and by this time more than 700 engines had been sold.

Throughout this period Otto had been working to reduce the noisy and explosive shocks that came with combustion. His solution came with the four-stroke engine that better controlled the gas inflow and worked more smoothly. For this he was awarded patent number 552 in 1877.[10] At the Paris Exhibition of 1878 the Otto engine again attracted much attention. From this point on, the firm's commercial success was assured. Its 2 hp engine sold for 2,100 marks, smaller engines for less (0.3 hp for 950 marks). In 1880, interestingly enough, book printers were the firm's top customers: with 1,396 engines they accounted for more than half of total sales. In 1889, the Langen & Otto company, with 700 workers, had become a large enterprise (Matschoss 1921).

At this time, conflict between Otto and the Daimler-Maybach team led to departure of the Swabian duo. They took knowledge of the Otto engine and its limitations with them. The Otto patent proved a fruitful constraint, for it dictated experimentation with variations that did not violate patent rights. Back in Swabia (Cannstadt), Daimler and Maybach eventually developed a more powerful and efficient engine, their progress slowed, however, by conflicts with their financial backers—a typical accompaniment of new industrial technologies. The Daimler Motor Company (DMC) that emerged in the 1890s produced stationary engines, motor boats, and autos. Not until the 1890s did it concentrate on automobiles, but like its competitor Benz & Cie in nearby Mannheim, the sharp competition from electrically powered motors encouraged it to do so.[11]

A high rate of entry and exit marked this young industry. As of 1900, 31 firms had begun production, followed between 1900 and 1910 by 115 new ones. Most successful were Daimler and Benz. Daimler, with its new model "Mercedes," became the industry's technological leader, Benz its top seller. In 1910, 80 firms still existed (and 66 firms had disappeared) (Horras 1982: 145). A census of 1907 counted 69 plants employing 13,423 persons and producing 4,283 motorized vehicles valued at 60.9 million marks. By 1912, its 124 plants employed more than 35,000 persons and produced vehicles worth 221.6 million marks. This was clearly an important and growing industry (Horras 1982: 342a,b). Despite the industry's progress, however, adoption of the automobile in Germany lagged well behind that of France, in 1914 the world's largest producer, and Great Britain, for both of which the "automobilization" process, ironically, owed much to the Otto engine (Laux 1976).

"Catching-Up Growth": A Balance

The driving forces of German industrial growth in this period were the iron and steel, chemicals, and engineering sectors. What did this mean for "catching-up growth"? The focus on German comparative strengths followed here up to now does not answer the question. Comparative productivity estimates of Broadberry and Burhop (2007) offer a more complete provisional answer.[12] Their estimates are listed in table 12.2.

The message is clear: German manufacturing had caught up to Great Britain before World War I, and Germany's chemical, engineering, and iron and steel industries had led the way. The case of engineering is not clear cut, for it is based on number of motor vehicles—arguably a poor indicator of that industry's growth contribution in the period, especially since it fails to mention electrical engineering, possibly Germany's technologically most progressive industrial branch.[13] Nevertheless, the main point

Table 12.2   **Germany/United Kingdom Labor Productivity c. 1907 (UK = 100)**

Industrial Sector	Germany/United Kingdom
General chemicals	126.6
Coke	98.9
Chemicals & allied	113.9
Iron & steel	137.8
Nonferrous metals	157.9
Motor vehicles	89.7
Metals & engineering	139.2
Cotton	85.6
Silk	74.9
Leather	67.8
Textiles & clothing	82.3
Brewing	90.5
Tobacco	28.3
Sugar	47.3
Food, drink & tobacco	66.9
Cement	108.1
Other manufacturing	108.1
Total manufacturing	105.0
Mining	78.7
Total industry	101.8

Source: Broadberry & Burhop 2007.

stands: Britain was strong in the big sectors of food and drink, clothing and textiles, and mining, sectors in which Germany was weaker. Moreover, by widening the perspective across services and tariff-protected agriculture, we have a somewhat less flattering picture of German "catching-up growth." In 1871 British output per head was nearly twice as high as Germany's, and in 1913 still about 40 percent higher (Burhop 2011). Germany had reduced the gap, but had not quite caught up.

Human Capital, Education, and Industrial Enterprise: General Considerations

The history of German enterprise is virtually inseparable from that of education and training. The sustained rise in levels of education attained by German top executives was one indication of this interest in education. As increasing numbers of industrial leaders recognized the connection between science and profit-generating innovations in the 1860s, they gave support to establishment of national public control of patents. As indicated earlier, public control came in 1877 at the national level with establishment of the German (Imperial) Patent Office.

German industrial entrepreneurs also showed their interest in science as a productive factor through the readiness with which they installed departments for research and development, especially in the chemicals and electro-technical industries. David Landes emphasized that "the more progressive industrial enterprises were no longer content to accept innovations and exploit them, but sought them by deliberate, planned experiment" (Landes 1969: 325; North 1981: 172). This observation also applies to a second aspect of this theme: the contribution of public institutions to technical education. Industrial entrepreneurs did not remain simply passive recipients of an industry-friendly government but sought to influence the latter's programs of technical education. Thus, the founding of the Aachen Technical College owed much to the financial and organizational efforts of entrepreneurs in mining and related branches (Laer 1982: 159–60). Industrial leaders were also behind the Association for Promotion of the German Chemical Industries. In 1886 it demanded uniform admission qualifications for the study of chemistry, uniform degree qualifications, and, finally, greater weight for the practical applications of chemistry. These steps were forthcoming, though not until 1897 (Burchardt 1975). Similarly, the Technical College of Berlin first began to devote a share of its curricula to the "chemistry of dyestuffs and textiles" in 1889, following intensive lobbying by local chemical firms. Still later (1910) came the founding of an Imperial Chemical Center, which provided government financial support of basic research in chemistry.

What deserves emphasis is the functional character of industrialists' high valuation of science and education. The rationalization of production methods and organizational structure of the steel industry, evident in the huge heat-energy economies realized in the 1880s, clearly reflected the increased employment of highly trained engineers and master steelworkers in these years (Krengel 1983). The development of metallurgical chemical research laboratories in steel companies by big enterprises such as Krupp (in 1887) furnishes another example, for it was such investment that yielded the high-quality steels, profits, and growing market shares associated with that firm (Boelcke 1970; James 2011).

The Importance of Large-Scale Enterprises

Large-scale enterprises played a major role in the technologically progressive sectors just discussed. This growth went hand in hand with the increasing availability of the corporation as organizational form. The corporate form offered capitalist owners limited liability, and hence, risk protection for their continued, nonactive participation, and it also made continuity of the enterprise much less dependent on the quality of the family members. The bubble that had followed the boom of the 1870s eventually led, in 1884, to a more restrictive law and set of legal rules, raising the minimum size of shares to 1,000 marks, and generally strengthening shareholders and the supervisory board (*Aufsichtsrat*) that represented shareholders with regard to the executive directors. This slowed the formation of corporations, but the biggest firms usually took this form. A study of the 100 largest German industrial enterprises for the years 1887 and 1907 identified four-fifths as corporations. Their capital grew rapidly. Between 1882 and 1913 the capital of industrial corporations grew from around 10 percent to more than 20 percent of the capital stock estimated for "industry and crafts" (Hoffmann 1965: table 34 and 224). Large-scale enterprises grew faster than the industrial sector as a whole.

Growth of enterprise size in the period tended to concentrate in the already dominant heavy industry, including mining and metallurgy; it also characterized chemicals, engineering, and electro-technical products. Together with the transportation sector, these branches mobilized the largest amounts of capital and made greatest use of the corporate enterprise form. In these branches, the trend was toward concentration. In the occupational census of 1907, enterprises with 50 employees or more employed around 70 percent of all workers in these branches, while for all industries the share was about 45 percent. The absolute numbers themselves were impressive: in 1907 the Krupp enterprise employed 64,000 workers, the Siemens-Schuckert firm 43,000, and the AEG around 31,000 (Kocka & Sigrist 1979). Giants such as these represented a radical change as compared with the situation of the 1850s or 1860s. Steering and coordinating the activities in such huge empires required complex internal organizational structures and stimulated the growth of large industrial bureaucracies. Size alone had consequences for the nature of competition between enterprises, turning market competition into a matter of negotiation between small numbers of rivals.

A somewhat anomalous aspect of German large-scale enterprise is that by the end of the period four of the five largest enterprises were state-owned and -operated: the Prussian-Hesse State Railway, the German Imperial Postal Service, the Prussian Mining Enterprises, and the Bavarian State Railway. Together this group employed almost 1.2 million persons—more than half of the total of 2.2 million employed by the country's 125 largest employers (Burhop 2011: 141–42).

Market shares offer one indicator of changes in competition. In Ruhr coal mining, for example, the number of independent enterprises fell from

100 in 1880 to 57 in 1913, while the market share of the 10 largest firms grew from 24 percent to 53 percent. Iron and steel experienced a similar decline in numbers, from 134 to 102, the market share of the biggest 5 producers rising moderately to about 30 percent. In the rapidly growing branch of electrical engineering, a more dramatic result is implied by the large share of the AEG Group and the Siemens-Schuckert Konzern—reportedly accounting for about one-half of total employment in 1907 (Pinner 1918, Kocka 1969, Feldenkirchen 1988).

Concentration is not identical to restraints on competition, but it does promote them. A branch-based cartel with a few dozen member firms was clearly easier to organize than one with hundreds of potential members. The founding of the Rhenish-Westphalian Coal Syndicate in 1893, for example, followed a wave of concentration in which dozens of mining firms relinquished their independence. The syndicate's 95 members represented about 87 percent of the district's productive capacity. Historians have long debated the syndicate's importance, but a definitive consensus has not been reached. Several careful studies suggest that its effects, if any, were quite small: thus, we have both evidence of continued competition among the members and evidence of a price stabilization in the 1893–1913 period, this latter usually attributed to the cartel (Feldenkirchen 1988, Peters 1989, Bittner 2005, Burhop & Lübbers 2009).[14] A look at Ruhr coal prices, shown in figure 12.1, suggests that the syndicate did affect the stability of prices.

The Rhenish-Westphalian industrial district appears to have offered fertile ground for cartel development. In the 1870s, as prices fell, iron and steel producers became active, forming the rail cartel in 1876, and a decade or so later the steelworks cartel, formalized in 1904. Cartels may have facilitated the growth of large-scale enterprise in heavy industry, where vertical integration of coal mines in steel works freed the latter from the higher cartel prices, and where—with the help of protective tariffs—those firms could stabilize their output in cyclical downturns by export "dumping" in foreign markets (Webb 1980; Burhop 2011: 158–60; Burhop & Lübbers 2009).

An additional form of cooperation developed: the pooling agreements known as "interest associations" (*Interessengemeinschaften*), the "IGs" that became so prominent toward the end of the nineteenth century, especially in the German chemical industry. These IGs typically exchanged shares, pooled their patents and licensing arrangements, and agreed on common purchasing and marketing facilities. By 1906 two powerful IGs had been formed. Both united three large dyestuff firms: one consisting of Hoechst, Leopold Casella & Co., and Kalle & Co.; the other consisting of the BASF, Bayer & Co., and the Berlin manufacturer, Agfa. The two IGs formed a duo-

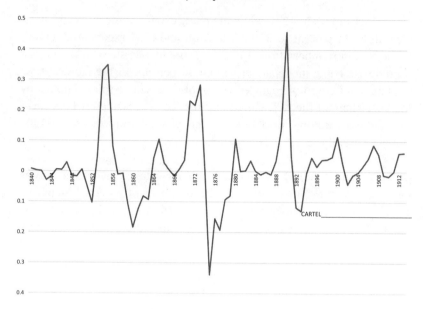

12.1 Annual Rate of Change of Ruhr Coal Prices, 1840–1913
Source: Holtfrerich 1973: 22–24.

poly by means of cartel agreement, and this controlled not only 95 percent of German dyestuffs, but thereby also about 80 percent of their world supply (Pohl 1978: 12).

So widespread and important were such cooperative arrangements between big firms in Germany that Alfred Chandler, the well-known historian of large-scale enterprises, classified that country's patterns of industrial organization as "Cooperative Managerial Capitalism"—a sharp contrast to the characterization he gave US patterns: "Competitive Managerial Capitalism" (Chandler 1990). To some extent, to be sure, small and medium-sized firms also made use of cooperative business forms—for example, exclusive, or long-run, supply contracts—but these usually involved big firms as partners. In this section, therefore, we are describing an important part of the German industrial economy, but only a part.

Large-Scale Industrial Enterprise and the Role of Organization

The success of German large-scale enterprises in applying science to production depended on some important changes in their organizational structure. Two of those changes probably enhanced the likelihood that science-based innovations contributed to enterprise success: integration and diversification. Around 1900 the top ten or twelve firms in iron and steel were vertically integrated. Each of them had their own coal mines, some of them iron ore mines. They produced their own pig iron and raw steel, worked these materials into finished and half-finished steel products, in some cases even manufacturing machine-driven equipment, vehicles, and other devices. These firms—the Krupp firm, the Gutehoffnungshütte, Gelsenberg, and Deutsch-Luxemburg are examples—were not only responding to the price-boosting effect of cartels, but also "internalizing external economies" by creating or acquiring separate departments or plants corresponding to the next higher stage of production. The *ex ante* risk of marketing a "new" product was zero if its intended destination was another department of the same firm, but uncertain if the taker belonged to a different enterprise.

Economic historians have often observed the relatively high degree of vertical integration—and internalization of external effects—that especially characterized German heavy industry, but which was markedly less evident in British industry. This difference is used to explain why and how the German steel industry overtook its British competitors between 1880 and 1913 (Webb 1980, Kindleberger 1975, Wengenroth 1986, Feldenkirchen 1980). Both the chemical and electro-technical industries give us further examples of German top firms far more integrated than the British ones in the same period (Landes 1969, Chandler 1990).

Forward vertical integration of marketing represented an enterprise strategy that characterized several German industries with large firms—except in a few cases where that function was transferred to a sales syndicate (cartel). Thus, Siemens developed its own marketing organization as early as the 1870s, a change then copied by the leading dyestuff firms of the chemical industry in the 1880s. A further example is the wide-ranging, international marketing system developed by Felix Deutsch for AEG in the 1890s—an important contributor to that firm's success (Kocka 1975). British competitors failed to develop similar marketing arrangements, possibly because foreign companies in Britain supplied domestic needs in these industries, obviating any need to mobilize independent dealers specialized by products. In the industries of tobacco, food, and drink, however, British firms did build successful marketing systems, branded and packaged their products, and advertised nationally (Chandler 1990: 262–63).

Diversification represented the second "strategic" change in organizational structure. More than half of the largest German industrial enterprises had diversified by the early 1900s. The historical study of the largest 100 firms by Kocka and Sigrist revealed that in iron and steel and chemicals, almost all the biggest firms produced and marketed a variety of individual products. They compare German firms with samples of the biggest British and American enterprises for the period between the 1880s and the 1900s. Their result emphasizes the similarity between German and American firms—both relatively integrated and diversified—and the contrast between those two and British ones (Kocka & Sigrist 1979, Chandler 1990). According to the theory of enterprise growth developed by Alfred Chandler and used by Kocka and Sigrist here, diversified and integrated structures promoted enterprise growth. This has been advanced as one reason why Germany's large industrial enterprises in key industries proved more innovative than their British counterparts. Supporting evidence, however, is limited to those industries in which Germany excelled.

In addition, in Britain's greatest industry, cotton textiles, vertical integration was not needed for success in the low-income markets on which it increasingly concentrated after 1870. This was because integration by individual firms meant sacrificing the comparative advantage of its well-organized specialized markets derived from economies of scale and long production runs (Brown 1995). This argument could also apply, with reservations, to other textiles, coal, tobacco, and a few other branches. The difficult question of the extent to which, and why, Britain—the first industrial country—after around 1870 began to relinquish its position as the world's industrial leader remains a puzzle to which we return below (chapter 14).[15]

Small and Medium-Sized Enterprises

The role of smaller enterprises (SME) in German industrialization deserves some attention here, though the topic necessarily remains somewhat elusive. Fewer micro-data are available except for the relatively few firms whose growth into large ones is documentable. German historiography long treated much of their history under the heading of *Handwerk*, or "handicraft," often as a threatened group.

Official statistics shed a little light. Thus, as total nonagricultural employment in Germany grew from a bit more than 7 million in 1882 to more than 14 million in 1907, the share working in the 3 million smallest firms (those employing 1–5 persons) in 1907 declined from about 60 percent to a little more than 30 percent. With about 1.5 persons per unit, these were small establishments indeed (table 12.3).

A somewhat more differentiated view is presented in table 12.4.

The numbers suggest that despite relative decline, smaller firms remained an important economic factor in the early twentieth century; though these statistics have their limits.[16] We can move a step further by

Table 12.3 Number & Size Class of Producing Units in Manufacturing and Shares of Total Number & Total Employment, 1882–1907 (in 1,000s & percent)

Year	Total Number (1,000s)	With 1–5 Employed (%)		With 6–50 Employed (%)		With More Than 50 Employed (%)	
		Units	Employed	Units	Employed	Units	Employed
1882	3,005	95.9	59.8	3.7	17.4	0.4	22.8
1895	3,145	92.8	41.8	6.5	24.7	0.8	33.5
1907	3,424	89.8	31.2	8.9	26.4	1.3	42.4

Source: Fischer 1976: 533; Reckendrees 2015.
Note: The units quantified here in the official censuses were *Betriebe*, or "operating units." Strictly speaking, they were not firms, since a relatively small number of firms maintained more than one unit (plant or branch).

Table 12.4 Number of Persons per Establishment in German Manufacturing Branches and Share in Plants with 50 Persons or More, 1882 & 1907

Branch of Industry	1882 Persons Per Plant	Share in Plants with More Than 50 Persons (%)	1907 Persons Per Plant	Share in Plants with More Than 50 Persons (%)
Mining & metallurgy	81.3	92.4	163.5	96.6
Quarrying, glass	6.6	33.1	16.2	52.5
Metal-working	2.8	18.7	6.1	47.0
Machines, apparatus	4.3	46.8	11.9	70.4
Chemicals	7.8	51.0	16.3	69.8
Textiles	2.6	38.2	8.0	67.5
Food & drink	3.0	20.0	4.0	21.8
Clothing	1.5	3.0	1.9	12.9
Average	2.6	26.2	5.2	45.5

Source: Burhop 2011: 139.

drawing on some older work by economic historians who took a closer look at the handicraft branches (*Handwerk*). In a memorably short article Wolfram Fischer suggested that the growth of certain groups of craft workers (such as bricklayers or tailors) could be coupled with available branch estimates of output (say, of building, or clothing) for the period from 1850 to 1913 (Fischer 1972: 338–48). He supplemented this argument with sample data taken from empirical studies of craft workers (carpenters, printers, mechanics, bakers, and so on), showing for the period from 1875 to 1907 a growth of output and capital and use of credit roughly comparable with industry as a whole. To some extent, then, we may look on these firms as SMEs, the forerunners of today's vaunted "middle class" enterprises. Nevertheless, the successful transition from a prospering small craft workshop to a medium-sized or large enterprise seldom happened, and the few cases for which we have evidence suggest that something more than technical handicraft competence was required to make it.[17] It may be useful to look at a few examples to illustrate what was involved.

It seems likely that family firms, constrained by the wish to maintain continuity of control, were well represented in the category of SMEs, often in what we may call "niche branches." Such was the case of the wire-weaving firm Haver & Boecker, founded in 1887 in Hohenlimburg (Sauerland) with twelve employees. Early attempts to mechanize wire-weaving and cut labor costs disappointed—and brought a dead loss of 20,000 marks written off (Pierenkemper & Tilly 1987). Stiff competition and labor costs in Hohenlimburg induced the firm to move to Oelde in eastern Westphalia, where wages were lower and market conditions more favorable (a railway connection, a nearby cement works). Here the firm mechanized its weaving operations, acquiring an Otto-type gas engine as power source. As its business prospered, it enlarged its labor force, which rose gradually from 25 persons in 1897 to 120 in 1907. Mechanized production paid off: between 1897 and 1907 (real) labor productivity rose by 44 percent, real wages by 4 percent. In 1914 the firm, with its capital of 135,000 marks, offers us an example of a successful middle-class enterprise.

Mechanics could also develop into family enterprises. The machine-maker Th. Calow & Co. in Bielefeld owed its start to the founder's employment as works-master in the Ravensburger Spinning Mill in the late 1850s. His work there familiarized him with the needs of the textile industry, and in 1863 he founded a new firm. It began with construction of transmission and bleaching equipment, gas meters, and boilers, later expanding into steam engines and a variety of machine tools. Begun in 1863 with 12 employees, by the 1870s his firm employed around 100 persons (Ditt 1982: 75). Many such firm histories exist, and available bibliographies suggest that the above-cited examples could easily be expanded (Pierenkemper 2000: 28–40).

Finally, it is useful to keep in mind that the viability of some big industries with a relatively small number of dominant producers—such was the automobile industry by the early twentieth century—depended on a large network of smaller enterprises that supplied inputs such as tires, electrical equipment, fuel, parts, repairs, sales, and other services, without which the attractiveness of automobiles, for instance, would have been much diminished (Horras 1982: 196–213). Their overall quantitative importance can only be guessed at, but the number of directly linked establishments grew from 66 in 1901 to 154 in 1906, their employment from 1,476 to 12,219 persons.

All of these firms began small, and many, if not most, remained so. Some made use of a new business form available since 1892, the private limited liability company (*Gesellschaft mit beschränkter Haftung*, or GmbH). Recent evidence on its emergence suggests that the GmbH was an institution better able to fit the needs of smaller firms than the corporation or the private partnership (Guinnane et al. 2007). That author shows that the share of industrial and commercial enterprises taking the GmbH form and reported in the 1907 census was already 10 percent—just as large as those organized as corporations (and the GmbH share of the sample of 130 "automobile enterprises" cited above was 17 percent). The GmbH share in total employment of labor was slightly lower, but in the relatively high-tech branches of chemicals and machinery, it was between 13 and 19 percent. With an average number of 64.3 workers per firm, they were dwarfed by corporations (with 458.1 persons), but still far above the average for all firms (5.2).[18] We return to its importance in the next chapter.

THIRTEEN

Industrial Finance, Money, and Banking

The growth of business enterprise depended decisively on finance, and company law played an important role. In 1870 the Prussian state replaced its strict joint-stock concession policy with a new law based on fulfillment of only a minimum of registration requirements. This facilitated the formation of hundreds of new companies—many of them flimsy constructions—and the notorious boom and bust of the 1870s. Both boom and bust involved many banks, and thus will deserve our attention again below. For now we note that one important consequence of the financial crisis was the public and political reaction to the hundreds of company failures, many of which were revealed to have been no more than empty joint-stock shells designed to enrich insider promoters and defraud gullible investors (Wirth 1874: 2:514–16; Rosenberg 1967: 70, 73; Kindleberger 1984: 125–26). Thus, in 1884, after long deliberation, a new law regulating corporations came into force that strengthened the rights of shareholders, raised the minimum share eligible for trade to 1,000 marks, lengthened the time between founding and eligibility for trade on the stock exchange, and so forth (Reich 1979, Tilly 1982, 1990, Schubert & Hömmelhof 1985).[1] The law gave established corporate enterprises more market power with respect to newcomer firms and probably promoted merger activity and concentration.

The Company Law of 1884 corresponded to the needs of large-scale enterprises, but proved less suitable for smaller ones. Critics of the law in the German Reichstag debate on it raised this point (Guinnane et al. 2007): they called for a hybrid between partnerships and corporations, and they pointed to the flexibility of the British corporate act of 1862 (which encouraged formation of SMEs) as a competitive advantage that Germany might copy. For the less capital-heavy needs of smaller enterprises (SMEs), ordinary partnerships came with the risks of unlimited liability and untimely dissolution (withdrawal of a partner and his or her capital), while corporations had high start-up costs and came with the risk of "minority oppression" (for instance, when one group of investors could not prevent another from actions with private benefits that reduced the value of the minority's shareholdings). We may thus see the law of 1892 authorizing the formation of private limited liability companies (*Gesellschaft mit beschränkter Haftung*, or GmbH), the ownership shares of which were not publicly tradable, as an answer to this deficit. In the year of its enactment the legal universe of German firms had three components:

ordinary partnership (*Offene Handelsgesellschaft*, or OHG): 90 percent of all firms

limited partnership (*Kommanditgesellschaft*, or KG): 9 percent of all firms (a small share of these as KGaA, or partnerhip limited by shares)

corporation (*Aktiengesellschaft*, or AG): about 1 percent of all firms

The GmbH found immediate acceptance. Its growth seems to have come largely at the expense of ordinary partnerships, whose share of all newly registered firms by 1912 had dropped to about 60 percent, with GmbHs increasing their share to one-third. By 1913 more than 26,000 such firms existed, representing a capital of more than 2 billion marks (compared with 5,486 joint-stock companies [*Aktiengesellschaften*] and a capital of almost 9 billion marks) (Reckendrees 2015: 254).[2] This might suggest that GmbHs were taking the place of partnerships that in the absence of the 1892 law would have continued to grow. Their sectoral distribution and size, however, raise the possibility that they also slowed the growth of the smaller corporations.

Money and Banking

The 1870s brought financial trouble to Germany, as we have seen, but it also gave birth to two important and constructive changes in the country's monetary system: (1) the introduction of a new national currency, the mark, based on the gold standard, the transition from silver facilitated by the reparations imposed on France in 1871, the "5 billion"; and (2) the creation of a truly national central bank of issue, the Reichsbank, whose operations began in 1876, simultaneously with the new currency. The Reichsbank built on the organizational and material structure of the Prussian Bank (whose assets and liabilities it absorbed), which had come to serve, if imperfectly, as central bank for most of northern Germany. The financial benefits of these two changes did not become visible in the 1870s, but by the 1880s both were rapidly becoming an integral, dependable part of the banking system. We make reference to their importance again below, but for a fuller picture we encourage readers to consult the available literature, and we offer no detailed discussion here (Borchardt 1976, Burhop 2011, Otto 2002, Flandreau 1996).

Turning away from those changes, we may look on the crisis of the 1870s as a shock that had long-run consequences for the development of German banking and industrial finance. The events of the 1870s offered certain opportunities utilized by the banks, a connection we attempt to interpret from an informational perspective. The following paragraphs discuss several of these.

To begin with, as mentioned above, the stock market boom of the 1870s included the founding of many new joint-stock banks, but by 1874 more than one-third of these had already failed, and many others were in trouble. The bust stimulated concentration processes in which the survivors emerged with larger market shares. The survivors—several of them the "great banks" of the future—began to drive out and replace the private bankers as well as their weaker joint-stock rivals. The Deutsche Bank offers perhaps the best example. Founded in 1870, it bought out the weak Berliner Bankverein and Deutsche Union-Bank in 1876. By the end of the decade it was Germany's biggest commercial bank (Gall et al. 1995: 23). The other big banks, however (for example, the Disconto-Gesellschaft, Berliner Handelsgesellschaft, or Darmstädter Bank), were not far behind.

The rise of the "great banks" also owed a great deal to the public's negative views on company promoters, views that were shared by many capitalist investors. The Company Law of 1884 built on this. By increasing the power of those who supplied the capital for new enterprises, it indirectly strengthened the banks' importance, especially that of the bigger banks centered in Berlin, location of the country's principal securities market. Private capitalists, many of whom had been burned in the crash, tended to avoid promoters and began to prefer investments associated with the joint-stock banks that operated in that market. The latter increasingly gained the capital market business formerly dominated by private bankers. Moreover, as corporate institutions, they developed organizational structures better able to operate supraregionally and to diversify their business than the private banking firms they began to replace (Da Rin 1996). Private bankers had founded many of the joint-stock banks and remained long associated with them; but their influence declined (Wallich 1978).

The crisis of the 1870s dramatically brought home to the banks the dangers of financing industry, and in its aftermath, they intervened decisively in the affairs of some of the heavily indebted Rhenish-Westphalian steel companies. Even the prestigious Krupp firm, saved from financial embarrassment by a Prussian government-sponsored loan of 10 million thalers (30 million marks), had to accept banker-monitoring conditions. The big Berlin bank Disconto-Gesellschaft undertook the most dramatic step. The efforts of the steel companies—Krupp, the Bochumer Verein, Rheinstahl, and Gutehoffnungshütte—to drive their rivals out of the market for steel rails by price cutting threatened them all and shocked the creditor banks into action. The Disconto-Gesellschaft demanded formation of a steel rail cartel, and its threat to one-sidedly support its own special client, the Dortmunder Union, proved sufficient to bring about the cartel in 1876 (James 2011: 74–76; Wellhöner 1989; Fischer 1965: 89; Wengenroth 1986).[3] Such intervention had the effect of a signal to "the market" that these banks were credit-worthy. To some extent, the many bankers registered on industrial supervisory boards then and in the years to follow represented the same kind of signaling.

The big banks operated on the basis of a banking business model that combined industrial lending with active participation in the issue and trading of securities on the capital market. This combination was risky, and it led the joint-stock banks to hold relatively large capitals. The larger their clients, the larger the capital the banks had to hold.[4] Again, we can interpret this as a signal the banks sent to the capital market to emphasize their willingness to pay the price of the risks they bore. The interesting fact that in 1913 the three largest German enterprises (by size of equity capital), and seventeen of the twenty-five largest, were banks reflects this stance. This was unique among the industrial countries of that time.

The readiness with which the big Berlin banks expanded rapidly from the 1880s on by establishing branch offices and, where local bankers were well established, by means of cooperation agreements with the local banks (called *Interessengemeinschaften*), throughout the country reflected in part a response to informational needs. This spatial growth enabled the big banks to acquire information about the regional and sectoral distributions of savings and investment needs and thus to diversify their business operations (Pohl 1986: 61–69). Similarly, the development of overseas connections via branch offices, participation in foreign banks, or cooperative agreements offered an additional way to secure better information on international financial conditions and diversification of their business operations. Most successful in this respect was the Deutsche Bank, but others, such as the Disconto-Gesellschaft or the Commerz- und Disconto Bank, also developed close foreign connections (Pohl 1982, Krause 1997, Tilly 1991b).

The business model used by Germany's big commercial banks as "universal banks" seems to have paid off in terms of stabilization of returns on bank shares, as shown in figure 13.1.

The strong position of the big banks in the German capital market underlay the important role they played in promoting and financing the country's larger industrial enterprises. In addition, however, the continuous monitoring of current account movements, indirect control over managers via the shareholder assembly and supervisory board, and direct participation in the issue and trading of shares and other securities on the security exchanges gave those "universal banks"—so-called due to simultaneous participation in normal commercial banking and in capital market operations—advantages that mitigated the classical problem of informational asymmetry usually connected with arms-length credit rela-

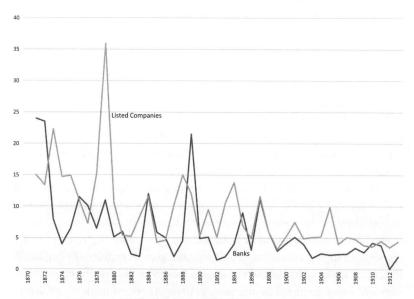

13.1 Standard Deviations of Rate of Return on Shares of Large German
Banks and of 34 Listed German Companies
Source: Own calculation from Tilly 1992.

tionships. The close, almost insider industrial role of the banks might be said to be one of the outstanding characteristics of German industrialization, a role long recognized by economists and economic historians (Marshall 1919: 223–24, 356–57, Schumpeter 1939, Gerschenkron 1962, Sylla & Toniolo 1991: 18–20, 181–84, Burhop 2002).[5]

Those economic historians have also long wondered about what or how much the big banks contributed to German industrial growth; a considerable literature on the subject exists.[6] Most historians agree that the banks' influence affected mainly large enterprises and wealthy capitalists, but their approaches to the problem have differed. Most recently, Carsten Burhop has found econometric evidence strongly suggesting presence of a positive influence of the banks on industry for the period from 1850 to 1882, but none for the following years to 1913 (Burhop 2006). That is consistent with the view, held by several contemporary observers and later by some economic historians, that the larger industrial enterprises from the 1880s on became increasingly independent from bank financing and even strong enough to exploit competition among the banks (Jeidels 1905; Riesser 1910; Gerschenkron 1962: 21; Wellhöner 1989). Other econometric studies, however, based on the concept of asymmetric information, found that presence of bank representatives in the supervisory boards of large industrial enterprises had an effect on how those companies financed their operations in the later period (Fohlin 1999, Burhop 2006, Becht & Ramirez 2003, Lehmann 2014). Yet a third approach took an Anglo-German comparative perspective, stressing the much stronger support that the German banks gave to industry, via both current account (short-term) credits and capital market services (Tilly 1999a). Despite differences, most authors agreed on the presence of close relations between the big banks and large-scale industry.

The historically unique syndrome of market power that came to connect the great banks with large-scale industrial enterprises built on two institutional preconditions. First, the Reichsbank, founded in 1876 as central bank, proved to be a reliable source of liquidity for the big banks when their relatively risky business of industrial finance brought them under pressure (as in the banking crisis of 1901). In addition, its nationwide giro system provided payments services that served and also complemented the great banks' operations. An interesting feature of the main branch offices located in bigger cities, such as Cologne, Leipzig, or Hamburg— was the advisory committees composed of local businessmen who were also Reichsbank shareholders, some of them bankers. This fact, coupled to a diversified branching network and close ties to the Reichsbank, gave the German banking system a degree of stability that contrasted sharply with the pre-1913 crisis-prone US banking system (Burhop, Guinnane & Tilly 2018).

By tradition the banks maintained close connections with the securities markets (especially in Berlin), and it was from these that a good part of their business influence derived. True, the government intervened in the organization of the securities exchanges, with increases in sales taxes in 1881 and 1885, and in 1896 it even enacted a ban on futures transactions. But, on the whole, these measures may have even tended to enhance the attractiveness of the big banks for potential investors, especially for securities issued by the banks' industrial customers.[7]

Qualifying the Role of the "Great Banks"

The well-documented role of the "great banks" should not blind us to the importance of other financial institutions and practices. Several of these are worth mentioning here.

A first important point concerns the German stock market in Berlin (mentioned above). Surprising results of recent research show that this central market played a more important role than earlier work had suggested. A recent econometric study by Lehmann-Hasemeyer and Streb argues that between 1892 and 1913 innovative firms (innovativeness as measured by their patent histories) achieved better IPO (initial public offering) pricing results when introduced for trading than less innovative ones.[8] High-tech industries, such as engineering and chemicals, were strongly represented in the sample tested. A particularly interesting finding is the significance of the subsequent performance of innovative firms for explaining their good IPO pricing results. This implies that investors not only knew the patent histories, but could pick "winners." An earlier publication by Lehmann-Hasemeyer also focused on IPO results, showing that big banks had no effect on those results, their oligopoly power diluted by competition (Lehmann 2014). Caroline Fohlin (2007), however, found that the long-term performance of bank-connected firms was better than independent ones, and that this positive bank influence derived from the link to the stock exchange. The ready acceptance of risk finance by stock market investors could help explain why big bank credit became less decisive for industrial growth in the 1890–1914 period. Berlin, moreover, was not the only stock exchange that mattered: exchanges in Frankfurt am Main, Leipzig, and Dresden, and Munich or Augsburg, also served the needs of smaller, regionally important firms. All told, capitalization of listed firms has been estimated (for 1913) at 20 billion marks (Burhop & Lehmann-Hasemeyer 2016: 429–51).

Declining influence of the big banks is a second point. Toward the end of the century, even heavy industry showed growing independence from the banks, as evidenced by the maintenance of multiple bank connections, useful as a bargaining tool to improve borrowing conditions. In some cases (Krupp, Bochumer Verein), this represented reaction to the 1870s, when banks had virtually dictated the conditions (Feldenkirchen 1982, Wellhöner 1989, Wengenroth 1986). Some evidence on large enterprises suggests that they financed their operations from retained earnings in leaner times (the 1880s and early 1890s), utilizing bank services above all when market conditions were especially buoyant, or when larger projects (such as mergers) were at stake (Fohlin 2007; Feldenkirchen 1982: 269–302; Wellhöner 1989; Tilly 2003: 108–10).[9]

A third qualification derives from an overall quantitative perspective. The macro-economic weight of "great banks" declined after 1880 (table 13.1). Taking the incorporated credit banks as a whole, we can trace a growing share in total assets held; but even so, they lagged behind the public savings banks. Moreover, we need to recognize that the activities financed by other institutions—urban infrastructure, urban housing, industrial investments of smaller firms, or agricultural improvements—were of at least equal economic importance. Table 13.1 offers an overview.

We look a bit more closely here at two institutions, whose growing importance stemmed from self-imposed limits of the great banks business model, especially its concentration on wealthy capitalists and large enterprises. This left out the financing of new, innovative but risky small and medium-sized enterprises, or of the capital investments in housing and infrastructure that came with urbanization (especially in the smaller cities)—

Table 13.1   German Financial Institutions, 1860–1913 (total assets in billions of marks)

	Institution	1860	1880	1900	1913
1	Note-issuing banks	0.95	1.57	2.57	4.03
2	Joint-stock credit banks	0.39	1.35	6.96	22.04
3	"Great banks"	—	0.90	3.30	8.40
4	Private bankers	1.50	2.50	3.50	4.00
5	Public savings banks[a]	0.51	2.78	9.45	23.56
6	Credit cooperatives[a]	0.01	0.59	1.68	6.17
7	Other[b]	0.89	4.71	16.34	31.20
8	Total, all institutions	4.25	13.50	40.50	91.0

Source: Goldsmith 1969, 1985, Holtfrerich 1989, Tilly 1986.
[a] Includes central offices. [b] Mortgage & land banks & insurance companies.

fields that were not neglected by the savings banks, the mortgage and land banks, and credit cooperatives.

The public savings banks, seen collectively, clearly came to represent Germany's largest financial institution. The growing stream of savings that accompanied rising living standards and the widening of the middle classes since the 1880s flowed largely into these savings banks, located as they were all over the country, in big and small cities and even in villages. Indeed, this savings potential supplied the main reason behind the readiness of the big banks in the 1890s to expand their network of branches and to cooperate with local, smaller private banks (Pohl 1986). As organs of local government, the savings banks followed a business model based on the "regional principle." That is, the savings they collected should serve local investment demands. Many local governments benefited especially from this practice, which eased borrowing. Recent work on just one of these banks suggests that the regional economy and local businesses could also benefit. An analysis of local lending by a savings bank in Württemberg for the period 1907–13 shows that a high proportion of mortgage-secured loans financed not simply real estate, but also the investment needs of small enterprises (and a surprising number of entrepreneurial "success stories") (Proettel 2013). Further exploration of local savings banks could be rewarding. If the lending experience of this savings bank was repeated across the country—terra incognita—it would mean that savings banks played a much more important role as agents of economic development than economic historiography has thought. That possibility would qualify certain limitations often associated with the savings banks business model, that is, that local savings and investment needs did not always coincide.

A second limitation, however—that savings deposits were not easily transferable, that is, by check or some other "cashless" medium—would still apply to the pre-1908 period. The development of supralocal organizations that linked savings banks with one another—begun regionally and crowned in 1884 by formation of the German-wide Deutsche Sparkassen- und Giroverband (German Savings Banks and Giro Association)—weakened the first limitation, and in 1908 a new law, which gave savings banks the right to offer their customers cashless payment services, eliminated the second one. These steps gradually gave the savings banks a more middle-class character, enhancing the competitive threat they posed for the private and corporate banks (Ashauer 1998, Deutsche Bundesbank 1976, Trende 1993 [1957], Born 1977).

Development of the credit cooperatives followed a more complex pattern than did savings banks, though important parallels can be recognized.

The pioneering Schulze-Delitzsch cooperatives, largely an urban phenomenon, served the needs of artisans, petty traders, and small workshop owners. Schulze-Delitzsch was a well-known liberal politician who saw cooperatives as an institution that could help workers, and especially craftsmen, to protect their interests against "monopolizing businessmen" (Guinnane 2013). Meanwhile, a separate type of cooperative (associated with the names of Raiffeisen and Haas) brought the principle of self-help to family farmers in rural areas. The success of these small-scale cooperatives built on their unique ability to "capitalize on the information and enforcement capabilities implicit in their small size and local organization." They operated in very small areas, 80 percent of them in districts with no more than 3,000 inhabitants. The importance of locality was reflected in the fact that loan applicants who lived outside of the cooperative's village had to supply collateral more frequently than did the "locals," who were more easily monitored by other members and the cooperative's management. Unlimited liability could draw community sanctions. One recent historian has called this "peasant nosiness the basis of their efficiency."[10]

In contrast to savings banks, the cooperatives were private entities, first acquiring juridical status with laws of 1867 and 1889. We cannot go into details here, but the measures (especially the spread of limited liability) were especially important for credit cooperatives, for they eased the creation of supralocal organizations designed to serve the needs of individual cooperatives. Like the saving banks, local cooperatives could face risky imbalances between assets and liabilities, and the central organizations helped spread the risk by monitoring and by providing welcome services (such as customer information or payment facilities). By 1913 the credit cooperatives had become an important part of the German financial world. They did not have the "clout" of the great banks or the public saving banks (see table 13.1), but with nearly 20,000 credit cooperatives spread across the country and more than 2.5 million members, their influence was not negligible (Guinnane 2013: 42–141; Deutsche Bundesbank 1976: 66–68).

In international comparative perspective, the German financial system is characterized as a "bank based" system and contrasted with the Anglo-American "market-based" system (Burhop, Guinnane & Tilly 2018). Raymond Goldsmith's older comparative estimates of financial wealth offer quantitative support for this view: though the importance of securities in Germany's estimated total financial assets grew from an average, 1875–85, of 17.4 percent to an average, 1912–14, of 20.0 percent, international comparison shows that in this regard, Germany was well behind its main competitors France, Great Britain, and the United States (1912–14) (Goldsmith 1985, tables 8.5, 8.6, 8.7):

France: 37.4 percent
Great Britain: 35.6 percent
United States: 42.2 percent

This, however, could reflect both dominance of the banking system in Germany and German use of foreign markets for securities transactions—two equally plausible explanations.

FOURTEEN

Germany in the World Economy, 1870s to 1914

Introduction

Between 1870 and 1914 Germany became a major player and partner in the world economy. That is, the world economy became more important for Germany, just as Germany became a more important economic factor for other nations. That interdependence is one of this chapter's themes. It reflected the advantages of an international division of labor, but brought with it political problems, both for Germany and for other nations similarly involved. The general theme of interdependence is too big for a book of this character. We therefore limit our discussion in this chapter to four sub-topics:

1. German industrial exports as a challenge to Britain's world leadership
2. The extent of German import dependence and the rise of protectionism
3. German capital exports and the question of international rivalry
4. Germany's transition from a land of emigration to land of "labor imports"

Before opening this discussion, a few comments and some statistics can help indicate the rough importance of Germany's foreign trade for its economy. Figure 14.1 shows the trend of commodity exports and imports.

The trend is accompanied by a reduction of the commodity trade deficit. The trade deficit in the period was offset by a surplus in services (freight and insurance earnings) plus net income from foreign investment (Torp 2005: 373; Burhop 2011: 104). The trend of the ratio between foreign trade and national product reflected an increasingly open economy. Between the 1870s and the last prewar years (1909–13) the export ratio grew from 8.5 percent to 15.8 percent, the import ratio from around 15 percent to

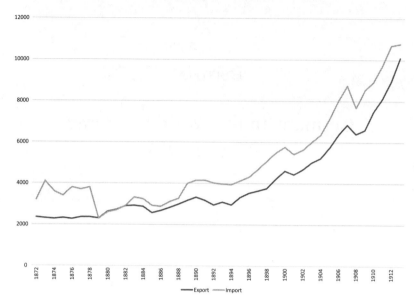

14.1 German Exports and Imports, 1872–1913 (in millions of marks in current prices)
Source: Torp 2005: 373.

Table 14.1 **Shares of 4 Countries in World Exports (percent)**

Country	1874–78	1879–83	1889–93	1899–1903	1909–13
Germany	9.5	10.0	10.4	11.5	12.2
France	11.7	10.2	9.4	8.4	7.5
Great Britain	17.3	16.7	15.9	14.2	13.5
United States.	10.0	12.1	12.0	14.3	12.7

Source: Torp 2005: 62.
Note: Important changes in the structure of German exports and imports took place, reflecting a shift
in the country's comparative advantage. Table 14.2 offers a rough summary of the changes.

just over 19 percent.[1] Table 14.1puts German exports between the 1870s
and 1913 in world context.

Most obvious is the decline of foodstuff exports. It reflected the "grain
invasion" of the 1870s, mentioned earlier (chapter 9) and growth of inter-
mediates, also the growing competitive advantage of the German sectors
producing intermediate goods (such as machines, steel structures, or chemicals). Most of the increase of raw materials exports was attributable to
coal. Imports reflected largely German industry's demand for raw materials
(such as special metals, ores, cotton, wool), offset by the declining shares
of intermediate and finished goods. The small share of finished goods im-

Table 14.2   **Structure of German Exports & Imports, 1880–1913**

Years	Foodstuffs[a]	Raw Materials	Intermediate Goods	Finished Goods
	Exports in Current Prices (in Percent of Total)			
1880–84	20.9	13.9	15.3	49.9
1910–13	10.2	15.5	21.0	53.3
	Imports in Current Prices (in Percent of Total)			
1880–84	33.4	36.4	19.3	11.9
1910–13	33.4	43.1	14.7	8.8

Source: Hoffmann 1965: 152–55.
[a] Includes drink & tobacco.

ports seems unusual—little more than one-third of British finished goods imports at this time (Deane & Cole 1969: 33).

The regional structure of Germany's foreign trade changed somewhat. Europe continued to absorb more than 75 percent of its exports, another 16–17 percent going to the Americas (mostly the United States). Imports, however, shifted away from Europe (falling from 73 percent to 57 percent), the difference absorbed by the United States, Asian countries, African countries, and countries in Oceania (Torp 2005: 76–83).

Anglo-German Trade Relations

The first theme considers German-British trade relations, for these have had an important place in the historical literature, have raised sensitive policy issues, and represent a kind of touchstone for evaluating the link between economic and political tensions. For both Great Britain and Germany we observe a continuing growth of exports, a growth marked by two characteristics and best illustrated in tabular form (see table 14.3).

The first point is that exports (measured nominally) grew roughly in step with the economy as a whole, rather slowly in the period 1880–96, more rapidly thereafter to 1913. This pattern characterized many countries, and also harmonized with the long cycles Spiethoff estimated for the German economy during these years.[2] That raises the question of causation: did Germany's economic growth simply reflect an (exogenous) increasing demand of the world economy for its exports, or did both of those changes depend on yet a third factor (such as prices)? Second, and unsurprisingly, the period from the 1870s to 1913 witnessed a considerable industrialization of German exports. Between 1872–74 and 1909–13 the share of in-

Table 14.3   World Exports and the Growth of Anglo-German Trade, 1880–1913 (annual rates of growth)

	1880–1896	1896–1913
World Exports		
Total	1.16	5.04
Finished goods	1.02	5.21
German Exports		
Total	1.17	6.19
Finished goods	2.14	6.32
Finished goods to Great Britain	2.02	4.58
British Exports		
Finished goods	0.82	4.31
British imports, finished goods	2.21	3.40

Source: Hilgert 1945; Buchheim 1983: 31, 132.

termediate and finished industrial goods in total exports grew from about 53 percent to 74 percent (Burhop 2011: 105).

Both of these observations on German exports bear on the question of Anglo-German trade rivalry. We begin our discussion by noting that German industrial exports grew more rapidly than those of Great Britain in both periods; the same applies to the growth of German industrial exports to Great Britain. In this respect, however, we see (in table 14.3) that the increase in the second period roughly reflects Britain's increased imports of finished goods—that is, the change was by no means particularly noteworthy.

The "industrialization" of German exports followed a similar pattern. In the 1860s agricultural goods and other primary products had considerable weight in German exports, while nearly one-quarter of Britain's grain imports came from Germany. In the 1870s that changed radically. In 1880 the share of nonindustrial exports to Britain was still more than 40 percent, but by the 1890s it had dropped to 33 percent and by 1913 to about 28 percent. The pattern reflected the structural change in all German exports, and thus a structural shift in the international comparative cost advantage of the German economy—away from land-intensive to capital and labor-intensive products. This change, blameless though it was, clearly transformed the complementary character of Anglo-German trade into a competitive relationship. The rivalry potential grew. Table 14.4 illustrates this development.

British concern about German competition first surfaced in the 1880s, based on worries associated with a loss of economic dynamism and ex-

Table 14.4 **Share of Industrial Finished Goods in Total Exports (in percent)**[a]

	1872	1880	1896	1913
Great Britain	86	84	82	76
Germany	53	60	70	72
World	38	38	37	38

Source: Hilgert 1945: 154–67.
[a] Based on values in $ prices.

pressed in an official Royal Commission on the Depression of Trade and Industry, which reported in 1886.[3] It complained about German exports invading the British domestic market, products alleged to be copies of British ones, such as musical instruments, toys, silken goods, also assorted implements of iron. The official report led to enactment of the "Merchandise Marks Act" in 1887, which came to be known as the "Made in Germany" law. Basing the law on the belief that the German products were of inferior quality, its sponsors expected it to drive German products from the British market, but just the opposite resulted: British consumers tended to associate the label with higher quality goods, and the German "export offensive" continued (Pollard 1987, Feldenkirchen 1980, Saul 1980).

Interpretation of the British reaction, however, deserves some differentiation by type of product. We look first at consumer goods (as in the case cited above). From 1880 to 1896 the small share of German imports in British consumption rose here from around 3 percent to 7 percent. Such a share may seem unimportant, but it included products used daily and which played an important role in the country's public consciousness: books, paper of various kinds, glassware, toys, or musical instruments. These were picked out by journalists in the 1890s to illustrate the "German Danger." A series of articles by E. E. Williams under the title "Made in Germany" seems to have touched a central nerve of British society, a shock effect that somehow encouraged development of a negative image of Germany in Britain. In fact, however, the field of producer goods represented the sector par excellence of German export success with respect to Britain. That point deserves some explanation.

According to Buchheim, "producers' goods"—defined as chemicals, iron and steel goods, noniron metals, machines, and vehicles—contributed 31 percent to the growth of German industrial exports to Great Britain between 1880 and 1896, but 51 percent to total German industrial exports. Between 1896 and 1913, however, 59 percent of German industrial export growth to Britain represented producers' goods (only slightly less than the

65 percent of its overall industrial export growth in this period). Here, one speculates, the imports from Germany should have induced a stronger re-action, but none was forthcoming. We are thus left with the impression that the initial "challenge" posed by German industrial power came as a shock in the 1890s, and given such negative political news as Kaiser Wil-helm's infamous "Krüger Telegram" in 1896 or his battleship-building policy announced in 1898, probably had foreign policy worries at its core rather than economic ones.

Nevertheless, the sources of German export success deserve attention in their own right. Various potential factors have been identified, by contem-poraries as well as by historians.[4] Many, if not most, interpretations had low wages at the top of their lists. In fact, most of the available evidence shows that German wages around 1880 were much lower than those in Britain, and even around 1900 amounted to hardly more than two-thirds of British wages (Brown 1995: 502; Broadberry & Burhop 2010). In indus-tries where the quality of labor and wage costs weighed heavily and both productivity and product quality came close to those of British producers, German exports had a competitive advantage. Such commodities as toys, musical instruments, or silken wares have been cited in this respect, but the same may have applied to branches of the producer goods sector. For ex-ample, German exports to Britain concentrated on commodities in which low wages had considerable weight, such as steel exports in the 1880s, but though these imports—in the form of low-cost inputs for the ship-building industry—benefited British industry, many Britons complained about Ger-man "starvation wages." In 1905, the British Board of Trade came out with a report on the money wages and cost of living of German workers com-pared to those of British workers. Its conclusion that German industrial workers were underpaid has found support in recent research on compara-tive productivity and real wages in Britain and Germany for this period (Broadberry & Burhop 2010).

We see a second important source of Germany's export dynamism in the growth of its science-based industries, above all, the chemical and electro-technical branches. These built on the country's celebrated educational and research institutions, rapidly developed since the 1860s. Germany had not only a larger share of world trade here than Great Britain (twice as large), but also a substantial export surplus with the latter country. The macro-economic weight of these industries was less than 3 percent, and perhaps this was the reason why British industrialists and other contemporaries showed little concern about this challenge. Economic historians, however, pointed out that "the English bourgeoisie should have been truly worried, for these were the industries of the future" (Pollard 1987, Saul 1980).[5]

Some of Germany's important export branches owed their superiority with respect to Britain to organizational features, especially in marketing. By the 1880s, vertical integration of large German enterprises had progressed much further than for their British competitors. This applies to the chemical, electro-technical, machinery-making, and steel industry. The larger enterprises of these branches ran their own foreign marketing organization, establishing thereby direct contact with their buyers. This avoided the frictional losses often associated with the British "merchant system," and made product innovation less risky and difficult to carry out. We add that the German marketing approach utilized knowledge of the foreign markets (language, customs, and so on) more fully than their British competitors, adapting their products to changing tastes.

Even in cottons, the staple of Britain's industrial revolution, Germany made some gains. The gains were slight (perhaps 3 percent of total exports), but they concentrated in high- and middle-income countries, thus representing intra-industry trade, while British exports concentrated increasingly in low-income countries, where marketing questions mattered little. But marketing played an important role in the Anglo-German rivalry in finished cottons (Brown 1995). This story of German relative success is interesting in several respects. First, its principal author, John Brown, emphasized that Germany's gain on British leadership was relative, for even in 1913 the world share of German exports of finished cloth was no more than one-fourth of Britain's. Second, he rejects the "low wage" argument for German growth by showing that lower wages mirrored lower productivity. The reason for this was that German mills—in contrast to their British rivals—were not specialized, frequently changed product specifications, and thus had to accept shorter production runs and higher set-up costs. Third, Brown attributes German success to the willingness of its producers to concentrate on high- and middle-income markets (United States, European countries, South American countries) and practice product differentiation, catering to the different tastes and fashions in these countries. Qualitative evidence confirms that German producers focused more on acquisition of information about their foreign markets than did British ones, and Brown's quantitative evidence does show results consistent with the models of intra-industry trade (Linder) and monopolistic competition: German exports were highly responsive to income differences, tariffs, and proximity (distance).

To some extent, finally, the German cartel system offered another kind of marketing advantage. In connection with protective tariffs, for example, the steel cartel could offset periods of weak domestic demand by selling at lower prices in foreign markets, thus stabilizing their output over the business cycle, while British producers, as Feldenkirchen observed, found it necessary to reduce production at such times (Feldenkirchen 1988). Repeated British complaints about German "dumping practices" were not unjustified. The balance of benefits and costs of such practices, however, may not have favored only Germany. The British economy could have compensated for the loss of comparative advantage in certain industries not only through cheaper or better imports, but also by the development of more profitable trading and financial services. After all, that was the core of the British free trade position. Sidney Pollard cited this argument, but added that "in the long run it could not be expected that suffering industries could remain satisfied with changes that benefited the economy but damaged their own interests" (Pollard 1981). Until 1914, the contrast between the two countries remained unchanged. In one respect, the shift of Britain's staple exports to the empire countries represented a kind of escape from Germany's tariff-supported competition and one part of the changes that seemed to point to a more harmonized world economy (Saul 1960).

The Extent of German Dependence on Imports and Tariff Protection

From a static welfare point of view, we can see the economic value of exports in the value of imports they make possible. According to the classical theory of trade that served as standard reference in these years (also in Germany), such an export-import exchange enabled an economy to achieve a greater welfare improvement than an expansion of domestic production alone. Many contemporary observers, however, did recognize certain negative aspects of that exchange, for example, reduced income for domestic producers of the goods imported, or increased dependence on foreign suppliers of key commodities (such as foodstuffs). Those statements, in shortened form, identify the economic core of the quasi-public debate that began in Germany in the 1890s, the question of "industrial state" versus "agrarian state." Noneconomic questions arose in this debate—questions to which we will return. The economic argument concentrated, perhaps unsurprisingly, on protectionism, that is, on commercial policy, the principal instrument of German economic policy of these years. The question it touched upon—the importance of protection of domestic producers from foreign competition—was surely one of the hottest political questions that marked the last decades of the Kaiserreich (Barkin 1970, Webb 1982, Puhle 1975, Wagner 1902).

The economic changes underlying protectionist interest reflected the transformation of the German economy from one having a comparative advantage in land-intensive goods to one based on skilled-labor, human capital-intensive goods. The balance of political power, however, favored the threatened producers of land-intensive goods.

Understanding this controversy requires going back to the 1870s, when the transition from a liberal to a protectionist policy began. That decade began with tariff reductions, which brought the average import duty to a little over 5 percent, keeping German rates roughly in step with liberalization in other European countries. The crisis that began in 1873, however, initiated a period of falling prices, including grain and iron, products that proved politically sensitive. The grain prices, of course, were related to the "European grain invasion" of these years (Lampe 2009, Torp 2005). As suggested earlier, this development affected the economic interests of East Elbian grain producers and of the heavy industrialists, who agitated for protection against imports. In the language of political economy, depression conditions transformed these interests into a "demand for protection." The "supply" derived from the interest of Bismarck in enlarged customs revenues for the central government (*Reichsregierung*), for it had virtually no other source of income. He utilized the protectionist arguments of the agrarians and industrialists, but his goal called for financially productive tariffs, that is, tariffs low enough to encourage taxable imports. The Tariff Law of 1879—by historians often celebrated as the "marriage of iron and rye"—corresponded in fact to Bismarck's aims: the duties were modest, and the Reich's revenues increased satisfactorily (Hardach 1967, Reuter 1977).

The protectionist spirit that Bismarck had legitimized, however, soon grew beyond the chancellor's aims. Agrarian interests increased their pressure. In 1885 and again in 1887 agricultural duties increased, initially from 10 marks to 30, then to 50 marks per ton of wheat or rye, which meant, in effect, protection worth 30 percent and 50 percent of the world price. This was politically risky: for foreign policy, because the tariffs affected mainly Russian grain exports; and indirectly because they worked against German industrial export interests in the Russian market (Müller-Link 1977). In 1890, with Bismarck's dismissal, high tariffs became dispensable. As part of Kaiser Wilhelm's "new program" (*Neuer Kurs*), a phase of "tariff experimentation" began. Caprivi, the new chancellor, pursued a more liberal tariff policy, and between 1891 and 1894, he concluded trade treaties with Austria-Hungary, Romania, and czarist Russia, which included substantial reductions of the duties on agricultural products. This seemed like a policy that would further German industrial export interests and, through lower duties on bread grains, indirectly lower the living costs of industrial workers (Torp 2005: 179–92).[6] It hardly had a chance to show its worth, however, for, quite fortuitously, in 1891 grain prices began to plummet. The agrarian interests remobilized, and with such effectiveness that a domestic political crisis arose, which ended Caprivi's government and served as context for the debate "industrial state or agrarian state."

This debate, carried on between members of the Kaiserreich's intellectual elite (mostly economists like Adolph Wagner, Max Sering, Lujo Brentano, or Max Weber) pitted an appeal, mixing romanticized judgments about agrarian life with protectionist arguments for preservation of a nationally self-sufficient agriculture (*Agrarstaat*), against advocates of lower tariffs and continued promotion of industrial and city growth (*Industriestaat*). Historians such as Wehler have seen this debate as a "sham battle," a smokescreen that obscured the true source of conflict, namely, the determination of the country's traditional elite to maintain their control over the political institutions of the Kaiserreich. The historian Harnisch agreed that the intellectual level of the debate was low, but he also noted that it had the virtue of bringing the protectionism question to the attention of a widening circle of middle-class Germans (Harnisch 1994b, Wehler 1995: 3:619–20). Of greatest importance, however, was the mobilization of the agrarian interests by the powerful Bund der Landwirte (German Agrarian League)—a mass organization encompassing several hundred thousand middle-class farmers, but dominated by the relatively small group of aristocratic owners of landed estates (Puhle 1975). Their electoral successes, beginning with the Reichstag election of 1893, soon gave them enough votes in the Reichstag and the Prussian Landtag to block any liberalization of tariff policy (Barkin 1970).

In the following years the agrarian lobby obtained an extension of protection to meat and animal imports by means of nontariff restrictions, thus ensuring the support by the many thousands of smaller and middle-sized farms engaged in "mixed farming." In 1902 the Caprivi trade treaties elapsed, and the so-called "Bülow reforms" initiated a further round of tariff increases, this time supported by the heavy industrialists organized in the CDI (Centralverband Deutscher Industrieller). The industrialists offered cooperation with the agrarian bloc as quid for the quo of legislation favoring their own interests (such as the bill authorizing naval expansion) (Kehr 1930, 1966, Berghahn 1971). The rise of German protectionism, though driven largely by the agrarian interests, thus had an important industrial component. The "market for protectionism" in the Kaiserreich produced, unsurprisingly, "winners" and "losers." We summarize our view of the "balance" in the following five points.

First, the big East Elbian grain producers—the main drivers of the movement—reaped the greatest gains, though smaller farmers also benefited. The view that agricultural protection of the Wilhelmine period one-sidedly served the political interests of the Junker estate owners long dominated German historiography, but a more differentiated interpretation now prevails (Webb 1982; Wehler 1995: 3:647–61; Burhop 2011: 110–17). Revision, pioneered by Steven Webb (1982), introduced the concept of "effective protection" into the tariff debate and showed that the small farms engaged mainly in animal farming also gained materially from protectionism ("effective protection" measures tariffs as a percentage of value-added rather than of price). This juncture was nicely characterized as an alliance of "pork and rye." The revision contradicted an older work by Alexander Gerschenkron (1943), whose position suggested that this group's support of grain tariffs was politically motivated, but economically irrational (since it raised their grain fodder costs and by helping the Junker raise domestic bread prices, may have also contributed to a weakening of urban domestic demand for meat and dairy products). The thousands of smaller farm owners more specialized in animal production who gave the lobby its votes, however, were in fact beneficiaries. This argument—reproducing Webb's estimates—is summarized in table 14.5. The duties on products rye and wheat alone generated a substantial transfer of income from German consumers to the grain producers estimated for the first decade of the twentieth century at 1 percent of the national net product per year. Moreover, if we include the effect of nontariff import restrictions—which kept cheaper foreign animal products from the German markets—the cost-benefit bal-

Table 14.5 **Effective Rates of Protection in Selected Branches of the German Economy (in percent)**

Sector	1883–85	1894–96	1900–1902	1911–13
Smelting & steelworks	12	11	28	8
Martin steelworks	—	—	—	−0.1
Rolling mills	—	—	−?	−?
Cast iron works	−9	−10	−10	−5
Rye	9	45	35	44
Wheat	7	33	28	36
Hogs & pork	−1	−3	26	27

Source: Webb 1982: 309–26.

ance would worsen for consumers, and they were thus clearly the main "losers" in the game of protection.[7]

Second, tariff protection could not halt the continued decline in the size of the agricultural sector, but it is highly probable that it slowed the process. That is, the proponents of *Agrarstaat* may not have been wholly unsuccessful. The hypothetical alternative of tariff-free imports of agricultural products—as suggested by British results—would have surely reduced the economic rents and income increases of owners of the factors of production in German agriculture, thus reducing incentives to invest in its expansion.[8] As it was, agricultural investment continued to increase, and toward the end of the nineteenth century, the sector's demand for labor led to a large-scale mobilization of seasonal foreign labor, mostly to the East Elbian producers. Without protection, that would have been unnecessary.

Third, in several respects it proved difficult to fault the arguments of the *Agrarstaat* defenders. One of these rested on the fact that German agriculture grew impressively over the 1880–1913 period, covering a rising food consumption and keeping roughly in step with population growth. Between 1871 and 1913 few staple products grew more slowly than population, barley remaining the major exception. Weighting the four main grain products plus potatoes and meat by market values, the share of imports in domestic consumption developed as follows (in percent):

1870–72: 5.2
1889–91: 15.5
1910–12: 9.3

The estimate, moreover, probably exaggerates the weight of imports, since it excluded items that played an increasing role in the food budget of German households, products such as milk, vegetables, and fruit, the markets for which depended on domestic suppliers. German agriculture did not remain static. It modernized. The productivity of agriculture increased over the period, and in certain areas, such as sugar beet production, the achievement of German producers even led the world, serving as a model of modern technology and organization (Perkins 1981).[9] When all is said and done, however, in key products—grains, root crops, and meat— German producers depended crucially on tariff protection, for agricultural productivity in other countries grew at least as fast as in Germany, and German products sold at prices that tended to lie above the world market price by approximately the height of the tariffs. Thus we are justified to conjecture that, in spite of some compensating effect of progress in German agriculture, the tariffs may well have slowed the country's rate of industrialization, its overall economic growth, and a rise in living standards. That conjecture also identifies a second *Agrarstaat* argument for protection: without it the mass migration out of East Elbia into the already growing cities would have been much greater and would have strained their capacity to absorb the newcomers without endangering social stability. On this reading, the *Agrarstaat* view represented wise "social policy."[10]

Fourth, German protectionism included several important industries. The steel industry offers the best illustration of this. Table 14.5, cited above, gives some examples. In contrast to agriculture, certain branches of the German steel industry enjoyed a comparative cost advantage in the world market; in such cases protective tariffs to ensure survival were redundant. As instrument of steel cartels, however, they had significant domestic redistributional effects: the tariff held domestic prices of pig iron and rolled steel goods above world prices, while tariffs kept imports out, thus enabling the German producers, strongly cartelized and vertically integrated, to gain at the expense of the no-cartelized branches of the economy. The short-run costs of this protection amounted to an estimated 7–8 percent of the value-added output of the entire metal-producing industry for the period from 1900 to 1913—less than the agrarian duties, but not negligible (Webb 1980: 318). Webb also offers a longer run perspective: the close link between steel cartel and tariff protection enabled the German producers to expand exports at "dumping prices" in times of slack domestic demand and thus achieve a stabilization of output and capacity utilization not otherwise possible. This would have reduced the ex ante risk perception of those producers and encouraged investment in more modern techniques and equipment, thus enabling them to improve their international competitive advantage. The crux of the conjectural argument is that the increased output of the protected branches of the steel industry may have been greater in value terms than the foregone production of the nonfavored branches (Webb 1980: 323–24). This is not implausible.

International Financial Relations

From the 1870s on, a growing web of financial flows, both long- and short-term, tightened the links between Germany and the world economy. By the 1900s, Germany had become both one of the world's largest exporters of capital and one of its largest short-term debtors. Here we look first at the country's role as foreign investor, often discussed under headings such as "Capital Export and Imperialism." We then go on to describe the development of short-term capital flows, which largely involved banks, interpreting this as one essential part of the gold standard that came to dominate international monetary flows in the period from the 1870s to 1914.

Germany's "capital exports" took largely the form of portfolio investments, that is, the purchase of shares or bonds issued by foreign firms or countries. In addition, German firms also engaged in direct investment: they created or purchased physical assets domiciled in foreign countries, usually as business firms that operated there and generated profits.

Historians have given much attention to the quantitative question: how large were Germany's capital exports? Unfortunately, exact figures on the extent of German capital exports before 1914 do not exist. Not only are flows of capital difficult to trace; but in the absence of balance of payments data, they are virtually impossible to specify. What information we have is based on contemporary estimates of stocks of assets at different points in time. Most of these derive from estimated portfolio investments and reflect published statistics on the issue of securities, reports in the financial press, and official tax data based on security exchange turnover.[11] For these we can draw on the summary of estimates by Christian Schaeffer, supplemented by an older estimate including direct investments (Schaeffer 1995: 100–102; Feis 1930: 68–73). Table 14.6 reproduces these estimates.

Thus, German foreign investments increased from 1 billion or 2 billion marks in the 1870s to perhaps around 25 billion marks on the eve of World War I. This made Germany the world's third most important exporter of capital, behind Great Britain with around 82 billion marks and France with about 40 billion marks of foreign holdings (Edelstein 1982, Platt 1986, Davis & Huttenback 1986, Feis 1965 [1930], Levy-Leboyer 1977). Between 60 percent and 70 percent of the sum for Germany represented securities (Schaeffer 1995: 101–2; Waltershausen 1907: 101–3; Arndt 1915: 445–60).

Historians have also shown great interest in the geographical distribu-

Table 14.6 **Estimates of German Foreign Investment, 1883–1913 (in billions of marks)**

Year	Schaeffer	Feis
1883	4–5	5
1892–93	10	10–13
1904–5	16	15–18
1913	20	22–25

Source: Schaeffer 1995, Feis 1930.
Note: This also includes estimates of direct investment.

Table 14.7   Geographic Distribution of German Foreign Investment, 1897–1914
(in billions of marks)

	New Issues		Total Foreign Investment, 1914	
Region	1897–1906	1907–14	All Investment[a]	Portfolio Investment
Europe				10.6
Austria/Hungary	7.1	5.5	12.5	5.4
Russia			3.0	2.3
Turkey			1.8	1.0
Balkan States			1.7	0.4
North America	4.0	1.1	3.7	2.6
Latin America	1.1	2.1	3.8	1.4
Asia	1.7	0.9	1.0	0.6
Africa		0.2	2.0	1.0
Total	13.7	9.0	23.5	17.9

Source: Arndt 1915, Schaeffer 1995: 101.
[a] Includes direct investment; Arndt 1915.

tion of Germany's foreign investments, not least of all because of the political sensitivity of some of the regions affected. A look at the regional studies, in addition, offers the possibility of a quantitative check on the accuracy of the overall estimates. We offer an example in table 14.7, which combines series on new issues (portfolio investments) with the German total, including direct investment, as of 1914.

We emphasize once more the crudeness of these estimates, a feature to some extent reflected in the discrepancies of the last two columns of table 14.7. Readers should note that these are gross figures—they exclude investments of foreign countries in Germany. In spite of such weaknesses, the numbers illustrate several features of German foreign involvement. We see a certain balance between the Americas and Europe as targets, with a shift in preference back toward Europe. Nevertheless, the greatest regional concentration of investment was for a time the United States. One study, indeed, has estimated German investments there at the end of 1913 at 1 billion dollars (or 4.2 billion marks).[12] German interest in Latin America grew, however, and some historians have seen the investments there as roughly equivalent to those in the United States (Feis 1965 [1930]). Finally, we note the relatively minor financial engagements in Africa and Asia. That deserves mention, if only because here was where Germany's colonial interests lay. These amounted to around 2 percent of total German foreign investments. However we interpret this, it seems that imperialism theories that link capital exports to politically dependent regions do not apply.[13]

Unsurprisingly, Germany's largest foreign investments after 1870 were in Austria-Hungary, a reflection of close economic ties as well as of the cultural and political affinity that bound the two countries together. In 1884 a contemporary estimated their value at 5.6 billion marks, about 40 percent larger than the sum estimated again for 1913. Most of this (about 60 percent) represented government debt and about half of this sum was issued by the Hungarian government. By setting free Austrian and Hungarian savings for industrial investment in Austria and Hungary, German capital helped promote economic growth, especially in Hungary (Komlos 1983, Eddie 1989, Good 1984, Tilly 1994).

German foreign investment, however, even where and when it reflected hard economic facts, could often lead into political conflicts. Czarist Russia offers a good example of this. In the 1860s, its government began an ambitious program of railroad building, enlisting to this end German financial capital, accompanied by the experienced productive services of German heavy industry, which began to supply needed material inputs, from locomotives to pig iron (Müller-Link 1977). The chronology of this investment mirrored both economic and political changes, for example, the condition of the German capital market, swings in Russian exports, or the Russo-Turkish War of 1877–78. Perhaps the most dramatic shift came in 1887, when Germany increased its tariffs on grain imports, and Russia raised its tariffs on iron and steel products, in addition limiting the right of Germans to buy land in Russian Poland. Bismarck responded with his famous "Lombard Verbot" (1887). With this measure Bismarck, as chancellor, ordered the Reichsbank to cease accepting Russian securities as collateral for loans, and this quickly led to collapse of the German market for those securities. Bismarck seems to have hoped that Russian dependence on German capital would cause the Russians to reverse their policies.[14] This hope failed to consider the potential importance of the alternative of French financial resources, which quickly came to dominate Russian capital imports; this shift also paved the way to the important Franco-Russian Alliance of 1894.

Nevertheless, despite the flight of Russian government securities from Berlin to Paris, the interest of German bankers in Russian railway finance remained strong. German-Russian trade was important, after all, not least as a link between loans and the returns they generated. Between 1890 and 1913, in any case, German holdings of Russian railway securities doubled, reaching by the period's end a market value of close to 2 billion marks. These were attractive investments, as we shall show, and good returns could strengthen banker resistance to government wishes (Schaeffer 1995: 544–57).[15]

Political considerations doubtless played a role in the development of German foreign investment after 1870, but they offer little help in the

search for a general explanation. We see the principal pervasive cause behind that investment to lie in its relatively high profitability. Thanks to the
availability of information on the market performance of securities traded
on the German stock exchanges, we can estimate rates of return realized by
German investors in domestic and foreign securities over the period 1870–
1913. Figure 14.2 shows the average returns of samples of foreign and domestic securities.[16]

We see at once that foreign securities yielded higher returns than domestic ones.[17] Under the assumption that period average returns reflected
expected returns and annual fluctuations around that mean expected risk,
we may interpret the results as follows. On the one hand, German investors
realized higher returns from foreign securities, though the higher volatility
of the latter—largely fixed-interest bonds—meant that investors had to accept higher risks than required for investment in comparable domestic securities.[18] On the other hand, these foreign securities were less volatile than
domestic industrial equity. We may take this to imply that they filled a gap
in German investors' portfolios, an argument occasionally made by bankers. Toward the end of the period, in any event, the differences diminished,
in part reflecting improvements in the international flow of information
between investors and the recipients of their capital.[19]

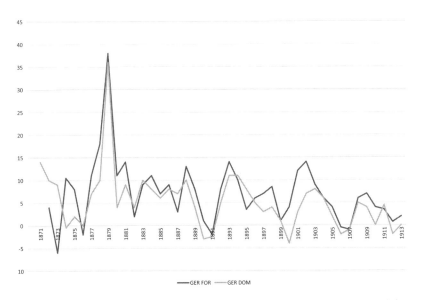

14.2 Annual Realized Rates of Return on German Foreign and Domestic Securities Traded
in German Capital Markets, 1871–1913 (in 1913 prices, in percent)
Source: Tilly 1992.

Table 14.8   Mean Realized Returns and Standard Deviations of Foreign & Domestic Securities Traded in German Capital Market for 2 Periods, 1871–1913

Securities	1871–91		1892–1913	
	Mean Returns	Standard Deviation	Mean Returns	Standard Deviation
All foreign	.0856	.0904	.0560	.0425
All domestic	.0675	.0693	.0335	.0400
Domestic bonds	.0451	.0318	.0237	.0320

Source: Tilly 1992.

Both figure 14.2 and table 14.8 show the long-run decline in returns over the period, a trend that reflects both a presumed diversification of German portfolios (result of a "learning process") and reduction of other types of perceived risks (such as default or political conflict). For this period, it seems, the returns to private investors in foreign securities justified their considerable investment, and did not represent a use of savings that came at the expense of growth of the German economy. German bankers, who initiated and then profitably intermediated the investment opportunities, thus contributed to the efficiency of the country's capital market.[20]

Readers familiar with financial economics and portfolio theory may wonder whether German bankers and investors also considered the covariance of individual security returns with overall market returns. A rational investor, after all, might even choose low-yield securities with negative covariances as a means to improve his or her portfolio (the return/variance ratio). The data used here did not reveal examples of such behavior. On the contrary, estimates of all security classes showed positive covariances. Under the stringent assumptions of the Capital Asset Pricing Model,[21] we estimated the expected return on a given security class as linearly dependent on its risk relative to other securities and the return on an riskless asset, using the "covariance" as the standard measure of portfolio risk.

Table 14.9, based on estimates of 33 classes of securities traded in the German market, attempts to offer one illustration of its usefulness. The lefthand regression shows our indicator of returns and the strongly positive covariance of the individual security groups with the market as a whole. The righthand regression shows the return to the security group relative to the market's riskless asset (Prussian consols). This is known in common parlance as the "risk premium," and it is shown here as the individual group's share in the risk of the market portfolio. It proved virtually useless as a tool for explanation of returns, but the negative signs on the variables OBL (bonds) and FOR (foreign securities) suggest a slight bias favoring

Table 14.9   Returns & Risk of Securities Traded in German Capital Market, 1871–1913

Independent Variable	Dependent Variable			
	Rit^a	t-statistic	$(Ri-Rf)//Cov(I,m)$	t-statistic
Constant	1.0475^b	118.86	5.2030	.69
Cov(I,m)	4.6570^b	3.43		
Dummy (OBL.)	−.0140	−1.72	−2.3528	−.28
Dummy (FOR)			−14.6800	−1.64
R2	.4556		.0211	
N	33		33	

Source: Tilly 1992.
[a] Rit = (At + (Pt − Pt − 1)/Pt − 1) − I. A = annual income of security as percent of par value. P = price of security as percent of par value. I = inflation rate of price level. Rf = Prussian consols.
[b] Significant at 1% level.

bonds and foreign securities—in effect by lowering the risk premium they would have borne.

Portfolio investment dominated Germany's capital exports during the period, but German industrialists and bankers also carried out a great deal of direct investment. Industrial firms such as Bosch founded subsidiary off-shoots in France and England to improve their marketing position there. The same applied to the large chemical companies, such as BASF, Bayer, or Hoechst, which set up dependent firms in Russia in the 1880s in response to that country's protective tariffs. Most direct investment, in fact, reflected marketing aims. Nevertheless, we do have examples of investment undertaken to ensure access to valuable natural resources, for example, by Krupp or Thyssen, which became partners (or shareholders) of Spanish, Swedish, or Russian companies owning iron ore properties.

Bankers initiated some of the most ambitious ventures, mixing portfolio investment with the creation of physical assets in the host countries. Perhaps the best known project was the Baghdad Railway, which grew out of participation of German banks in loans made to the Turkish government in the 1880s. The railway's historical notoriety derived from its connection with politics of the "Great Powers" (Great Britain, Germany, France, and Russia) and the following run-up into World War I. That story has been well told elsewhere and needs no repeating here.[22]

South America gives us an instructive example, however: the Deutsche Überseeische Elektrizitäts-Gesellschaft (DÜEG), founded in 1898 in Buenos Aires. It followed in the footsteps of the Deutsche Bank, which had founded a South American bank in 1886—the Deutsche Übersee-Bank (German Overseas Bank), with branches in Argentina, Chile, Bolivia, and

Uruguay. Emil Rathenau and his AEG (General Electric Company) developed the project in concert with Berlin bankers, the negotiations being then conducted with the city of Buenos Aires through the Deutsche Bank's Overseas Bank. The DÜEG was conceived to build, own, and operate power stations and urban transport and lighting facilities, first in Buenos Aires, then in other parts of Argentina and other South American countries. This program eventually absorbed large sums, and by 1913 the DÜEG's capital amounted to 200 million marks, most of which was raised in the Berlin capital market. Its assets were more than twice as large. This seemed risky at the start, but the power stations performed well, and the program represented perhaps Germany's most successful instance of foreign direct investment up to 1914.[23] Its success, we speculate, reflected the fact that it combined two of Germany's most important competitive advantages: its prowess in electro-technical matters and its risk-taking big banks.[24]

Short-term Capital and the International Money Market

German banks also provided their customers with credit and payment services for international transactions. For this service they drew on the facilities of the international money market, mainly in London, secondarily also in Paris. Bankers and traders in most countries saw "bills on London" as the standard international means of payment. Since the 1870s, however, nationalist-minded journalists and politicians had repeatedly voiced resentment about this "dependence" and hoped German banks would correct it.[25] That this did not happen reflected two important dimensions of the international money market.

First, German banks drew on London and later, increasingly, on Paris for short-term credit because it was cheaper there than in Berlin or other German financial centers. When the discount rate gap between these centers changed (in the period 1880–1913), short-term capital responded by moving accordingly. Considerable sums were involved—at one point in 1913, for example, 1.4 billion marks from London—and in these last prewar years, at times more than 1 billion marks from Paris were employed in Berlin. Cheapness and availability were the reasons why the Deutsche Bank, Germany's biggest, had maintained (since the 1870s) a subsidiary in London, where it executed most of its foreign business.[26]

Second, the mobilization of foreign credit reflected not only the strong demand and relative scarcity of capital in Germany, but also the increasing attractiveness of the German money market for foreign bankers and capitalists. The establishment of the gold standard in conjunction with

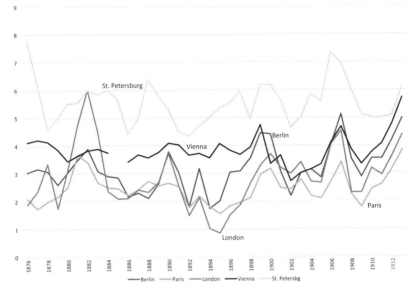

14.3 Money Market Discount Rates in 5 European Cities, 1876–1913 (in percent)
Source: Own calculation from Reichsbank 1925.

the country's expansion of foreign trade and investment gradually turned the mark into an internationally respected and usable currency. A foreign banker could see his capital in Berlin as a relatively secure and liquid asset, one that normally brought a higher return than in Paris or London. By the turn of the century the mark had become a "key currency," and German banks operated as international financial intermediaries, borrowing short-term funds and using them to finance long-term investments, in the process earning the difference between interest rates (fig. 14.3).

As some wary contemporaries noted, however, this development brought with it certain risks—inadequate liquidity and dependence on foreign creditors (Plenge 1913). Up to 1914 the system worked well, but the extent to which the international ties of German banking represented stabilizing diversification or simply greater risks remains an open question.

International Migration of Labor

Between 1870 and 1913 Germany experienced considerable population movements across its borders. Up to the early 1890s, emigration clearly dominated; thereafter and up until 1914, emigration declined while inmigration increased. By the 1900s the latter may have outweighed emigration. We focus here on the outward flow, a mass migration, largely to the United States, which formed, economically speaking, part of an emerging transatlantic labor market.[27] The quantitative dimensions of this European flow to the "New World" were enormous, between 1850 and 1914 including possibly as many as 40 million persons! A huge wage and income disparity generated powerful incentives. By 1870 US average incomes were a good deal higher than those in Europe.[28] More relevant was the level of US real wages (for unskilled workers), which may have been more than three times as high as those in Europe.[29] Accordingly, economic historians have emphasized the transnational labor flows as responses to international wage and income differences.

A striking feature of this interpretation is the demonstration that those wage and income differentials declined over the period from 1850 to 1914—a finding that supports the notion of "convergence." This applies to a sample of (mostly European) countries. The European countries of emigration experienced (excluding the United States and Canada) an even higher degree of convergence, reflecting the more rapid wage growth in North America.[30]

The aggregate, rather benign view of European migration history just discussed, however, may not fit the German case so well. By the 1870s, Germany was a relatively big country, and though its contribution of around 4 million persons to transatlantic migration between 1850 and 1914 was substantial, its emigration was conditioned by several factors, some of them peculiar to Germany (for instance, its ongoing population growth, or its important links with Eastern Europe). The real wages of German unskilled workers rose by well over 60 percent in the period, but because real wages rose faster in the United States, the transatlantic gap remained. In the smaller Scandinavian countries and Ireland, in contrast, the rate of emigration was higher, and its positive impact on domestic labor and wages naturally much stronger. Here the gap declined. The data presented in table 14.10 confirm this.

Nevertheless, North American wage levels doubtless remained a relevant factor for German emigration decisions over the period, working as a more or less constant magnet, or "pull force," in complex concert with "push" factors, such as population pressure or dwindling employment opportunities at home. One of the most important elements in the German case was the fateful decline of prices and the economic depression that swept across the agrarian East Elbian provinces in the 1870s, for it was in this region that the mass exodus of the 1880s—between 1880 and 1893 some 1.8 million persons left Germany—found its readiest recruits.

Table 14.10 Percentage Rate of Change of Real Wage Ratio of Home to Receiving Countries and Rate of Net Migration per 1,000 Inhabitants in a Sample of European Countries, 1870–1913

Countries	Ratio, Rate of Change	Net Migration Rate
Scandinavia[a]	55	−4.08
Ireland	27.4	−11.24
Germany	−2.1	−0.73
Europe[b]	23.3	−3.51

Source: Williamson 1996.
[a] Average of Denmark, Norway & Sweden. [b] Average of 10 European countries without Germany.

Table 14.11 Emigration from Prussian Provinces in Relation to German Emigration, 1871–94

Number	Region	1871–79	1880–89	1890–94	1871–94
(1)	5 East Elbian provinces[a]	170,830	444,943	163,971	779,744
(2)	Row (1) + Brandenburg	192,419	512,533	190,046	894,998
(3)	Germany	508,639	1,361,900	462,160	2,332,699
(4)	(1) as % of (3)	34	33	35	33

Source: Mönckmeier 1912.
[a] East Prussia, West Prussia, Pomerania, Posen, Silesia.

Table 14.11 illustrates the importance of the "classic" East Elbian agrarian provinces for German emigration in this period.[31]

The imposing outward flow of the 1880s, largely of young persons, stimulated nationalistic-minded worries, shared by politicians, journalists, and academics, and even provoked discussion of colonies as an alternative to the "strengthening of Germany's rivals" feared from emigration (Wehler 1995: 980–85, Bade 1980). There is no need to pursue such concerns further here: German colonies could never serve as a serious alterative to America, which by mid-century had already become not only a land of immigrants but also an important market for German exports and target of German foreign investment. More interesting are the contemporary critics, who mixed worries about East Elbian out-migration—often described as *Landflucht*, or "flight from the land"—with analyses of its putative causes. Two of these deserve attention: the shortage of land for smallholders and high rates of natural increase, the combination of which meant "popula tion pressure." Contemporaries seem to have regarded these as conflicting hypotheses, but more recent work shows them as complementary.[32] Modest increases in small holdings and labor-intensive peasant family farming took place, but big owners' hold on land over the period remained strong, while improved nutrition lowered mortality rates. The combination produced a regional excess supply of labor that chose out-migration.[33]

Out-migration from East Elbia did not necessarily mean emigration. By the 1880s, Germany's growing industrial regions had just about exhausted local labor potential, and employers began to look eastward for recruits. Thus, as the last great wave of German emigration moved abroad, a nearly equal flow of labor from East Elbia to the west took place within the country. Emigration slowed to a trickle in the mid-1890s, but the east-west movement of labor, stimulated by industrial and urban growth, continued. Here, our concern is the importance of out-migration of about 1 million persons for the agrarian regions they left.[34] As early as the 1880s, the larger landowners were complaining about labor scarcity (*Leutenot*) and found an answer in the recruitment of foreign laborers from neighboring Russian Poland and Galicia. They valued this source of labor, not only for its cheapness but also for its adaptability to the seasonality of their labor needs—a condition that reflected the spread of root crops and mechanization of threshing and reaping. To some extent, the policy adopted doubtless reflected anti-Polish sentiments shared by Prussian political leaders. The historian Klaus Bade has emphasized this aspect: "the idea was above all to insure that the needed supply of labor from the east did not become permanent immigrants, that they remained a part of a transnational reserve seasonally mobilizable" (Bade 1982: 194). In the 1890s it led to a system of "foreigner control" supported by the government, symbolized in 1907 by the transfer of power to confer "temporary residential rights and work permits" to the so-called "Prussian Field Worker Central." The strict enforcement of reverse migration eastward when the seasonal work load ended (*Rückkehrzwang*), added to this rather dark chapter of German migration history (Bade 1980).

Thus Germany became an importer of labor services but not a land of immigrants. This chapter of German migration history, however, may have had a positive side. German employers in mining and urban construction in need of manpower for heavy and onerous tasks (such as ditch-digging)—for which the supply of willing and able German workers was limited—copied East Elbian agrarian employers and drew on mobile reserves in neighboring countries. Bade rightly called this the employers' "foreign reserve army." When business conditions were good, employers could and did obtain exceptions from the seasonal "reverse migration" rule. Since the opposite applied in slack times, foreign labor played a contracyclical role in the developing Prussian-German labor market. The "foreign reserve army" had a second feature, which hurt German workers in the short run: it intensified competition for employment on the lowest rungs of the work world. We speculate, however, that in the long run, the willingness of foreign workers to fill the jobs with the lowest social status and greatest disutility probably accelerated the upward movement of natives into more skilled types of employment, directly, in the case of those leaving East Elbia for the industrial regions farther west (Bade 1980, Kaelble 1983). But in concluding, finally, it is important not to forget that the control system clearly reflected nationalistic interest supported by government and would not have come about without it.

Germany in the World Economy in Perspective

Between 1870 and 1914 Germany became a major player in the world economy. Here we briefly review its role in the light of its impact on the international political climate. We see none of the four dimensions of Germany's growing economic importance in the world as a direct threat to the peaceful and conflict-free development of international relations. The absolute and relative growth of German exports to Great Britain evolved, not as part of an international zero-sum game, but as an element in the structural changes of an expanding world economy, changes marked, for example, by the transformation of Great Britain from workshop of the world to world banker. German protectionism, in contrast, had a more negative character. Initially, of course, it represented a response to increased grain exports from other countries. Its continuation, however, derived more from domestic political conflicts and interests than from international influences, and some observers have seen it as an income-raising factor that could benefit other countries. German capital exports also represented a complementary element in the international division of labor, and we see no strong correlation between the expansion of foreign investment and political conflicts, though certain commitments (such as Turkey) later surfaced as conflict-laden. The fourth dimension, international migration, effected an income-promoting redistribution of labor in the world without influence on world conflict potential. Germany's restrictive "labor import" policy, however, did include some antiharmonious nationalistic elements.

The connection between Germany's international economic relations and global political conflict in the late nineteenth century appeared, it seems, in indirect form. The growing weight of its economy in the world tended to strengthen the claim of its leaders to Great Power status, while the spread of its foreign economic interests did increase the probability of conflicts with other Great Powers. Where national political aims came to coincide with economic interests that collided with those of other countries, as in the Near East or in the navy-building program of 1898, international tensions could grow.

FIFTEEN

Urban Growth, 1871–1914

Economic and Social Dimensions

This chapter focuses on urbanization—the relative growth of population living in cities—and some of the more important economic and social changes that accompanied it: population growth and migration; living standards, including housing and health conditions; educational opportunities; and economic inequality. These were changes that affected the human capital, growth potential, and welfare of the German population in these years. As such, they called forth political reactions, from both the population and the state. Of course, within the scope of this book, we can only touch on the issues raised by such topics and indicate where interested readers can learn more about them.

Population Growth and Demographic Transition

Population is obviously not an exclusively urban phenomenon, but it is included here because of its relevance for all of the other subtopics that follow. The chronological pattern of births and deaths, shown in figure 15.1, is a starting point.

The surplus of births over deaths produced a rate of growth of 1.1 percent per year, 1870–1913, and between 1900 and 1913, a rate of more than 1.4 percent p.a. This happened despite considerable emigration in the 1880s. Noteworthy above all is the decline of death and birth rates toward the century's end. They embodied together one of the most momentous social changes of the entire period, their coincidence representing "the demographic transition." At the period's beginning, German mortality was relatively high in comparison with England or France, its urban death rates higher than rural ones. Improvements in health conditions, discussed below, brought city mortality rates down and below those of rural areas by

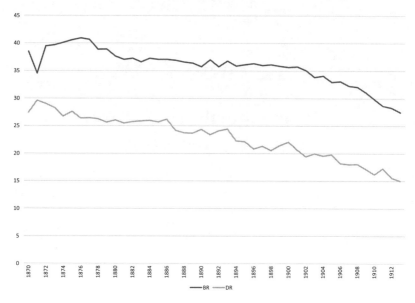

15.1 Birth and Death Rates in Germany, 1870–1913 (per 1,000 inhabitants)
Source: Hoffmann et al. 1965: 173–74.

1913. Birth rates fell by nearly one-third between 1875 and 1913, a change attributable mainly to a remarkably rapid decline in marital fertility (Guinnane 2003: 53–55; Spree 1981: 78–79, 179–81). We hypothesize that it reflected couples' desire for smaller families, an interest probably aided by increasing availability of contraceptives in the 1900s.

Such arguments necessarily draw on contemporary work on fertility decline, and this work has roots going far back to the 1970s and the Princeton European Fertility Project, to a seminal study by John Knodel on Germany, one of the project's fruits (Knodel 1974). Knodel used indices based on the number of legitimate births per 1,000 married women with ages from fifteen to forty-nine as proportions of the same ratio of Hutterite married women. He saw the abruptness of Germany's fertility decline as a "revolution in reproductive behavior" difficult to attribute to specific socioeconomic changes (Knodel 1974: 241–45). Nevertheless, his indices did show a clear urban-rural difference for Prussian districts 1880–1911 (fig. 15.2).

In recent years, moreover, the consensus has seemed to favor interpretations of the decline in German fertility as dependent on economic and social changes. A detailed (county-level) study of Prussia's fertility between 1875 and 1910 stresses a combination of such changes (for instance, improvements in education, development of financial institutions, development

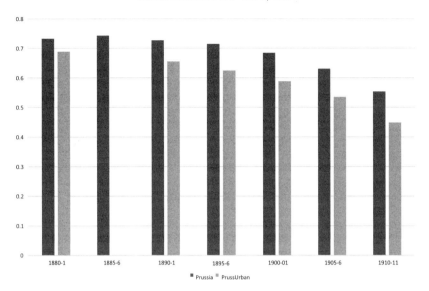

15.2 Indices of Decline of Total and Urban Marital Fertility in Prussia, 1880–81 to 1910–11
Source: Knodel 1974: 32.

of communications and transportation infrastructure, reduction in infant mortality) as "the forces that drove fertility in nineteenth-century Prussia" (Galloway, Hammel & Lee 1994: 58). A similar study of Bavaria's fertility, by identifying socioeconomic varables (such as urbanization and female employment in industry) as co-determinants of fertility decline, points in the same direction (Brown & Guinnane 2002).[1] The decline of fertility, finally, raises the question of the extent to which it reflected a change in family demographic strategy adapted to changing social and economic circumstances, a trade-off favoring more investment per child, that is, more human capital (Galor 2011). Some evidence from a recent study of patent history that links high-tech patents (science-based innovations) with research and development departments of firms, income growth, and fertility decline at the county level supports this speculation (Cinnirella & Streb 2017: 222–23).[2]

Urban Growth and Migration

We begin our discussion by considering the dimensions of city growth, which accelerated in the period. Between 1871 and 1910, cities with at least 20,000 inhabitants grew at an annual rate of 4.2 percent, while large cities (those with 100,000 or more inhabitants) grew at an annual rate that exceeded 5 percent! Table 15.1 illustrates this trend.

Table 15.1   **Population and City Growth in Prussia & Germany, 1871–1910**

	Prussia		Germany		
Year	Total (in 1,000s)	% in Cities ≥ 20,000	Total (in 1,000s)	% in Cities ≥ 20,000	% in Cities ≥ 100,000
1871	24,691	13.0	41,059	12.5	4.8
1890	29,957	22.9	49,428	21.9	12.1
1910	40,165	37.1	64,926	34.7	21.3

Source: Hohorst et al. 1978: 43.

Table 15.2   **Regional Differences in Prussian Urbanization, 1871–1910**

	Northeast[a]		Rest of Prussia	
Indicator	1871	1910	1871	1910
Population (in 1,000s)	6,153	7,584	18,537	32,581
% in places < 2,000	75	62.2	58	33
% in cities ≥20,000	7	18	15	41
% in cities ≥ 100,000	1.9	10.7	6.3	25.1
Population density (per km)	50.85	63	70.8	115.2

Source: Hohorst et al. 1978: 42–43.
[a] Provinces East & West Prussia, Pomerania, and Posen.

The table shows two noteworthy changes: population growth accelerated after 1890 (from about 1 percent per annum 1871–90 to about 1.4 percent 1890–1910); and more than 80 percent of the total increase was in cities having at least 20,000 inhabitants. The rate of growth of the larger cities was more than three times as high as that of the country as a whole, and between 1871 and 1910 their share of the total population rose from about 12 percent to more than 34 percent! Seen in comparative perspective, this made Germany one of the world's most rapidly urbanizing countries. Nowhere in Europe was city growth more rapid.

The overall growth picture of table 15.1 conceals one important disparity: the lagging development of northeastern Prussia. Table 15.2 lists a few of the relevant indicators.

Incomparably slower urban growth in this region meant that many of the changes associated with that growth were missing or remained less developed here. That difference will become evident in the discussion that follows.[3]

Most of this city growth came from migration. The 1907 census showed that about half of the German population had been born elsewhere. That share for big cities was higher (about 60 percent), most of the migrants

Table 15.3   City Typology and Population Growth in Prussian Cities, 1875–1905

Type of City (no.)	Population Increase (1875 = 100)	Share of Net Migration (%)	Mean Size (1905 in 1,000s)	Absolute Growth (in 1,000s)
Commerce & finance (13)	264	75	174	1,410
Administrative cities (10)	210	70	53	280
University/rentier cities (8)	208	73	55	229
Heavy industry (9)	373	59	101	519
Textile industry (7)	185	25	85	274
Other industry (15)	327	59	75	784
Diversified cities (24)	225	60	101	1,346
Berlin	211	67	2,040	1,073
All cities (87)	240	64	68	5,915

Source: Laux 1989.

coming from neighboring districts (Köllmann 1974b: 117). One study of a group of representative large cities in Prussia between 1865 and 1905 placed net migration (estimated by the "residual method") at more than 70 percent of population growth: that is, in eight periods of 3–4 years, net migration gains were about twice as large as natural increase.[4] These gains mirror the direct effect of migration. In the Prussian northeast, cited above, negative net migration was substantial, the main reason for the region's slow urban growth.[5]

Birth rates in the city sample of table 15.3 correlated highly with migration gains three to five years earlier. Actual population growth here between 1875 and 1905 was 1.76 times higher than that simulated by a model assuming growth by natural increase and no "residual" net migration gains. Note, however, that net migration gains actually "caused" a share of the subsequent natural increase registered over this long period (Laux 1989: 133–35). This is because of the relatively young age of migrants and a correspondingly high marriage rate. Urban migrants largely belonged to the age group 15–30. The estimated average marriage ages were 24–25 for women and 26–27 for men (Bleek 1989). For one big city, Hamburg, we have data showing migration as the principal factor driving marriage rates: in the 1880s, for example, more than half of all recorded marriages involved no native of Hamburg, while only 17 percent came about without migrants. Some evidence suggests that city born inhabitants had fewer children, perhaps reflecting the contrast between urban and rural or small-town traditions (Köllmann 1974b, Reulecke 1985, Jackson 1979, 1980, Kamphoefner 1983, Tilly & Wellenreuther 1985). Urbanization and migration belong together.

Migration reflected largely the hope for material improvement. Both "push" and "pull" factors played a role, as in the case of transnational migration, discussed earlier. The East Elbian agricultural regions were a major source of city-directed "push" that involved long-distance movement—especially to the Rhenish-Westphalian districts (Bade 2005: 232–34).[6] The movement to specific regions and cities also reflected the "pull" of employment and higher incomes obtainable there. A wage gap favoring cities prevailed throughout most of the nineteenth century, but urban migration fluctuated, concentrating mostly in phases reflecting economic expansion, as has been shown for Berlin, Hamburg, Duisburg, or Dortmund (Tilly & Wellenreuther 1985, Jackson 1979, 1980, Wischermann 1983).

Migration indirectly contributed to one of the most distinctive features of German urbanization in this period: the growth of housing. Migration led to increased rates of marriage and household formation and, coupled to rising levels of income, raised the demand for housing. As scarcity pressed house prices (and rental levels) upward, the supply side responded positively. Wage levels and interest rates seem to have played a role, but it was demand that drove the increasing supply.[7] Once in place and occupied, new housing had indirect effects on the urban economies. It fueled the demand for consumer goods and services, and it called forth the need for substantial investments in the local infrastructure, for example, in streets, lighting, water, sewerage disposal, and so forth. The migration-housing syndrome thus represented an important link in the economic growth of this period. In figure 15.3, we offer a few crude estimates of the result described.

The discontinuous character of this urban growth, with its long swings and shorter cycles, deserves some emphasis. In addition, estimates of yearly movements to and from cities (mobility index) suggest an even higher degree of measured instability than that shown here, as the work of several researchers has confirmed (Heberle & Meyer 1937, Langewiesche 1977, Reulecke 1985: 72). A vast sociological literature has connected this mass movement with social disintegration, violent protests, and criminality, but the issue remains controversial (Köllmann 1974b; Brepohl 1957: 206; Reulecke 1985: 139–47; C. Tilly, L. Tilly & R. Tilly 1975; Bergmann et al. 1986).

In fact, since migration involved costs, moves to cities must have reflected a kind of positive cost-benefit calculation, a behavior pattern not consistent with the disorientation emphasized in that older sociological literature. Migrants most likely reflected a process of positive selection. Moreover, there is evidence that mobility tended to end with marriage. Workers became permanent residents (Bleek 1989).

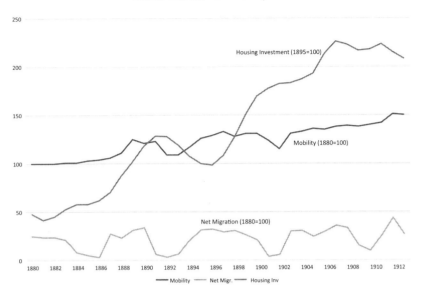

15.3 Indices of Urban Mobility, Net Migration, and Housing
Investment in Germany, 1880–1913
Source: Laux 1989; Hoffmann 1965: 259–60; Langewiesche 1977.

Germany's large cities differed from one another considerably, depending on their function (administration, commerce, residential, and so on), but they were all residentially segregated (by status, wealth, education, and occupation). These growing cities grew spatially, into neighboring communities, often annexing them. This reflected migrants' need for low-rent housing, and tended to enhance the divide between working-class districts and those of other social strata. It was not the only instance of spatial segregation, but it was clearly the most important one. By the end of the century the development of local mass transport (for instance, streetcars) had affected the spatial link between workplace and residence. Nevertheless, segregation continued. Rental levels and land prices offer one explanation of this continuity, but income levels seem to have been at least as important, if not more so. In any case, comparisons of urban spatial structures leave no doubt about the closeness of the relationships between income, social status, and quality of housing (Fritzsche 1985: 159–61).

The Place of Housing

Income inequality played a major role in determination of housing policy and its effects. In cities distributional inequality had a particular intensity,

for (in Prussia and several other states) it was tied to the three-class system of voting that could determine social policy, and in cities it influenced
municipal decisions related thereto. This meant, for example, that in some
cases two-thirds of the taxpayers in Class III (mostly working-class households) would control just one-third of the votes, no more than the 5–6 percent of wealthy taxpayers in Class I controlled, while Class II (mostly quite
well-off households, with incomes well over 2,000 marks) was likely to
produce representatives sharing interests with those of Class I. These two
classes (I and II) were also the principal property owners in most cities.
Given this political context, it was perhaps unsurprising that government
intervention in urban housing remained limited during the Kaiserreich.
This is a point deserving some discussion.

The empirical studies of urban housing in this period clearly reflected
the relatively free play of market forces. During the first big housing boom
of the early 1870s, reformer complaints about the shortage of housing and
the spread of "usurious" rental prices dominated. In the collapse of the
later 1870s, attention turned to the fraudulent character of many real estate development companies and to their dubious business practices. It
was at this point that the newly founded Verein für Socialpolitik launched
its first series of "scientific" investigations on housing (Teuteberg 1986).
Two main principles became evident, which henceforth marked the position of the "social reformers." First, they called for a building program that
assigned "small apartments" (or "workers' dwellings") the highest priority,
to be financed by public funds. Second, they saw the necessity of restricting the market determination of urban land prices, drawing as they did on
the view that high real estate prices derived from monopoly-like control of
urban land and that this explained the "excessively" high rental prices.

This critical view of market-determined housing formed the basis on
which liberal defenders of the market developed their counterarguments. In
their view, excess demand for existing housing caused higher rents, which,
in turn, produced higher land prices, and not the reverse.[8] When the reformers spoke of a "supply gap," they assumed that sufficient demand prevailed, but by this they meant working-class families' need (or desire) for
better housing, not at all identical with the idea of market demand. A second argument took the reformers' recommendation of "workers' houses"
as its target, pointing out that the construction of such houses needed to
be financed, and since the houses were unlikely to be profitable, this would
involve subsidies, and thus would be paid by taxes on the wealthy.[9]

Nevertheless, despite the social reformers, residential housing remained
very largely the product of market forces up to 1914. This reflected the fact

that investment in housing faced virtually incalculable risks—related to the uncertainty on both supply and demand sides. An individual builder had to reckon with competing house-builders, who influenced his costs, while the demand for new housing, strongly affected by uneven swings in migration, also remained uncertain. Government-sponsored housing could not elude such risks, and public housing achievements up to 1914 remained "modest." Nevertheless, there was improvement. One reason was that toward the century's end, real wages were rising, making better housing affordable (Pierenkemper 2015). Another reason was policy, for some reaction did result: by the 1900s the share of small (one-room) apartments in big cities like Hamburg, Berlin, or Frankfurt am Main rose considerably. The share of working-class housing designated as "poor" declined (Teuteberg 1985, 1986, Wischermann 1986), and the the role of government in housing did not remain negligible. With compulsory fire insurance, deed registries, and building regulations that gradually raised minimum sanitary standards, state policy determined much of the institutional framework, and there was more at the local level.

Labor and Social Policy: Political Background

Wage workers dominated urban immigration in this period: so, the historians' consensus (Hochstadt 1981, Bade 2005, Köllmann 1974b, Reulecke 1985, Jackson 1980). The cities in which they arrived were already segregated by class, social status, and income. The arrivals concentrated themselves accordingly, enlarging and extending the urban working-class districts. This development doubtless enhanced the solidarity and class-consciousness among wage workers, just as it caused worries among middle-class social reformers, who hoped to integrate the working class into the growing capitalist society. On the surface, at least, it appeared that in these segregated "worker communities," costs of solidarization and organization were low, and that just the opposite was happening, for it was in many of these cities that the labor movement—with its free labor unions and its "outsider" Social Democratic Party (SPD) found its strongest support (Wehler 1995: 772–804, especially 796; Ritter & Niehuss 1980). Here we find the greatest concentrations of a working class—increasingly marked by a kind of class-consciousness, a difficult concept we need to explain.

Class-consciousness derived from the experience of inequality. Materially this turned on both the inequality of means of sustenance and the inequality of political rights—social justice in its wider sense. Material improvement in living standards over the period could have weakened the effects of economic inequality. Workers' real wages and living standards were obviously crucial. The historians' consensus is clearly that these were rising in the period. Evidence on the development of wages, food consumption, housing, and mortality is unambiguous: these elements of working-class living standards improved, even if the extent of improvement varied from indicator to indicator. The standard estimate of real wages, for instance, rose between 1880 and 1913 by an annual rate of 1.4 percent—just as fast as the economy as a whole—while child mortality fell among working-class families: among skilled workers by 25 percent, though among unskilled workers and household help by only 10 percent. Housing conditions also improved for workers, but the decline of housing designated as "poor" and the improvements of working-class dwellings registered were considerably smaller than the same variables showed for urban housing as a whole.[10]

Nevertheless, the overall increase in welfare, however welcome, could not mask substantial differences between the top, middle, and bottom of the social structure. Many contemporary critics found these differences relevant for "the social question," dominated as it was by the idea of social justice and disbelief that unreformed capitalist methods could lead to its realization. For the social reformers—the so-called *Kathedersozialisten*, or "lectern socialists"—that idea meant less inequality in the distribution of income between rich and poor, but especially less inequality between income from capital and income from labor. In fact, reformers such as Karl Bücher or Adolph Wagner saw the fundamental social problem of the Kaiserreich in the contradiction between "capital" and "labor."[11] Against this background, it is of interest that empirical investigations of personal income in Prussia have revealed the following results: (1) inequality rose significantly in the 1880s and 1890s, then remained at the higher level up to World War I; (2) income inequality was substantially higher in cities than in rural areas, and urban inequality correlated positively with the size of cities; and (3) viewed over time, the inequality of personal income appears to have correlated positively with the share of income from capital (Dumke 1991, Grant 2005: chap. 9).[12]

Class-consciousness, however, permeated the entire social pyramid, top, middle, and bottom. At the national level we see in the 1870s a conservative constellation at the top dominated by Bismarck and his class-ridden aristocratic compatriots. These men were determined to maintain a society governed by men of property, landed, commercial, and industrial, and one free of socialist aspirations. Best known are the measures associated with Reich-Chancellor Bismarck's program of social insurance, introduced in the 1880s. The political historiography has emphasized its importance as an attempt to wean the working class from socialist influence (Wehler 1995: 902–15). This lay behind his support of the one-man, one-vote electoral law of 1871. His target was the urban working class. Events foiled his plans. The first was an impressive surge of labor movement activity in the early 1870s, expressed in a great wave of worker strikes, some of them successful, and supplemented by growth and consolidation of the movement's political arm—its socialist party—strengthened as it was in 1875 with the merger of Lassalle's ADAV (General German Workers' Association) and Bebel and Liebknecht's SDAP (Social-Democratic Workers' Party of Germany). This development called forth a reactive response from the ruling conservative faction, for labor's apparent organizing success, its disregard for Bismarck's plans, and its radical ideas and rhetoric, enhanced the fears and misgivings of the chancellor and his allies. The Reichstag election of 1877, which showed the Sozialistische Arbeiter Partei (SAP, Socialists Workers' Party) as the fourth-strongest party, strengthened these fears. Two assassination attempts on the Kaiser's life in 1878 gave Bismarck a chance to act. It led to the fateful repressive Socialist Law of 1878, which forced the SAP to disband and to cease all political activity. Thus began a long period of isolation of labor leaders from political responsibility at the national level.[13]

Social Policy: Implementation

The program of social insurance was Bismarck's "carrot," following the "stick" of 1878, and it came in three variants. The first of these was the Workers Sickness Insurance Law of 1883, with coverage that grew from 4.3 million industrial workers in 1885 to 13.6 million workers (including nonindustrial ones) in 1913. Workers paid for one-half to two-thirds of its costs, and its representatives were co-administrators of the branch offices (*Krankenkassen*) that ran it. It was not Germany's first social insurance collective, but it was by far the most comprehensive, about eight times the size of existing programs. Its most important forerunner—the Knappschaften (KV) organized and run by miners and mine owners, and whose origins went back to medieval times—administered a sickness and disability program covering 465,000 members, which was integrated into the Reich's system.[14] The 1883 law surely strengthened the demand for medical care. Indeed, another recent study of the Knappschaften argues that the "moral hazard" problem of an inability to observe the state of another person's health could encourage workers to simulate illness (Guinnane & Streb 2011). The study shows that compulsory membership, the size of a Knappschaft's membership, the amount of sick pay, paid sick days, and share of costs borne by employers were factors enhancing simulation.[15] Toward the end of the period, more careful monitoring by the KVs seems to have reduced simulation. This judgment probably applies to the Reich sickness insurance system as a whole.

The second step was the Accident Insurance Law of 1884. Contemporaries had long recognized the problem of industrial accidents, and the law represented an improvement over the Liability Law of 1871, which had placed the burden of proof on the injured worker. Its costs were borne by industrial firms bundled together in groups (*Berufsgenossenschaften*) of related branches, and it provided compensation to injured workers in a routine way. It suffered, however, from design weaknesses that limited its effectiveness: its undifferentiated method of assessing the insurance costs for individual firms—which varied considerably in degree of riskiness—gave those firms little incentive to invest in safety-reducing changes. This helps explain why accident rates—including many fatalities—continued to rise until 1905, when policy improvements helped them to level off and begin to fall.[16]

The third measure was the Old Age and Invalidity Insurance Law of 1889. Organized on a decentralized basis with administrative centers in the individual states (*Landesversicherungsanstalten*), it emphasized the right of all male workers—at the age of seventy or over—to claim payments that were fixed by law. The Reich contributed 50 marks per insured to the program's funding, while the rest was shared equally by employers and employees. Contributions took between 1 percent and 1.5 percent of a worker's annual wages; the old age benefit annually paid out 110–80 marks, and the invalids' pension (in 1911) amounted to an estimated 187 marks (Hentschel 1983: 21–29). In 1911 it reportedly supported 1.1 million invalids. Opinions on its impact differ. One recent study of personal saving accounts in Prussian public savings banks, however, has suggested that the law's benefits sufficed to "crowd out" the personal savings of a large group of workers (Lehmann-Hasemeyer & Streb 2018).[17] That is an argument supporting its effectiveness.

The Bismarckian social insurance program, modest though it was, represented a considerable achievement that offered workers more security and protection. To Bismarck's chagrin, however, it failed to weaken the socialist movement, which moved from one electoral success to another (in the Reichstag election of 1890 polling 1.5 million votes).

The state-sponsored insurance programs contributed to health improvement by increasing the population's access to medical care facilities, such as

Table 15.4   Indicators of Health Care Facilities in Germany, 1876–1910

Indicator (per 10,000 persons)	1876	1887	1900	1909
Number of MDs	3.2	3.4	4.9	4.8
Number of nurses		3.1		10.8
Number of hospital beds	24.6[a]	32.3[b]	48.3[c]	63.1[d]

Source: Hohorst et al. 1975: 151–52.
[a] 1877. [b] 1886. [c] 1901. [d] 1910.

doctors and hospitals. Supported by central and local governments, these facilities expanded considerably during the Kaiserreich period. Table 15.4 offers a few examples. The number of medical doctors (MDs) kept a bit ahead of population growth, but great differences in this respect between urban and rural districts persisted. In 1876, for example, the corresponding rate for the Prussian northeast was 2.0 doctors per 10,000 persons, and in 1899, 3.2.

Doctors began to play an increasingly important role, helped by their integration in the sickness insurance program, by government support for better medical training at the university level, and by the attempts to eliminate amateur practitioners from the medical market. Big cities were relatively well supplied with qualified MDs. Thus, in 1910–11, 23 big cities reported an average of 8.3 MDs per 10,000 persons, well above the national average. They became articulate advocates of hygienic improvements (including disinfection of dwellings) and advised local governments on improvement of public health conditions (Spree 1981: 96–114). In spite of such contributions, the consensus of medical historians is that changes in the urban water supply systems, in sewage treatment, in street cleaning, and in the sanitary equipment available in housing were of greater immediate importance for observed improvements in health conditions (Spree 1981: 115–33; Brown 1988). We return to the extent and agents of these changes in the section on local government, below.

Mortality Changes

Changes in mortality are arguably the best indicator of overall health conditions in nineteenth century Germany. As mentioned earlier, mortality rates in Germany remained higher and declined later than in other Western European states (such as Great Britain or France). More to the point, city mortality rates remained higher than rural ones until early in the twentieth century, life expectancy at birth remained correspondingly lower. Spree's

Table 15.5   Infant Mortality[a] in Prussia by Occupational Status of Father (1877–79 to 1912–13)

Social Group	1877–79	1889–91	1898–99	1906–7	1912–13
Civil service officer	17.5	16.3	14.7	11.0	8.3
Skilled worker	18.9	19.6	19.0	16.2	13.1
Unskilled worker	20.6	22.2	22.2	19.7	17.4
Domestic servant	29.6	29.9	28.6	25.5	22.5
Prussian state	20.1	20.6	19.9	17.3	14.8
Prussia, rural	20.0			18.3	16.2

Source: Spree 1981: 171, Hohorst et al. 1978: 36.
[a] Percent of births (includes illegitimate births).

study cites estimates for 22 Prussian big cities in 1876 and 1900, comparing their mortality rates to Prussia as whole (Spree 1981: 34–35, 169). For the 22 big cities, the mortality rate per 1,000 inhabitants was 30.0 in 1876, falling to 21.3 in 1900. For Prussia as a whole, the mortality rate per 1,000 inhabitants fell from 27.5 in 1876 to 22.3 in 1900—now higher than in cities .

The relative improvement of big-city populations reflected in aggregate figures, however, did not extend to age groups thirty and over, whose mortality rates remained higher than the Prussian average, possibly reflecting the cumulative effect of the less healthy conditions of city life. The decline in aggregate mortality began in the late 1890s, that of infant mortality in the early 1900s. Both of these were deeply affected by differences in social class. Table 15.5 shows the importance of these differences for three very different social groups. The results reflect income and educational differences, and possibly also indirect effects of the decline in fertility noted earlier.

The Role of Education

The growth of educational institutions in the Kaiserreich period depended on the policies of local and state governments, and was financed largely by the local governments. Most attention focused on the elementary schools. By 1871, they had already achieved results—regular attendance of 86–90 percent of the school-age population, an overall literacy rate of 87 percent—that put Germany close to the top of Western countries. For most Germans in this period, elementary schools defined the limits of formal education. Worst off were the one-class rural schools, where in 1911 1 teacher educated 51 pupils. Big cities were most progressive here, as elementary schools expanded instruction to a seven-class (later ten-class)

Table 15.6 **Prussian Schools, 1910–11**

Number of Prussian Schools	Number of Teachers	Number of Pupils
Elementary schools: 38,684	117,162	6,572,140
Middle schools:[a] 632	6,134	180,729
Higher schools (Gymnasia): 881	13,731	260,019

Source: Hohorst et al. 1978: 157–59.
[a] 1910.

level. The number of teachers doubled to 187,500 in 1914, the number of pupils grew from 6 million to more than 10 million (Wehler 1995: 1191–94). Table 15.6 for 1910 and 1911 is revealing.[18]

The elementary and middle schools together constituted a supply of potential applicants to the higher schools, but for more than 90 percent of this potential, the school fees and other costs (such as foregone earnings) were too high. Those schools thus remained a privileged field of education reserved largely to upper-class families, but also open to ambitious middle-class families willing to pay the price (Wehler 1995: 1201–4). Big cities contributed a disproportionately high share of higher school enrollment. For 1910–11 a sample of 23 big cities with a total population of slightly over 10 million (15 percent of the German total) had 168,481 pupils in higher schools—about 42 percent of the estimated total (*Statistisches Jahrbuch deutscher Städte* 1913: 710–31). Unsurprisingly, industrial cities, with their large working-class populations, did less well. The same was true of cities with relatively large Catholic populations. The average share of school pupils in higher schools was 16.5 percent for the big cities, and 9.5 percent for industrial/Catholic cities. Despite such shortcomings, there is no doubt that Germany's educational system contributed positively to the wellbeing of its population, helping them to better adapt to change and control their lives.

Vocational Education as Social Policy

One of the most striking shifts in labor-related policy focused on handicraft workers and rehabilitation of their guild organizations. The heyday of liberal policy that had marked the middle decades of the nineteenth century and weakened both craft workers and their guilds came to an end in the 1870s. This reflected their growing political importance as an organized interest group (Allgemeine Deutsche Handwerkerbund, or ADHB) and the declining influence of economic liberalism. In 1881 guilds gained legal status as public organizations, and they began to play a larger role in handicraft occupations. The Handicrafts Law of 1897 strengthened guild control over craft practices, and the apprenticeship system and master-journeyman hierarchy that came with it. In 1908 a supplementary law limited supervisory positions in guild-dominated occupations to master craftsmen, the so-called *Kleine Befähigungsnachweis* (proof of qualification). Initially, this development had little to do with vocational education, which had begun earlier at the local government level and in connection with so-called "Sunday" or "industry" schools. By the 1870s and 1880s, however, the state had become the principal promoter of their further evolution into the vocational secondary schools (*gewerbliche Fortbildungsschulen*) familiar in our times. In part this resulted from deficiencies of both industrial and handicraft training programs recognized by social reformers (such as Karl Bücher) in the 1870s. By 1884 more than 1,600 such schools operated in Prussia, most of them in the larger industrial towns. During the 1870s, moreover, most German states made vocational school attendance mandatory for all fourteen- to eighteen-year-olds employed in industry and handicraft trades. The basic curriculum included religion, German, arithmetic (later geometry), drafting and sketching, and bookkeeping (Lee 1978: 453–59; Wehler 1995: 680–85; Laer 1977: 195–224).

Interpretation of this institutional development needs to recognize its dual character. It raised the skill levels of labor force entrants, so to speak, adding to their "human capital," and it influenced the social attitudes they developed. That factory and workshop employers cooperated willingly reflected the growing recognition that the vocational schools promoted not merely useful technical skills, but also a conservative ideology. After all, most employers, factory owners and handicraft masters alike, will have welcomed public-sponsored efforts to shield labor-force recruits from Marxist-socialist influence, particularly when mixed with the transmission of productivity-enhancing practical knowledge. This element was what made vocational education social policy.

The Role of Local Government

Municipal governments became key actors as regulators and providers of the urban infrastructure—virtually a necessity of city life—including street-building and traffic regulation facilitating the movement of persons and goods; construction of water works and sewage facilities, contributing decisively to maintenance of public health; organizing and reorganizing of the local schools; provision of lighting systems, which contributed to public security, and so on. Here, local government assumed functions for which private actors seemed unsuitable, since cost-benefit calculations pointed to substantial discrepancies between social and private interests for these services. The modernization of German cities, so apparent to knowledgeable observers by the end of the century, reflected in large part the work of local officials and their technicians. Serious technical difficulties, for example, in the development of an adequate water supply or sewage disposal facility, called for engineering expertise that could be mobilized through a cooperative network developed in this period and which linked city managers and officials with one another (Reulecke 1985).

Improvement of the urban infrastructure and the expertise it embodied, however, depended first and foremost on finance. To illustrate a typical case, we take the example of Prussian cities and the relatively heavy spending on elementary schools and on public health and welfare, especially for the poor.[19] Such expenditures had to be financed by taxes. In Prussia this meant surtaxes imposed on the state income tax—a tax that fell disproportionately on the well-off citizens. This disproportionate burden, however, bound as it was to the three-class electoral system, also gave the wealthiest households considerable power they could use to their advantage in local city councils. In addition, in many cities the right to vote and to run for political office depended on property ownership, which de facto precluded the use of taxes on urban land (Reulecke 1985: 110, 112, 221).[20] By the 1880s we see a situation in which many city governments chose surtaxes on the income tax, which chronically exceeded 200 percent; 65–90 percent of municipal revenues came from the surtaxes, mostly from the wealthy taxpayers, though as much as 50–60 percent of this revenue flowed into education, poor relief, and public health spending. In industrial cities, such as Bochum or Krefeld, by the late 1870s and 1880s the share of income surtax revenues borne by the top 2–3 percent of taxpayers grew from about one-third to more than half. Complaints about the tax burden became chronic, accompanied by the argument that health and education benefited society—and the state—as a whole, and should be financed at the central government level, and not by municipalities.

The Prussian state, in fact, did react to the situation with a reform of public finance in 1891 and 1893, a set of measures we will return to below. At this point it is important to emphasize the sustained expansion of muncipal spending that marked the 1870–1913 period. According to Hoffmann (1965), municipal spending on consumption goods and services grew at an annual rate of nearly 6 percent, and by 1913 accounted for roughly 6 percent of the net social product. For a group of larger cities we can also identify investment expenditures, and these—measured as per head of city population—grew at a rate of 3–4 percent per year, or faster than social product. They accounted for about half of all public construction spending and around 5 percent of the total estimated for Germany as a whole (Hoffmann 1965, Tilly 1997). This growth of investment resulted from the needs of growing cities, but it also served as prerequisite for their further growth.[21]

A rough picture of the growth of municipal spending in the period may be seen in table 15.7.

In 1891 came the "Miquel tax reform" (named after the Prussian finance minister). It introduced the principle of universal taxability of all citizens and juridical entities, and of all sources of income, and the general obligation to submit a declaration of income and to reveal all financial details related to income to the responsible fiscal authorities. It also listed the kinds of deductions (such as costs) allowed, and it listed penalities for violation of tax obligations. Finally, it raised the minimum taxable income to 900 marks and set tax rates that were modestly progressive (in the income bands up to 100,000 marks).[22] The Tax Law of 1891 was coupled to the Municipal Tax Law of 1893. This law—often called the KAB (Kommunale Abgaben Gesetz)—assigned the taxes of business firms, land, and buildings to municipalities, partly in the hope to brake cities' use of the surtax on income. That practice did not stop, but social and political change did affect how the wealthier citizens—industrialists, bankers, managers—reacted to their tax burden and the condition of the less well-off social strata. In the next paragraph we offer a speculative interpretation of that interaction.

From roughly the second half of the 1890s, the distribution of urban incomes appears to have become less unequal, probably due to the economic growth and spread of income growth to the middle and lower classes ob-

Table 15.7 Annual Expenditures Per Capita of Samples of German Cities, 1869–1911 (in marks)

Category	1869	1876	1883–84	1891–92	1911
Administration	4.6	8.3	6.6	5.1	13.5
Social welfare	4.4	5.1	6.5	7.2	18.7
Education	4.2	9.3	9.4	10.0	21.5
Transportation	4.3	13.7	7.1	8.7	19.8
Debt service	2.4	5.3	4.0	5.3	31.7
Total	22.1	54.3	48.3	56.6	127.7

Source: Bolenz 1965: 55.
Note: Expenditures of varying sample of German large cities (includes extraordinary spending).

served for this period (Müller & Geisenberger 1972, Dumke 1991). In this same time span we see the rise of the Center Party (Zentrumspartei)—often associated with middle-class craftsmen and shopkeepers, as well as a part of the working class—as an actor in local urban politics. In many big cities, in addition, the Social Democrats began to make themselves felt in local affairs. These changes could well be seen as grounds for political representatives of the wealthy elite to seek cooperation with the middle classes and work toward measures that could contribute to the integration of the working classes in local communities. We have a good example of this for the Rhenish industrial city, Krefeld, whose local government in 1893 set up a Commission for the Social Question. Its task was to support certain expenditures intended to especially benefit the poorer citizens, even if the costs were borne largely by the wealthy. Such were, for example, spending on public education or financing of welfare payments.

We may doubt, however, whether the wealthy urban elite would have pursued a cooperative political course wholly on their own initiative. That they did do so was owing to the emergence of a new factor in German urban life—an increasingly powerful municipal bureaucracy, which gradually became a virtually autonomous social and political force. We draw here on the Prussian "magistrate system" to illustrate the role played by these official actors, but similar developments also took place in other states. By the 1870s the key actor was the *Bürgermeister*, in the larger cities the *Oberbürgermeister*. The *Oberbürgermeister* was elected by the local city council for a relatively long period, but his election needed confirmation by the Prussian state. He was, in effect, the municipality's chief executive officer (CEO), but at the same time he represented the authority of the state in the city he served. This duality gave him greater freedom of action with regard to both city councils and the state. As urbanization continued, the city's problems became more complex and often required legal and technical expertise. A municipal bureaucracy grew, increasingly professional and encompassing an expanding number of departments (of education, health, welfare, security, and so on), gradually becoming a sort of bourgeois elite. Complexity gave the bureaucracy informational advantages and bargaining power relative to the city council and the local interests it represented.

Out of this complexity emerged, encouraged by the city CEO and his staff of experts, an answer to municipal financial problems: the development of city-owned and -managed utility enterprises that provided water, gas and electricity, transportation, and even public bathing facilities. Some of these had started as private companies based on concessions, but by 1890 their "communalization" had become popular. Once in place, these local public monopolies proved profitable, though the cost and profit calculations of the city managers were often kept secret—impenetrable even for members of the city councils. Despite some complaints from the public and the council, the revenues they produced—for services rendered—generated less resistance from the public than taxes. They could not reduce the local tax load, but they clearly limited its growth. From a sample of some 40–50 larger cities, we estimate that per capita taxes rose from about 16 marks in 1890 to more than 38 marks in 1912, while municipal enterprise net revenues increased from about 3.5 marks to 18 marks in 1912. The tax reductions they implied, however, varied greatly from city to city (Reulecke 1985, Tilly & Bieber 1991, Matzerath 1985, Kwack 1989, Tilly 1997, Steitz 1984, Krabbe 1985).

We may see the *Oberbürgermeister* and his staff of experts as an independent force in local city politics. It proved able to resist the demands of local interests represented in city councils for special treatment, for example, property owners or enterprises. This official thus served, at least to some extent, the interests of the lower income groups who—disadvantaged as they were by the three-class voting system—were underrepresented in the city councils. This independence doubtless explains why so many cities by around 1900 had begun to introduce taxes on city real estate transactions.

We thus see the powerful position of these local executives as a driving force behind the expansion of municipal services after 1890, especially those financed by the profits—virtually uncontrolled by city councils—of the city-run enterprises. The 45,000 salaried civil servants and employees of the 110 largest Prussian cities represented in 1908 a collective, historically specific answer to the challenge of urbanization and the "social question," a kind of state intervention at the local level—we might term it "municipal socialism"—and one of the most remarkable characteristics of the German "industrial state."

German Industrialization from a Twentieth-Century Perspective

Here we look back to the long time span of development of the German economy that ended in 1914. That year was long ago, and we inevitably see that time span through the prism of the country's experience since then: two world wars, two major inflations, two postwar recoveries, and profound changes in its social and political structure, nevertheless producing to date, as in 1914, one of the world's most developed economies. We feel justified to ask at this point whether there is anything "special" about its development? Is there a "German model" of development that distinguishes Germany from other countries?

The historiography has made two important attempts to classify German industrial development. The first, and most important, typology was Alexander Gerschenkron's concept that posited "advantages of economic backwardness" of countries whose industrial development followed that of the pioneer industrializer, Great Britain. This seemed to correspond to certain structural characteristics of German industrial development: learning from a more advanced country; importing the newest technologies, with emphasis on producers' goods; dominance of big banks, large-scale enterprises, and cartels; the combination generating more rapid growth but a less liberal and competitive economy than had characterized Britain's industrial revolution. In the 1960s this "model" found favor among German historians because it built on two popular paradigms—the "growth" paradigm of economists and the "special way" (*Sonderweg*) debate on Germany's development path among historians. The *Sonderweg* implied modernization of the economy, but without the democratization of society associated with the "norm," as represented by British, French, and American development (Eric Hobsbawm's "double revolution").

A second classification attempt focused on the late nineteenth century and saw a "corporativist" production regime based on big enterprises of heavy industry and of the science-related chemical and electro-technical industries, organized as they were for cooperation within powerful lobbying associations and with organs of the state. The politically still important East Elbian agrarian interests helped to ensure a system of protective tariffs that shielded the "production regime" from foreign competition. This regime permeated the network of relationships that formed "organized capitalism," a coalition of big enterprise, organized labor, and state bureaucracy that collectively took the places of market and democratic processes in determination of production and the distribution of incomes.

Although both of these typologies accurately identify some components of Germany's industrialization, we found, as our plan for this book materialized, that they were missing some important themes. We now contend that those typologies convey no more than a description of the tip of an iceberg. There is no single "German model" of industrialization, there are several. The following concluding remarks illustrate what we mean by this.

We see the starting point of German industrialization in the growth and spread of rural industries based on exports that so clearly marked the eighteenth century. This "proto-industrialization," consisting mostly but not exclusively of textiles, was a regional phenomenon, but it affected many regions and places: the Rhineland with Aachen; Krefeld; the Wuppertal towns of Barmen and Elberfeld; the northern Sauerland region of Westphalia; eastern Westphalia; in Saxony the Vogtland, Erzgebirge, and Chemnitz regions; lower Silesia; Württemberg. Collectively, they accounted for most of Germany's nonagricultural exports, and significantly reduced the seasonally caused underemployment of the rural population, the resultant income increase contributing to food demands that stimulated agricultural expansion. By the early nineteenth century textiles represented by far the largest industry, and in its more successful centers its expansion gave birth to the important mechanical engineering industry. Simplifying somewhat, but noting that in the eighteenth century exports grew faster than estimated income in Germany, this experience could be summarized as "export based" growth. A second "German model"? Hardly, for it covers just one phase and layer of relationships; but it carries us one part of the way to a satisfactory characterization.

The state and its bureaucracy represented another force that shaped eighteenth- and early nineteenth-century development. Prussia is the case that stands out. Its leaders mobilized an emerging "educated middle class"—the *Bildungsbürgertum*—to create an increasingly effective civil bureaucracy. This instrument of state-initiated reforms facilitated an effective response to the challenge of the French Revolution and Napoleonic hegemony: promotion of a relatively rapid transition to a market economy, reforms carried out though under nondemocratic conditions. In contrast to early industrialization in Great Britain, the United States, and France, in almost all German states a capable yet authoritarian "modernization bureaucracy" was a crucially important agent of change. This was the "heroic" phase, but its presence would be felt throughout the country's industrialization, sometimes as enemy of entrepreneurial initiatives. It became an important, though ambivalent, part of the "German model."

We move on to agriculture, often neglected in short accounts of German industrialization. During the first half of the nineteenth century agriculture represented in several respects a "growth factor": first, agricultural expansion sufficed to feed a growing population, its productivity increase permitting the growth of the nonagricultural labor force and also, by producing cheaper food, freeing income for other demands (clothing, home furnishings, services). Second, during the early stages of industrialization, agrarian households were probably the most important source of increased demand for domestically produced nonagricultural goods, including the demand for iron products (which in the 1840s and 1850s was approximately equivalent in aggregate to the demand of railroads). Nevertheless, agriculture does not qualify, for historians show its modernization to have depended strongly on demand emanating from industrializing or already industrialized centers. In international comparative perspective, moreover, the weight of food in household budgets remained high, and its protection from foreign competition since the 1870s probably slowed German industrialization.

More promising would seem to be "Smithian growth" based on a widening of Germany's domestic market, which could encourage regional specialization and realization of benefits of division of labor. Reduction in the number of independent German states and borders that came with the French Napoleonic period and its conclusion was a start. More important, surely, was the development of the Zollverein and the accompanying transportation improvements, especially those brought by expansion of the railway network, both driven forward by a curious coalition of mercantile and state-bureaucratic initiative. Here we have a second "German model" that explains part of the story.

Population growth since the second half of the eighteenth century tended to exceed the ability of the German economy to supply employment opportunities at above-subsistence levels. Regional discrepancies enhanced the mismatch, producing in the middle third of the nineteenth century a chronic labor surplus. A look at the migration patterns and develoment of real wages in this period thus suggests the relevance of the "labor surplus" model of Arthur Lewis, particularly if coupled to evidence on the distribution of income between owners of capital and laborers. Were the rising levels of investment and rapid growth of heavy industry and related sectors in this period—financed and in part organized by "universal type" banks—proof of yet a third, Lewis-type "German model" of growth? The case is strong; but the importance of skilled workers in the heavy industrial growth complex of that period suggests a dualism that raises some doubts.

Our story of German industrialization up to now reads a bit like "*Hamlet* without the prince" (or princes): human capital and technological change. Acceleration of German industrial growth since the 1850s was driven by the spread and growth of steam power. Steam power, in combination with coal and coal's properties as industrial input and locational force, may be regarded as a "general purpose technology" (GPT) that strongly shaped Germany's emerging and increasingly concentrated industrial landscape. From this GPT evolved waves of innovations leading to new industries: dyestuffs based on coal tars, organic chemistry, and heavy chemicals; and mechanical engineering, which gave birth to gas engines, which led to the automobile, and so forth. At the end of the nineteenth century the coal/steam power syndrome was eclipsed by development of a new GPT based on electricity, which created a new industry based on electrical engineering, and relaxed, even reversed, some of the centralizing effects of coal and steam on industrial location. Technological change, however, was and is inseparable from human capital. Inventors and innovating entrepreneurs themselves embodied human capital, of course. But the diffusion and spread of their new products and processes depended on the widespread availability of actors endowed with the human capital needed to imitate and apply the new knowledge. Here, Germany profited from its developing educational system—at the primary, secondary, and tertiary levels—and it was this, perhaps more than any other factor, that brought Germany, by the early twentieth century, to the top of the world's leading industrial nations. The syndrome of human capital and technological change, perhaps, comes closest to a "German model" of industrialization.

Our concluding summary would be incomplete without consideration of two further parts of the industrialization story. One of these was the rapid growth of cities—urbanization of the population—that marked the period 1870–1914. It represented a consequence of the changes already described, but it also had important effects on those changes. Agglomeration economies, such as pools of skilled labor, easier communication of new knowledge, and lower transportation costs, could enhance productivity growth. The urban concentration of population also caused congestion, housing and sanitary problems that stimulated protest politics (socialist labor movement), and also the beginning of a state-sponsored social policy that probably improved the general welfare. By 1914 we can see here a materially better off urban working class, most of which supported the socialist labor movement, its criticism of the atavastic power structure that ruled Germany, and its vain attempts to control that structure. This was surely one of the distinctive features of the German industrialization model.

German industrial growth, finally, benefited greatly from the global expansion of world trade and capital flows that characterized the period 1850–1914. It reflected the acceptance of liberal capitalist policies by the ruling circles of most of the industrializing countries—including the system of fixed exchange rates that virtually precluded a domestic montary policy. How important this global environment was for the health of the German economy and its population became abundantly clear in the so-called "Thirty Years' War" that began in 1914.

NOTES

INTRODUCTION

1. According to Frank's study on regional disparities during German industrialization between 1849 and 1939, until 1914 the small group of industrial advanced regions (*Regierungsbezirke*, "administrative districts") was formed by Berlin; the Rhenish-Westphalian regions of Cologne, Arnsberg, and Düsseldorf; as well as the Saxon regions of Leipzig, Dresden, and Zwickau (Frank 1994: 93).

2. For the following more general remarks on institutions and economic growth during the later early modern period, c. 1750–1850, in Germany, see Kopsidis and Bromley (2016, 2017) as well as Ogilvie and Carus (2014).

3. It is now recognized that security of property rights "was a matter of gradation rather than outright presence or absence" (Ogilvie & Carus 2014: 406).

4. The Becker-Woessmann study has the merit of offering a useful sketch of human capital, of its operationalization, and of information on the research potential of the iPEHD (Institut für Wirtschaftsforschung Prussian Economic History Database) and its county-level source materials.

5. As the historian Jonathan Sperber writes, "In such a context, the bureaucratic political initiatives of the first decades of the nineteenth century may be seen as an intervention in an ongoing process of social change rather than as the origination of a new socioeconomic order" (Sperber 1985: 293).

6. For a full critique of Acemoglu et al.'s (2011) model, see Kopsidis and Bromley (2016, 2017).

CHAPTER ONE

1. During the period 1740–1815, "the decline of the death rate was temporarily interrupted by episodes in which deaths exceed births, which mostly reflect periods of European-wide famines . . . Such episodes occurred in 1740, 1757–8, 1761–3 (both possibly in connection with the Seven Years' War), 1772—the worst mortality crisis on the national level during the period under study—, 1795, possibly 1807/8 and 1814" (Pfister & Fertig 2019: 7).

2. For Germany, reliable data on birth rates and death rates are only available since the 1730s. We do not know when the death rate started to develop exogenously or whether Germany ever was a full-scale Malthusian economy.

CHAPTER TWO

1. This brief summary draws on the work of Ulrich Pfister (2004, 2008). See also Haupt (2002). A contrasting, more negative view on guilds is presented by Ogilvie (1996, 1997a, 1997b).

2. In 1853, 61.5 percent of all farm land belonged to farms between 5.5 and 41.5 hectares, and 9.6 percent to farms smaller than 5.5 hectares (Kopsidis & Pfister 2013: 10).

3. Thanks to the debt guarantee offered by Leipzig's wealthy merchants, Saxony successfully stabilized its finances. These creditors maintained their control of the funds created for this purpose, even intervening against state policy, for example, in 1766, when they stopped an expensive rearmament planned by the electoral prince and his noble advisors. The reformers consciously opted for Saxony as a peaceful state refraining from any foreign policy adventures but investing in infrastructure. In addition, the debt commission created by the Saxon reformers may have formed the role model for Great Britain in organizing its debt service after its defeat in the War of American Independence (Däbritz 1906, Schlechte 1958, Schmitt-Sasse 1987).

4. The continental system prohibited all imports of manufactured goods into France and the kingdom of Italy. At the same time all non-French parts of the grand empire were forced to open their markets for French imports.

5. See F. Crouzet (1958, 1964) on the gap. In a long-run historical perspective from, say, 1760 to 1850, the French and Napoleonic War period 1790–1814, but even more so the period of continental blockade, 1806–14, appears as reversal of a long-term expansion of world trade affecting many countries, including ones overseas (O'Rourke 2006). The locus classicus on this is Eli Heckscher, *The Continental System* (1922), who interprets it as applied mercantilism.

6. Readers should note that home laborers in these industries, using their own machines and homes, had substantial fixed costs—a condition that encouraged self-exploitation and depressed their wage levels. On this see Karlsch and Schäfer (2006: 32–33) and the interesting commentary by Frederick Engels on the persistence of this practice decades later (1887).

7. A similar continuum of accelerated industrial development and economic reform policy—begun under the ancien régime, continuing more slowly in the short French period, then finally completed under Prussian auspices—is identifiable for the second large industrial region of the Rhein-Ruhr area: the upland *Bergische Land* containing the Wupper valley (Engelbrecht 1996).

8. On the Saar see Banken (2003).

9. Langewiesche labeled Württemberg's constitution of 1819 an "authoritarian constitution [*obrigkeitliche Verfassung*]" because constitutional checks and balances to control the central government and authorities were only poorly developed, but at least Württemberg had a constitution and the parliament had some rights. Prussia's bureaucracy did not face any parliamentary controls (Langewiesche 1974: 72). This made a difference.

10. This unique industrial organization emerged to integrate dispersed immobile industrial workers who owned farm land in the countryside into the industrial production process (Megerle 1982: 221–23).

11. Annual demographic growth rates were negative in Württemberg during the decade 1846–55 (–0.28 percent) compared to +0.64 percent for all of Germany.

CHAPTER THREE

1. Adding labor generated diminishing marginal returns but increased total output—important for poor peasants.

2. Exemplarily for the peasant-friendly modern historiography, see Berthold 1962; Müller 1964, 1967; Harnisch 1984, 1986, 1989; Groß 1968: 38–79; Kopsidis & Pfister 2013; Pfister & Kopsidis, 2015; Kopsidis 2015; Henn 1973; Grüne 2011; Dehlinger 1897: 49–58; Mahlerwein 2001; Prass 2016: 75–148.

3. We remind readers at this point that the English word "peasant" is not quite equivalent to the German term *Bauer,* and the distinction between "peasant" and "farmer" is much stronger than the difference between *Bauer* and *Landwirt.*

4. We note here that the estate boom was fueled by estate landowners speculating with mortgage credits supplied by the Prussian *Landschaften* (created, ironically, by Frederick the Great to save those landowners from "speculators"). A study of the resultant debt crisis might be rewarding (Behrens 1985: 150). A recent study by Wandschneider suggests that the *Landschaften* were efficient monitors of credit-worthiness (Wandschneider 2013, 2015).

5. The expansion of potato cultivation gained momentum in Saxony at the end of the eighteenth century (Kopsidis & Pfister 2013). Potatoes brought more calories per hectare than grain and could more easily feed a rising population. In addition, the reaction of potatoes to seasonal weather conditions differed from that of grain. Hence, a mix of grain and potato farming provided a better diversification of food risk than reliance on grain farming alone (shown for Saxony 1792–1811 by Uebele & Grünbaum [2013]).

6. These are briefly discussed above (in chapter 4; see Kopsidis et al. [2017]); on credit and land banks, Wehler (1987b: 39). The same argument applies to the other German states. For Bavaria, see Böhm (1995).

7. Dickler's data are rough estimates, a good deal less reliable and replicable than those for Westphalia (table 3.2).

CHAPTER FOUR

1. For a summary of the rich supply of recent research on the Prussian manorial system, see Eddie (2013: 29–156). East German historians, such as Liselott Enders (1989, 1991, 1992, 2000), Hartmut Harnisch (1976, 1978b, 1982, 1984, 1996), Jan Peters (1970), Hans-Heinrich Müller (1964, 1967), and Rudolf Berthold (1962, 1974, 1978), and, from the United States, William Hagen (1986, 1995, 2002), have established a more differentiated and peasant-friendly view of Prussian agricultural development between 1650 and 1850.

2. The plan failed because peasants found redemption costs too high, and, given the absence at this time of a market for peasant produce, there was no way to finance them (Harnisch 1994a).

3. For a more critical position on the absolutist Prussian peasant policy, see Corni (1986) and Berdahl (1988: 77–106), who interpret royal agricultural policy as simple "nobility-protection." However, a basic assumption of this critical view—that coerced labor disappeared spontaneously when agrarian capitalism started because it could not compete with more profitable wage labor—is simply wrong. Coerced labor never disappeared automatically when capitalism started, and Prussia was no exception. In any case massive state action was required even only to push back non-free labor. This was definitely true for the eighteenth and early nineteenth centuries.

4. Harnisch (1994a: 21) shows this directly only for the Brandenburg province, but his estimates of land distribution at the end of the century show most of it being worked by peasant farmers.

5. *Erbzins* (or hereditary tenure) was roughly equivalent to the English "copyhold."

6. "Interlocked factor markets" have been and still are widespread in the rural areas of developing economies whose agriculture experience a process of commercialization. They can be defined as "the contractual tying of the terms of exchange in one market to those in other markets" (Ellis 1996: 156). Interlocked factor and commodity markets under the conditions of the large estate's based manorial economy (*Gutsherrschaft*) were governed by strong 'non- market elements' which characterized all relations between lords and their laborers to a large extent. However, during the second half of the 18th century even in the east commercialization processes had a strong impact on the arrangement of all labor and credit relationships on manorial estates as well as on local commodity markets, including the fixing of payments in kind (Hagen 2002: 391–422).

7. These were noble landed estates that the king freed from vassalage claims, replaced by a light tax.

8. In 1740 around half of the Prussian revenues came from the leasing of royal domains. In the province *Kurmark* 13.5 percent of the total area belonged to the royal domains (240,000 acres agricultural land and 1 millon acres forest land [Heegewaldt 2012: 163]).

9. According to Adam Smith, not more than 1 percent of the population should serve in the army, to avoid economic stagnation and fiscal ruin. However, throughout the second half of the eighteenth century Prussia had put constantly equivalent in numbers to 4 percent of the population into the military, and no economic or fiscal collapse occurred. Quite the opposite was true (Behrend 1985: 88).

10. For state finances, Schremmer (1994: 116–17, comparisons with Great Britain and France, 14–16, 62). See also Braun (1975). We note that the domain revenues were large, making Prussia much less dependent on taxes than either Great Britain or France. That enhanced the monarch's independence.

11. For example, the capability of a region to industrialize after 1816 and to benefit economically from rising enrollment rates was rooted deep in the early modern period. To properly integrate these manifold and interactive historical factors into an econometric model is almost impossible.

12. Frederick II thought juridical interpretation of existing law by courts was dangerous. On reasons for this, see Prümm (2012), which shows certain limits to the monarch's understanding of legal issues but also the dilemma of a "monocratic" government.

13. As Koselleck put it, "the Prussian bureaucracy consciously opted for Adam Smith and against Napoleon to chase the one with the other" (1967: 14; our translation).

14. General calculations convinced reformers that an agrarian structure based on viable family farms would produce much more taxable income per unit of land compared to what was available from large estate farms based on wage labor (Eddie 2013: 277).

15. In contrast to Prussia and Great Britain the revolutionary French civil code interpreted the common rights of peasants as infrangible private property rights. Thus, as a heritage of the peasant-friendly French Revolution, nineteenth-century France only knew voluntary enclosures (Grantham 1978, 1980, Jones 2012). The situation was completely different in Prussia. In the course of its "defensive modernization," Prussian legislators saw common rights as a relic of barbarian times that had to be

removed completely and as quickly as possible to enable agricultural growth for the good of all. In Prussian understanding even "holy" private property rights could be suspended when they impaired the general welfare (defined as maximum economic growth). No part of Germany experienced more rapid enclosures than the Prussian core lands east of the river Elbe (Brakensiek 2004: 164–65). These post-1821 eastern enclosures may have proceeded even faster than the parliamentary enclosures in the United Kingdom.

16. The juridical negotiations between lords and peasants were mediated by general commissions appointed by the state and could be activated by both parties. Noble estates were "winners" of the reforms (to the extent of roughly 1 million hectares of peasant land from commutation of feudal dues, eviction of peasants, and outright purchases from peasants plus cash payments by peasants in place of land), and their role as "agrarian capitalists" strengthened (Harnisch 1984: 147; Harnisch 1989: 35–40).

17. Johann Christian Friederich Scharnweber, the Prussian chief agrarian reformer, succeeded in rejecting many demands of the nobility. In tenacious struggles during 1811–16, he gained redemption of feudal obligations—except in Silesia—for many peasants who had very weak property rights. He also managed to reduce substantially the number of evicted peasants, and he managed to save 500,000 to 750,000 hectares of peasant land from seizure by the nobility. In addition, he reduced substantially the redemption payments of peasants in land and money to their former lords in exchange for full property rights in their farms (Harnisch 1976: 78–82; Harnisch 1978b: 273–75).

18. The very different treatment of dependent peasants on state domains in the course of the agrarian reforms in Württemberg and Prussia paradigmatically demonstrates the radical nature of the Prussian reform approach as compared with French-influenced states or those French model states where the agrarian reforms completely failed. They failed not so much because of war troubles as because of Napoleon's nobility-friendly policy to stabilize his empire (Berding 1973, Fehrenbach 1983, Kopsidis & Bromley 2017, 2016, Keimer 1915, Schotte 1912, Keinemann 1987, Heitzer 1959, Berding 2008, Dehtlefs 2008). Württemberg delayed the liberation of its domain peasants until 1848, mainly for shortsighted fiscal reasons, but also because it lacked the strategic approach of Prussian reformers (Harnisch 1984: 75–83; Eddie 2013: 185–92; Hippel 1977: 279, 311–12, 335; Medick 1990: 71).

19. Towns limited acquisition of a license to a trade to their own citizens, excluding migrants. The historian Jonathan Sperber (1985: 282) noted the contrast to Prussian practice and concluded: "Possibly the most important contribution of Prussian state policy to fostering economic growth, although still a surprisingly little-investigated one, was the authorities' stubborn insistence on retaining freedom of occupation, residence, and mobility, an adherence to laissez-faire unmatched by the other German states before 1850."

20. In Germany, a "coup d'état of the bureaucracy" was the only way to bring about profound economic reforms against the will of old elites (Vogel 1980: 17; Vogel 1983: 31, 48–72; Nolte 1990: 26–28, 39–42; Fehrenbach 2008).

21. Reinhart Koselleck (1967) was the first who analyzed the trade-off between political and economic reforms in Prussia/Germany during the early nineteenth century. A broad consensus among German historians supports the "Koselleck thesis." In the early nineteenth century German conservatives uniformly denounced the Prussian economic reforms as "Jacobinism" (Dipper 1996a: 142).

CHAPTER FIVE

1. On this see Ferguson (1998: 124–25). The loan was listed on all the principal European capital markets—a novum in London. See also Jenks,(1971: 38 and 350).

2. Useful surveys on Prussia's post-1815 public finance and tax system are to be found in Schremmer (1994: 123–49) and Spoerer (2004). Spoerer shows how policy affected the problem of imbalance between the old and new Prussian provinces.

3. Dumke (1994) showed that the border length/area ratios correlated strongly with estimated collection costs.

4. In the form of potentially lost benefits of trade that weakened its bargaining position with respect to Prussia.

5. Of some interest is the fact that this agreement was preceded by political and violent popular protests that caused the prince to abdicate in favor of his son, who then signed the treaty (Dumke 1994, Ploeckl 2010).

6. Ploeckl (2010) adds that Prussia exploited the isolated condition of the Thuringian states by forcing them to join *en bloc* and obtain as one collective member just one vote.

7. The Zollverein as constituted consisted of seven full members with equal voting (and veto) rights, and twenty-six nonvoting members, all with claims on a share of net revenues based on population. Changes in tariff duties and acceptance of new members had to be voted unanimously. A congress of members was to meet every three years, and a small office staff was to monitor revenue development and matters of weights and measures.

8. Resistance to Prussia would have encouraged alliance with Austria for these states, but ended duty-free access to the coastal ports (Henderson 1968, Böhme 1966).

9. An appendix in the Dumke study shows that in 1837 the South Zollverein imported commodities with a value of nearly 24 million thaler—more than 16 percent of average total Zollverein imports, 1836–38, as reported in von Borries (1970: 90).

10. In another paper Ploeckl (2010) presents a similar (if less compelling) argument based on Saxony's accession.

11. The numbers for the German Confederation for 1850: canals = 3,528 km of total c. 12,200 km waterways (Fischer et al. 1982: 80).

12. Kopsidis (1996: 266–344). Uebele (2011) treats transportation costs indirectly with a variable "distance." See also Fremdling & Hohorst (1979).

13. Both base their findings on grain price movements, but, oddly, neither offers data on transportation costs, and only Kopsidis deals directly with supply changes and their effects.

14. Notably, David Landes in his masterful study of European industrialization, *The Unbound Prometheus* (1969), or *The Wealth and Poverty of Nations* (1998), where "Pursuit of Albion" is the theme.

15. Recent discussion of German national accounts suggests that Hoffmann's (1965) NNP per capita benchmark estimates for 1850 are too low (Burhop & Wolff 2005; Fremdling 1988, 1995; Pfister 2019c). Since Maddison's GDP estimates are based on Hoffmann, his figures may not do full justice to German catching up.

CHAPTER SIX

1. Problems are related to the link with agricultural self-employment. We have several regional studies (east Westphalia, lower Silesia, Württemberg, for example) that

provide some benchmarks, and we also have much andecdotal evidence (Boldorf 2009, Kwasny 2009, Wischermann 1992). See also for wage data Gömmel (1979).

2. Figure 6.2, however, attempts to simplify an argument made by Hans-Heinrich Bass (1991: 42–45) based on a complicated demographic indicator he calculated. The indicator "Relative Rate of Population Increase" (RRPI), as he calculated it, is based on ten-year (centered) growth rate averages thought to reflect "normal" demographic behavior in Prussia, while deviations of –50 percent or more from that average are defined as "crises."

3. Thanks to the courageous research of Rudolf Virchow (a prominent physician), we know that Upper Silesia was an especially hard-hit region, for its 1846–47 harvests proved catastrophic and caused the spread of the so-called typhus epidemic (Virchow 1849).

4. Foodstuffs, which represented a significant share of household budgets, were an example of what economists call "Giffen goods," the demand for which can increase when their price rises. In the jargon of economics, "income effects" overwhelm "price effects," and less income remains for other wants.

5. Note that this account of the German revolution of 1848–49 makes no attempt to describe its politics—the connection between unification and liberty, and international complications (on this see Winkler 2000: 98–130).

PART THREE

1. We note here that this corresponds roughly to the upswing phase of the "Bourgeois Kondratieff" (from 1843 to 1870–75) that Schumpeter used to describe the period from 1843 to 1897 (1939: 1:170–71, 305–13). More on this below (chapter 12).

CHAPTER SEVEN

1. The Allgemeine Deutsches Handelsgesetzbuch. We return to this issue again below (chapters 12 and 14).

2. A further liberalizing step came with the General Mining Law of 1865.

3. For these questions, see the discussion in Spree (1977: 65–85), where the relative neglect of social product (or national income) for growth cycle analysis is justified. New work by Pfister (2019c) bears in this issue—too late for incorporation into this book.

4. Spree (1977: 75): "The [original] index may be seen, roughly speaking, as depicting the change in the economic climate." It consists of 21 volume variables (tons of coal, number of bankruptcies, and so on) and 27 value variables (financial asset prices, wholesale prices, and so on). When the number of rising variables falls below that of falling ones, the curve depicts a downward turning point. Our version is based on 16 volume variables and 26 value variables.

5. Fremdling (1986: 307–8, 347) shows that German bar iron (and rail) producers had costs only slightly higher than British and Belgian competitors, while German pig iron capacity was both high-cost and quantitatively inadequate. The reason for encouragement of imports was less German inability to master the technique of coke smelting than the enormous pull of the demand that stemmed from the railroad-building in the 1840s.

6. The Ruhr's deep shafts required continuous pumping by steam-driven machinery to keep them free of water, but this dictated costs of labor, coal, and other overheads that motivated mining companies to limit output reduction (Holtfrerich 1973: 120).

7. There are other historical examples of this phenomenon, such as US canal-building in the early nineteenth century, or the "overexpansion" of privately owned railroads in Germany in the 1860s and 1870s. On this see Fremdling (1985) and Ransom (1970).

8. The Berlin firm of August Borsig alone delivered 1,195 of those 2,647 locomotives. In 1860 his firm employed more than 3,000 persons; his success probably contributed a good deal to Berlin's importance as center of the industry (Wagenblass 1973: 88–89, 256–64; Redlich 1944: 121–48).

9. Notwithstanding the fact that the first railroads were responses to demand and profitable, as Fremdling (1985) argued; but see Hornung (2014b).

10. This is known (in English) as "the social savings controversy," related to Robert Fogel's locus classicus, *Railroads and American Economic Growth* (1964). For this see Fremdling (1985: 234–36).

11. Pierenkemper (1979) documents the slow rise of the 1850s (17 applications) to the 380 and 863 applications of the 1860s and 1870s for the counties of the eastern Ruhr district.

12. This Westphalian district (Arnsberg) had 554 workshops with 12,422 persons (and 3 percent of the total population) (data from iPEHD ifo Prussian Economic History DataBase, Gewerbetabelle 1849, occ. "Crafts").

13. This judgment is subject to the qualification that the Becker (1962) sample is quite restrictive: it corresponds to the 1875 definition for Prussia (producers with at least 50 employees and using steam power), that is, 1,196 firms compared with the full definition of 44,390.

CHAPTER EIGHT

1. In classical perspective, labor surplus in the subsistence sector means that labor supply to the modern sector is infinitely elastic at the subsistence level (Lewis 1954).

2. For Prussia, rough estimates of the agricultural population for 1849 are possible. Assuming a constant participation rate and for the 14/15–60 age group a rate of population growth of 0.75 percent, we get an estimate of 9,780,581—an excess of more than 1 million persons.

3. Köllmann (1974a) and Megerle (1979: 116–23); Megerle, however, emphasizes above all absence of the classic "leading sectors," railroads and heavy industry.

4. German pre-1877 history depended on the individual German states. Prussian law involved examination by state-appointed "experts," while Saxon law followed the liberal British system, and so on. This raised problems for inventors. For a study of patents filed in Baden in this period, most by applicants from other German states, see Donges and Selgert (2019).

5. For both measures, "northeast" includes the provinces of East and West Prussia, Pommerania, Posen, and Silesia; "central" includes Brandenburg and Saxony; and "west" covers Rhineland and Westphalia. Enrollment data are from the iPEHD ifo Prussian Economic History Data Base.

6. Cinirella and Hornung's arguments are based on panel regressions using county-level data. We note here that the authors claim to have adequately identified the supply of primary schooling with the indicators "school density" and teacher-pupil ratio (unresponsive to land concentration), while enrollments, the "peasant demand," proved responsive. This raises the question whether supply and demand have actually been identified. In addition, there is the problem that enrollment was not identical with actual attendance. On this, see Denkschrift "Die öffentlichen

Volksschulen im preussischen Staate," 13 Ergänzungsheft zur Zeitschrift des Königlich preussischen statistischen Bureaus (1883).

7. A new study of nineteenth-century German real wages by Ulrich Pfister (2017a) makes it possible to revise results of the older sources (Kuczynski 1909, Gömmel 1979, Hoffmann 1965, Spree 1977). It offers a more suitable cost-of-living index than hitherto available. For trough-to-trough estimates, however, the differences are small. They confirm the view taken here that real wages grew very little in the period from around 1850 to 1880. Pfister even suggests a decline relative to the 1820s. It should be added that the evidence cited does not suggest any change in hours worked. The results are obviously to some extent sensitive to the choice of years (1845, 1850; 1875 or1880, and so on).

8. Burhop and Wolff's modifications of Hoffmann confirm a rate significantly higher than Pfister's (and Gömmel's) real wages. See also Hoffmann (1965: 171–72, 826–27).

9. Prussian tax officials were ordered not to inquire too deeply into the financial affairs of taxpayers, and the literature on the subject correctly assumes that a significant share of capital income remained undeclared. The tax data show a substantial increase in measured inequality between 1852 and 1875, but the true degree of inequality was surely higher (Tilly 2010). Please note that the new study by Pfister (2019c) offers new estimates of capital income not discussed here.

10. For further explanation of these measures, see Dumke (1991: 125–30).

CHAPTER NINE

1. Johann Heinrich von Thünen anticipated this process in his famous agricultural location model of the "isolated state"—which seems to perfectly fit the contemporary German experience (Kopsidis & Wolf 2012; Kopsidis 2006: 101–35). In the same direction argued the famous statistician Ernst Engel (1866, 1867).

2. These counties were endowed with high-quality soil (Kopsidis 1996: 97–101).

3. The data on land rents, urban population, and agricultural characteristics were produced by a massive contemporary study by August Meitzen (1868) covering all 342 Prussian counties in the mid-1860s. It was intended to serve as the basis for a reform of the land tax. These were the basis for an econometric study of the relationships, described above, published by Kopsidis and Wolf in 2012.

4. According to Grant (2009: table 2), East Elbia's net value-added per worker in agriculture, 1905–7, lay, with an average of 1,134 marks, well above the German-wide average of 982 marks.

5. Within Germany, however, catching-up growth seems to have taken place, leveling out the productivity gap between lagging eastern and leading western regions (Grant 2002, 2005: 225–52).

CHAPTER TEN

1. The word "government" is set in quotation marks here to indicate that neither the Prussian Bank nor its successor, the Reichsbank, were purely government organs; in fact, they were a mixture in which commercial interests were paramount (Borchardt 1976).

2. There are many histories of individual savings banks. A modern summarizing study would be useful.

3. Local chambers of commerce and industry apparently reported on these institutions. For Saxony, these were said to have considerably reduced rates of interest (cited for various places around Leipzig in the Wirtschaftsarchiv, Leipzig).

CHAPTER ELEVEN

1. The two price-deflated estimates are roughly equal. These numbers reflect the use of logarithms: (LOG NSPt-LOG NSP t-1)/LOG NSP-t-1. The use of period averages yields higher growth rates.

2. Hoffmann (1965: 492–94, 598–99); Gömmels estimates of real incomes in Fischer et al. (1982: 155–56) and Pierenkemper (2015: 148).

3. An abundant supply of theories is on offer, to be sure. Burhop (2011: 67–80) summarizes most of the literature. See also Spiethof (1955), Akerman (1960), Spree (1978), Schröder & Spree (1981), Schumpeter (1939).

4. Urban infrastructure investment also played a role (Tilly 1990: 80–81; Reulecke 1985: 68–70; Tilly & Wellenreuther 1985: 273–300).

5. Both Spree (1978) and a more recent publication by Sarferaz & Uebele (2009) agree on this periodization.

6. Nevertheless, as we shall see, the German securities markets (in Berlin) eventually became an important source of equity finance.

7. In Schumpeter's *Business Cycles* (1939: 313–97) these years corresponded roughly to the downswing phase of the "Bourgeois" Kondratieff long wave during which the productivity effects of innovations (mainly transportation) became manifest. On these long waves see Solomou (1987) and also Grabas (1992).

8. This was based on an article Rosenberg had written back in 1940, in which he saw the period as part of the *lange Wellen der Konjunktur* ("long wave" or "long economic cycle") as proposed by Kondratieff in the 1920s.

9. Nine-tenths of the Vereinigung's members owned the prestigious landed estates, the *Rittergüter* (Rosenberg 1967: 162–63).

10. Schumpeter labeled this upswing the start of "The Neo-Mercantilist Kondratieff" (1939: 397–448). Nikolai Kondratieff was a Russian economist whose "Long Wave" concept, first published in German in 1926, appeared in English in *Review of Statistics* (1935): "The Long Waves in Economic Life." His long waves of c. fifty-year length are based on selected time series charting English, French, American, and German nineteenth-century development (Spiethoff 1955: 130–39).

CHAPTER TWELVE

1. This represented about 10 percent of all patents held between 1877 and 1918 (Streb et al. 2006: 352–53).

2. Richter & Streb (2011: 1017–19) also discuss patent applications of American machine-tool makers.

3. In 1891 a public demonstration of the usefulness of alternating current (AC) in this respect widened electricity's potential for industry (Gutberlet 2014).

4. This is not an appeal to a "great men" interpretation of industrial history, but a plea for caution in the weight attributable to the number of patents.

5. Gutberlet (2014) based her estimates on comparison of the employment censuses of 1875, 1895, and 1907.

6. Steel required 0.1–2.0 percent carbon, wrought iron less than 0.1 percent, and cast iron a good deal more than 2.0 percent. Complete decarburization left iron soft, malleable, in the extreme too easily bent and worn. An excellent account of steel development in this period is Landes (1969: 242–69).

7. Webb cites empirical evidence on prices and costs of German producers that support this claim (Webb 1980: 323–25). He also cites dumping in foreign markets by

German producers in recession phases as part of an "over the cycle" stabilization that encouraged investment.

8. By 1897 a BASF competitor, Hoechst AG, had developed a marketable indigo blue, this leading to a joint marketing agreement. This and other interesting material in von Hippel (2003: 73–76).

9. Murmann (2003) offers a wealth of comparative information on the British and German dyestuffs industry.

10. Otto's first experiments had been based on the four-stroke cycle (intake, compression, ignition, and exhaust strokes), but due to technical difficulties it was then abandoned. Matschoss (1921) and Laux (1976: 5) suspected that Otto did not realize the significance of his discovery.

11. Until 1901 Benz had been the industry's leader, but development of the "Mercedes" model propelled Daimler Motor Company to the top (Feldenkirchen 2003: 59–63).

12. Broadberry and Burhop offer estimates extending beyond 1913 but not discussed here.

13. The Broadberry & Burhop estimates are based on physical productivity in branches for which good comparable employment data exist.

14. Neither stock prices nor production efficiency of member firms showed a reaction to the cartel (Bittner 2005, Burhop & Lübbers 2009).

15. Some years ago, this issue was debated under the heading "Did Victorian Britain Fail?" For a critical discussion see Crafts, Leybourne & Mills (1991).

16. For contemporary criticism of these statistics see Tooze (2001: 50–63).

17. The first (and classic) statement of handicraft decline was Gustav Schmoller's *Zur Geschichte der deutschen Kleingewerbe im 19. Jahrhundert* (1870). Still worth reading is the critical treatment of this historiography—going back to the "Historical School"—by Wolfram Fischer (1972). His output data are taken from Hoffmann (1965). See also the articles by Kaufhold (1976b) and Fischer (1976) and the dissertation by Adolf Noll (1969). A modern survey is in Pierenkemper (2000: 115–16; 1994: 61–73).

18. Note that about 97 percent of all firms counted were sole proprietorships. These data are from unpublished work by Tim Guinnane (2007).

CHAPTER THIRTEEN

1. The prestigious British weekly, *The Economist,* praised this law and recommended similar legislation for Britain, which came in 1900 (*The Economist,* 9 and 16 February 1884, 1901: 474).

2. Guinnane et al. (2007 [online 2015]: 687–732) offer a comparative discussion of this enterprise form.

3. For the banks the cartel helped to overcome informational asymmetry favoring steel companies.

4. As late as the 1900s the paid-up capital of German banks amounted to about one-third of total assets—a stark contrast to the corresponding share for British commercial banks, of about 12 percent (Sheppard 1971: 118–19; Deutsche Bundesbank 1976: 56–7).

5. A more recent and more skeptical view is in Fohlin (2007).

6. A recent survey is in Burhop (2011: 167–90); see also Fohlin (2007: 101–5).

7. Among other things, this served as the basis of the banks' control of proxy votes at shareholder assemblies.

8. Lehmann-Hasemeyer and Streb (2016) examine 474 IPOs. Unfortunately, no data on the size of these issues are given.

9. Rettig (1978: 140–41) shows for 50 listed companies an average internal-finance quotient of 59 percent for 1880–1911, though a declining trend.

10. These points are documented quantitatively in Guinnane (2001: 366–89).

CHAPTER FOURTEEN

1. Burhop (2011: 103); Lampe & Wolf (2015: 282) have slightly different numbers.

2. This reflected largely the behavior of prices (discussed in this chapter above under the heading "boom and bust").

3. Much of this section derives from the account in Buchheim (1983). The older literature on Britain's "Great Depression" in the 1870s and 1880s is cited there.

4. Grant (2005: 263–65) offers a short overview.

5. Floud (1976) notes that German exports of machine tools to France after around 1880 far exceeded British ones, but the British producers still saw the United States as their most dangerous competitor.

6. It is worth adding, however, that railway tariff rate adjustments and nontariff measures ensured continued protection of agrarian interests (Gerschenkron 1943). Gerschenkon failed to mention that west German farmers also pressed for railroad rates to protect their share of the grain market in the west against East Elbian competition. (Hailer 1902: 1–13; Wiedenfeld 1909: 781–83; Hardach 1967: 94–97, 112–15).

7. Readers may note here that the results for animal producers suggest that the thousands of smaller farm owners so specialized and who had supported the Bund der Landwirte, did not do so for ideological reasons alone, as, for example, Gerschenkron once (1943) suggested.

8. British agriculture, of course, had a much different social structure. Its large landowners, a relatively small number, were politically expendable, not so German agriculture, with its large number of small farm owners (Tilly 1999b).

9. See also Webb (1982), who points out the importance—and ultimate absurdity—of export subsidies for this branch.

10. A modern variant of this argument is presented by Oliver Grant, who estimates growth rates of German cities rising to more than 8 percent p. a. in a free trade scenario as a result of a collapsing agricultural sector (Grant 2005: 218).

11. Well known, but worth mentioning, are the facts that (1) securities issued in Germany could soon be held in other countries; and that (2) German banks carried out new issues in other countries via intermediaries.

12. To some extent this reflected the close ties between German bankers and the German-Jewish banking community in New York (Carosso 1970, Kabisch 1982, Wilkins 1989).

13. For the role of imperialism theories, see Barth (1995).

14. Even though, as Müller-Link pointed out, his financial advisors had counseled otherwise. As background, Wehler (1995: 3:775–77) emphasizes Bismarck's encouragement of a policy of "Germanization" of the eastern provinces and even Polish territories, which ensured the support of the East Elbian *Agrarier*.

15. In the case of Russia, to be sure, German government policy became more accommodating after Bismarck's departure in the 1890s.

16. The sample consists of 34 groups of securities, 25 foreign and 9 domestic. The do-

mestic securities are weighted at 1900–1913 market prices. The sample is described in Tilly (1992).

17. Estimated annual returns $(R_{it}) = (A_t + (P_t - P_{t-1})/P_{t-1}) - I$. A = annual income as % of par value; P = security price as % of par value; I = Annual rate of inflation.

18. We note here that while about 80 percent of the foreign securities were bonds, only a little more than half of domestic securities were, and domestic shares were more volatile than foreign securities.

19. For Germany see Tilly (1992), cited above. This was a general phenomenon. See, for example, Neal (1985), Tilly (1999b), and Taylor (1999).

20. We have reason to believe that bankers profited more from the issue of foreign securities than from that of domestic ones. For a sample of 16 transactions involving Eastern and Central European securities (1880–1913) we calculated a return of 4.85 percent of the issue volume, in most cases for engagements lasting less than one year (Tilly 1994: 208–10). For a skeptical view see Schaeffer (1995: 526–33). A full estimate of the risks involved, however, is not possible.

21. Those are: (1) that investors based portfolio decisions solely on the bases of expected mean returns and risks; (2) that they chose the highest returns for given levels of risk; (3) that ex post returns measure expected returns; (4) that expected returns were realized; (5) that investors were risk avoiders; and (6) that all investors had identical market information.

22. The Deutsche Bank played a major role here (Feis 1930: 313–60; Barth 1995: 202–74; Schaeffer 1995: 345–75).

23. A good account is in Seidenzahl (1970: 125–31). For the DÜEG's balance sheet, see Salings Börsenjahrbuch, 1912–13 and 1914–15, pt. 2.

24. All of Berlin's important banks participated, but it was not until 1907 that the "syndicate" could offer DÜEG shares and bonds on the capital market (Seidenzahl 1970: 130).

25. Tilly (1991b: 106, citing Rosendorff [1904] and Hauser [1906]).

26. On these points: Lindert (1969), Borchardt (1976), Bloomfield (1963); and for the Deutsche Bank's "agency," see Pohl (1973).

27. This is an important point, for German historiography has tended to see that emigration largely as a German problem. The principal prophet of an econometric approach to the question of nineteenth-century mass migration has been Jeffrey Williamson (1995, 1996, 1997).

28. Except possibly Great Britain. See Easterlin (1961) for an early interpretation of European emigration along these lines.

29. Williamson and his various collaborators have contributed many articles linking migration flows to these wage statistics (see Williamson 1996, or Taylor & Williamson 1997).

30. Williamson (1996) emphasizes the anomalous role of US growth in the history of migration and convergence, one that seemed to defy the "Heckscher-Ohlin" view of factor mobility.

31. Adding the agrarian districts of Schleswig-Holstein and the two Mecklenburgs would raise the total for the entire period 1871–94 by more than 200,000 emigrants (Mönckmeier 1912: 86–90).

32. Klaus Bade's full-length study (2005) is the standard German authority. But see the still relevant PhD dissertation by Robert A. Dickler (1975a: 321–23). See also Oliver Grant (2005: 56–214) for econometric results. Two noteworthy contemporaries cited by these authors were Max Sering (1910) and Theodor von der Goltz (1893).

33. Dickler (1975a) and others have pointed out that technical change since the 1860s did have a labor-absorbing component, but the spread of mechanical threshing and, somewhat later, of reapers was clearly labor-saving and thus migration-inducing.
34. In this period, out-migration from East Elbia was nearly twice as high as the region's estimated contribution to overseas emigration, and it continued after the latter peaked around 1894. A comparison of Dickler (1975a) with Burgdorfer's or Mönckmeier's figures confirms this claim.

CHAPTER FIFTEEN

1. Both of the studies cited used county-level data (in contrast to Knodel's use of the larger administrative districts). Both also show that Catholic districts maintained significantly higher fertility levels (and experienced less decline) in this period than others. Thus, to the extent that fertility decline promoted human capital, the "Protestant ethic," as Becker and Woesmann (2009) suggested, had consequences for the creation of human capital.
2. Cinnirella & Streb (2017) show that the negative impact of literacy on fertility was significantly larger in counties marked by technologically more advanced economies—where returns to education were presumably higher.
3. An interesting article by Lucas (1988) stressed the potential agglomeration economies and network effects of concentration of labor in big cities for human capital formation (citing Jane Jacobs, *The Economics of Cities*).
4. On these results see Laux (1989), Tilly & Wellenreuther (1985), and Matzerath (1985). The "residual method" takes the difference between population increase and estimated natural increase as the measure of net migration.
5. The balance for 1907 showed a loss of nearly 2 million persons that just about matched the net gains of the regions Berlin/Brandenburg and Rhineland/Westphalia (table in Hohorst et al. 1978: 40).
6. This was the source of the large Polish population of Ruhr mining towns (Wehler 1961).
7. This is the principal finding of Thomas Wellenreuther's important doctoral dissertation (Wellenreuther 1989). We return to the importance of housing below.
8. Nevertheless, despite its role as liberal voice of German wealth owners, the *Deutsche Oeconomist* even favored government expropriation of private land needed for public infrastructural projects. On this and other aspects see Wellenreuther (1989: app. 3, citing the *Deutsche Oeconomist*, 1883–1913).
9. To be paid for by higher taxes on the well-off, the *Deutsche Oeconomist* feared. Private builders and real estate specialists, and landowners, might also have feared a "crowding out" effect of public housing investments.
10. For wages, see Gömmel (1979), Orsagh (1969), Bry (1968), and Hoffmann (1965); a summary is in Pierenkemper (2015). For mortality, Spree (1981); for food consumption, Teuteberg & Wischermann 1972; and for housing, Teuteberg (1983, 1986), Wischermann (1986), and Niethammer & Bruggemeier (1976).
11. The *Kathedersozialisten* all called for more state intervention in the economy and saw socialism as the ultimate goal, but they differed on the nature of capitalism's replacement. Karl Bücher, for example, was more skeptical of government management of the economy than was Adolph Wagner (Wagner-Hasel 2011).
12. These results are subject to the reservation that the "raw" data used have not been made public.

13. The Socialist Law of 1878 was repealed in 1890, coinciding with Kaiser Wilhelm's dismissal of Bismarck (Wehler, 1995: 902–15).

14. T. A. Jopp (2013) interprets the development of the Knappschaften (1850–1920) from the perspective of their efficiency as insurance institutions against the background of changes in membership size, costs, and benefits.

15. The authors point out that rheumatism—frequently recorded as reason for miners' absence from work—was impossible to observe and, hence, unverifiable (Guinnane & Streb 2011).

16. This was when enforcement of safety regulation began to become effective. See Guinnane & Streb (2015) for an empirical treatment of this "institutional failure."

17. The "counterfactual" being the higher amount of savings deposits the model predicts (with "Bismarck" as a negative coefficient).

18. Prussia's "middle schools" were a collection of schools that offered an advanced elementary school education (with a foreign language) for middle-class aims (skilled artisans, shopkeepers), integrated into the Prussian state system in 1872. "Higher schools" included the *Oberrealschulen, Realprogymnasium*, and so on—institutions that paved the way to the coveted "one year" military service and to study at a university or technical college.

19. "Education" (mainly schools) accounted for the largest share of Prussian municipal expenditures in this period (Tilly & Bieber 1991).

20. In Prussia tax law was made at the central government level, but even here considerable resistance virtually blocked tax increases on land.

21. Municipal investment was reflected in the growth of municipal debt, indirectly (and incompletely) captured by the budget item "debt service."

22. Further details are reported in Schremmer (1994).

REFERENCES

Abel, W. 1962. *Geschichte der deutschen Landwirtschaft.* Stuttgart: Ulmer.

Abel, W. 1966. *Agrarkrisen und Agrarkonjunktur. Eine Geschichte der Land- und Ernährungswirtschaft seit dem hohen Mittelalter.* Hamburg: Paul Parey.

Abel, W. 1977. *Massenarmut und Hungerkrisen im vorindustriellen Deutschland.* Göttingen: Vandenhoeck & Ruprecht.

Abelshauser, W., ed. 2003. *BASF. Eine Unternehmensgeschichte.* Munich: Beck.

Acemoglu, D. 2005. "Institutions as a Fundamental Cause of Long-run Growth." In P. Aghion & S. N. Durlauf, eds., *Handbook of Economic Growth, Vol. IA* (Amsterdam: Elsevier), 385–472.

Acemoglu, D., D. Cantoni, S. Johnson & J. A. Robinson. 2011. "The Consequences of Radical Reform: The French Revolution." *American Economic Review* 101:3286–307.

Ackermann, O. 1911. *Die Entwicklung der Landwirtschaft auf den Vorwerken der schönburgischen Herrschaften Wechselburg und Penig vom 16. Jahrhundert bis zur Gegenwart.* Weida: Thomas & Hubert.

Adelmann, G. 1986. "Strukturwandel der rheinischen Leinen- und Baumwollgewerbe zu Beginn der Industrialisierung." In Adelmann, *Vom Gewerbe zur Industrie im kontinentalen Nordwesteuropa, Zeitschrift für Unternehmensgeschichte,* suppl. 38, 84–106.

Adelmann, G. 2001. *Die Baumwollgewerbe Nordwestdeutschlands und der westlichen Nachbarländer beim Übergang von der vorindustriellen zur frühindustriellen Zeit 1750–1815.* Stuttgart: Franz Steiner.

Akerman, J. 1960. *Theory of Industrialism.* Lund: Gleerup.

Albers, H., & U. Pfister. 2018. *The Great Moderation: Market Integration vs. Climate Change, Germany 1650–1790.* European Historical Economics Society Working Papers 135. www.ehes.org.

Allen, R. C. 1992. *Enclosure and the Yeoman.* Oxford: Clarendon Press.

Allen, R. C. 2000. "Economic Structure and Agricultural Productivity in Europe, 1300–1800." *European Review of Economic History* 4:1–26.

Allen, R. C. 2001. "The Great Divergence in European Wages and Prices from the Middle Ages to the First World War." *Explorations in Economic History* 38:411–47.

Allen, R. C. 2009. *The British Industrial Revolution in Global Perspective.* Cambridge: Cambridge University Press.

Arndt, P. 1915. "Wesen und Zweck der Kapitalanlage im Ausland." *Zeitschrift für das gesamte Staatswissenschaft* 6:445–60.

Ashauer, G. 1998. "Die ökonomische und soziale Bedeutung der preussische Sparkassen im 19. Jahrhundert, Bankhistorisches Archiv." *Zeitschrift für Bankengeschichte* 24, no. 2:55–86.

Aubin, H. 1922. "Das rheinische Wirtschaftsleben: Agrargeschichte." In Gesellschaft für rheinische Geschichtskunde, ed., *Geschichte des Rheinlandes von der ältesten Zeit bis zur Gegenwart*, vol. 2, 115–48. Essen: G. D. Baedecker.

Baar, L. 1966. *Die Berliner Industrie in der Industriellen Revolution*. Berlin: Akademie Verlag.

Bade, K. 1980. "Massenwanderung und Arbeitsmarkt im deutschen Nordosten von 1880 bis zum Ersten Weltkrieg: überseeische Auswanderung, interne Abwanderung und kontinentale Zuwanderung." *Archiv für Sozialgeschichte* 20: 265–323.

Bade, K. 1982. "Transnationale Migration und Arbeitsmarkt im Kaiserreich. Vom Agrarstaat mit starker Industrie zum Industriestaat mit starker agrarischer Basis." In T. Pierenkemper & R. Tilly, eds., *Historische Arbeitsmarktforschung: Entstehung, Entwicklung und Probleme der Vermarktung von Arbeitskraft* (Göttingen: Vandenhoeck & Ruprecht), 182–210.

Bade, K. 2005. *Land oder Arbeit? Transnationale und interne Migration im deutschen Nordosten vor dem Ersten Weltkrieg*. Osnabrück: IMIS. URN: urn:nbn:de:gbv:700-201001304775.

Baltzer, M. 2007. *Der Berliner Kapitalmarkt nach der Reichsgründung 1871*. Berlin: LIT.

Banken, R. 2003. *Die Industrialisierung der Saarregion 1815–1914*. 2 vols. Stuttgart: Steiner.

Barkhausen, M. 1954. "Der Aufstieg der rheinischen Industrie im 18. Jahrhundert und die Entstehung eines industriellen Großbürgertums." *Rheinische Vierteljahrsblätter* 19:135–77.

Barkhausen, M. 1958. "Staatliche Wirtschaftslenkung und freies Unternehmertum im westdeutschen und im nord- und südniederländischen Raum bei der Entstehung der neuzeitlichen Industrie im 18. Jahrhundert." *Vierteljahrsschrift für Sozial- und Wirtschaftsgeschichte* 45:168–241.

Barkin, K. 1970. *The Controversy over German Industrialization 1890 to 1902*. Chicago: University of Chicago Press.

Barth, B. 1995. *Die deutsche Hochfinanz und die Imperialismen. Banken und Aussenpolitik vor 1914*. Stuttgart: Steiner.

Bass, H.-H. 1991. *Hungerkrisen in Preußen während der ersten Hälfte des 19. Jahrhunderts*. St. Katharinen: Scripta Mercaturae.

Baten, J. 1999. *Ernährung und wirtschaftliche Entwicklung in Bayern (1730–1880)*. Stuttgart: Steiner.

Becht, M., & C. Ramirez. 2003. "Does Bank Affiliation Mitigate Liquidity Restraints?" *Southern Economic Journal* 70, no. 2:254–72.

Becker, G. 1964. *Human Capital: A Theoretical and Empirical Analysis, with Special Reference to Education*. Chicago: University of Chicago Press.

Becker, S., F. Cinnirella & L. Woessmann. 2013. "Does Women's Education Affect Fertility? Evidence from Pre-Demographic Transition Prussia." *European Review of Economic History* 17:24–44.

Becker, S., E. Hornung & L. Woessmann. 2011. "Education and Catch-up in the Industrial Revolution." *American Economic Journal: Macroeconomics* 3, no. 3:92–126.

Becker, S., & L. Woesmann. 2009. "Was Weber Wrong? A Human Capital Theory of Protestant Economic History." *Quarterly Journal of Economics* 124:531–96.

Becker, W. 1960. "Die Bedeutung der nichtagrarischen Wanderung für die Herausbildung des industriellen Proletariats in Deutschland, unter besonderer Berücksichtigung Preussens von 1850 bis 1870." In H. Mottek, ed., *Studien zur Geschichte der Industriellen Revolution in Deutschland* (Berlin: Akademie Verlag).

Becker, W. 1962. "Die Entwicklung der deutschen Maschinenbau von 1850 bis 1870." In A. Schröter & W. Becker, *Die deutsche Maschinenbau in der industriellen Revolution* (Berlin: Akademie Verlag), 137–258.

Behre, O. 1979 (1905). *Geschichte der Statistik in Brandenburg-Preußen bis zur Gründung des Königlich Statistischen Bureaus*. Berlin: Carl Heymanns.

Behrens, C. B. A. 1985. *Society, Government and the Enlightenment. The Experiences of Eighteeth-Century France and Prussia*. London: Thames & Hudson.

Bein, L. 1884. *Die Industrie des sächsischen Voigtlandes*. Vol. 2, *Die Textilindustrie*. Leipzig: Dunker & Humblot.

Benaerts, P. 1933. *Les origines de la grande industrie allemande*. Paris: Turot.

Berdahl, R. M. 1988. *The Politics of the Prussian Nobility. The Development of a Conservative Ideology, 1770–1848*. Princeton, NJ: Princeton University Press.

Berding, H. 1973. *Napoleonische Herrschafts- und Gesellschaftspolitik im Königreich Westphalen 1807–1813*. Göttingen: Vandenhoeck & Ruprecht.

Berding, H. 1980. "Die Reform des Zollwesens in Deutschland unter dem Einfluss der napoleonischen Herrschaft." *Geschichte und Gesellschaft* 6, no. 4:523–37.

Berding, H. 1996. "Zur historischen Einordnung der Reformen im frühen 19. Jahrhundert." In H.-P. Ullmann & C. Zimmermann, eds., *Restaurationssystem und Reformpolitik. Süddeutschland und Preußen im Vergleich* (Munich: Oldenbourg), 17–24.

Berding, H. 2008. "Das Königreich Westphalen als napoleonischer Modell- und Satellitenstaat (1807–1813)." In G. Dehtlefs, A. Owzar & G. Weiß, eds., *Modell und Wirklichkeit. Politik, Kultur und Gesellschaft im Großherzogtum Berg und im Königreich Westphalen 1806–1813* (Paderborn: Schöningh), 15–29.

Berdrow, W. 1927. *Alfred Krupp*. 2 vols. Berlin: Hobbing.

Berger, H., & M. Spoerer. 2001. "Economic Crises and the European Revolutions of 1848." *Journal of Economic History* 61:293–326.

Bergfeld, C. 1987. "Preussen und das Allgemeine Deutsche Handelsgesetzbuch." *Ius Commune* 14:101–14.

Berghahn, V. 1971. *Der Tirpitzplan. Genesis und Verfall einer innenpolitischen Krisenstrategie unter Wilhelm II*. Düsseldorf: Droste.

Berghoff, H., & T. Möller. 1994. "Tired Pioneers and Dynamic Newcomers: A Comparative Essay on English and German Entrepreneurial History." *Economic History Review* 47, no. 2:262–87.

Bergmann, J. 1976. "Ökonomische Voraussetzungen der Revolution von 1848." *Geschichte und Gesellschaft*, special issue: 254–87.

Bernert, G. 1982. "Die französischen Gewerbegerichte (Conseils de Prud'hommes) und ihre Einführung in den linksrheinischen Gebieten zwischen 1808 und 1813." In K. O. Scherner & D. Willoweit, eds., *Vom Gewerbe zum Unternehmen. Studien zum Recht der gewerblichen Wirtschaft im 18. und 19. Jahrhundert* (Darmstadt: WBG), 112–51.

Berthold, R. 1962. "Einige Bemerkungen über den Entwicklungsstand des bäuerlichen Ackerbaus vor den Agrarreformen des 19. Jahrhunderts." In Berthold, ed., *Beiträge zur deutschen Wirtschafts- und Sozialgeschichte des 18. und 19. Jahrhunderts* (Berlin: Akademie Verlag).

Berthold, R. 1974. "Der sozialökonomische Differenzierungsprozess der Bauernschaft in der Provinz Brandenburg während der industriellen Revolution." *Jahrbuch für Wirtschaftsgeschichte* 2:13–50.

Berthold, R. 1978. "Die Veränderungen im Bodeneigentum und in der Zahl der Bauernstellen, der Kleinstellen und Rittergüter in den preußischen Provinzen Sachsen, Brandenburg und Pommern während der Durchführung der Agrarreformen des 19.

Jahrhunderts in Preußen und Russland." *Jahrbuch für Wirtschaftsgeschichte*, special issue: 7–134.

Beyer, P. 1978. *Leipzig und die Anfänge des deutschen Eisenbahnbaus*. Weimar: Böhlau.

Binswanger, H. P., K. Deininger & G. Feder. 1995. "Power, Distortions, Revolt and Reform in Agricultural Land Relations." In H. B. Chenery & T. N. Srinivasan, eds., *Handbook of Development Economics, Vol. IIIB* (Amsterdam: North Holland), 2659–772.

Birtsch, Gü., & D. Willoweit. 1998. *Reformabsolutismus und ständische Gesellschaft. Zweihundert Jahre Preußisches Allgemeines Landrecht*. Berlin: Duncker & Humblot.

Bittner, T. 2005. "An Event Study of the Rhenish-Westphalian Coal Syndicate." *European Review of Economic History (EREH)* 9:337–64.

Blanning, T. C. W. 1974. *Reform and Revolution in Mainz 1743–1803*. Cambridge: Cambridge University Press.

Blanning, T. C. W. 1983. *The French Revolution in Germany: Occupation and Resistance in the Rhineland 1792–1802*. Oxford: Clarendon Press.

Blanning, T. C. W. 1989. "The French Revolution and the Modernization of Germany." *Central European History* 22:109–29.

Blanning, T. C. W. 2016. *Frederick the Great: King of Prussia*. London: Penguin.

Blaschke, K. 1967. *Bevölkerungsgeschichte von Sachsen bis zur industriellen Revolution*. Weimar: Böhlau.

Blaschke, K. 1974. "Wollerzeugung und Wollhandel im östlichen Mitteldeutschland bis 1700." In M. Spallanzani, ed., *La lana come materia prima. I fenomeni della sua produzione e circolazione nei secoli XIII—XVII. Atti della "Prima settimana di studio" (18—24 aprile 1969)* (Florence: Olschki), 67–74.

Blaschke, K. 1984. "Entwicklungstendenzen im sächsischen Städtewesen während des 19. Jahrhunderts (1815-1914)." In H. Matzerath, ed., *Städtewachstum und innerstädtische Strukturveränderungen* (Stuttgart: Klett-Cotta).

Blaschke, K. 2000. "Sachsen zwischen den Reformen 1763 bis 1831." In U. Schirmer, ed., *Sachsen 1763–1832. Zwischen Rétablissement und bürgerlichen Reformen* (Beucha: Sax), 9–23.

Bleek, S. 1989. "Mobilität und Sesshaftigkeit in deutschen Grossstädten während der Urbanisierung." *Geschichte und Gesellschaft* 15:5–33.

Blickle, P. 2006. *Von der Leibeigenschaft zu den Menschenrechten. Eine Geschichte der Freiheit in Deutschland*. Munich: Beck.

Bloomfield, A. 1963. *Short-Term Capital Movements under the Pre-1914 Gold Standard*. Princeton Studies in International Finance 11. Princeton, NJ: Princeton University Press.

Blumberg, H. 1960. *Die Finanzierung der Neugründung und Erweiterungen von Industriebetrieben in Form der Aktiengesellschaft während der fünfziger Jahre des neunzehnten Jahrhunderts in Deutschland am Beispiel der preußischen Verhältnisse erläutert*. Berlin: Akademie-Verlag.

Blumberg, H. 1965. *Die deutsche Textilindustrie in der industriellen Revolution*. Berlin: Akademie-Verlag.

Boch, R. 1991. *Grenzenloses Wachstum? Das rheinische Wirtschaftsbürgertum und seine Industrialisierungsdebatte 1814–1857*. Göttingen: Vandenhoeck & Ruprecht.

Boch, R. 2004. *Staat und Wirtschaft im 19. Jahrhundert*. Enzyklopädie deutscher Geschichte 70. Munich: Oldenbourg.

Boch, R. 2016. "Das Bergische Land im 19. Jahrhundert (1814-1914)." In S. Gorißen, H. Sassin & K. Wesoly, eds., *Geschichte des Bergischen Landes. Das 19. und 20. Jahrhundert* (Bielefeld: Verlag für Regionalgeschichte), 171–267.

Bodemer, H. 1856. *Die industrielle Revolution mit besonderer Berücksichtigung auf die erzge-birgschen Erwerbsverhältnisse*. Dresden: Kuntze.

Boelcke, W. A. 1970. *Krupp und die Hohenzollern in Dokumenten*. Frankfurt am Main: Akademische Verlagsgesellschaft Athenaion.

Boelcke, W. A. 1973. "Wege und Probleme des industriellen Wachstums im Königreich Württemberg." *Zeitschrift für Württembergische Landesgeschichte* 32: 436–520.

Böhme, H. 1966. *Deutschlands Weg zur Großmacht*. Cologne: Kiepenheuer & Witsch.

Boldorf, M. 2004. "Märkte und Verlage im institutionellen Gefüge der Leinenregion Niederschlesien des 18. Jahrhunderts." In K.-P. Ellerbrock & C. Wischermann, eds., *Die Wirtschaftsgeschichte vor der Herausforderung durch die New Institutional Economics* (Dortmund: Gesellschaft für Westfälische Wirtschaftsgeschichte).

Boldorf, M. 2006. *Europäische Leinenregionen im Wandel. Institutionelle Weichenstellungen in Schlesien und Irland (1750–1850)*. Cologne: Böhlau.

Boldorf, M. 2009. "Entwicklung in die Sackgasse. Das niederschlesische Textilgewerbe im 19. Jahrhundert." In Toni Pierenkemper, ed., *Regionen und regionale Industrialisierung. Zur wirtschaftlichen Entwicklung ostmitteleuropäischer Regionen im 19. Jahrhundert* (Aachen: Shaker), 33–47.

Bolenz, J. 1965. "Wachstum und Strukturwandlungen der kommunalen Ausgaben in Deutschland 1849-1914." PhD diss., University of Freiburg.

Bölsker-Schlicht, F. 1990. "Sozialgeschichte des ländlichen Raumes im ehemaligen Regierungsbezirk Osnabrück unter besonderer Berücksichtigung des Heuerlingswesens und einzelner Nebengewerbe." *Westfälische Forschungen* 40:223-50.

Borchardt, K. 1961. "Zur Frage des Kapitalmangels in der ersten Hälfte des 19. Jahrhunderts in Deutschland." *Jahrbuch für Nationalökonomie und Statistik* 173:401-21.

Borchardt, K. 1966. "Regionale Wachstumsdifferenzen in Deutschland im 19. Jahrhundert unter besonderer Berücksichtigung des West-Ost-Gefälles." In W. Abel et al., eds., *Wirtschaft. Geschichte und Wirtschaftsgeschichte. Festschrift zum 65. Geburtstag von F. Lütge* (Stuttgart: Gustav Fischer), 325–39.

Borchardt, K. 1976. "Währung und Wirtschaft." In Deutsche Bundesbank, ed., *Währung und Wirtschaft in Deutschland, 1876–1975* (Frankfurt am Main: Knapp).

Borght, R. v. d. 1883. *Statistische Studien über die Bewährung der Aktiengesellschaft*. Jena: G. Fischer.

Born, K.-E. 1977. *Geld und Banken im 19. und 20. Jahrhundert*. Stuttgart: Kröner.

Borries, B. von. 1970. *Deutschlands Aussenhandel 1836 bis 1856. Eine statistische Untersuchung zur Frühindustrialisierung*. Stuttgart: Fischer.

Boserup, E. 1965. *The Conditions of Agricultural Growth: The Economics of Agrarian Change under Population Pressure*. London: Allen & Unwin.

Boserup, E. 1981. *Population and Technology*. Oxford: Blackwell.

Boserup, M. 1972 (1963). "Agrarstruktur und Take Off." In R. Braun, W. Fischer, H. Großkreutz & H. Volkamann, eds., *Industrielle Revolution. Wirtschaftliche Aspekte* (Cologne: Kiepenheuer), 309–30.

Bösselmann, K. 1939. *Die Entwicklung des deutschen Aktienwesens im 19. Jahrhundert. Ein Beitrag zur Frage der Finanzierung gemeinwirtschaftlicher Unternehmungen und zu den Reformen des Aktienrechts*. Berlin: de Gruyter.

Bracht, J. 2013. *Geldlose Zeiten und überfüllte Kassen. Sparen, Leihen und Vererben in der ländlichen Gesellschaft Westfalens (1830–1866)*. Stuttgart: Lucius & Lucius.

Brakensiek, S. 1991. *Agrarreform und ländliche Gesellschaft. Die Privatisierung der Marken in Nordwestdeutschland 1750–1850*. Paderborn: Schöningh.

Brakensiek, S. 2004. "Die Auflösung der Marken im 18. und 19. Jahrhundert. Probleme und Ergebnisse der Forschung." In U. Meiners & W. Rösener, eds., *Allmenden und Marken vom Mittelalter bis zur Neuzeit* (Cloppenburg: Museumsdorf Cloppenburg), 157–69.

Bräuer, H. 1990. "Das zünftige Handwerk in Sachsen und die 'Landes-Oeconomie- Manufactur- und Commercien-Deputation' im 18. Jahrhundert." In K. Czok & H. Bräuer, eds., *Studien zur älteren sächsischen Handwerksgeschichte* (Berlin: Akademie Verlag), 50–84.

Braun, R. 1975. "Taxation, Sociopolitical Structure, and State-Building: Great Britain and Brandenburg-Prussia." In C. Tilly, ed., *The Formation of States in Western Europe* (Princeton, NJ: Princeton University Press).

Brepohl, W. 1957. *Industrievolk im Wandel von der agraren zur industriellen Daseinsform, dargestellt am Ruhrgebiet.* Tübingen: Mohr.

Broadberry, S., & C. Burhop. 2007. "Comparative Productivity in British and German Manufacturing before World War II: Reconciling Direct Benchmark Estimates and Time Series Projections." *Journal of Economic History* 67:315–46.

Broadberry, S., & C. Burhop. 2010. "Real Wages and Labor Productivity in Britain and Germany, 1871–1938: A Unified Approach to International Comparison of Living Standards." *Journal of Economic History* 70:400–427.

Broadberry, S., & K. O'Rourke, eds. 2010. *The Cambridge Economic History of Modern Europe.* Cambridge: Cambridge University Press.

Broadberry, S. N. 1997. "Anglo-German Productivity Differences, 1870–1990: A Sectoral Analysis." *European Review of Economic History* 1–2:247–67.

Brockhage, B. 1910. *Zur Entwicklung des preussisch-deutschen Kapitalexports.* Staats- und Sozialwissenschaftliche Forschungen 148. Leipzig: Duncker & Humblot.

Brown, J. 1988. "Coping with Crisis: The Diffusion of Waterworks in Late Nineteenth-Century German Towns." *Journal of Economic History* 48, no. 2:307–318.

Brown, J. 1995. "Imperfect Competition and Anglo-German Trade Rivalry: Markets for Cotton Textiles before 1914." *Journal of Economic History* 55:494–527.

Brown, J., & T. Guinnane. 2002. "The Fertility Transition in Bavaria." *Population Studies* 56:35–49.

Brown, J., & T. Guinnane. 2018. "Infant Mortality and Urban Bavaria: Fertility Decline, Economic Transformation, Infant Care and Inequality in Bavaria and Munich, 1825–1910." *Economic History Review* 71:853–86.

Bry, G. 1968. *Wages in Germany, 1871–1908.* Oxford: Oxford University Press.

Buchheim, C. 1983. *Deutsche Gewerbeexporte nach England in der zweiten Hälfte des 19. Jahrhunderts.* Ostfildern: Scripta Mercaturae.

Burchardt, L. 1975. *Wissenschaftspolitik in Wilhelminischen Deutschland. Vorgeschichte, Gründung und Aufbau der Kaiser-Wilhelms-Gesellschaft zur Förderung der Wissenschaft.* Göttingen: Vandenhoeck & Ruprecht.

Burhop, C. 2002. "Die Entwicklung der deutschen Aktienkreditbanken von 1848 bis 1913." *Bankhistorisches Archiv* 2:103–28.

Burhop, C. 2006. "Did Banks Cause the German Industrialization?" *Explorations in Economic History* 43:39–63.

Burhop, C. 2010. "The Transfer of Patents in Imperial Germany." *Journal of Economic History* 70, no. 4:921–39.

Burhop, C. 2011. *Wirtschaftsgeschichte des Kaiserreichs 1871–1918.* Göttingen: UTB.

Burhop, C., T. Guinnane, & R. Tilly. 2018. "The Financial System in Germany." In T. Beck & R. Levine, eds., *Handbook of Finance and Development.* Elgar Online.

Burhop, C., & S. Lehmann-Hasemeyer. 2016. "The Berlin Stock Exchange and the Geography of German Stock Markets in 1913." *European Review of Economic History* 20, no. 4:429–51.

Burhop, C., & T. Lübbers. 2009. "Cartels, Managerial Incentives, and Production Efficiency in German Coal Mining, 1881–1913." *Journal of Economic History* 69:500–527.

Burhop, C., & T. Lübbers. 2010. "Incentives and Innovation: R & D Management in Germany's Chemical and Electrical Engineering Industries around 1900." *Explorations in Economic History* 47:100–111.

Burhop, C., & G. Wolff. 2005. "A Compromise Estimate of German Net National Product, 1851–1913." *Journal of Economic History* 65:613–57.

Büsch, O. 1962. *Militärsystem und Sozialleben im alten Preußen 1713–1807. Die Anfänge der sozialen Militarisierung der preußisch-deutschen Gesellschaft.* Berlin: de Gruyter.

Büsch, O. 1980. "Linien und Perioden der gewerblichen Entwicklung in Brandenburg von 1800 bis 1850." In B. Vogel, ed., *Preußische Reformen 1807–1820* (Königstein: Verlagsgruppe Athenäum-Hain-Scriptor-Hanstein), 132–49.

Cameron, R. 1961. *France and the Economic Development of Europe 1800–1914.* Chicago: Rand McNally & Co.

Cantoni, D., & N. Yuchtman. 2014. "Medieval Universities, Legal Institutions, and the Commercial Revolution." *Quarterly Journal of Economics* 129:823–87.

Carosso, V. 1970. *Investment Banking in America: A History.* Cambridge: Cambridge University Press.

Carsten, F. L. 1959. *Princes and Parliaments in Germany: From the Fifteenth to the Eighteenth Century.* Oxford: Clarendon Press.

Carsten, F. L. 1968. *Die Entstehung Preußens.* Cologne: Kiepenheuer & Witsch.

Chandler, A. 1990. *Scale and Scope: Dynamics of Industrial Capitalism.* Cambridge, MA: Harvard University Press at the Belknap Press.

Cinnirella, F., & E. Hornung. 2016. "Landownership Concentration and the Expansion of Education." *Journal of Development Economics* 121:135–52.

Cinnirella, F., & J. Streb. 2017. "The Role of Human Capital and Innovation in Economic Development: Evidence from Post-Malthusian Prussia." *Journal of Economic Growth* 22:193–227.

Clapham, J. H. 1964. *An Economic History of Modern Britain, Vol. 1.* Cambridge: Cambridge University Press.

Clark, G. 2007. *A Farewell to Alms: A Brief Economic History of the World.* Princeton, NJ: Princeton University Press.

Conze, W. 1954. "Vom Pöbel zum Proletariat. Sozialgeschichtliche Voraussetzungen für den Sozialismus in Deutschland." *Vierteljahrsschrift für Sozial- und Wirtschaftsgeschichte* 41:333–64.

Corni, G. 1986. "Absolutistische Agrarpolitik und Agrargesellschaft in Preußen." *Zeitschrift für die historische Forschung* 13:285–313.

Coym, P. 1971. "Unternehmensfinanzierung im 19. Jahrhundert—dargestellt am Beispiel der Rheinprovinz und Westfalen." Diss., University of Hamburg.

Crafts, N. 1985. *British Economic Growth during the Industrial Revolution.* New York: Oxford University Press.

Crafts, N., S. Leybourne & T. Mills. 1991. "Britain." In R. Sylla & G. Toniolo, eds., *Patterns of European Industrialization: The Nineteenth Century* (New York: Routledge).

Crouzet, F. 1958. *L'économie britannique et le Blocus Continental, 1806–13.* 2 vols. Paris: Presses Universitaires de France.

Crouzet, F. 1964. "Wars, Blockade, and Economic Change in Europe, 1792–1815." *Journal of Economic History* 24, no. 4:567–88.

Crüger, H. 1912. "Der Staat und das Genossenschaftswesen." *Schmollers Jahrbuch* 36: 305–23.

Cubells, M. 2005. "Parlamente." In H. Reinalter, ed., *Lexikon zum aufgeklärten Absolutismus in Europa. Herrscher—Denker—Sachbegriffe* (Vienna: Böhlau/UTB), 457–62.

Däbritz, W. 1906. *Die Staatsschulden Sachsens in der Zeit von 1763 bis 1837.* Leipzig: Teubner.

Däbritz, W. 1925. "Entstehung und Aufbau des rheinisch-westfälischen Industriebezirks." *Beiträge zur Geschichte der Technik und Industrie* 15:13–107.

Däbritz, W. 1931. *Gründung und Anfänge der Disconto-Gesellschaft.* Berlin: Duncker & Humblot.

Da Rin, M. 1996. "Understanding the Development of the German Kreditbanken, 1850–1914: An Approach from the Economics of Information." *Financial History Review* 3, no. 1:29–47.

Davis, L., & R. Huttenback. 1986. *Mammon and the Pursuit of Empire: The Economics of British Imperialism.* Cambridge: Cambridge University Press.

Deane, P., & W. A. Cole. 1969. *British Economic Growth, 1688–1959.* 2d ed. Cambridge: Cambridge University Press.

De Cecco, M. 1974. *Money and Empire: The International Gold Standard, 1890–1914.* Oxford: Oxford University Press.

Dehlinger, G. 1897. "Überblick über die Entwicklung der Landwirtschaft in Württemberg seit der Mitte des 18. Jahrhunderts." *Württembergische Jahrbücher für Statistik und Landeskunde* 1:49–76.

Dehtlefs, G. 2008. "Gewerbefreiheit—Patentsteuer—Aufhebung der Zünfte in Westfalen 1808–1820. Münster und Osnabrück im Vergleich." In G. Dehtlefs, A. Owzar & G. Weiß, eds., *Modell und Wirklichkeit. Politik, Kultur und Gesellschaft im Großherzogtum Berg und im Königreich Westphalen 1806–1813* (Paderborn: Schöningh), 389–408.

Demel, W. 2010. *Vom aufgeklärten Reformstaat zum bürokratischen Staatsabsolutismus.* Munich: Oldenbourg.

Desai, A. V. 1968. *Real Wages in Germany 1871–1913.* Oxford: Clarendon Press.

Deutsche Bundesbank, ed. 1976. *Währung und Wirtschaft in Deutschland, 1876–1975.* Frankfurt am Main: Knapp.

Dickler, R. 1975a. "Labor Market Pressure Aspects of Agricultural Growth in the Eastern Region of Prussia, 1840–1914." PhD diss., University of Pennsylvania.

Dickler, R. 1975b. "Organization and Change in Productivity in Eastern Prussia." In W. N. Parker & E. L. Jones, eds., *European Peasants and Their Markets* (Princeton, NJ: Princeton University Press), 269–92.

Diefendorf, J. M. 1980. *Businessmen and Politics in the Rhineland, 1789–1834.* Princeton, NJ: Princeton University Press.

Dieterici, C. F. W. 1844. *Statistische Übersicht der wichtigsten Gegenstande des Verkehrs und Verbrauchs: Als Fortsetzung d. Ferberschen Beitr./aus amtlichen Quellen, 3. Fortsetzung. 2: Im deutschen Zollvereine, Zeitraum von 1840–1842.* Berlin: Mittler.

Dieterici, C. F. W. 1846. *Der Volkswohlstand im Preussischen Staate.* Berlin: Mittler.

Dipper, C. 1980. *Die Bauernbefreiung in Deutschland 1790–1850.* Stuttgart: Kohlhammer.

Dipper, C. 1989. "Bauernbefreiung, landwirtschaftliche Entwicklung und Industrialisierung in Deutschland. Die nichtpreußischen Staaten." In T. Pierenkemper, ed., *Landwirtschaft und industrielle Entwicklung* (Stuttgart), 61–75.

Dipper, C. 1996a. "Wirtschaftspolitische Grundsatzentscheidungen in Süddeutschland." In H.-P. Ullmann & C. Zimmermann, eds., *Restaurationssystem und Reformpolitik. Süddeutschland und Preußen im Vergleich* (Munich: Oldenbourg), 129–61.

Dipper, C. 1996b. "Übergangsgesellschaft. Die ländliche Sozialordnung in Mitteleuropa um 1800." *Zeitschrift für historische Forschung* 23:57–87.

Ditt, K. 1982. *Industrialisierung, Arbeiterschaft und Arbeiterbewegung in Bielefeld.* Dortmund: Ges. für Westfälische Wirtschaftsgeschichte.

Donges, A., & F. Selgert. 2019. "Technology Transfer via Foreign Patents in Germany, 1843–77." *Economic History Review* 72, no. 1:182–208.

Dufraisse, R. 1981. 'Französische Zollpolitik, Kontinentalsperre und Kontinentalsystem im Deutschland der Napoleonischen Zeit." In H. Berding & H.-P. Ullmann, eds., *Deutschland zwischen Revolution und Restauration* (Königstein: Verlagsgruppe Athenäum-Hain-Scriptor-Hanstein), 238–352.

Dumke, R. 1981. "Die wirtschaftlichen Folgen des Zollvereins." In W. Abelshauser & D. Petzina, eds., *Deutsche Wirtschaftsgeschichte im Industriezeitalter* (Düsseldorf: Athenäum-Verlag), 241–73.

Dumke, R. 1984. "Der Deutsche Zollverein als Modell ökonomischer Integration." In H. Berding, ed., *Wirtschaftliche und politische Integration in Europa im 19. und 20. Jahrhundert* (Göttingen: Vandenhoeck & Ruprecht), 71–101.

Dumke, R. 1991. "Income Inequality and Industrialization in Germany, 1850–1913: The Kuznets Hypothesis Re-examined." In Y. S. Brenner, H. Kaelble & M. Thomas, eds., *Income Distribution in Historical Perspective* (Cambridge: Cambridge University Press).

Dumke, R. 1994 (1977). "The Political Economy of German Economic Unification: Tariffs, Trade and Politics of the Zollverein Era." PhD diss., University of Wisconsin.

Easterlin, R. 1961. "Influences in European Overseas Emigration before World War I." *Economic Development and Cultural Change* 9:331–51. Reprinted in Fogel & Engermann, eds., *The Reinterpretation of American Economic History* (New York: Harper & Row: 1971).

Ebeling, D. 2000. "Zunfthandwerk, Heimarbeit und Manufakturwesen in den Rheinlanden während des 18. Jahrhunderts." In Ebeling, ed., *Aufbruch in eine neue Zeit. Gewerbe, Staat und Unternehmer in den Rheinlanden des 18. Jahrhunderts.* (Cologne: DuMont), 10–32.

Eddie, S. 1989. "Economic Policy and Economic Development in Austria-Hungary, 1867–1913." In *Cambridge Economic History of Europe, Vol. 8* (Cambridge: Cambridge University Press).

Eddie, S. A. 2013. *Freedom's Price: Serfdom, Subjection, and Reform in Prussia, 1648–1848.* Oxford: Oxford University Press.

Edelstein, M. 1982. *Overseas Investment in the Age of High Imperialism: The United Kingdom, 1850–1914.* (London: Methuen).

Edwards, J. 2018. "A Replication of 'Education and Catch-up in the Industrial Revolution' (*American Economic Journal: Macroeconomics*, 2011)." *Economics: The Open-Access, Open-Assesment E-Journal* 12, no. 3:1–33. http://dx.doi.org/10.5018/economics-ejournal.ja.2018-3.

Ehmer, J. 1991. *Heiratsverhalten, Sozialstruktur, ökonomischer Wandel: England und Mitteleuropa in der Formationsperiode des Kapitalismus.* Kritische Studien zur Geschichtswissenschaft 92. Göttingen: Vandenhoeck & Ruprecht.

Ellis, F. 1996. *Peasant Economics: Farm Households and Agrarian Development.* Cambridge: Cambridge University Press.

Enders, L. 1989. "Bauern und Feudalherrschaft der Uckermark im absolutistischen Staat." *Jahrbuch für Geschichte des Feudalismus* 13:247–83.

Enders, L. 1990. "Produktivkraftentwicklung und Marktverhalten. Die Agrarproduzenten der Uckermark im 18. Jahrhundert." *Jahrbuch für Wirtschaftsgeschichte*, no. 3:81–105.

Enders, L. 1991. "Bauern und Feudalherr in der Mark Brandenburg vom 13. bis zum 18. Jh." *Jahrbuch für Wirtschaftsgeschichte*, no. 2:9–20.

Enders, L. 1992. *Die Uckermark. Geschichte einer kurmärkischen Landschaft vom 12. bis zum 18. Jahrhundert.* Cologne: Böhlau.

Enders, L. 2000. *Die Prignitz. Geschichte einer kurmärkischen Landschaft vom 12. bis zum 18. Jahrhundert.* Potsdam: Verlag für Berlin-Brandenburg.

Engel, E. 1856. "Die physische Beschaffenheit der militärpflichtigen Bevölkerung im Königreich Sachsen." *Zeitschrift des Statistischen Bureaus des Königlich Sächsischen Ministeriums des Innern* 4–5:61–116.

Engel, E. 1857. "Die vorherrschenden Gewerbzweige in den Gerichtsämtern mit Beziehung auf die Productions- und Consumtionsverhältnisse des Königreichs Sachsens." *Zeitschrift des Statistischen Bureaus des Königlich Sächsischen Ministeriums des Innern* 8–9:153–82.

Engel, E. 1861. "Die Getreidepreise, die Ernteerträge und der Getreidehandel im preußischen Staate." *Zeitschrift des Königlich Preussischen Statistischen Bureaus* 1, no. 10: 249–87.

Engel, E. 1866. "Die Grösse, Beschaffenheit und Besteuerung der Fläche des preussischen Staatsgebietes." *Zeitschrift des Königlich Preussischen Statistischen Bureaus* 6:1–31, 162–209.

Engel, E. 1867. "Wie hoch belastet in Preussen die Grundsteuer die Landwirtschaft?" *Zeitschrift des Königlich Preussischen Statistischen Bureaus* 7:93–157.

Engel, E. 1868. "Die Eregerbnisse der Classensteuer, der classificierten Einkommensteuer und der Mahl-uns Schlachtsteuer im Preussischen Staate." *Zeitschrift des Königlich Preussischen Statistischen Bureaus* 8:25–84.

Engel, E. 1875. "Die Klassensteuer und klassifizierte Einkommensteuer im Preussischen Staat in den Jahren 1852 bis 1875." *Zeitschrift des Königlich Preussischen Statistischen Bureaus* 15:105–48.

Engel, E. 1880. *Die deutsche Industrie 1875 und 1861.* Berlin: Verl. des Königlichen Statistischen Bureaus.

Engelbrecht, J. 1996. *Das Herzogtum Berg im Zeitalter der Französischen Revolution. Modernisierungsprozesse zwischen bayerischem und französischem Modell.* Paderborn: Schöningh.

Engelbrecht, T. H. 1907. *Bodenbau und Viehstand in Schleswig Holstein.* Kiel: Verlag der Landwirtschaftskammer.

Engels, F. 1954 (1887). "Gegenwart und Zukunft der ländlichen Hausindustrie." In *Zur Wohnungsfrage.* In *Marx-Engels-Lenin-Stalin: Zur deutschen Geschichte* (Berlin: Dietz), 1037–46.

Erickson, C. 1959. *British Industrialists, 1850–1950.* Cambridge: Cambridge University Press.

Ewert, Ulrich C. 2006. 'The Biological Standard of Living on the Decline: Episodes from Germany during Early Industrialisation." *European Review of Economic History* 10:51–88.

Faust, H. 1967. *Die Zentralbank der Deutschen Genossenschaften. Vorgeschichte, Aufbau und Entwicklung der deutschen Genossenschaftskasse.* Frankfurt: Dt. Genossenschaftskasse.

Fehrenbach, E. 1983. *Traditionelle Gesellschaft und revolutionäres Recht. Die Einführung des Côde Napoléon in den Rheinbundstaaten.* Göttingen: Vandenhoeck & Ruprecht.

Fehrenbach, E. 2008. *Vom Ancien Regime zum Wiener Kongress.* Munich: Oldenbourg.

Feig, J., & W. Mewes. 1911. *Unsere Wohnungsproduktion.* Göttingen: Vandenhoeck & Ruprecht.

Feis, H. 1965 (1930). *Europe: The World's Banker, 1870–1914.* New York: W. W. Norton.

Feldenkirchen, W. 1980. "Die wirtschaftliche Rivalität zwischen Deutschland und England im 19. Jahrhundert." *Zeitschrift für Unternehmensgeschichte* 25:77–107.

Feldenkirchen, W. 1982. *Die Eisen- und Stahlindustrie des Ruhrgebiets, 1879–1914*. Wiesbaden: Steiner.

Feldenkirchen, W. 1988. "Concentration in German Industry 1870–1939." In Hans Pohl, ed., *The Concentration Process in the Entrepreneurial Economy since the Late Nineteenth Century, Zeitschrift für Unternehmensgeschichte*, suppl. 55 (Wiesbaden: Steiner).

Feldenkirchen, W. 2003. "Vom Guten das Beste." *Von Daimler und Benz zur DaimlerChrysler AG. I. Die ersten 100 Jahre*. Munich: Herbig.

Ferguson, N. 1998. *The House of Rothschild: Money's Prophets, I*. New York: Viking.

Fernihough, A., & K. H. O'Rourke. 2014. "Coal and the European Industrial Revolution." *University of Oxford—Discussion Papers in Economic and Social History* 124.

Fertig, G. 2007. *Äcker, Wirte, Gaben. Ländlicher Bodenmarkt und liberale Eigentumsordnung im Westfalen des 19. Jahrhunderts*. Berlin: Akademie Verlag.

Fertig, G., & U. Pfister. 2014. "When Did Germany Cease to Be Malthusian? The Evolution of the Preventive and Positive Checks, 1730–1870." Contribution to First European Conference on Historical Demography, Alghero.

Fertig, G., C. Schlöder, R. Gehrmann, C. Langfeldt & U. Pfister. 2018. "Das postmalthusianische Zeitalter: Die Bevölkerungsentwicklung in Deutschland, 1815–1871." *Vierteljahrschrift für Sozial- und Wirtschaftsgeschichte* 105, no. 1:6–33.

Finck von Finckenstein, W., Graf von. 1960. *Die Entwicklung der Landwirtschaft in Preussen und Deutschland 1800–1930*. Würzburg: Holzner.

Fircks, A. von. 1879. "Rückblick auf die Bewegung der Bevölkerung im preussischen Staate." *Preußische Statistik* 48A. Berlin: Verlag des Königlichen Statistischen Bureaus.

Fischer, W. 1961. *Die Bedeutung der preußischen Bergrechtsreform (1851 bis 1856) für den industriellen Aufbau des Ruhrgebiets*. Dortmund: Ardey Verlag.

Fischer, W. 1965. *Herz des Reviers. 125 Jahre Wirtschaftsgeschichte des Industrie- und Handelskammerbezirks Essen, Mülheim, Oberhausen*. Essen: Bacht.

Fischer, W. 1972. "Die Rolle des Kleingewerbes im wirtschaftlichen Wachstumsprozess in Deutschland 1850–1914." In W. Fischer, *Wirtschaft und Gesellschaft in der Industrialisierung* (Göttingen: Vandenhoeck & Ruprecht), 338–48.

Fischer, W. 1976. "Bergbau, Industrie und Handwerk." In H. Aubin & W. Zorn, eds., *Handbuch der deutschen Wirtschafts- und Sozialgeschichte* (Stuttgart: Klett), 2:527–62.

Fischer, W., & G. Bajor. 1967. *Die Soziale Frage*. Stuttgart: Koehler.

Fischer, W., J. Krengel & J. Wietog. 1982. "Materialien zur Statistik des Deutschen Bundes 1815–1870." In *Sozialgeschichtliches Arbeitsbuch, Vol.1*. Beck: Munich.

Flandreau, M. 1996. "The French Crime of 1873: An Essay on the Emergence of the International Gold Standard, 1870–1880." *Journal of Economic History* 56:862–97.

Flik, R. 1990. *Die Textilindustrie in Calw und Heidenheim 1750–1870*. Stuttgart: Steiner.

Floud, R. 1976. *The British Machine-Tool Industry, 1850–1914*. Cambridge: Cambridge University Press.

Fogel, R. 1964. *Railroads and American Economic Growth*. Baltimore: Johns Hopkins Univ. Press.

Fohlin, C. 1999. "Universal Banking in Pre-World War I Germany: Model or Myth?" *Explorations in Economic History* 36:305–43.

Fohlin, C. 2007. *Finance Capitalism and Germany's Rise to Industrial Power*. Cambridge: Cambridge University Press.

Forberger, R. 1958. *Die Manufaktur in Sachsen vom Ende des 16. bis zum Anfang des 19. Jahrhunderts*. Berlin: Akademie Verlag.

Forberger, R. 1982. *Die industrielle Revolution in Sachsen 1800–1861. Vol. 1, pt. 1: Die Revolution der Produktivkräfte in Sachsen1800–1830*. Berlin: Akademie Verlag.

Forberger, R. 1999. *Die industrielle Revolution In Sachsen 1800–1861. Vol. 2, pt. 1: Die Revolution der Produktivkräfte in Sachsen1831–1861.* Stuttgart: Steiner.

Forstmann, W. 1995. "Christian Jakob Kraus und die Männer der preußischen Reform." In Heinz Ischreyt, ed., *Königsberg und Riga* (Tübingen: Niemeyer), 123–42.

Franck, F. 1902. *Die Veränderungen in den Betriebsgrößen und Anbauverhältnissen sowie in der Viehhaltung der württembergischen Landwirtschaft in der zweiten Hälfte des 19. Jahrhunderts.* Diss. Halle: Pritschow.

Frank, H. 1994. *Regionale Entwicklungsdisparitäten im deutschen Industrialisierungsprozess 1849–1939.* Münster: LIT.

Fremdling, R. 1985. *Eisenbahnen und deutsches Wirtschaftswachstum 1840–1879. Ein Beitrag zur Entwicklungstheorie und zur Theorie der Infrastruktur.* 2d ed. Dortmund: Gesellschaft für westfälische Wirtschaftsgeschichte.

Fremdling, R. 1986. *Technologischer Wandel und internationaler Handel im 18. und 19. Jahrhundert.* Berlin: Duncker & Humblot.

Fremdling, R. 1988. "German National Accounts for 19th and Early 20th Century: A Critical Assessment." *Vierteljahrschrift für Sozial- und Wirtschaftsgeschichte* 75:339–57.

Fremdling, R. 1995. "German National Accounts for the 19th and Early 20th Century." *Scandinavian Economic History Review* 43:77–100.

Fremdling, R. & G. Hohorst. 1979. "Marktintegration der preußischen Wirtschaft im 19. Jahrhundert." In R. Fremdling & R. H. Tilly, eds., *Industrialisierung im Raum: Studien zur regionalen Differenzierung im Deutschland des 19. Jahrhunderts* (Stuttgart: Klett-Cotta), 56–104.

Freymark, H. 1898. *Die Reformen der Handels- und Zollpolitik von 1800–1821.* Jena: Fischer.

Friedeburg, R. 1996. "Heimgewerbliche Verflechtung, Wanderarbeit und Parzellenbesitz in der ländlichen Gesellschaft des Kaiserreichs." *Archiv für Sozialgeschichte* 36:27–50.

Fritzsche, B. 1985. "Mechanismen der sozialen Segregation." In H.-J. Teuteberg, ed., *Homo Habitans* (Münster: Coppenrath).

Gailus, M. 1984. *Pöbelexzesse und Volkstumulte in Berlin: zur Sozialgeschichte der Straße (1830–1980).* Berlin: Verlag Europäischen Perspektiven.

Gailus, M. 1990. *Straße und Brot. Sozialer Protest in den deutschen Staaten unter besonderer Berücksichtigung Preußens, 1847–1849.* Göttingen: Vandenhoeck & Ruprecht.

Gall, L., G. Feldman, H. James, C.-L. Holtfrerich & H. Büschgen. 1995. *Die Deutsche Bank, 1870–1995.* Munich: C. H. Beck.

Galloway, P., A. Hammel & R. Lee. 1994. "Fertility Decline in Prussia, 1875–1910: A Pooled Cross Section Time Series Analysis." *Population Studies* 48:35–158.

Galor, O. 2005. "From Stagnation to Growth: Unified Growth Theory." In P. Aghion & S. N. Durlauf, eds., *Handbook of Economic Growth, Vol. IA* (Amsterdam: Elsevier B. V.), 171–293.

Galor, O. 2011. *Unified Growth Theory.* Princeton, NJ: Princeton University Press.

Galor, O., & D. N. Weil. 2000. "Population, Technology and Growth: From the Malthusian Regime to the Demographic Transition and Beyond." *American Economic Review* 90:806–28.

Garber, J. 1979. "Spätaufklärerischer Konstitutionalismus und ökonomischer Frühliberalismus. Das Staats- und Industriebürgerkonzept der postabsolutistischen Staats-, Kameral- und Polizeiwissenschaft (Chr. D. Voss)." In J. H. Schoeps, ed., *Revolution und Demokratie in Geschichte und Literatur. Zum 60. Geburtstag von Walter Grab* (Duisburg: Braun), 61–94.

Gehrmann, R. 2000. *Bevölkerungsgeschichte Norddeutschlands zwischen Aufklärung und Vormärz.* Berlin: Berlin Verlag.

Gerschenkron, A. 1943. *Bread and Democracy in Germany*. Ithaca, NY: Cornell University Press.

Gerschenkron, A. 1962. *Economic Backwardness in Historical Perspective*. Cambridge, MA: Belknap Press of Harvard University Press.

Gerschenkron, A. 1968. *Continuity in History and Other Essays*. Cambridge, MA: Harvard University Press.

Gleitsmann, R.-J. 1980. "Rohstoffmangel und Lösungsstrategien. Das Problem vorindustrieller Holzknappheit." In F. Duve, ed., *Technologie und Politik* 16 (Reinbek: Rowohlt), 104–54.

Gleitsmann, R.-J. 1982. "Haubergswirtschaft als Beispiel für ressourcenschonende Kreislaufwirtschaft." *Scripta Mercaturae* 16, no. 1:21–54.

Goldsmith, R. 1969. *Financial Structure and Development*. New Haven, CT: Yale University Press.

Goldsmith, R. 1985. *Comparative National Balance Sheets: A Study of Twenty Countries, 1688–1978*. Chicago: University of Chicago Press.

Goltz, Th. von der. 1893. *Die ländliche Arbeiterklasse und der Preussische Staat*. Jena: G. Fischer.

Gömmel, R. 1979. *Realeinkommen in Deutschland. Ein internationaler Vergleich (1810–1914)*. Nuremberg: By the author.

Good, D. 1984. *The Economic Rise of the Habsburg Empire, 1750–1914*. Berkeley: University of California Press.

Gorißen, S. 1992. "Die Steuerreform in der Grafschaft Mark 1791. Ein Modell für die Stein-Hardenbergschen Reformen?" In S. Brakensiek et al., eds., *Kultur und Staat in der Provinz* (Bielefeld: Verlag für Regionalgeschichte), 189–212.

Gorißen, S. 2000. "Gewerbe, Staat und Unternehmer auf dem rechten Rheinufer." In D. Ebeling, ed., *Aufbruch in eine neue Zeit. Gewerbe, Staat und Unternehmer in den Rheinlanden des 18. Jahrhunderts* (Cologne: DuMont), 58–85.

Gorißen, S. 2002. *Vom Handelshaus zum Unternehmen. Sozialgeschichte der Firma Harkort im Zeitalter der Protoindustrie (1720–1820)*. Göttingen: Vandenhoeck & Ruprecht.

Gorißen, S. 2016a. "Interessen und ökonomische Funktion merkantilistischer Privilegienpolitik. Das Herzogtum Berg und seine Textilgewerbe zwischen 16. und 18. Jahrhundert." In G. Garner, ed., *Die Ökonomie des Privilegs, Westeuropa 16.–19. Jahrhundert* (Frankfurt am Main: Klostermann), 279–329.

Gorißen, S. 2016b. "Gewerbe im Herzogtum Berg vom Spätmittelalter bis 1806." In S. Gorißen, H. Sassin & K. Wesoly, eds., *Geschichte des Bergischen Landes bis zum Ende des alten Herzogtums 1806* (Bielefeld: Verlag für Regionalgeschichte), 407–67.

Gothein, E. 1903. *Geschichtliche Entwicklung der Rheinschiffahrt im XIX. Jahrhundert*. Leipzig: Duncker & Humblot.

Gould, J. D. 1972. *Economic Growth in History*. London: Methuen.

Grabas, M. 1992. *Konjunktur und Wachstum in Deutschland von 1895 bis 1914*. Berlin Duncker & Humblot.

Grant, O. 2002. "Productivity in German Agriculture: Estimates of Agricultural Productivity from Regional Accounts for 21 German Regions: 1880/4, 1893/7 and 1905/9." *Oxford University Discussion Paper in Economic and Social History* 47.

Grant, O. 2005. *Migration and Inequality in Germany 1870–1913*. Oxford: Oxford University Press.

Grant, O. 2009. "Agriculture and Economic Development in Germany, 1870–1939." In P. Lains & V. Pinilla, eds., *Agriculture and Economic Development in Europe since 1870* (London: Routledge), 178–209.

Grantham, G. 1978. "The Diffusion of the New Husbandry in Northern France." *Journal of Economic History* 38, no. 2:311–37.

Grantham, G. 1980. "The Persistence of Open-Field Farming in Nineteenth-Century France." *Journal of Economic History* 40, no. 3:515–31.

Grantham, G. 1989. "Agricultural Supply during the Industrial Revolution: French Evidence and European Implications." *Journal of Economic History* 49:43–72.

Grantham, G. 1999. "Contra Ricardo: On the Macroeconomics of Pre-industrial Economies." *European Review of Economic History* 3, no. 2:199–232.

Gray, M. W. 1973. "Schroetter, Schön, and Society: Aristocratic Liberalism versus Middle-Class Liberalism in Prussia, 1808." *Central European History* 6:60–82.

Groß, Reiner. 1968. *Die bürgerliche Agrarreform in Sachsen in der ersten Hälfte des 19. Jahrhunderts*. Weimar: Hermann Böhlaus Nachfolger.

Grumbach, F. 1957. "Statistische Untersuchungen über die Einkommensentwicklung in Deutschland." PhD diss., University of Münster.

Grüne, N. 2011. *Dorfgesellschaft—Konflikterfahrung—Partizipationskultur. Sozialer Wandel und politische Kommunikation in Landgemeinden der badischen Rheinpfalz (1720–1850)*. Stuttgart: Lucius & Lucius.

Grüne, N. 2016. "Marktorientierte Agrarproduktion als dörflicher (Des-)Integrationsfaktor. Ressourcenzugang und Sonderkulturen in der badischen Pfalz." In J. Ebert & W. Troßbach, eds., *Dörfliche Erwerbs- und Nutzungsorientierungen (Mitte 17. Bis Anfang 19. Jahrhundert) Bausteine zu einem überregionalen Vergleich* (Kassel: Kassel University Press).

Gudermann, Rita (2000) *Morastwelt und Paradies. Ökonomie und Ökologie in der Landwirtschaft am Beispiel der Meliorationen in Westfalen und Brandenburg (1830–1880)*. Paderborn: Schöning.

Guinnane, T. W. 2001. "Cooperatives as Information Machines: German Rural Credit Cooperatives, 1883–1914." *Journal of Economic History* 61:366–89.

Guinnane, T. W. 2002. "Delegated Monitors, Large and Small: Germany's Banking System, 1800–1913." *Journal of Economic Literature* 40:73–124.

Guinnane, T. W. 2003. "Population and the Economy in Germany, 1800–1990." In S. Ogilvie & R. Overy, eds., *Germany: A New Social and Economic History, Vol. 3 (Since 1800)* (London: Arnold).

Guinnane, T. W. 2013. "Zwischen Selbsthilfe und Staatshilfe: Die Anfänge genossenschaftlicher Zentralbanken in Deutschland (1864–1914)." In *Die Geschichte der DZ Bank. Das genossenschaftliche Zentralbankwesen vom 19. Jahrhundert bis Heute* (Munich: C. H. Beck).

Guinnane, T. W. 2018. "German Company Law 1794–1897." In H. Wells, ed., *The Research Handbook on the History of Corporate and Company Law* (Cheltenham, UK : Edward Elgar).

Guinnane, T. W., R. Harris, N. Lamoreaux & J. L. Rosenthal. 2007. "Putting the Corporation in its Place." *Enterprise and Society* 8, no. 3:687–729.

Guinnane, T. W., & J. Streb. 2011. "Moral Hazard in a Mutual Health-Insurance System: German Knappschaften, 1867–1914." *Journal of Economic History* 71:70–104.

Guinnane, T. W., & J. Streb. 2015. "Incentives That (Could Have) Saved Lives: Government Regulation of Accident Insurance Associations in Germany, 1884–1914." *Journal of Economic History* 75:1196–227.

Gutberlet, T. 2013. "Mechanization, Transportation, and the Location of Industry in Germany 1846–1907." PhD diss., University of Arizona.

Gutberlet, T. 2014. "Mechanization and the Spatial Distribution of Industries in the German Empire, 1875 to 1914." *Economic History Review* 67:463–91.

Gysin, J. 1989. *"Fabriken und Manufakturen" in Württemberg während des ersten Drittels des 19. Jahrhunderts.* St. Katharinen: Scripta Mercaturae Verlag.

Hagen, W. W. 1986. "The Junkers' Faithless Servants: Peasant Subordination and the Breakdown of Serfdom in Brandenburg-Prussia, 1763–1811." In R. J. Evans & W. R. Lee, eds., *The German Peasantry* (London: Croom Helm), 71–101.

Hagen, W. W. 1995. "Der bäuerliche Lebensstandard unter brandenburgischer Gutsherrschaft im 18. Jahrhundert." In J. Peters, ed., *Gutsherrschaft als soziales Modell, Historische Zeitschrift,* suppl., n.s. 18:179–96.

Hagen, W. W. 1998. "Village Life in East-Elbian Germany and Poland, 1400–1800." In T. Scott, ed., *The Peasantries of Europe: From the Fourteenth to the Eighteenth Centuries* (London: Longman), 145–89.

Hagen, W. W. 2002. *Ordinary Prussians: Brandenburg Junkers and Villagers, 1500–1840.* Cambridge: Cambridge University Press.

Hagen, W. W. 2005. "Two Ages of Seigniorial Economy in Brandenburg-Prussia: Structural Innovation in the Sixteenth Century, Productivity Gains in the Eighteenth Century." In P. Janssens & B. Y. Casallila, eds., *European Aristocracies and Colonial Elites: Patrimonial Management Strategies and Economic Development, Fifteenth to Eighteenth Centuries* (Aldershot, UK: Ashgate), 137–53.

Hahn, M. 2000. "Handwerkliches Unternehmertum und Unternehmerpotential eines entwickelten sächsischen Gewerbezentrums—Das Beispiel der Chemnitzer Zeug- und Leinweberinnung." In U. Schirmer, ed., *Sachsen 1763–1832. Zwischen Rétablissement und bürgerlichen Reformen* (Beucha: Sax), 109–27.

Hailer, H. 1902. *Studien über den deutschen Brot-Getreidehandel in den Jahren 1880–1899 insbesondere über den Einfluss der Staffeltarife und der Aufhebung des Identitätsnachweises.* Jena: Fischer.

Hammer, M. 1997. *Volksbewegungen und Obrigkeiten. Revolution in Sachsen 1830/31.* Weimar: Böhlau.

Hansen, J. 1906. *Gustav von Mevissen.* 2 vols. Berlin: Reimer.

Hardach, K. 1967. *Die Bedeutung wirtschaftlicher Faktoren bei der Wiedereinführung der Eisen- und Getreidezölle in Deutschland.* Berlin: Duncker & Humblot.

Harnisch, H. 1976. "Agrarpolitische und volkswirtschaftliche Konzeption einer kapitalistischen Agrarreform bei Christian Friedrich Scharnweber." *Wissenschaftliche Mitteilungen. Historikergesellschaft der Deutschen Demokratischen Republik* 2–3:66–87.

Harnisch, H. 1977. "Die Bedeutung der kapitalistischen Agrarreform für die Herausbildung des inneren Marktes und die Industrielle Revolution in den östlichen Provinzen Preussens in der ersten Hälfte des 19. Jahrhunderts." *Jahrbuch für Wirtschaftsgeschichte* 18, no. 4:63–82.

Harnisch, H. 1978a. "Produktivkräfte und Produktionsverhältnisse in der Landwirtschaft der Magdeburger Börde von der Mitte des 18. Jahrhunderts bis zum Beginn des Zuckerrübenanbaus in der Mitte der dreißiger Jahre des 19. Jahrhunderts." In H.-J. Rach & B. Weissel, eds., *Landwirtschaft und Kapitalismus. Zur Entwicklung der ökonomischen und sozialen Verhältnisse in der Magdeburger Börde vom Ausgang des 18. Jahrhunderts bis zum Ende des Ersten Weltkrieges,* vol. 1, pt. 1 (Berlin: Akademie Verlag), 67–173.

Harnisch, H. 1978b. "Vom Oktoberedikt des Jahres 1807 zur Deklaration von 1816. Problematik und Charakter der preußischen Agrarreformgesetzgebung zwischen 1807 und 1816." *Jahrbuch für Wirtschaftsgeschichte,* special issue, 231–93.

Harnisch, H. 1982. "Die kapitalistischen Agrarreformen in den preußischen Ostprovinzen und die Entwicklung der Landwirtschaft in den Jahrzehnten vor 1848. Ein Beitrag zum Verhältnis zwischen kapitalistischer Agrarentwicklung und Industrieller Revolution," *Jahrbuch für Wirtschaftsgeschichte*, special issue, 135–254.

Harnisch, H. 1984. *Kapitalistische Agrarreform und industrielle Revolution. Agrarhistorische Untersuchungen über das ostelbische Preußen zwischen Spätfeudalismus und bürgerlich-demokratischer Revolution 1848/49 unter besonderer Berücksichtigung der Provinz Brandenburg.* Weimar: Böhlau.

Harnisch, H. 1986. "Peasants and Markets: The Background to the Agrarian Reforms in Feudal Prussia East of Elbe, 1760–1807." In Richard J. Evans & W. R. Lee, eds., *The German Peasantry* (London: Croom Helm), 37–70.

Harnisch, H. 1989. "Bäuerliche Ökonomie und Mentalität unter den Bedingungen der ostelbischen Gutsherrschaft in den letzten Jahrzehnten vor Beginn der Agrarreformen." *Jahrbuch für Wirtschaftsgeschichte*, no. 3:87–108.

Harnisch, H. 1994a. "Der preußische Absolutismus und die Bauern. Sozialkonservative Gesellschaftspolitik und Vorleistung zur Modernisierung." *Jahrbuch für Wirtschaftsgeschichte*, no. 1:11–32.

Harnisch, H. 1994b. "Agrarstaat oder Industriestaat. Die Bedeutung der Debatte um die Bedeutung der Landwirtschaft in Wirtschaft und Gesellschaft Deutschlands an der Wende vom 19. Zum 20. Jahrhundert." In H. Reif, ed., *Ostelbische Agrargesellschaft im Kaiserreich und in der Weimarer Republik* (Berlin: Akademie Verlag), 33–50.

Harnisch, H. 1996. "Wirtschaftspolitische Grundsatzentscheidungen und sozialökonomischer Modernisierungsprozess in Preußen während der ersten Hälfte des 19. Jahrhunderts." In H.-P. Ullmann & C. Zimmermann, eds., *Restaurationssystem und Reformpolitik. Süddeutschland und Preußen im Vergleich* (Munich: Oldenbourg), 163–87.

Haun, F. J. 1892. *Bauer und Gutsherr in Kursachsen.* Strassburg: Türmer.

Haupt, H.-G. 2002. "Neue Wege zur Geschichte der Zünfte in Europa." In Haupt, ed., *Das Ende der Zünfte: ein europäischer Vergleich* (Göttingen: Vandenhoeck & Ruprecht), 9–37.

Hauser, A. 1904. *Die deutschen Banken im Überseeverkehr.* Berlin: Duncker & Humblot.

Hayami, Y. 1998. "The Peasant in Economic Modernization." In C. K. Eicher & J. M. Staatz, eds., *International Agricultural Development*, 3d ed. (Baltimore: Johns Hopkins University Press), 300–315.

Heberle, R., & F. Meyer. 1937. *Die Grossstädte im Strome der Binnenwanderung.* Leipzig: Hirzel.

Heckscher, E. 1922. *The Continental System: An Economic Interpretation.* Oxford: Clarendon Press.

Heegewaldt, W. 2012. "Friderizianische Domänenpolitik am Beispiel der Kurmark." In F. Göse, ed., *Friedrich der Große und die Mark Brandenburg* (Berlin: Lukas), 163–82.

Heitzer, H. 1959. *Insurrectionen zwischen Weser und Elbe. Volksbewegungen gegen die französische Fremdherrschaft im Königreich Westfalen (1806–1813).* Berlin: Rütten & Loening.

Helling, G. 1966. "Berechnung eines Index der Agrarproduktion in Deutschland im 19. Jahrhundert." *Jahrbuch für Wirtschaftsgeschichte.*

Henderson, W. O. 1968 (1939). *The Zollverein.* London & Edinburgh: Frank Cass & Co.

Henn, V. 1973. "Zur Lage der rheinischen Landwirtschaft im 16. bis 18. Jahrhundert." *Zeitschrift für Agrargeschichte und Agrarsoziologie* 21:173–88.

Henning, F.-W. 1973. *Die Industrialisierung in Deutschland 1800 bis 1914.* Paderborn: Schöningh.

Henning, F.-W. 1978. *Landwirtschaft und ländliche Gesellschaft in Deutschland, Vol. 2.* Paderborn: Schöningh.

Hentschel, V. 1983. *Geschichte der deutschen Sozialpolitik, 1880–1980.* Frankfurt am Main: Suhrkamp.

Hermes, G. 1930. "Statistische Studien zur wirtschaftlichen und gesellschaftlichen Struktur des zollvereinten Deutschlands." *Archiv für Sozialwissenschaft und Sozialpolitik* 63, no. 1:121–62.

Herzog, B., & K. Mattheier. 1979. *Franz Haniel, 1779–1868. Materialien, Dokumente und Untersuchungen zu Leben und Werk des Industriepioniers Franz Haniel.* Bonn: Ludwig Rohrscheid.

Herzog, S. 2000. "Kursachsens Städte im 18. Jahrhundert—Materialien der Restaurationskommission von 1762/63 zum Städtewesen." In U. Schirmer, ed., *Sachsen 1763– 1832. Zwischen Rétablissement und bürgerlichen Reformen* (Beucha: Sax), 101–8.

Hilgert, F. 1945. *Industrialisation and Foreign Trade.* New York: League of Nations.

Hintze, O. 1967 (1896). "Preußische Reformbestrebungen vor 1806." In G. Oestreich, ed., *Otto Hintze. Regierung und Verwaltung. Gesammelte Abhandlungen zur Staats-, Rechts-, und Sozialgeschichte Preußens* (Göttingen: Vandenhoeck & Ruprecht), 504–29.

Hintze, O. 1898. "Zur Agrarpolitik Friedrichs des Großen." *Forschungen zur Brandenburgischen und Preußischen Geschichte* 10:275–309.

Hintze, O. 1967 (1900). "Staat und Gesellschaft unter dem ersten König." In G. Oestreich, ed., *Otto Hintze. Regierung und Verwaltung. Gesammelte Abhandlungen zur Staats-, Rechts-, und Sozialgeschichte Preußens* (Göttingen: Vandenhoeck & Ruprecht), 313–418.

Hintze, O. 1967 (1920). "Preußens Entwicklung zum Rechtsstaat." In G. Oestreich, ed., *Otto Hintze. Regierung und Verwaltung. Gesammelte Abhandlungen zur Staats-, Rechts-, und Sozialgeschichte Preußens* (Göttingen: Vandenhoeck & Ruprecht), 97–163.

Hippel, W. von. 1976. "Bevölkerungsentwicklung und Wirtschaftsstruktur im Königreich Württemberg 1815/65." In U. Engelhardt, V. Sellin & H. Struke, eds., *Soziale Bewegung und politische Verfassung* (Stuttgart: Ernst Klett), 270–371.

Hippel, W. von. 1977. *Die Bauernbefreiung im Königreich Württemberg, Vol. 1.* Boppard am Rhein: Harald Boldt.

Hippel, W. von. 2003. "Auf dem Weg zum Weltunternehmen (1865–1900)." In W. Abelshauser, ed., *BASF. Eine Unternehmensgeschichte* (Munich: Beck).

Hirschman, A. O. 1958. *The Strategy of Economic Development.* New Haven, CT: Yale University Press.

Hochstadt, S. 1981. "Migration and Industrialization in Germany, 1815–1870." *Social Science History* 5:445–68.

Hoffmann, W. G. 1965. *Das Wachstum der deutschen Wirtschaft seit Mitte des 19. Jahrhunderts.* Berlin: Springer.

Hoffmann, W. G. 1969. "Die Entwicklung der Sparkassen im Rahmen des Wachstums der deutschen Wirtschaft (1850 bis 1967)." *Zeitschrift für die gesamte Staatswissenschaft* 125:561–605.

Hofmann, W. 1974. *Zwische Rathaus und Reichskanzlei. Die Oberbürgermeister in der kommunal- und Staatspolitik des Deutschen Reiches von 1890 bis 1933.* Stuttgart: Kohlhammer.

Hohorst, G. 1975. *Wirtschaftswachstum und Bevölkerungsentwicklung in Preussen 1816 bis 1914.* New York: Arno Press.

Hohorst, G., J. Kocka & G. Albert. 1978. *Materialien zur Statistik des kaiserreichs 1870– 1914.* Munich: Beck.

Holtfrerich, C.- L. 1973. *Quantitative Wirtschaftsgeschichte des Ruhrkohlenbergbaus im 19. Jahrhundert*. Dortmund: Ges. für Westfäl. Wirtschaftsgeschichte.

Holtfrerich, C.-L. 1989. "The Monetary Unification Process in Nineteenth-Century Germany: Relevance and Lessons for Europe Today." In M. De Cecco & A. Giovanni, eds., *Monetary Regimes and Monetary Institutions: Issues and Perspectives* (Cambridge: Cambridge University Press), 216–43.

Horn, N., & J. Kocka, eds. 1979. *Recht und Entwicklung der Grossunternehmen im 19. Und frühen 20. Jahrhundert*. Göttingen: Vandenhoeck & Ruprecht.

Hornung, E. 2014a. "Immigration and the Diffusion of Technology: The Huguenot Diaspora in Prussia." *American Economic Review* 104, no. 1:84–122.

Hornung, E. 2014b. "Railroads and Growth in Prussia." Available at SSRN: https://ssrn.com/abstract=2399352 or http://dx.doi.org/10.2139/ssrn.2399352.

Horras, G. 1982. *Die Entwicklung des deutschen Automobilmarktes bis 1914*. Munich: Florentz.

Horster, P. 1908. *Die Entwicklung der sächsischen Gewerbeverfassung (1780–1861)*. Crefeld: Wilhelm Greven.

Hoth, W. 1983. "Die Entwicklung der Industrien in Wuppertal." In K. Düwell & W. Köllmann, eds., *Rheinland -Westfalen im Industriezeitalter, Vol. 1* (Wuppertal: Hammer), 96–113.

Hötzsch, O. 1902. "Der Bauernschutz in den deutschen Territorien vom 16. bis ins 19. Jahrhundert." *Jahrbuch für Gesetzgebung, Verwaltung und Volkswirtschaft im Deutschen Reich* 26:1137–69.

Jackson, J. 1979. "Wanderungen in Duisberg während der Industrialisierung." In W. H. Schröder, ed., *Moderne Stadtgeschichte* (Stuttgart: Klett-Cotta), 217–37.

Jackson, J. 1980. "Migration and Urbanization in the Ruhr Valley." PhD diss., University of Minnesota.

Jacobs, A. & H. Richter. 1935. *Die Grosshandelspreise in Deutschland von 1792–1934*. Berlin: Hanseatische Verl.-Anst.

James, H. 2011. *Deutsche Leg ende und globales Unternehmen*. Munich: Beck.

Jantke, C. 1965. "Zur Deutung des Pauperismus." In C. Jantke & D. Hilger, eds., *Die Eigentumslosen*. Munich: Karl Alber.

Jeidels, O. 1905. *Das Verhältnis der deutschen Grossbanken zue Industrie mit besonderer Berücksichtigungder Eisenindustrie*. Leipzig: Duncker & Humblot.

Jenks, L. 1971. *The Migration of British Capital to 1875*. London: Nelson.

Jones, P. M. 2012. "The Challenge of Land Reform in Eighteenth- and Nineteenth-Century France." *Past and Present* 216:107–42.

Jones, C. & P. Romer. 2010. "The New Kaldor Facts: Ideas, Institutions, Population, and Human Capital." *American Economic Journal: Macroeconomics* 2, no. 1:224–45.

Jopp, T. A. 2013. *Insurance, Fund Size, and Concentration: Prussian Miners' Knappschaften in the Nineteenth- and Early Twentieth Centuries and Their Quest for Optimal Scale*. Berlin: Akademie Verlag.

Jovanovic, B., & P. Rousseau. 2005. "General Purpose Technologies." In P. Aghion & S. Durlauf, eds., *Handbook of Economic Growth* (Amsterdam: Elsevier).

Kaak, H. 1991. *Die Gutsherrschaft. Theoriegeschichtliche Untersuchungen zum Agrarwesen im ostelbischen Raum*. Berlin: Walter de Gruyter.

Kabisch, T. R. 1982. *Deutsches Kapital in den USA*. Stuttgart: Klett-Cotta.

Kaelble, H. 1983. *Soziale Mobilität und Chancengleichheit im 19. und 20. Jahrhundert*. Göttingen: Vandenhoeck & Ruprecht.

Kaelble, H., & Volkmann. H. 1986. "Streiks und Einkommensverteilung im späten Kai-

der Grossunternehmen im 19. und frühen 20. Jahrhundert (Göttingen: Vandenhoeck & Ruprecht).

Köhler, L. 1891. *Das Württembergische Gewerbe-Recht von 1805 bis 1870*. Tübingen: Laupp'sche Buchhandlung.

Kölling, B. 1999. *Agrarstatistik der Provinz Brandenburg 1750–1880*. Quellen und Forschungen zur Historischen Statistik von Deutschland 25. St. Katharinen: Scripta Mercaturae.

Köllmann, W. 1960. *Sozialgeschichte der Stadt Barmen im 19. Jahrhundert*. Tübingen: Mohr.

Köllmann, W. 1974a. "Bevölkerung und Arbeitskräftepotential in Deutschland 1815–1865." In W. Köllmann, *Bevölkerung in der industriellen Revolution* (Göttingen: Vandenhoeck & Ruprecht), 61–98.

Köllmann, W. 1974b. "Industrialisierung, Binnenwanderung und 'soziale Frage.'" In Köllmann, *Bevölkerung in der industriellen Revolution* (Göttingen: Vandenhoeck & Ruprecht), 106–24.

Köllmann, W. 1990. "Beginn der Industrialisierung." In Köllmann et al., eds., *Das Ruhrgebiet im Industriezeitalter. Geschichte und Entwicklung*, Vol. 1 (Düsseldorf: Schwann), 11–79.

Kollmer-von Oheimb-Loup, G. 1996. *Zollverein und Innovation. Die Reaktion württembergischer Textilindustrieller auf den Deutschen Zollverein 1834–1874*. St. Katharinen: Scripta Mercaturae.

Komlos, J. 1983. *The Habsburg Monarchy as a Customs Union: Economic Development in the Nineteenth Century*. Princeton, NJ: Princeton University Press.

König, A. 1899. *Die sächsische Baumwollen-Industrie am Ende des 18. Jahrhunderts und während der Kontinentalsperre*. Leipzig: Teubner.

Kopitzsch, F. 2003. "Die wirtschaftliche Entwicklung 1721–1830." In U. Lange, ed., *Geschichte Schleswig-Holsteins* (Neumünster: Wachholtz), 287–303.

Kopsidis, M. 1996. *Marktintegration und Entwicklung der westfälischen Landwirtschaft 1780–1880*. Münster: LIT.

Kopsidis, M. 1998. "Der westfälische Agrarmarkt im Integrationsprozeß 1780–1880. Phasen und Einflußfaktoren der Marktentwicklung in historischen Transformationsprozessen." *Jahrbuch für Wirtschaftsgeschichte*, no. 2:169–98.

Kopsidis, M. 2002. "The Creation of a Westphalian Rye Market 1820–1870: Leading and Following Regions, a Co-Integration Analysis." *Jahrbuch für Wirtschaftsgeschichte*, no. 2:85–112.

Kopsidis, M. 2006. *Agrarentwicklung. Historische Agrarrevolutionen und Entwicklungsökonomie*. Stuttgart: Steiner.

Kopsidis, M. 2009. "Boserup Meets Thuenen: Markets and Farming Intensity in Preindustrial Westphalian Peasant Agriculture, circa 1830." In V. Pinilla, ed., *Markets and Agricultural Change in Europe from the Thirteenth to the Twentieth Century*, Rural History in Europe 2 (Turnhout: Brepols), 107–35.

Kopsidis, M. 2012. "Peasants and Markets: Market Integration and Agricultural Development in Westphalia 1780–1880." In P. van Cruyningen & E. Thoen, ed., *Food Supply, Demand and Trade: Aspects of the Economic Relationship between Town and Countryside (Middle Ages–19th Century)*, CORN Publication Series 14 (Turnhout: Brepols), 189–215.

Kopsidis, M. 2013. "North-west Germany, 1750–2000." In L. Van Molle & Y. Segers, eds., *The Agro-Food Market: Production, Distribution and Consumption*, series Rural Economy and Society in North-western Europe, 500–2000 (Turnhout: Brepols), 292–328.

Kopsidis, M. 2015. "North-west Germany, 1750–2000." In E. Thoen & T. Soens, eds.,

Struggling with the Environment: Land Use and Productivity, series Rural Economy and Society in North-western Europe, 500–2000 (Turnhout: Brepols), 340–80.

Kopsidis, M., & D. W. Bromley. 2014. "The French Revolution and German Industrialization: The New Institutional History Rewrites History," *IAMO Discussion Paper* 149.

Kopsidis, M., & D. W. Bromley. 2016. "The French Revolution and German Industrialization: Dubious Models and Doubtful Causality," *Journal of Institutional Economics* 12, no. 1:161–90.

Kopsidis, M., & D. W. Bromley. 2017. "Expliquer la modernization économique allemande. La Révolution francaise, les réformes prussiennes et l'inévitable continuité du changement." *Annales HSS* 72, no. 4:1117–56.

Kopsidis, M., O. Dube & G. Franzmann. 2014. "Die Entwicklung der sächsischen Pflanzenproduktion 1791–2010." *Zeitschrift für Agrargeschichte und Agrarsoziologie* 62:46–79.

Kopsidis, M., & H. Hockmann. 2010. "Technical Change in Westphalian Peasant Agriculture and the Rise of the Ruhr, circa 1830–1880." *European Review of Economic History* 14, no. 2:209–37.

Kopsidis, M., & K. Lorenzen-Schmidt. 2013. "North-west Germany, 1000–1750." In L. Van Molle & Y. Segers, eds., *The Agro-Food Market: Production, Distribution and Consumption,* series Rural Economy and Society in North-western Europe, 500–2000 (Turnhout: Brepols), 260–91.

Kopsidis, M., & U. Pfister. 2013. "Agricultural Development during Early Industrialization in a Low Wage Economy: Saxony, c. 1790–1830." *EHES Working Papers in Economic History* 39.

Kopsidis, M., U. Pfister, F. Scholten & J. Bracht. 2017. "Agricultural Output Growth in a Proto and Early Industrial Setting: Evidence from Sharecropping in Western Westphalia and the Lower Rhineland, c. 1740–1860." *Rural History* 28, no. 1:1–26.

Kopsidis, M., & N. Wolf. 2012. "Agricultural Productivity across Prussia during the Industrial Revolution: A Thünen Perspective." *Journal of Economic History* 72, no. 3:634–70.

Koselleck, R. 1962. "Staat und Gesellschaft in Preußen 1815–1848." In W. Conze, ed., *Staat und Gesellschaft im deutschen Vormärz 1815–1848* (Stuttgart: Ernst Klett), 79–112.

Koselleck, R. 1967. *Preußen zwischen Reform und Revolution. Allgemeines Landrecht, Verwaltung und soziale Bewegung von 1791–1848.* Stuttgart: Klett Cotta.

Kötzschke, R. 1953. *Ländliche Siedlungen und Agrarwesen in Sachsen.* Remagen: Verlag der Bundesanstalt für Landeskunde.

Krabbe, W. 1985. *Kommunalpolitik und Industrialisierung. Die Entfaltung der städtischen Leistungsverwaltung in Deutschland bis zum Ersten Weltkrieg.* Stuttgart: Kohlhammer.

Kraus, A. 2007 (1980). *Quellen zur Bevölkerungsstatistik Deutschlands 1815–1875.* GESIS Cologne, Germany. ZA8276 data file version 1.0.0. https://histat.gesis.org/histat.

Krause, D. 1997. "Die Anfänge der Commerz- und Diskontobank in Hamburg." *Bankhistorisches Archiv* 23:20–55.

Krengel, Rolf. 1983. *Die deutsche Roheisenindustrie 1871–1913.* Berlin: Duncker & Humblot.

Kriedte, P. 2007. *Taufgesinnte und großes Kapital. Die niederrheinisch-bergischen Mennoniten und der Aufstieg des Krefelder Seidengewerbes.* Göttingen: Vandenhoeck & Ruprecht.

Kriedte, P., H. Medick & J. Schlumbohm. 1977. *Industrialisierung vor der Industrialisierung. Gewerbliche Warenproduktion auf dem Land in der Formationsperiode des Kapitalismus.* Göttingen: Vandenhoeck & Ruprecht.

Krüger, A. 1925. *Das Kölner Bankiergewerbe vom Ende des 18. Jahrhunderts bis 1875.* Essen: Baedeker.

Krüger, H. 1958. *Zur Geschichte der Manufakturen und Manufakturarbeiter in Preussen.* Berlin: Rütten & Loening.

Krüger, K. 2003. *Die Landständische Verfassung.* Enzyklopädie deutscher Geschichte 67. Munich: Oldenbourg.

Kubitschek, H. 1962. "Die Börsenverordnung vom 24. Mai 1844 und die Situation im Finanz- und Kreditwesen Preussens in den vierziger Jahren des 19. Jahrhunderts." *Jahrbuch für Wirtschaftsgeschichte* 3, no. 3:57–78.

Kuczynski, J. 1960–66. *Die Geschichte der Lage der Arbeiter unter dem Kapitalismus.* 3 vols. East Berlin: Akademie Verlag.

Kuczynsyki, R. R. 1909. *Die Entwicklung der gewerblichen Löhne seit der Begründung des Deutschen Reiches, 1871–1908.* Berlin: G. Reimer.

Kumpmann, K. 1910, *Die Entstehung der Rheinischen Eisenbahngesellschaft, 1830–1844.* Essen: Baedeker.

Küpker, M. 2008. *Weber, Hausierer, Hollandgänger. Demografischer und wirtschaftlichere Wandel im ländlichen Raum.* Frankfurt: Campus.

Kuske, B. 1949. *Wirtschaftsgeschichte Westfalens in Leistung und Verflechtung mit den Nachbarländern bis zum 18. Jahrhundert.* Münster: Aschendorff.

Kussmaul, A. 1990. *A General View of the Rural Economy of England 1538–1840.* Cambridge: Cambridge University Press.

Kutz, M. 1974. "Deutschlands Außenhandel von der Französischen Revolution bis zur Gründung des Zollvereins." *Vierteljahrschrift für Sozial- und Wirtschaftsgeschichte,* suppl. 61 (Wiesbaden: Steiner).

Kwack, T.-Y. 1989. "Die Entwicklung von kommunalunternehmen in Deutschland im 19. Und frühen 20. Jahrhundert—unter besonderer Berücksichtigung finanz- und sozialpolitischer Aspekte." Diss., University of Münster.

Kwaśny, Z. 2009. "Die gewerbliche Entwicklung Niederschlesiens in der ersten Hälfte des 19. Jahrhunderts außerhalb von Kohle und Leinen." In Toni Pierenkemper, ed., *Regionen und regionale Industrialisierung. Zur wirtschaftlichen Entwicklung ostmitteleuropäischer Regionen im 19. Jahrhundert* (Aachen: Shaker), 49–62.

Laer, H. von. 1977. *Industrialisierung und Qualität der Arbeit.* New York: Arno Press.

Laer, H. von. 1982. "Der Arbeitsmarkt für Techniker in Deutschland: von der industriellen Revolution bis zum 1. Weltkrieg." In T. Pierenkemper & R. H. Tilly, eds., *Historische Arbeitsmarktforschung: Entstehung, Entwicklung und Probleme der Vermarktung von Arbeitskraft* (Göttingen: Vandenhoeck & Ruprecht), 152–75.

Lampe, M. 2009. "Effects of Bilateralism and the MFN Clause on International Trade: Evidence for the Cobden-Chevalier Network (1860–1875)." *Journal of Economic History* 69:1012–40.

Lampe, M., & N. Wolff. 2015. "Binnenhandel und Aussenhandel." In T. Rahlf, ed., *Deutschland in Daten. Zeitreihen zur historischen Statistik* (Bonn: Bundeszentrale für politische Bildung), 276–91.

Landes, D. S. 1969. *The Unbound Prometheus: Technological Change and Industrial Development in Western Europe from 1750 to the Present.* Cambridge: Cambridge University Press.

Landes, D. S. 1980. "Reformpolitik und Industrialisierung in Japan und Preußen. Ein Vergleich." In B. Vogel, ed., *Preußische Reformen 1807–1820* (Königstein: Verlagsgruppe Athenäum-Hain-Scriptor-Hanstein), 30–48.

Landes, D. S. 1998. *The Wealth and Poverty of Nations: Why Some Are So Rich and Some So Poor.* London: Little, Brown.

Lange, G. 1976. *Das ländliche Gewerbe in der Grafschaft Mark am Vorabend der Industrialisierung.* Cologne: Rheinisch-Westfälisches Wirtschaftsarchiv.

Langewiesche, D. 1974. *Liberalismus und Demokratie in Württemberg zwischen Revolution und Reichsgründung.* Düsseldorf: Droste.

Langewiesche, D. 1977. "Wanderungsbewegungen in der Hochindustrialisierungsperiode. Regionale, interstädtische und innerstädtische Mobilität in Deutschland, 1880–1914." *Vierteljahrschrift für Sozial- und Wirtschaftsgeschichte* 64:1–40.

Laux, H.-D. 1989. "The Components of Population Growth in Prussian Cities, 1875–1905 and Their Influence on Urban Population Structure." In W. R. Lee & R. Lawton, eds., *Urban Population Development in Western Europe from the Late-Eighteenth Century to the Early-Twentieth Century* (Liverpool: Liverpool University Press).

Laux, J. 1976. *In First Gear: The French Automobile Industry to 1914.* Liverpool: Liverpool University Press.

Lazer, D. 1999. "The Free Trade Epidemic of the 1860s and Other Outbreaks of Economic Discrimination." *World Politics* 51, no. 4:447–83.

Lee, J. J. 1978. "Labor in German Industrialization." In *Cambridge Economic History of Europe, Vol. 7* (Cambridge: Cambridge University Press).

Lee, R. D. 1986. "Maltus and Boserup: A Dynamic Synthesis." In D. Coleman & R. Schofield, eds., *The State of Population Theory* (Oxford: Blackwell), 96–130.

Lehmann, S. 2014. "Taking Firms to the Stock Market: IPOs and the Importance of Large Banks in Imperial Germany, 1896–1913." *Economic History Review* 67:92–122.

Lehmann-Hasemeyer, S., & J. Streb. 2016. "The Berlin Stock Exchange in Imperial Germany—A Market for New Technology?" *American Economic Review* 106:3358–76.

Lehmann-Hasemeyer, S. & J. Streb. 2018. "Does Social Security Crowd Out Private Savings? The Case of Bismarck's System of Social Insurance." *European Review of Economic History* 22:298–321.

Leiskow, H. 1930. *Spekulation und öffentliche Meinung in der ersten Hälfte des 19. Jahrhunderts.* Jena: Gustav Fischer.

Levy, H. 1935. *Industrial Germany: A Study of Its Monopoly Organizations and Their Control by the State.* Cambridge: Cambridge University Press.

Levy-Leboyer, M. 1977. *La position international de la France: Aspects économiques et financiers, 19e–20e siècle.* Paris: Bibliothèque Générale de l'École des Hautes Études en Sciences Sociales.

Lewis, W. A. 1954. "Economic Development with Unlimited Supplies of Labour." *Manchester School of Economic and Social Studies* 22:139–91.

Lichter, J. 1994. *Landwirtschaft und Landwirtschaftskammer in der Rheinprovinz am Vorabend des Ersten Weltkriegs.* Cologne: Botermann & Botermann.

Lincke, C. A. 1842. *Die sächsische und altenburgische Landwirthschaft.* Leipzig: Gebrüder Reichenbach.

Lindert, P. 1969. *Key Currencies and Gold, 1900–1913.* Princeton, NJ: Princeton University Press.

Lindert, P. H. 2004. *Growing Public: Social Spending and Economic Growth since the Eighteenth Century.* Cambridge: Cambridge University Press.

List, F. 1841. *Das nationale System der Politischen Ökonomie.* Stuttgart: Cotta.

Lorenzen-Schmidt, K. 2003. "Neuorientierung auf den deutschen Wirtschaftsraum—Wirtschaftliche Entwicklung 1864–1918." In U. Lange, ed., *Geschichte Schleswig-Holsteins* (Neumünster: Wachholtz), 384–99.

Loreth, H. 1974. *Das Wachstum der württembergischen Wirtschaft von 1818 bis 1918*. Stuttgart: Statistisches Landesamt Baden-Württemberg.

Lorsbach, J. 1956. *Hauberge und Hauberggenossenschaften des Siegerlandes*. Karlsruhe: C. F. Müller.

Lucas, R. 1988. "On the Mechanics of Economic Development." *Journal of Monetary Economics* 22:3–42.

Lütge, F. 1957. *Die mitteldeutsche Grundherrschaft und ihre Auflösung*. Stuttgart: Fischer.

Lütge, F. 1963. *Geschichte der deutschen Agrarverfassung vom frühen Mittelalter bis zum 19. Jahrhundert*. Stuttgart: Eugen Ulmer.

Maddison, A. 2000. *The World Economy: A Millennial Perspective*. Paris: OECD.

Mahlerwein, G. 2001. *Die Herren im Dorf. Bäuerliche Oberschicht und ländliche Elitenbildung in Rheinhessen 1700–1850*. Mainz: Zabern.

Marchand, H. 1939. *Säkularstatistik der deutschen Eisenindustrie*. Essen: Essener Verlagsanstalt.

Marshall, A. 2006 (1919). *Industry and Trade*. New York: Cosimo Inc.

Martin, R. 1895. "Der Fleischverbrauch im Königreich Sachsen." *Zeitschrift des Königlich Sächsischen Bureaus*: 133–50.

Matschoss, C. 1921. *50 Jahre Gasmotorfabrik Deutz*. Berlin: Verlag des Vereins Deutscher Ingenieure.

Matz, K.-J. 1980. *Pauperismus und Bevölkerung. Die gesetzlichen Ehebeschränkungen in den süddeutschen Staaten während des 19. Jahrhunderts*. Stuttgart: Klett-Cotta.

Matzerath, H. 1985. *Urbanisierung in Preussen, 1815–1914*. Stuttgart: Kohlhammer.

Matzerath, J. 2000. "Adelsrecht und Ständegesellschaft im Kursachsen des 18. Jahrhunderts." In U. Schirmer, ed., *Sachsen 1763–1832. Zwischen Rétablissement und bürgerlichen Reformen* (Beucha: Sax), 24–39.

Matzerath, J. 2006. *Aspekte sächsischer Landtagsgeschichte: die Spätzeit der sächsischen Ständeversammlung (1763–1831)*. Dresden: Sächsischer Landtag.

Mauer, H. 1907. *Das landschaftliche Kreditwesen Preussens*. Strassburg.

Medick, H. 1985. "Teuerung, Teuerungspolitik und Hunger in Württemberg 1816 und 1817 (mit einem Vergleich zu 1846/7)." In Deutscher Historiker-Verband, *Bericht über die 33d Versammlung* (Stuttgart).

Medick, H. 1990. "Von der Bürgerherrschaft zur Staatsbürgerlichen Gesellschaft—Württemberg zwischen Ancien régime und Vormärz." In L. Niethammer et al., eds., *Bürgerliche Gesellschaft in Deutschland* (Frankfurt am Main: Fischer TB), 52–79.

Medick, H. 1997. *Weben und Überleben in Laichingen 1650–1900*. Göttingen: Vandenhoeck & Ruprecht.

Meerwein, G. 1914. *Die Entwicklung der Chemnitzer bzw. Sächsischen Baumwollspinnerei von 1789–1879*. Berlin: Ebering.

Megerle, K. 1979. "Regionale Differenzierung des Industrialisierungsprozesses: Überlegungen am Beispiel Württembergs." In R. Fremdling & R. Tilly, eds., *Industrialisierung und Raum: Studien zur regionalen Differenzierung im Deutschland des 19. Jahrhunderts* (Stuttgart: Klett-Cotta), 105–31.

Megerle, K. 1982. *Württemberg im Industrialisierungsprozess Deutschlands*. Stuttgart: Klett-Cotta.

Mehring, F. 1975 (1893). *Die Lessing Legende*. Berlin: Dietz.

Meinert, R. 1958. "Die Entwicklung der Arbeitszeit in der deutschen Industrie im 19. Jahrhundert." Diss., University of Münster.

Meitzen, A. 1868. *Der Boden und die landwirthschaftlichen Verhältnisse des Preussischen Staates*. 4 vols. Berlin: Wiegandt & Hempel.

Meitzen, A., & F. Grossmann. 1901. *Der Boden und die landwirthschaftlichen Verhältnisse des Preussischen Staates, Vol. 6.* Berlin: Paul Parey.

Metz, R. 2015. "Volkswirtschaftliche Gesamtrechnung." In T. Rahlf, ed., *Deutschland in Daten. Zeitreihen zur Historischen Statistik* (Bonn: Bundeszentrale für politische Bildung).

Mitchell, B. A. 1973. "Statistical Appendix." In C. Cipolla, ed., *The Fontana Economic History of Europe*, vol. 4, part 2. Glasgow: Collins.

Mitchell, B. A. 1975. *European Historical Statistics, 1750–1970.* London: Macmillan.

Mönckmeier, W. 1912. *Die deutsche Uebersee-Auswanderung.* Jena: G. Fischer.

Mooser, J. 1984. *Ländliche Klassengesellschaft 1770–1848. Bauern und Unterschichten, Landwirtschaft und Gewerbe im östlichen Westfalen.* Göttingen: Vandenhoeck & Ruprecht.

Mottek, H. 1964. *Wirtschaftsgeschichte Deutschlands. Ein Grundriss, vol. 2 (Von der Zeit der Französischen Revolution bis zur Zeit der Bismarckschen Reichsgründung.* Berlin: VEB Deutscher Verlag der Wissenschaften.

Mottek, H. 1966. "Die Gründerkrise. Produktionsbewegung, Wirkungen, theoretische Problematik." *Jahrbuch für Wirtschaftsgeschichte* 7, no. 1:51–128.

Müller, H.-H. 1964. "Der agrarische Fortschritt und die Bauern in Brandenburg vor den Reformen von 1807." *Zeitschrift für Geschichtswissenschaft* 12, no. 4:629–48.

Müller, H.-H. 1965. "Domänen und Domänenpächter in Brandenburg-Preußen im 18. Jahrhundert." *Jahrbuch für Wirtschaftsgeschichte* 6:152–92.

Müller, H.-H. 1966. "Bauern, Pächter und Adel im alten Preußen." *Jahrbuch für Wirtschaftsgeschichte* 7: no. 1:259–83.

Müller, H.-H. 1967. *Märkische Landwirtschaft vor den Agrarreformen von 1807.* Potsdam: Veröffentlichungen des Bezirksheimatmuseum Potsdam.

Müller, J. H., & S. Geisenberger. 1972. *Die Einkommensstruktur in verschiedenen deutschen Ländern 1874–1913, unter Berücksichtigung regionaler Verschiedenheiten.* Berlin: Duncker & Humblot.

Müller-Link, H. 1977. *Industrialisierung und Aussenpolitik, Preussen-Deutschland und das Zarenreich 1860–1890.* Göttingen: Vandenhoeck & Ruprecht.

Müller-Wille, W. 1981. *Westfalen. Landschaftliche Ordnung und Bindung eines Landes.* Münster: Aschendorff.

Münch, P. 1996. "The Growth of the Modern State." In S. Ogilvie, ed., *Germany: A New Social and Economic History, Vol. 2: 1630–1800* (London: Arnold), 196–232.

Mura, J., ed. 1985. "Der öffentliche Auftrag der Sparkassen in der historischen Entwicklung." In *Sparkassenhistorisches Symposium* (Bonn: Deutscher Sparkassenverlag).

Murmann, J. P. 2003. *Knowledge and Competitive Advantage. The Coevolution of Firms, Technology and National Institutions.* Cambridge: Cambridge University Press.

Mütter, B., & R. Meyer. 1995. *Agrarmodernisierung im Herzogtum Oldenburg zwischen Reichsgründung und Erstem Weltkrieg.* Hannover: Hahnsche Buchhandlung.

Neal, L. 1985. "Integration of International Capital Markets: Quantitative Evidence from the Eighteenth to Twentieth Centuries." *Journal of Economic History* 45:219–26.

Neidlinger, K. 1930. *Studien zur Geschichte der deutschen Effektenspekulation von ihren Anfängen bis zum Beginn der Eisenbahnspekulation.* Jena: Fischer.

Neugebauer, W. 1985. *Absolutistischer Staat und Schulwirklichkeit in Brandenburg-Preussen.* Berlin: de Gruyter.

Neugebauer, W. 2009. "Brandenburg-Preußen in der Frühen Neuzeit. Politik und Staatsbildung im 17. und 18. Jahrhundert." In Neugebauer, ed., *Handbuch der preußischen Geschichte, Vol. 1: Das 17. und 18. Jahrhundert und große Themen der Geschichte Preußens* (Berlin: de Gruyter), 113–407.

Nicholas, T. 2014. "Technology, Innovation and Economic Growth in Britain since 1870." In Roderick Floud et al., eds., *Cambridge Economic History of Modern Britain, Vol. 2: Growth and Decline, 1870 to the Present* (Cambridge: Cambridge University Press).

Niedhart, G. 1979. "Aufgeklärter Absolutismus oder Rationalisierung der Herrschaft." *Zeitschrift für Historische Forschung* 6:199–211.

Niethammer, L., & F. Bruggemeier. 1976. "Wie wohnten Arbeiter im Kaiserreich?" *Archiv für Sozialgeschichte* 16:61–134.

Nipperdey, T. 1983. *Deutsche Geschichte 1800–1866* Munich: Beck.

Nocken, U. 1993. "Die grosse Deflation: Goldstandard, Geldmenge und Preise in den U.S.A. und Deutschland, 1870 bis 1896." In E. Schremmer, ed., *Geld und Währung vom 16. Jahrhundert bis zur Gegenwart, Vierteljahrschrift für Sozial- und Wirtschaftsgeschichte*, suppl. 106 (Stuttgart: Steiner).

Noll, A. 1969. "Sozio-ökonomischer Strukturwandel des Handwerks in der zweiten Phase der Industrialisierung." Diss., University of Münster.

Nolte, P. 1990. *Staatsbildung als Gesellschaftsreform. Politische Reformen in Preußen und den süddeutschen Staaten 1800–1820.* Frankfurt: Campus.

North, D. 1981. *Structure and Change in Economic History.* New York: W. W. Norton.

Obenaus, H. 1980. "Finanzkrise und Verfassungsgebung. Zu den sozialen Bedingungen des frühen deutschen Konstitutionalismus." In B. Vogel, ed., *Preussische Reformen 1807–1820* (Königstein: Hain), 244–65.

Obermann, K. 1972. "Wirtschafts- und sozialpolitische Aspekte der Krise 1845–1847 in Deutschland, insbesondere Preussen." *Jahrbuch für Wirtschaftsgeschichte* 7:141–74.

Ogilvie, S. 1996. "The Beginnings of Industrialization." In Ogilvie, ed., *Germany: A New Social and Economic History, Vol. 2: 1630–1800* (London: Arnold), 263–308.

Ogilvie, S. 1997a. *State Corporatism and Proto-industry: The Württemberg Black Forest, 1580–1797.* Cambridge: Cambridge University Press.

Ogilvie, S. 1997b. "Soziale Institutionen, Korporatismus und Protoindustrie. Die Württembergische Zeugmacherei (1580–1797)." In D. Ebeling & W. Mager, eds., *Protoindustrie in der Region. Europäische Gewerbelandschaften vom 16. bis zum 19. Jahrhundert* (Bielefeld: Verlag für Regionalgchichte), 105–38.

Ogilvie, S. 1999. "The German State: A Non-Prussian View." In E. Hellmuth & J. Brewer, eds., *Rethinking Leviathan: The Eighteenth-Century State in Britain and Germany* (Oxford: Oxford University Press), 167–202.

Ogilvie, S. 2003. *A Bitter Living: Women, Markets, and Social Capital in Early Modern Germany.* Oxford: Oxford University Press.

Ogilvie, S., & A. W. Carus. 2014. "Institutions and Economic Growth in Historical Perspective." In *Handbook of Economic Growth, Vol. 2A* (Amsterdam: Elsevier B.V.), 403–513.

Ohnishi, T. 1973. *Zolltarifpolitik Preußens bis zur Gründung des deutschen Zollvereins. Ein Beitrag zur Finanz- und Außenpolitik Preußens.* Göttingen: Schwartz.

O'Rourke, K. 1997. "The European Grain Invasion, 1870–1913." *Journal of Economic History* 57:775–801.

O'Rourke, K. H. 2006. "The Worldwide Economic Impact of the French Revolutionary and Napoleonic Wars, 1793–1815." *Journal of Global History* 1:123–49.

Orsagh, T. J. 1969. "Löhne in Deutschland 1871–1913." *Zeitschrift für die gesamten Staatswissenschaften* 125:476–83.

Otto, F. 2002. *Die Entstehung eines nationalen Geldes: Integrationsprozesse der deutschen Währungen im 19. Jahrhundert.* Berlin: Duncker & Humblot.

Pannwitz, K. von. 1998. *Die Entstehung der allgemeinen Deutschen Wechselordnung.* Frankfurt am Main: Lang.

Perkins, J. A. 1981. "The Agricultural Revolution in Germany, 1850–1914." *Journal of European Economic History* 10, spring 1981: 71–118.

Peters, J. 1970. "Ostelbische Landarmut—Statistisches über landlose und landarme Agrarproduzenten im Spätfeudalismus." *Jahrbuch für Wirtschaftsgeschichte* 1:97–126.

Peters, L. 1989. "Managing Competition in German Coal, 1893–1913." *Journal of Economic History* 49:419–33.

Pfetsch, F. 1970. "Scientific Organization and Science Policy in Imperial Germany, 1871–1914: The Foundation of the Imperial Institute of Physics and Technology." *Minerva* 8: 557–80.

Pfister, U. 1992. *Die Züricher Fabriques. Protoindustrielles Wachstum vom 16. zum 18. Jahrhundert.* Zürich: Chronos.

Pfister, U. 2004. "Protoindustrielle Produktionsregimes in institutionenökonomischer Perspektive." In K.-H. Ellerbrock & C. Wischermann, eds., *Die Wirtschaftsgeschichte vor der Herausforderung durch die New Institutional Economics* (Dortmund: Gesellschaft für Westfälische Wirtschaftsgeschichte), 160–78.

Pfister, U. 2008. "Craft Guilds, the Theory of the Firm, and Eraly Modern Proto-Industry." In S. R. Epstein & M. Prak, eds., *Guilds, Innovation and the European Economy, 1400–1800* (Cambridge: Cambridge University Press), 25–51.

Pfister, U. 2011. "Economic Growth in Germany, 1500–1850." Unpublished contribution to "Quantifying Long Run Economic Development" conference, University of Warwick in Venice, 22–24 March 2011.

Pfister, U. 2015. "The Quantitative Development of Germany's International Trade during the Eighteenth and Early Nineteenth Centuries." *Revue de l'OFCE* 140:175–221.

Pfister, U. 2017a. "The Timing and Pattern of Real Wage Divergence in Pre-industrial Europe: Evidence from Germany, c. 1500–1850." *Economic History Review* 70, no. 3: 701–29.

Pfister, U. 2017b. "Germany: A Positive Institutional Shock." Contribution to Waterloo Project conference, Institute of Historical Research, London, 23–24 June.

Pfister, U. 2018. "Real Wages in Germany during the First Phase of Industrialization, 1850–1889." *Jahrbuch für Wirtschaftsgeschichte* 59, no. 2:567–96.

Pfister, U. 2019a. "The Inequality of Pay in Pre-modern Germany, Late Fifteenth Century to 1889." *Jahrbuch für Wirtschaftsgeschichte* 60, no. 1:209–43.

Pfister, U. 2019b. "Economic Inequality in Germany, c. 1500–1800." Unpublished paper.

Pfister, U. 2019c. "The Crafts-Harley View of German Industrialization: An Independent Estimate of the Income Side of Net National Product, 1851–1913." *European Review of Economic History.* https://doi.org/10.1093/ereh/hez009.

Pfister, U., & G. Fertig. 2010. "The Population History of Germany: Research Strategy and Preliminary Results." MPIDR Working Paper WP 2010–035.

Pfister, U., & G. Fertig. 2019. "From Malthusian Disequilibrium to the Post-Malthusian Era: The Evolution of the Preventive and Positive Checks in Germany, 1730–1870." Unpublished paper.

Pfister, U., & M. Kopsidis. 2015. "Institutions versus Demand: Determinants of Agricultural Development in Saxony 1660–1850." *European Review of Economic History* 19: 275–93.

Pfister, U., & M. Kopsidis. 2016. "Strukturelle Transformation hin zum 'Industriestaat' unter den Bedingungen der Grundherrschaft: die Entwicklung der sächsischen Landwirtschaft vom späten 17. bis zur Mitte des 19. Jahrhunderts." In Sächsisches Staatsarchiv, ed., *Wissen—Wolle—Wandel. Merinozucht und Agrarinnovation in Sachsen im 18. und 19. Jahrhundert* (Halle: Mitteldeutscher Verlag), 11–41.

Pfister, U., J. Riedel & M. Uebele. 2012. "Real Wages and the Origins of Modern Economic Growth in Germany. Sixteenth to Nineteenth Centuries." *EHES Working Papers in Economic History* 17.

Pierenkemper, T. 1979. *Die westfälischen Schwerindustriellen 1852–1913. Soziale Struktur und unternehmerischer Erfolg.* Göttingen: Vandenhoeck & Ruprecht.

Pierenkemper, T. 1987. *Arbeitsmarkt und Angestellte im Deutschen Kaiserreich, 1880–1913.* Stuttgart: Steiner.

Pierenkemper, T. 1994. *Gewerbe und Industrie im 19. und 20. Jahrhundert.* Munich: Oldenbourg.

Pierenkemper, T. 2000. *Unternehmensgeschichte.* Steiner: Stuttgart.

Pierenkemper, T. 2015. "Arbeit, Einkommen und Lebensstandard." In T. Rahlf, ed., *Deutschland in Daten. Zeitreihen zur historischen Statatistik* (Bonn: Bundeszerale für politische Bildung).

Pierenkemper, T., & R. Tilly.1987. *Die Geschichte der Drahtweberei. Dargestellt am Beispiel der Firma Haver & Boecker, Oelde aus Anlaß des einhundertjährigen Bestehens 1887—1987.* Stuttgart: Steiner.

Pinner, F. 1918. *Emil Rathenau und das elektrische Zeitalter.* Leipzig: Akademische Verlagsgesellschaft.

Platt, D. C. M. 1986. *Britain's Investment on the Eve of the First World War: The Use and Abuse of Numbers.* London: Palgrave.

Plenge, J. 1913. *Von der Diskontpolitik zur Herrschaft über den Geldmarkt.* Berlin: Springer.

Ploeckl, F. 2009. "The Zollverein and the Sequence of a Customs Union." *Australian Economic History Review* 33:277–300.

Ploeckl, F. 2010. "The Zollverein and the Formation of a Customs Union." *Oxford Economic and Social History Working Papers* 34.

Ploeckl, F. 2013. "The Internal Impact of a Customs Union. Baden and the Zollverein." *Explorations in Economic History* 50:387–404.

Pohl, H. 1978. "Die Konzentration in der deutschen Wirtschaft vom ausgehenden Jahrhundert bis 1945." In W. Treue & H. Pohl, eds., *Zeitschrift für Unternehmensgeschichte,* suppl. 11 (Wiesbaden: Steiner).

Pohl, M. 1973. "Hundert Jahre Deutsche Bank London Agency." In Deutsche Bank, ed., *Beiträge zu Wirtschafts- und Währungsfragen und Bankgeschichte 10* (Frankfurt am Main: Deutsche Bank).

Pohl, M. 1982. *Konzentration im deutschen Bankwesen, 1848–1980.* Frankfurt am Main: Knapp.

Pohl, M. 1986. *Entstehung und Entwicklung des Universalbankensystems.* Frankfurt am Main: Knapp.

Pollard, S. 1965. *The Genesis of Modern Management: A Study of the Industrial Revolution in Great Britain.* Cambridge, MA: Harvard University Press.

Pollard, S. 1981. *Peaceful Conquest: The Industrialization of Europe 1760–1970.* Oxford: Oxford University Press.

Pollard, S. 1987. "'Made in Germany'—die Angst vor der deutschen Konkurrenz im spätviktorianischen England." *Technikgeschichte* 53:183–95.

Poschinger, H. von. 1878–79. *Bankwesen und Bankpolitik in Preussen.* 3 vols. Berlin: Springer,.

Prass, R. 2016. *Grundzüge der Agrargeschichte. Vom Dreißigjährigen Krieg bis zum Beginn der Moderne (1650–1880), Vol. 2.* Cologne: Böhlau.

Preussische Statistik. 1884. *Die Ergebnisse der Berufszählung vom 5. Juni 1882, Vol. 76, Pt. 3: Landwirtschaftsbetriebe sowie Hauptberuf und Religionsbekenntnis der Bevölkerung des preussischen Staates nach den Ergebnissen der Berufszählung vom 5. Juni 1882*. Berlin: Verlag des Königlichen Statistischen Bureaus.

Proettel, T. 2013. "Die Darlehensvergabe der Oberamtssparkasse Kirchheim unter Teck 1907 bis 1913." *Zeitschrift für Unternehmensgeschichte*: 1–25.

Prümm, H. 2012. "Friedrich von Preussen und das Recht. Das Interpretationsverbot in ALR, der Prozess des Müllers Arnold und der Überfall auf Sachsen." *Zeitschrift des Studiengangs*. zjs-online.com/dat/artikel/2012.

Puhle, H.-J. 1975. *Agrarische Interessenpolitik und preussischer Konservatismus im Wilhelminischen Reich, 1893–1914*. Bonn: Verlag Neue Gesellschaft.

Quataert, J. H. 1995. "Survival Strategies in a Saxon Textile District during the Early Phases of Industrialization, 1780–1860." in D. M. Hafter, ed., *European Women and Preindustrial Craft* (Bloomington: Indiana University Press), 153–78.

Ransom, R. L. 1970. "Social Returns from Public Transport Investment: A Case Study of the Ohio Canal." *Journal of Political Economy* 78:1041–80.

Rätzer, S. 1914. *Die Baumwollmanufaktur im sächsischen Vogtlande von ihren Anfängen bis zum Zusammenbruch des napoleonischen Kontinentalsystems*. Mylau: Carl Krüger.

Reckendrees, A. 2015. "Unternehmen, Industrie und Handwerk." In T. Rahlf, ed., *Deutschland in Daten. Zeitreihen zur historischen Statistik* (Bonn: Bundeszentrale für politische Bildung).

Redlich, F. 1944. "The Leaders of the German Steam Engine Industry during the First Hundred Years." *Journal of Economic History* 4:121–48.

Reekers, S. 1968. "Beiträge zur statistischen Darstellung der gewerblichen Wirtschaft Westfalens um 1800, Teil 5: Grafschaft Mark." *Westfälische Forschungen* 21:98–161.

Reich, N. 1979. "Auswirkungen der deutschen Aktienreform von 1884 auf die Konzentration der Wirtschaft." In N. Horn & J. Kocka, eds., *Recht und Entwicklung der Großunternehmen im 19. und frühen 20. Jahrhundert* (Göttingen: Vandenhoeck & Ruprecht), 255–73.

Reichsbank. 1925. *Vergleichende Notenbankstatistik: Organisation und Geschäftsverkehr wichtiger europäischer Notenbanken 1876–1913 statistisch dargestellt*. Berlin: Reichsdruckerei.

Reinalter, H., & H. Klueting, eds. 2002. *Der aufgeklärte Absolutismus im europäischen Vergleich*. Vienna: Böhlau.

Reinicke, C. 1989. *Agrarkonjunktur und technisch-organisatorische Innovationen auf dem Agrarsektor im Spiegel niederrheinischer Pachtverträge 1200–1600*. Cologne: Böhlau.

Reininghaus, W. 1995. *Die Stadt Iserlohn und ihre Kaufleute*. Dortmund: Gesellschaft für westfälische Wirtschaftsgeschichte e.V.

Reininghaus, W. 2002. "Zünfte und Zunftpolitik in Westfalen und im Rheinland am Ende des Alten Reichs." In H.-G. Haupt, ed., *Das Ende der Zünfte. Ein europäischer Vergleich* (Göttingen: Vandenhoeck & Ruprecht), 71–86.

Rettig, R. 1978. *Das Investitions- und Finanzierungsverhalten deutscher Grossunternehmen 1880–1911*. Diss., University of Münster.

Reulecke, J. 1980. "Nachzügler und Pionier zugleich. Das Bergische Land und der Beginn der Industrialisierung in Deutschland." In S. Pollard, ed., *Region und Industrialisierung* (Göttingen: Vandenhoeck & Ruprecht), 52–68.

Reulecke, J. 1985. *Geschichte der Urbanisierung in Deutschland*. Frankfurt am Main: Suhrkamp.

Reuter, H.-G. 1977. "Schutzzollpolitik und Zolltarife für Getreide 1880–1900." *Zeitschrift für Agrargeschichte und Agrarsoziologie* 25:129–213.

Richter, E. 1869. *Das Preussische Staatsschuldenwesen und die Preussischen Staatspapiere*. Breslau: Maruschke & Berndt.

Richter, R., & J. Streb. 2011. "Catching-up and Falling Behind: Knowledge Spillover from American to German Machine Tool Makers." *Journal of Economic History* 71:1006–31.

Riesser, J. 1910. *Die deutschen Grossbanken und ihre Konzentration.* 3d ed. Jena: Fischer.

Ritter, G. 1997. *Goldbugs and Greenbacks: The Antimonopoly Tradition and the Politics of Finance in America.* Cambridge: Cambridge University Press.

Ritter, G. A. 1963. *Die Arbeiterbewegung im Wilhelminischen Reich. Die sozialdemokratische Partei und die freie Gewerkschaften 1890–1900.* Berlin: Colloqium Verlag.

Ritter, G. A. 1983. *Sozialversicherung in Deutschland und England. Entstehung und Grundzüge im Vergleich.* Munich: Beck.

Ritter, G. A., & M. Niehuss, eds. 1980. *Wahlgeschichtliches Arbeitsbuch.* Munich: Beck.

Ritter, G. A., & K. Tenfelde. 1992. *Arbeiter im Deutschen Kaiserreich 1871–1914.* Bonn: Dietz.

Rittmann, H. 1975. *Deutsche Geldgeschichte 1484–1914.* Munich: Battenberg.

Robisheaux, T. W. 1998. "The Peasantries of Western Germany, 1300–1750." In T. Scott, ed., *The Peasantries of Europe: From the Fourteenth to the Eighteenth Centuries* (London: Longman), 111–42.

Roehl, H. 1900. *Beiträge zur Preußischen Handwerkerpolitik vom Allgemeinen Landrecht bis zur Allgemeinen Gewerbeordnung von 1845.* Leipzig: Duncker & Humblot.

Rohrscheidt, K. von. 1976 (1898). *Vom Zunftzwang zur Gewerbefreiheit.* Berlin: Heymanns.

Roscher, W. 1852. *Über Kornhandel und Theurungspolitik.* Stuttgart: Cotta.

Rosenberg, H. 1974 (1934). *Die Weltwirtschaftskrise, 1857–1859.* 2d ed. Göttingen: Vandenhoeck & Ruprecht.

Rosenberg, H. 1958. *Bureaucracy, Aristocracy and Autocracy: The Prussian Experience 1660–1815.* Cambridge, MA: Harvard University Press.

Rosenberg, H. 1967. *Grosse Depression und Bismarckzeit.* Berlin: De Gruyter.

Rosendorff, R. 1906. *Die deutschen Überseebanken.* Jena: G. Fischer.

Rostow, W. W. 1960. *The Stages of Economic Growth: A Non-Communist Manifesto.* Cambridge: Cambridge University Press.

Rostow, W. W. 1962. *The Process of Economic Growth.* Rev. ed. New York: W. W. Norton.

Rumler, M. 1921ff. "Die Bestrebungen zur Befreiung der Privatbauern in Preußen, 1797–1806." *Forschungen zur Brandenburgischen und Preußischen Geschichte* 33:179–92, 327–67; 34:1–24, 265–97; 37:31–76.

Sarfarez, S. & M. Uebele. 2009. "Tracking Down the Business Cycle: A Dynamic Model for Germany, 1820–1914." *Explorations in Economic History* 46:368–87.

Saul, B. 1960. *Studies in British Overseas Trade 1870–1914.* Liverpool: Liverpool University Press.

Saul, S. B. 1980. *Industrialization and De-industrialization? The Interaction of the German and British Economies before the First World War.* London: German Historical Institute.

Schaefer, K. C. 1995. *Deutsche Portfolioinvestitionen im Ausland 1870–1914.* Münster: LIT.

Schäfer, M. 2016. *Eine andere Industrialisierung. Die Transformation der sächsischen Textilexportgewerbe 1790–1890.* Stuttgart: Steiner.

Schattkowsky, M. 2007. *Zwischen Rittergut, Residenz und Reich. Die Lebenswelt des kursächsischen Landadeligen Christph von Loß auf Schleinitz (1574–1620).* Leipzig: Leipziger Universitäts-Verlag.

Schirmer, U. 1996. "Der Bevölkerungsgang in Sachsen zwischen 1743 und 1815." *Vierteljahrschrift für Sozial- und Wirtschaftsgeschichte* 83:25–58.

Schlechte, H. 1958. *Die Staatsreform in Kursachsen 1762–1763.* Berlin: Rütten & Loening.

Schlumbohm, J. 1994. *Lebensläufe, Familien, Höfe. Die Bauern und Heuerleute des osna-*

brückischen Kirchspiels Belm in proto-industrieller Zeit, 1650–1860. Göttingen: Vandenhoeck & Ruprecht.

Schmidt, E. 1980. *Beiträge zur Geschichte des preußischen Rechtsstaates*. Berlin: Duncker & Humblot.

Schmitt-Sasse, J. 1987. "Der Patriot und sein Vaterland. Aufklärer und Reformer im sächsischen Rétablissement." In H. E. Bödekerand & U. Herrmann, eds., *Aufklärung als Politisierung—Politisierung der Aufklärung* (Hamburg: Felix Meiner), 237–52.

Schmoller, G. 1975 (1870). *Zur Geschichte der deutschen Kleingewerbe im 19. Jahrhundert*. New York: Georg Olms.

Schmoller, G. 1886. "Die preußische Kolonisation des 17. und 18. Jahrhunderts." *Schriften des Vereins für Socialpolitik* 32:1–43.

Schmoller, G. 1906. "Das Verhältnis der Kartelle zum Staat." In *Schriften des Vereins für Socialpolitik* 116:237–71.

Schnee, H. 1953–55. *Die Hoffinanz und der moderne Staat*. 3 vols. Berlin: Duncker & Humblot.

Schomerus, H. 1977. *Die Arbeiter der Maschinenfabrik Esslingen*. Stuttgart: Klett-Cotta.

Schöne, B. 1982. "Posamentierer—Strumpfwirker—Spitzenklöpplerinnen. Zu Kultur und Lebensweise von Textilproduzenten im Erzgebirge und im Vogtland während der Periode des Übergangs vom Feudalismus zum Kapitalismus (1750–1850)." In R. Weinhold, ed., *Volksleben zwischen Zunft und Fabrik* (Berlin: Akademie Verlag), 107–64.

Schotte, H. 1912. "Die rechtliche und wirtschaftliche Lage des westfälischen Bauernstandes bis zum Jahre 1815." In E. Frhr. von Kerckerinck zur Borg, ed., *Beiträge zur Geschichte des westfälischen Bauernstandes* (Berlin: Parey), 3–106.

Schremmer, E. 1987. "Die Badische Gewerbesteuer und die Kapitalbildung in gewerblichen Anlagen und Vorräten in Baden und in Deutschland, 1815–1913." *Vierteljahrschrift für Sozial- und Wirtschaftsgeschichte* 74:18–61.

Schremmer, E. 1994. *Steuern und Staatsfinanzen während der Industrialisierung Europas. England, Frankreich, Preussen und das Deutsche Reich 1800 bis 1914*. New York: Springer.

Schröder, W. H., & R. Spree, eds. 1980. *Historische Konjunkturforschung*. Stuttgart: Klett-Cotta.

Schröter, A., & W. Becker. 1962. *Die deutsche Maschinenbauindustrie in der industriellen Revolution*. East Berlin: Akademieverlag.

Schubert, W., & P. Hommelhoff. 1985. *Hundert Jahre modernes Aktienrecht. Eine Sammlung von Texten und Quellen zur Aktienrechtsreform 1884 mit zwei Einführungen*. Berlin: De Gruyter.

Schulte, F. 1959. "Die Entwicklung der gewerblichen Wirtschaft in Rheinland-Westfalen im 18. Jahrhundert." Cologne: Rheinisch-Westfälisches Wirtschaftsarchiv.

Schultheis-Friebe, M. 1969. "Die französische Wirtschaftspolitik im Roer-Department 1792–1814." PhD diss., University of Bonn.

Schultz, T. 1961. "Investment in Human Capital." *American Economic Review* 51, no. 1:1–17.

Schultze, C. 2011. "Die Chemnitzer Schmiedeinnungen im 19. Jahrhundert und ihre Auflösung durch das Königlich Sächsische Gewerbegesetz von 1861." Master's thesis, TU Chemnitz.

Schumpeter, J. 1939. *Business Cycles: A Theoretical, Historical and Statistical Analysis of the Capitalist Process*. New York: McGraw-Hill.

Schwann, M. 1915. *Ludolf Camphausens Denkschriften, wirtschaftspolitische Arbeiten und Briefe*. Vols. 1 and 2. Essen: Baedeker.

Sedatis, H. 1979. *Liberalismus und Handwerk in Südwestdeutschland. Wirtschafts- und Gesellschaftskonzep-tionen des Liberalismus und die Krise des Handwerks im 19. Jahrhundert.* Stuttgart: Klett-Cotta.

Seidenzahl, F. 1970. *Hundert Jahre Deutsche Bank.* Frankfurt am Main: Deutsche Bank.

Sen, A. 1982. *Poverty and Famines: An Essay on Entitlement and Deprivation.* 2d ed. Oxford: Oxford University Press.

Sensch, J. 2004 (1847–2002). Histat-Datenkompilation online: Geschichte der deutschen Bevölkerung seit 1815. GESIS, Cologne. ZA8171 data file. https://histat.gesis.org/histat.

Sering, M. 1910. "Die Verteilung des Grundbesitzes und die Abwanderung vom Lande." *Rede im Königlichen Landesökonomiekollegium am 11.2.1910.* Berlin: Parey.

Seybold, G. 1974. *Württembergs Industrie und Außenhandel vom Ende der Napoleonischen Kriege bis zum Deutschen Zollverein.* Stuttgart: W. Kohlhammer.

Sheppard, D. 1971. *The Growth and Role of UK Financial Intermediaries 1880–1962.* London: Methuen.

Sieber, S. 1967. *Studien zur Industriegeschichte des Erzgebirges.* Cologne: Böhlau.

Siemann, W. 1985. *Die deutsche Revolution von 1848/49.* Frankfurt am Main: Suhrkamp.

Siemann, W. 2016. *Metternich. Stratege und Visionär. Eine Biographie.* Munich: Beck.

Simms, B. 1999. "Reform in Britain and Prussia, 1797–1815: (Confessional) Fiscal-Military State and Military-Agrarian Complex." In T. C. W. Blanning & P. Wende, eds., *Reform in Great Britain and Germany 1750–1850*, Proceedings of the British Academy 100 (Oxford: Oxford University Press), 79–100.

Slicher van Bath, B. H. 1963. *The Agrarian History of Western Europe A.D. 500–1850.* London: Edward Arnold.

Smith, A. 1988 (1776). *An Inquiry into the Nature and Causes of the Wealth of Nations.* Ed. K. Sutherland. Oxford: Oxford University Press.

Soetbeer, A. 1874. *Die fünf Milliarden. Betrachtungen über die Folgen der grossen Kriegsentschädigung für die Wirtschaftsverhältnisse Frankreichs und Deutschlands.* Berlin: Carl Cabel.

Soetbeer, A. 1886. *Materialien zur Erläuterung und Beurteilung der wirtschaftlichen Edelmetallverhältnisse und der Währungsfrage.* 2d ed. Berlin: Schriften des Vereins zur Wahrung der Wirthschaftlichen Interessen von Handel und Gewerbe.

Sokoll, T. 2007. "Kameralismus." In *Enzyklopädie der Neuzeit*, 16 vols. (Stuttgart: Metzler), 6:290–99.

Solomou, S. 1987. *Phases of Economic Growth, 1850–1973: Kondratieff Waves and Long Swings.* Cambridge: Cambridge University Press.

Sombart, W. 1919. *Die deutsche Volkswirtschaft im neunzehnten Jahrhundert.* 4th ed. Berlin: Bondi.

Sperber, J. 1985. "State and Civil Society in Prussia: Thoughts on a New Edition of Reinhart Koselleck's *Preussen zwischen Reform und Revolution.*" *Journal of Modern History* 57, no. 2:278–96.

Spiethoff, A. 1955. *Die wirtschaftlichen Wechsellagen.* 2 vols. Tübingen: Mohr.

Spoerer, M. 2004. *Steuerlast, Steuerinzidenz, Steuerwettbewerb. Verteilungswirkungen der Besteuerung in Preußen und Württemberg (1815—1913).* Berlin: Akademie Verlag.

Spree, R. 1977. *Die Wachstumszyklen der deutschen Wirtschaft von 1840 bis 1880.* Berlin: Dunker & Humblodt.

Spree, R. 1978. *Wachstumstrends und Konjunkturzyklen in der deutschen Wirtschaft von 1820 bis 1913.* Göttingen: Vandenhoek & Ruprecht.

Spree, R. 1981. *Soziale Ungleichheit vor Krankheit und Tod.* Göttingen: Vandenhoek & Ruprecht.

Spree, R. 2011. *Die Industrialisierung Deutschlands im 19. Jahrhundert.* Online publication. rspree.wordpress.com.

Steindl, H. 1986. "Die Einführung der Gewerbefreiheit." In H. Coing, ed., *Handbuch der Quellen und Literatur der neueren europäischen Privatrechtsgeschichte, Vol. 3: Das 19. Jahrhundert, Pt. 3: Gesetzgebung zu den privatrechtlichen Sondergebieten* (Munich: Beck), 3527–633.

Steitz, W. 1974. *Die Entehung der Köln-Minden Eisenbahn.* Cologne: Rheinisch-Westfälischen Wirtschaftsarchiv.

Steitz, W. 1984. "Kommunale Infrastruktur und in der Zeit der deutschen Hochindustrialisierung." In K. Düwell & W. Köllmann, eds., *Rheinland-Westfalen im Industriezeitalter, Vol. 2: Von der Reichsgründung bis zur Weimarer Republik* (Wuppertal: Hammer).

Stern, F. 1977. *Gold and Iron: Bismarck, Bleichröder and the Building of the German Empire.* New York: Alfred A. Knopf.

Straubel, R. 2010. *Adlige und bürgerliche Beamte in der friderizianischen Justiz- und Finanzverwaltung. Ausgewählte Aspekte eines sozialen Umschichtungsprozesses und seiner Hintergründe (1740–1806).* Berlin: BWV.

Strauss, R. 1960. *Die Lage und die Bewegung der Chemnitzer Arbeiter in der ersten Hälfte des 19. Jahrhunderts.* Berlin: Akademie Verlag.

Streb, J., J. Baten & S. Yin. 2006. "Technological and Geographical Spillover." *Economic History Review* 59:347–73.

Streb, J., J. Wallusch & S. Yin. 2007. "Knowledge Spill-over from New to Old Industries: The Case of German Synthetic Dyes and Textiles 1878–1913." *Explorations in Economic History* 44:203–23.

Stulz, P., & A. Opitz. 1956. *Volksbewegungen in Kursachsen zur Zeit der Französischen Revolution.* Berlin: Rütten & Loening.

Stürmer, M., G. Teichmann & W. Treue. 1989. *Wägen und Wagen. Sal. Oppenheim jr. Et Cie. Geschichte einer Bank und einer Familie.* Munich: Piper.

Sylla, R., R. Tilly & G. Tortella, eds. 1999. *The State, the Financial System, and Economic Modernization.* Cambridge: Cambridge University Press.

Sylla, R. & G. Toniolo, eds. 1991. *Patterns of European Industrialization: The Nineteenth Century.* London & New York: Routledge.

Tàrle, E. 1914. "Deutsch-französische Wirtschaftsbeziehungen zur napoleonischen Zeit." *Schmollers Jahrbuch für Gesetzgebung, Verwaltung und Volkswirtschaft* 38:167–212.

Taylor, A. 1999. "Sources of Convergence." *Economic Review:* 1621–45.

Taylor, A., & J. G. Williamson. 1997. "Convergence in the Age of Mass Migration." *European Review of Economic History* 1:27–63.

Tenfelde, K. 1977. *Sozialgeschichte der Bergarbeiterschaft an der Ruhr im 19. Jahrhundert.* Bonn–Bad Godesberg: Neue Gesellschaft.

Teuteberg, H. J. 1985. *Homo Habitans. Zur Sozialgeschichte des ländlichen und städtischen Wohnens in der Neuzeit.* Münster: Coppenrath.

Teuteberg, H. J. 1986. *Stadtwachstum, Industrialisierung, Sozialer Wandel. Beiträge zur Erforschung der Urbanisierung im 19. und 20. Jahrhundert.* Berlin: Duncker & Humblot.

Teuteberg, H. J., & G. Wiegelmann. 1972. *Der Wandel der Nahrungsgewohnheiten unter dem Einfluss der Industrialisierung.* Göttingen: Vandenhoeck & Ruprecht.

Thorp, W. 1926. *Business Annals.* New York: National Bureau of Economic Research.

Thorwart, F. 1883. "Die Entwicklung des Banknotenumlaufs in Deutschland von 1851–1880." *Jahrbücher für Nationalökonomie und Statistik* 41.

Thünen, J. H. von. 1990 (1826). *Der isolierte Staat in Beziehung auf Landwirtschaft und Nationalökonomie.* Ed. H. Lehmann with L. Werner. Berlin: Akademie Verlag.

Tilly, C., ed. 1975. *The Formation of National States in Western Europe*. Princeton, NJ: Princeton University Press.

Tilly, C., L. A. Tilly & R. H. Tilly. 1975. *The Rebellious Century: 1830–1930*. Cambridge, MA: Harvard University Press.

Tilly, R. H. 1966. *Financial Institutions and Industrialization in the Rhineland*. Madison: University of Wisconsin Press.

Tilly, R. 1967. "Los von England. Probleme des Nationalismus in der deutschen Wirtschaftsgeschichte." *Zeitschrift für die gesamte Staatswirtschaft* 124:179–96.

Tilly, R. H. 1974. "The Growth of Large-Scale Enterprise in Germany since the Middle of the Nineteenth Century." In H. Daems & H. Van der Wee, eds., *The Rise of Managerial Capitalism* (Leuven: Leuven University Press).

Tilly, R. H. 1978. "Capital Formation in Germany in the Nineteenth Century." In P. Mathias & M. M. Postan, eds., *The Cambridge Economic History of Europe*, vol. 7 (Cambridge: Cambridge University Press), 382–441.

Tilly, R. H. 1981. "Herbert Kisch und sein Werk. In H. Kisch, *Die hausindustriellen Textilgewerbe am Niederrhein vor der industriellen Revolution* (Göttingen: Vandenhoeck & Ruprecht), 9–24.

Tilly, R. H. 1982. "Mergers, External Growth, and Finance in the Development of Large-Scale Enterprises in Germany, 1880–1913." *Journal of Economic History* 42:629–58.

Tilly, R. H. 1985. "Some Problems in the Measurement of Economic Growth in Germany in the Nineteenth Century." Paper presented at Workshop on Quantitative Economic History, University of Groningen.

Tilly, R. H. 1986. "German Banks, 1850–1914: Development Assistance for the Strong." *Journal of Economic History* 15:113–52.

Tilly, R. H. 1990. *Vom Zollverein zum Industriestaat. Die wirtschaftlich-soziale Entwicklung Deutschlands 1834 bis 1914*. Munich: dtv.

Tilly, R. H. 1991a. "Germany." In R. Sylla & G. Toniolo, eds., *Patterns of European Industrialization: The Nineteenth Century* (London: Routledge), 175–96.

Tilly, R. H. 1991b. "International Aspects of the Development of German Banking." In R. Cameron & V. I. Bovykin, eds., *International Banking, 1870–1914* (New York: Oxford University Press).

Tilly, R. H. 1992. "Der deutsche Kapitalmarkt und die Auslandsinvestitionen von 1870 bis 1913." *IFO Studien* 2:199–225.

Tilly, R. H. 1994. "German Banks and Foreign Investment in Central and Eastern Europe before 1939." In D. F. Good, ed., *Economic Transformations: Legacies from the Past and Lessons for the Future* (London: Routledge), 201–30.

Tilly, R. H. 1996. "'Perestroika à la Prusse.' Preußens liberale Reformen am Anfang des 19. Jahrhunderts im Lichte des Transformationsparadigmas." *Jahrbuch für Wirtschaftsgeschichte* 37, no. 2: 147–60.

Tilly, R. H. 1997. "Investitionen der Gemeinden im Deutschen Kaiserreich." In K.-H. Kaufhold, ed., *Investitionen der Städte im 19. Und 20. Jahrhundert* (Cologne: Böhlau).

Tilly, R. H. 1999a. "Public Policy, Capital Markets and the Supply of Industrial Finance in Nineteenth-Century Germany." In R. Sylla, R. H. Tilly & G. Tortella, eds., *The State, the Financial System, and Economic Modernization* (Cambridge: Cambridge University Press).

Tilly, R. H. 1999b. *Globalisierung aus historischer Sicht und das Lernen aus der Geschichte*. Kölner Vorträge zur Sozial- und Wirtschaftsgeschichte 41. Cologne: Forschungsinstitut für Sozial- und Wirtschaftsgeschichte.

Tilly, R. H. 2000. "Die deutsche Wirtschaftskrise von 1900/01 und der Fall der Leipziger

Bank." In R. H. Tilly, ed., *Bankenkrisen in Mitteleuropa im 19. und 20. Jahrhundert*, Geld und Kapital 3 (Stuttgart: Steiner), 69–100.

Tilly, R. H. 2003. *Geld und Kredit in der Wirtschaftsgeschichte*. Stuttgart: Steiner.

Tilly, R. H. 2010. "The Distribution of Personal Income in Prussia, 1852 to 1875: An Exploratory Study." *Jahrbuch für Wirtschaftsgeschichte* 51, no. 1:175–94.

Tilly, R. H. 2015. "Geld und Kredit." In T. Rahlf, ed., *Deutschland in Zahlen. Zeitreihen zur historischen Statistik*. Bonn: Bundeszentrale für politische Bildung, 212–23.

Tilly, R. H., & G. Bieber. 1991. "Die Entwicklung der kommunalen Finanzen in Preussen, 1870–1913, am Beispiel der Städte Bochum, Krefeld und Muenster." *Prace naukowe* 560 (Wroclaw [Breslau]).

Tilly, R. H., & T. Wellenreuther. 1985. "Bevölkerungswanderung und Wohnungsbauzyklen." In H.-J. Teuteberg, *Homo Habitans* (Münster: Coppenrath), 273–300.

Tipton, F. B. 1976. *Regional Variations in the Economic Development of Germany during the Nineteenth Century*. Middletown, CT: Wesleyan University Press.

Tooze, A. 2001. *Statistics and the German State, 1900–1945*. Cambridge: Cambridge University Press.

Torp, C. 2005. *Die Herausforderung der Globalisierung. Wirtschaft und Politik in Deutschland 1860–1914*. Göttingen: Vandenhoeck & Ruprecht.

Trende, A. 1993 (1957). *Geschichte der deutschen Sparkassen bis zum Anfang des 20. Jahrhunderts*. Sparkassen in der Geschichte 2. Stuttgart: Deutscher Sparkassenverlag.

Treue, W. 1937. *Wirtschaftszustände und Wirtschaftspolitik in Preußen, 1815–1825*. Stuttgart: Kohlhammer.

Treue, W. 1951. "Adam Smith in Deutschland. Zum Problem des 'Politischen Professors' zwischen 1776 und 1810." In W. Conze, ed., *Festschrift für Hans Rothfels* (Düsseldorf: Droste), 101–33.

Troeltsch, W. 1897. *Die Calwer Zeughandlungskompagnie und ihre Arbeiter*. Jena: Gustav Fischer.

Troßbach, W., & C. Zimmemann. 2006. *Die Geschichte des Dorfes. Von den Anfängen im Frankenreich zur bundesdeutschen Gegenwart*. Stuttgart: Ulmer.

Uebele. M. 2011. "Deutsche Weizenpreise 1806–1855. Eine Comovement-Analyse nationaler und internationaler Marktintegration." In R. Walter, ed., *Globalisierung in der Geschichte. Erträge der 23. Arbeitstagung der Gesellschaft für Sozial- und Wirtschaftsgeschichte 18. bis 21. März 2009 in Kiel, Vierteljahrschrift für Sozial- und Wirtschaftsgeschichte*, suppl. 214 (Stuttgart: Steiner), 175–97.

Uebele, M., & D. Gallardo-Albarrán. 2015. "Paving the Way to Modernity: Prussian Roads and Grain Market Integration in Westphalia, 1821–1855." *Scandinavian Economic History Review* 63, no. 1:69–92.

Ullmann, H.-P. 1986. *Staatsschulden und Reformpolitik. Die Entstehung moderner öffentlicher Schulden in Bayern und Baden 1780–1820*. 2 vols. Göttingen: Vandenhoeck & Ruprecht.

Ullmann, H.-P. 2009. *Staat und Schulden. Öffentliche Finanzen in Deutschland seit dem 18. Jahrhundert*. Göttingen: Vandenhoeck & Ruprecht.

Vanhaute, E., R. Paping & C. O'Grada. 2006. "The European Subsistence Crisis of 1845–1850: A Comparative Perspective." Paper presented at International Economic History Conference, session 123.

Vann, J. A. 1984. *The Making of a State: Württemberg, 1593–1793*. Ithaca, NY: Cornell University Press.

Van Zanden, J. L. 1991. "The First Green Revolution: The Growth of Production and Productivity in European Agriculture, 1870–1914." *Economic History Review* 44, no. 2: 215–39.

Van Zanden, J. L. 1999. "The Development of Agricultural Productivity in Europe, 1500–1800." In B. J. P. Van Bavel & E. Thoen, eds., *Land Productivity and Agro-Systems in the North Sea Area* (Turnhout: Brepols), 357–75.

Van Zanden, J. L., & B. van Leeuwen. 2012. "Persistent But Not Consistent: The Growth of National Income in Holland 1347–1807." *Explorations in Economic History* 49:119–30.

Vierhaus, R. 1976. "Land, Staat und Reich in der politischen Vorstellungswelt deutscher Landstände im 18. Jahrhundert." *Historische Zeitschrift* 223:40–60.

Virchow, R. 1849. "Mitteilungen über die in Oberschlesien herrschende Typhus-Epidemie." In *Archiv für pathologische Anatomie und Physiologie und für klinische Medizin*, 2 vols. (Berlin: G. Reimer).

Vogel, B. 1980. "Einleitung. Die preußischen Reformen als Gegenstand und Problem der Forschung" In Vogel, ed., *Preußische Reformen 1807–1820* (Königstein: Verlagsgruppe Athenäum-Hain-Scriptor-Hanstein), 1–27.

Vogel, B. 1983. *Allgemeine Gewerbefreiheit. Die Reformpolitik des preußischen Staatskanzlers Hardenberg (1810–1820)*. Göttingen: Vandenhoeck & Ruprecht.

Vogel, B. 1988. "Beamtenliberalismus in der Napoleonischen Ära." In D. Langewiesche, ed., *Liberalismus im 19. Jahrhundert. Deutschland im europäischen Vergleich* (Göttingen: Vandenhoeck & Ruprecht), 11–63.

Voigt, F. 1950. *Der volkswirtschaftliche Sparprozess*. Berlin: Duncker & Humblot.

Volckart, O. 1999. "Politische Zersplitterung und Wirtschaftswachstum im Alten Reich, ca. 1650–1800." *Vierteljahrsschrift für Sozial- und Wirtschaftsgeschichte* 86, no. 1:1–38.

Volckart, O. 2002. *Wettbewerb und Wettbewerbsbeschränkung im vormodernen Deutschland 1000–1800*. Tübingen: Mohr Siebeck.

Vopelius, M.-E. 1968. *Die altliberalen Ökonomen und die Reformzeit*. Stuttgart: Gustav Fischer.

Wagenblass, H. 1973. *Der Eisenbahnbau und das Wachstum der deutschen Eisen- und Maschinenbauindustrie 1835 bis 1860*. Stuttgart.

Wagner, A. 1902. *Agrar- und Industriestaat. Die Kehrseite des Industriestaats und die Rechtfertigung agrarischen Zollschutzes mit besonderer Rücksicht auf die Bevölkerungsfrage*. 2d ed. Jena: G. Fischer.

Wagner-Hasel, B. 2011. *Die Arbeit der Gelehrten*. Frankfurt: Campus.

Wallich, H., & P. Wallich. 1978. *Zwei Generationen im deutschen Bankwesen 1833–1914*. Frankfurt am Main: Knapp.

Waltershausen, S. von. 1907. *Das volkwirtschaftliche System der Kapitalanlage im Ausland*. Berlin: G. Reimer.

Wandschneider, K. 2014. "Lending to Lemons: Landschafts-Credit in Eighteenth-Century Prussia." In E. N. White, K. Snowdon & P. Fishback, eds., *Housing and Mortgage Markets in Historical Perspective*. National Bureau of Economic Research Conference Report. Chicago: University of Chicago Press.

Wandschneider, K. 2015. "Landschaften as Credit Purveyors—The Example of East Prussia." *Journal of Economic History* 75, no. 3:791–818.

Webb, S. 1977. "Tariff Protection for the Iron Industry, Cotton Textiles and Agriculture in Germany, 1879–1914." *Jahrbücher für Nationalökonomie und Statistik* 192, nos. 3–4:336–57.

Webb, S. 1980. "Tariffs, Cartels, Technology and Growth in the German Steel Industry." *Journal of Economic History* 40: 309–30.

Webb, S. 1982. "Agricultural Protection in Wilhelminian Germany: Forging an Empire with Pork and Rye." *Journal of Economic History* 42:309–26.

Weber, M. 1952 (1906). "Kapitalismus und Agrarverfassung." *Zeitschrift für die gesamte Staatswissenschaft* 108, no. 3:431–52.

Wehler, H.-U. 1961. "Die Polen im Ruhrgebiet." *Vierteljahrschrift für Sozial- und Wirtschaftsgeschichte* 48:203–35.

Wehler, H.-U. 1987a. *Deutsche Gesellschaftsgeschichte, Vol. 1: Vom Feudalismus des Alten Reiches bis zur Defensiven Modernisierung der Reformära 1700–1815.* Munich: C. H. Beck.

Wehler, H.-U. 1987b. *Deutsche Gesellschaftsgeschichte, Vol. 2: Von der Reformara bis zur industriellen und politischen "Deutschen Doppelrevolution," 1815–1845/49.* Munich: C. H. Beck.

Wehler, H.-U. 1989. "Wirtschaftlicher Wandel in Deutschland 1789–1815." In H. Berding, E. François & H.-P. Ullmann, eds., *Deutschland und Frankreich im Zeitalter der Französischen Revolution* (Frankfurt a. M.: Suhrkamp), 100–120.

Wehler, H.- U. 1995. *Deutsche Gesellschaftsgeschichte, Vol. 3: Von der "Deutschen Doppelrevolution" bis zum Beginn des Ersten Weltkrieges 1849–1914.* Munich: C. H. Beck.

Weidmann, W. 1968. *Die pfälzische Landwirtschaft zu Beginn des 19. Jahrhunderts.* Saarbrücken: Verlag J. Paul.

Wellenreuther, T. 1989. *Wohnungsbau und Industrialisierung. Eine ökonometrische Untersuchung am Beispiel Deutschlands von 1850 bis 1913.* Bergisch-Gladbach: Eul.

Wellhoener, V. 1989. *Grossbanken und Grossindustrie im Kaiserreich.* Göttingen: Vandenhoeck & Ruprecht.

Wengenroth, U. 1986. *Unternehmensstrategien und technischer Fortschritt. Die deutsche und die britische Stahlindustrie, 1865–1895.* Göttingen: Vandenhoeck & Ruprecht.

Weyermann, M. 1910. *Geschichte des Immobiliarkreditwesens in Preussen.* Karlsruhe: Braun.

Whale, P. B. 1930. *Joint-Stock Banking in Germany.* London: Macmillan.

Wieck, F. G. 1840. *Industrielle Zustände Sachsens.* Chemnitz: Expedizion des Gewerbeblattes für Sachsen.

Wiedenfeld, K. 1909. "Die Organisation des Getreidehandels." In *Handwörterbuch der Staatswissenschaften,* 8 vols. (Jena: Gustav Fischer), 4:770–83.

Wienfort, M. 2001. *Patrimonialgerichte in Preußen. Ländliche Gesellschaft und bürgerliches Recht 1770–1848/49.* Kritische Studien zur Geschichtswissenschaft 148. Göttingen: Vandenhoeck & Ruprecht.

Wilkins, M. 1989. *The History of Foreign Investment in the U.S. to 1914.* Harvard Studies in Business History 41. Cambridge, MA: Harvard University Press.

Wilkins, M. 1991. "Foreign Banks and Foreign Investment in the United States before 1914." In R. Cameron & V. I. Bovykin, eds., *International Banking, 1870–1914* (New York: Oxford University Press).

Williamson, J. 1995. "The Evolution of Global Labor Markets since 1830: Background, Evidence and Hypotheses." *Explorations in Economic History* 32:141–96.

Williamson, J. 1996. "Globalization, Convergence, and History." *Journal of Economic History* 56:277–306.

Winkler, H. A. 2000. *Deutsche Geschichte vom Ende des Alten Reiches bis zum Untergang der Weimarer Republik.* Vol. 1 of *Der lange Weg nach Westen.* Munich: Beck.

Wirth, M. 1874. *Die Geschichte der Handelskrisen.* 2d ed. Frankfurt: Sauerländer.

Wirtz, R. 1981. *"Widersetzlichkeiten, Excesse, Crawalle, Tumulte und Skandale."* Berlin: Ullstein.

Wischermann, C. 1983. "Hungerkrisen im vormärzlichen Westfalen." In K. Düwell &

W. Köllmann, eds., *Rheinland—Westfalen im Industriezeitalter, Vol. 1: Von der Entstehung der Provinzen bis zur Reichsgründung* (Wuppertal: Hammer), 126–47.

Wischermann, C. 1986. "Wohnungsmarkt, Wohnungsversorgung und Wohnmobilität in deutschen Grossstädten, 1870–1913." In H.-J. Teuteberg, ed., *Stadtwachstum, Industrialisierung, Sozialer Wandel: Beiträge zur Erforschung der Urbanisierung im19. und 20.Jahrhundert* (Berlin: Duncker & Humblot).

Wischermann, C. 1992. *Preußischer Staat und westfälische Unternehmer zwischen Spätmerkantilismus und Liberalismus.* Cologne: Böhlau.

Wischermann, C., & A. Nieberding. 2004. *Die Institutionelle Revolution. Eine Einführung in die deutsche Wirtschaftsgeschichte des 19. und frühen 20. Jahrhunderts.* Stuttgart: Steiner.

Wittich, W. 1896. *Die Grundherrschaft in Nordwestdeutschland.* Leipzig: Duncker & Humblot.

Witzleben, A. von. 1985. *Staatsfinanznot und sozialer Wandel.* Wiesbaden: Steiner.

Wolf, N. 2009. "Was Germany Ever United? Evidence from Intra- and International Trade, 1885–1933." *Journal of Economic History* 69, no. 3:846–81.

Wolf, N., & T. Huning. 2019. "How Britain Unified Germany: Endogenous Trade Costs and the Formation of a Customs Union (March 2019)." CEPR Discussion Paper No. DP13634. Available at SSRN: https://ssrn.com/abstract=3363547.

Wrigley, E. A. 1987. *People, Cities and Wealth: The Transformation of a Traditional Society.* Oxford: Blackwell.

Wrigley, E. A. 1988. *Continuity, Chance and Change: The Character of the Industrial Revolution in England.* Cambridge: Cambridge University Press.

Wunder, H. 1996. "Agriculture and Agrarian Society." In S. Ogilvie, ed., *Germany: A New Social and Economic History, Vol. 2: 1630–1800* (London: Arnold), 63–99.

Zachmann, K. 1997. "Die Kraft traditioneller Strukturen. Sächsische Textilregionen im Industrialisierungsprozess." In U. John & J. Matzerath, eds., *Landesgeschichte als Herausforderung und Programm. Karlheinz Blaschke zum 70. Geburtstag* (Leipzig: Verlag der Sächsischen Akademie der Wissenschaften), 509–35.

Ziegler, D. 1996. *Eisenbahnen und Staat im Zeitalter der Industrialisierung. Die Eisenbahnpolitik der deutschen Staaten im Vergleich.* Stuttgart: Steiner.

Ziekow, J. 1992. *Freiheit und Bindung des Gewerbes.* Berlin: Duncker & Humblot.

Zimmermann, A. 1885. *Blüthe und Verfall des Leinengewerbes in Schlesien.* Breslau: Korn.

Zwahr, H. 1981. *Zur Konstituierung des Proletariats als Klasse. Strukturuntersuchung über das Leipziger Proletariat während der industriellen Revolution.* Munich: C. H. Beck.

Zwahr, H. 1996. *Revolutionen in Sachsen. Beiträge zur Sozial- und Kulturgeschichte.* Weimar: Böhlau.

INDEX

Aachen, 27, 38, 42–43, 47–48, 136, 159, 252
Aachen Technical College, 185
Accident Insurance Law of 1884, 242
Acemoglu, D., 5–7, 47, 257n6
ADHGB of 1861, 121
AEG, 175, 180, 186–89, 224
Africa, 25, 207, 219
Agfa, 179, 188
agrarian institutions. *See* manorial system
agrarian protectionism, 154, 169. *See also* protectionism
agrarian reforms, 6; in French influenced states, 261n18 (*see also* agriculture); in Prussia, 59, 62–65, 68–70, 78–84, 260nn14–15, 261n17, 261nn19–20, 268n3; and the Revolution of 1848–49, 49, 116–17; in Saxony, 27, 117
Agrarstaat vs. *Industriestaat* (debate on), 214–17
agricultural markets, 61, 71–72; and agricultural productivity, 39, 59, 62–67, 155–56, 252–53; importance of railroads for, 150–54; Rhine-Ruhr region as, 150–53. *See also* grain invasion
agriculture: the crises of the 1840s and, 104–13, 116; early industrialization and, 31–33, 38, 44, 49, 56–62, 253; employment and, 2, 18, 139, 252; the Great Depression and, 168–70; industrial breakthrough and, 119, 124, 138–41, 149–53, 253; industrial power and, 165, 168, 201; markets and, 65–67,

260n6; old regime and, 2–3, 6; Prussian agrarian reforms and, 62–65, 82; the state and, 69–73; the world economy and, 184, 213–17, 228. *See also* agrarian reforms; farming
Allgemeine Deutsche Credit-Anstalt Leipzig, 160
Allgemeine Deutsche Handwerkerbund (ADHB), 245–46
ALR (Allgemeine Landrecht für den Preussischen Staaten), 76–79
Amtsbürger, 52
ancien régime, 4–5, 26, 45, 71, 104, 258n7
Anholt, 63
Argentina, 223–24
aristocracy, 3–4, 33, 74, 79–83, 104, 117–18, 158, 169, 214, 240. *See also* Junker
Arnsberg, 27, 140, 173–75, 257n1
artisans, 4, 55, 143, 203, 271n18
A. Schaaffhausen & Co., 114–15
Asia, 207, 219
Association for Promotion of the German Chemical Industries, 185
Association of Tax and Economic Reformers, 169, 266n9
Atlantic economy, 3, 11, 30, 40, 46, 51, 71
Augsburg, 54, 200
Austria, 20, 25, 97, 101, 114, 167, 219–20, 262n8
Austria-Hungary, 213, 219–20
authoritarianism, 7, 82–83, 253, 258n9
autocracy, 55
automobiles, 181–83, 192–93, 254